## About Island Press

Island Press is the only nonprofit organization in the United States whose principal purpose is the publication of books on environmental issues and natural resource management. We provide solutions-oriented information to professionals, public officials, business and community leaders, and concerned citizens who are shaping responses to environmental problems.

In 2006, Island Press celebrates its twenty-first anniversary as the leading provider of timely and practical books that take a multidisciplinary approach to critical environmental concerns. Our growing list of titles reflects our commitment to bringing the best of an expanding body of literature to the environmental community throughout North America and the world.

Support for Island Press is provided by the Agua Fund, The Geraldine R. Dodge Foundation, Doris Duke Charitable Foundation, The William and Flora Hewlett Foundation, Kendeda Sustainability Fund of the Tides Foundation, Forrest C. Lattner Foundation, The Henry Luce Foundation, The John D. and Catherine T. MacArthur Foundation, The Marisla Foundation, The Andrew W. Mellon Foundation, Gordon and Betty Moore Foundation, The Curtis and Edith Munson Foundation, Oak Foundation, The Overbrook Foundation, The David and Lucile Packard Foundation, The Winslow Foundation, and other generous donors.

The opinions expressed in this book are those of the author(s) and do not necessarily reflect the views of these foundations.

# Communicating Nature

# Communicating Nature

## How We Create and Understand

## Environmental Messages

Julia B. Corbett

**ISLAND**PRESS

Washington, Covelo, London

Copyright © 2006 Island Press

ISLAND PRESS is a trademark of the Center for Resource Economics.

Chapter 6, Faint-Green: Advertising and the Natural World, is adapted from Julia B. Corbett, "A Faint Green Sell: Advertising and the Natural World," in *Enviropop: Studies in Environmental Rhetoric and Popular Culture.* Mark Meister and Phyllis M. Japp, eds. (Westport, CT: Praeger, 2002). Cartoons by Kirk Anderson; reprinted with permission. Drawings in Figure 2.1 and Box 4.1 by Valerie Jar.

*Library of Congress Cataloging-in-Publication Data.*

Corbett, Julia B.
  Communicating nature : how we create and understand environmental messages / Julia B. Corbett.
     p.    cm.
  Includes bibliographical references and index.
  ISBN 1-59726-067-3 (cloth : alk. paper) — ISBN 1-59726-068-1 (pbk. : alk. paper)
  1. Nature—Effect of human beings on.   2. Human ecology—Social aspects.
3. Communication in science—Social aspects.   I. Title.
  GF75.C697 2006
  333.72—dc22                                                    2006017426

Printed on recycled, acid-free paper ✪

Manufactured in the United States of America
10  9  8  7  6  5  4  3  2  1

*To my students—past, present, and future.*

*And to my parents, who gave me profound childhood experiences of the natural world.*

# Contents

**9**

Battle for Spin: The Public Relations Industry 247

**10**

Communication and Social Change 281

# Acknowledgments

The seed for this book was planted in undergraduate communication classes I taught at the University of Utah. It quickly became apparent that we couldn't discuss just news coverage of the environment, because each news story was sandwiched between ads for bottled water and humongous trucks. Concentrating on the environmental movement left students with the idea that the environment was the domain of activists and didn't much concern them. Students (and much of the general public) needed environmental communication brought home and made relevant to their everyday lives. Thus the first acknowledgment is to my students; this book is a direct outgrowth of your questions and passions. And now we can be done with bulky reading packets!

I also am grateful to my colleagues in the Department of Communication. As a die-hard "journalism and mass communication" type, I have benefited greatly by being in your midst. Your breadth and open-mindedness for research gave me the freedom to explore environmental communication from all its angles. Department Chair Ann Darling has been a superb leader and friend—wise with her counsel, unflagging in her support, and wonderfully quick to laugh. Thanks also to the university for a fellowship and sabbatical in support of this project.

I'm indebted to Todd Baldwin at Island Press, first for believing in this project, and then for his gentle guidance in steering a massive manuscript into a cohesive, cogent book.

Three cheers for all my supportive friends! Two friends helped launch this creative endeavor by gifting me with seclusion at their cabins—Debora's in the desert and Dennis's in the mountains. Sara, Jan, Natalie, Camille, Carol, and Donna have supported my soul, made me laugh, taken me away to play, and when appropriate, left me alone. Peg offered rousing support from the beginning and eagerly read early drafts. Marc, thanks for your friendship and sage advice about the world of book publishing.

Despite what they say, writing this book was not lonely, for Tobie and Kaya were always "in position" in my office, sometimes before I was. It's such a delight to write amid admirers who love you though they have never read your work.

Finally, thanks to Dad, whose love, support, and generosity I treasure more each year. You taught me the value and pride of hard, excellent work.

# Introduction

Two decades ago, abundant mountain snowfall and an abrupt spring melt sent City Creek roaring through downtown Salt Lake City, Utah. Fish slapped against the wall of sandbags in a muddy torrent past department stores and pawn shops. City Creek was one of seven streams flowing from seven mountain canyons into the valley and one of the first to be diverted and treated for drinking water by the pioneers. And like all seven streams, once sufficient water was removed and treated, the remainder of the flow was banished into the storm drain. But in 1983, the meltwater and rainwater overwhelmed the storm drain, and City Creek went barreling into its city; the spectacle of flood waters on State Street made national news.

In the 1990s, the city and the Mormon Church spent over a million dollars to bring City Creek back up to the surface for an additional mile—before banishing it once more into the storm drain. Landscapers got involved. In the new City Creek Park, the tracks of birds and small mammals were pressed into concrete and identified. Rocks were glued into streambanks that would never shift or accommodate, lined with exotic plants and Kentucky bluegrass. A waterwheel churns peacefully in the summer, dumping its load without a true purpose but evoking some sort of enterprising pioneer spirit. Without a park sign, you wouldn't recognize it as the same creek whose unfettered waters upstream form a narrow, shrubby oasis in the desert foothills.

City Creek Park communicates volumes about our relationship with the natural world or nonhuman environment. Some of the communication is written (such as park signs and news reports about the project), but the bulk of the messages are received while walking through the park. Its landscaping communicates what is valued, what is considered "natural," and what is desired. The

1

cemented creek banks send a message about the control of nature and the desire for nature to be tidy and predictable. Sending the city's namesake water source into a storm drain communicates that the best use of this natural resource is human utility and enjoyment, a human-centered or *anthropocentric* view of nature. This park, like many parks, has a taken-for-granted quality to the average visitor. You understand the message being communicated and you accept it—it's a park because it has green grass, benches, walking paths, interpretive signs, and is designed for humans.

All of these messages are examples of *environmental communication*, the various ways we communicate about the natural world. A news story, an advertisement, a speech, a letter, a photo, a Web site—these are easy to recognize as messages. These forms of communication are intentional and purposeful, sent by people who want to achieve a particular outcome. But our actions and practices—including those that are second nature and subconscious—also send messages about the natural world and our relationship with it, just like City Creek Park or your own backyard. A great deal of what is communicated

**Figure I.1**
Photo of City Creek Park.

about the environment is almost entirely unrecognized and unstated, and we might not recognize that it's "communication" at all: roads without sidewalks, drive-through service, bottled water, disposable washcloths, food served without dishes, office windows that don't open, big houses, garbage cans. These everyday things have a taken-for-granted quality, particularly for those who feel that the environment exists somewhere "out there" and distant from their lives.

Every day practices are so ingrained that we might forget there are other options. For example, an alternative scenario for City Creek might allow it to flow its natural course above ground, winding through the length of the city. On each side of the creek could be a public greenbelt used by walkers, joggers, rollerbladers, and bird watchers. Students could take field trips to learn about water quality, hydrology, and the native vegetation lining the creek. A few picnic tables could sit on small patches of native grass, but otherwise the park would have a wilder feel. Or, City Creek could run the same natural course it had for centuries. Along the creek, native vegetation would grow thick and tangled. The creek occasionally would flood in spring and the volume year-round would be much greater because the majority of the water had been left in the creek for nonhuman use. In a few spots, water pools would be large enough to support fish populations, aided by the work of beavers and muskrats. People would hike and visit the creek on rough trails.

These scenarios communicate very different things about our relationship with the natural world and stem from different belief systems. In City Creek Park, humans dominate and alter the original habitat to fit human desires. The second scenario still caters to human desires but there is a lighter hand in controlling and altering the natural world. In the last scenario, humans are just one part of the biotic community and do not dominate and control, but let the natural system unfold as it will with minimal interference. These scenarios are not just about development versus conservation or preservation. Each reflects, and thus communicates, a belief system of humans toward the natural world, and each tells a story based on those beliefs. Each scenario tells us how nature fits into daily life and leisure and what the environment is "good for."

If you're sitting near a window, look outside and see if you can see a tree. If it's in your backyard, maybe you planted it. If the tree is on a city street or campus, maybe it too was planted. Perhaps the tree grew there "naturally," which we would understand to mean that humans were not involved with the tree's placement.

Now think about a tree you noticed in some sort of "wild" setting, perhaps in a wilderness area or forest, or on another patch of ground that looked "natural." What are the differences between these two trees? The two are wood and branches and roots and leaves or needles. They both need sunlight and moisture and soil. But do you perceive them differently? Is one more valued than the other? Does one tree "need" you more than the other?

Isn't it curious how we make such distinctions, how we draw boundaries between elements of nature existing near to us every day and elements living quite apart and independent of us. We are forced to recognize that "wild" nature has no need for our existence or assistance and that it is indeed "other." In wild areas, "we need no reminder that a tree has its own reasons for being, quite apart from us. The same is less true in the gardens we plant and tend ourselves; there it is easier to forget the otherness of the tree. . . . The tree in the garden is in reality no less other, no less worthy of our wonder and respect than the tree in an ancient forest. . . . Both trees stand apart from us; both share our common world."[1]

Some semesters I ask my students to draw a picture of "nature." Other semesters, I ask them to draw one of "the environment." Invariably, the nature pictures are people-less and predictable, like the quintessential painting in the motel room with a mountain, water, a meadow, flowers, and a deer. The environment pictures, on the other hand, produce varied results. Sometimes they have people and sometimes they have factories spewing smoke. The meanings that these students attach to the environment are often more politicized, while meanings of nature are idealized and untouched. In both cases, nature and environment tend to be places where we humans are not.

In an evocative and persuasive essay, historian William Cronon says historically and culturally we have become accustomed to seeing and valuing nature in some places and not others. If we think we are in *real* nature only when we are in less-peopled places like wild parks or wilderness, how then are we likely to treat the nature that exists in our backyards and cities? Cronon says:

[T]o the extent that we live in an urban-industrial civilization but at the same time pretend to ourselves that our real home is in the wilderness, to just that extent we give ourselves permission to evade responsibility for the lives we actually lead. We inhabit civilization while holding some part of ourselves—what we imagine to be the most precious part—aloof from its entanglements. We work our nine-to-five jobs in its institutions, we eat its food, we drive its cars . . . , we benefit from the intricate and all too invisible networks with which it shelters us, all the while pretending that these things are not an essential part of who we are. By imagining that our true home is in the wilderness, we forgive ourselves the homes we actually inhabit.[2]

Our tendency to equate "wilderness" with the most pristine kind of "nature" has historical roots. Early visual representations of the West (particularly paintings and landscape photography) defined nature as "untouched" and separate from human culture. To this day, many environmental groups remain most concerned with preserving what they believe to be the most unsullied places in the natural world. According to one scholar, this narrow focus has allowed us to ignore "industrialism's progressive plundering of the planet" and to not concern ourselves with "nature" in our inhabited environments.[3]

Think of the lines we draw between nature and culture every day. The news media feature a conflict over logging in a national forest, but don't cover the far more extensive daily displacement of hosts of trees, plants, and animals by development. We value bodies of water where we go to boat or fish, but consider it acceptable to waste water or pollute water where we live. All of these communicate about our culture and the natural world—not just the words of environmental groups and journalists, but the ordinary words and actions in our lived-in spaces.

The way we describe and understand the nonhuman world is of course entangled with the human one. Does "nature" exist separate from our conceptualization of it? After all, "What we mean when we use the word 'nature' says as much about ourselves as about the things we label with that word."[4] Depending on the individual, "nature" may be the state park or the most remote corner on earth; "nature" may be the Garden of Eden, or something you buy at The

Nature Company; "nature" may be the Rainforest Café or Disney World. "Nature" may be angelic or demonic and avenging, such as when "natural" disasters like hurricanes occur.

In short, "nature," and in a different way "environment," are complicated cultural concepts, not just words. Nevertheless, they *communicate*. The words and how we use them interpret and define what exists beyond humans. This is nature, that is not. This is an environmental issue, but this is not. The definitions and meanings to a certain extent influence our behaviors and practices and our communication about it.

That is not to say, however, that nature or environment or whatever we want to call it is one big social construction and doesn't really exist out there independent of us and our definition of it. The physical, nonhuman world does exist; ecosystems and their inhabitants would unfold and continue just fine without humans. *Social construction*—the definitions and meanings we come to accept through our social interaction—is just one component. Other components are the historical and cultural contexts in which we live and the unique sets of individual experience we carry with us. When a forest is portrayed on TV as dangerous, it doesn't match my own experience because I grew up playing in the woods and have a strong affinity for that type of habitat. A lifelong Manhattan resident likely has a different notion of what nature is good for and where it exists than a Kansas farmer or an Alaskan bush pilot.

For all these reasons, environmental communication is a complex and multi-layered phenomenon. All environmental messages have ideological roots that are deep and that are influenced by individual experience, geography, history, and culture. Communication takes place at the individual level, in small social interactions, and at the macro level in our cultural institutions. Environmental communication involves sending and receiving words and pictures, but also actions. We read news about genetically modified organisms and drilling on public lands. We get direct mail from environmental groups. We hear about the price of oil in the Middle East. These messages may make the environment seem distant and a nonsalient feature of daily life. Yet how we build and landscape homes, how we travel to workplaces, how we consume resources, and what we do in our leisure time—these also involve communication (direct or implied) about the natural world. Even food choices can be considered environmental acts for they bear serious consequences for the use of land and animals, the use of water and chemicals, and for food waste and waste disposal. Essentially everything we do bears a relationship to (and has consequences for) the natural world. Each and every individual is surrounded by—and participates in—communication about the natural world on a daily basis.

A recent story in the *Los Angeles Times* reported that at the same time that the city was spending $1 million to raise awareness about how the tap water was perfectly safe to drink, various city departments had been buying bottled water. Several years ago, I went to an environmental communication conference and they handed me bottled water with my registration packet. I see water bottles littering hiking trails and I see them wheeled out by the caseload from discount stores; Americans spend over $8 billion a year on bottled water. Some of my colleagues, friends, and students buy it.

There is a lot of communication going on here. Advertising communicates that bottled water is safer and better than tap water, carries social status, and that the product is pure, healthy, and comes from pristine mountain snows or springs. Waiters ask if you want "a water." At the same time, news stories report that bottled water receives far less testing and is often less pure, not to mention the energy and waste in its distribution and consumption. The cheap price communicates that it's a good consumer choice (even though numerous environmental costs are *not* reflected in that price). What these messages "say" to me may not be the same thing they say to you. To many people, they say "convenience" and "better than tap water." To others, they say plentiful resources exist solely for human convenience and immediate human desires. But it's hard to deny that all these messages and actions about bottled water take place on the same stage with other messages about water—an activist arguing for minimum stream flows, a journalist writing about water conservation, a kid telling his parent to turn off the water while washing dishes, and a municipal water department trying to convince residents that tap water is safe to drink.

Because we communicate about the natural world on many levels, it follows that the solutions to environmental problems are similarly complex. Part of that solution is a bigger and broader understanding of how we "talk" to each other—in word, thought, and practice—about natural resources and our relationship with them. This book provides a comprehensive, introductory understanding of how we individually develop environmental beliefs and ideologies, how we express those through communication, how we are influenced by the communication of pop culture and social institutions, and how all this communication becomes part of the larger social fabric of this thing called "the environment."

This book endeavors to enlarge the definition of environmental messages and where we find them, and to encourage readers to go beyond their face value. The premise is that recognizing multiple levels of everyday communication—individual belief and ideology, popular culture, and discourse by social institutions—is vital for understanding the subtle complexities of environmental communication. The chapters explore and develop the premises that environmental communication is:

> Expressed in values, words, actions, and everyday practices
> Individually interpreted and negotiated
> Historically and culturally rooted
> Ideologically derived and driven
> Embedded in a dominant societal paradigm that assigns instrumental value to the environment and believes it exists to serve humans
> Intricately tied to pop culture, particularly advertising and entertainment
> Framed and reported by the media in a way that generally supports the status quo
> Mediated and influenced by social institutions like government and business

The first section of this book explores environmental communication at the individual level and the cultural contexts and conditions that shape it. The first chapter in this section explores how each person—environmentalist or not—develops an environmental belief system based on experiences in childhood and adolescence, a sense of place, and historical and cultural influences. Chapter 2 discusses these belief systems as fully developed environmental ideologies and places them along a spectrum of environmental thought.

Many people associate environmentalism with beliefs such as "conservation" and "preservation"; however, these ideologies represent only a narrow (and fairly conservative) piece of the spectrum. Less human-centered belief systems such as deep ecology, ecofeminism, and Native American ideologies also are discussed. Chapter 3 explores how these ideologies shape individual attitudes and behaviors toward the natural world. Our beliefs also are expressed in interpersonal communication, everyday practices, and public opinion. Decades of research exploring values, attitudes, and pro-environmental behaviors have discovered that there's a complex (and not entirely consistent) relationship between how we feel, think, and act. The cultural context of our working lives and how they drive our consumer culture is the topic of chapter 4. We tend to think of most jobs as utterly divorced from the natural world, though in truth they are impossible to separate. Our jobs also enable our participation in the "buyosphere" of consumer culture.

The second section of the book shifts the focus to the various forums where environmental communication takes place: leisure, advertising, animal communication, news media, government and business, and environmental groups. Chapter 5 moves beyond the workplace to examine how nonwork or leisure is commodified and sold as an experience. From parks to tourism and entertainment, communication directs our experiences and attaches meaning and value to the natural world, often in the form of a product. Ubiquitous advertising is the subject of chapter 6. Many ads utilize the natural world, often as an idealized backdrop, and present it as sublime and entirely for human desires and benefit. In ads and in many other messages, animals are the perfect "shorthand" to communicate an environmental message. Chapter 7 investigates our perceptions of animals and how they are influenced by myth, history, pop culture, and even news media.

The last three chapters in this section concern several forms of "mediated" communication about the environment. Much of the information we receive about the environment is not the result of personal experience or personal reality, but of a mediated social reality that's shaped by social institutions and social values. While pop culture messages (such as from advertising and the entertainment industry) intercede in our perception of nature and environment, their aim is to sell products (and meanings) to mass audiences. The aim of some social institutions in entering the environmental discussion differs. News media, government, business and corporations, and environmental groups all shape and filter messages that are related to the natural world and our use of it. When news media (discussed in Chapter 8) present a story concerning the environment, they choose a story "frame" that encourages us to view the event one way and not another. The choice of news sources lets some humans speak for the environment, but not others. This chapter discusses how environmental stories are instigated, chosen, reported, and framed. Environmental groups strive to frame the environment as a social change issue; that is, to varying degrees, they must argue that the current situation is unacceptable and posit an alternative vision. Chapter 9 examines public relations and the "battle for spin" by government and business in environmental communication. Increasingly, corporations are participating in the communication and perception of environmental issues, not just related to the products they sell but in relation to their environmental image. They are funneling millions of dollars into advertising and public relations to change the definition of "green" and the nature of the environmental dialogue. Government agencies are charged with the role of "guardians," protecting natural resources and public health, yet fulfilling an obligation to the commercial sector. In essence, the battle for spin is not over physical things like wilderness or fish, but over the meaning and value attached to those physical things, which affects their destiny. The final chapter is concerned with the social change sought by environmental groups and the communication constraints they face as "challengers" to the status quo. Ultimately, for messages of change to be effective, they must come from many sources.

For anyone born after the first Earth Day in 1970, the environment you will pass on to your children will not be the same one your parents passed along to you—in some ways better but in some ways worse. Rivers may no longer catch on fire (as did Cleveland's Cuyahoga in the 1960s), but numerous waterways remain endangered and aquifers are being sucked dry. Our cars now use unleaded gas and catalytic converters, but we travel more and more miles in larger and larger cars, which means worsening air quality that threatens the life and lungs of children and healthy adults alike. Roadways may be more litter free, but chemical "litter" now appears in beluga whales in the Arctic and mothers' breast milk. Bald eagles and peregrine falcons have returned to our skies, but innumerable plant and animal species leave us for good every year. And the newest, most intractable environmental problem of all, global climate change, is already altering the very cycles of life on earth. Bird and animal migrations and behavior are changing as temperatures warm and native northern villages occupied for centuries are being evacuated.

These are the on-the-ground conditions. But what we do with this information and how we continue to communicate about it is another matter. What indeed matters is how we individually and collectively translate what this means, determine the implications for daily life, and agree whether this is acceptable or not. The power and persuasiveness of human communication will then be thoroughly tested.

"The environment" may be relatively new as a prominent social issue, but it is unlikely to be far from public concern for the remainder of this century. Environmental issues are not just the purview and concern of scientists and policymakers, but involve every single individual. Whether or not you consider yourself a radical tree-hugger, a concerned conservationist, or just an average citizen with other things to think about, environmental communication and practices affect you every single day. They involve what you eat, the air you breathe, the water you drink, and profoundly affect the nonhuman species that share our planet. Understanding how we communicate about the natural world—both individually and collectively, verbally and nonverbally—provides important insights into the challenges that lie before us.

# 1

## The Formation of Environmental Beliefs

If you've seen one redwood tree, you've seen them all.

*—Ronald Reagan*

Something will have gone out of us as a people if we ever let
the remaining wilderness be destroyed. . . . We need wilderness
preserved—as much of it as is still left, and as many kinds—
because it was the challenge against which our character as a
people was formed. The reminder and the reassurance that it is
still there is good for our spiritual health even if we never once
in ten years set foot in it.

*—Wallace Stegner*

All environmental communication stems from a complex, evolving
system of beliefs about the natural world. Regardless of how well it is
understood or recognized, an environmental belief system inhabits
each individual and informs her or him about where humans "fit"
in relation to the rest of the nonhuman world. How you value redwoods, insects, and ecosystems—as well as the environmental messages you send and receive—all have roots in this belief system.

Like most people, you probably have not given much thought
to your environmental belief system or what influenced it. You may
think of "the environment" as something out there that people tend
to fight over and wring hands about, but not as something that's a
part of you. But we breathe an atmosphere, drink a watershed, participate in a climate, and live in a habitat that supplies us with food.

Famed naturalist and writer Wallace Stegner wrote that environmental beliefs "have roots as deep as creosote rings, and live as long, and grow as slowly. Every action is an idea before it is an action, and perhaps a feeling before it is an idea, and every idea rests upon other ideas that have preceded it in time."[1] All environmental messages are crafted from a perspective, informed by a worldview, reference personal relationships and experiences, and are used to justify words and actions.

A fully formed environmental belief system is an *environmental ideology*, or a way of thinking about the natural world that a person uses to justify actions toward it. Ideology articulates a relationship to the land and its creatures, and to some extent, guides the way we act toward it. The next chapter discusses a full spectrum of specific environmental ideologies. These ideologies become the lens through which we interpret words and behavior—received from literature, education, film, news media, advertising, and pop culture—about the natural world. But first, it's important to explore what forms and shapes these beliefs, which is the focus of this chapter.

## Development of Environmental Belief Systems

Your belief system is both an individual and a cultural product. The environmental history of this country, your childhood and adult experiences with the natural world, the beliefs of your parents and significant others—these all helped to develop your environmental beliefs. The process begins in childhood, particularly through direct experiences with nature and through deep connections to physical places. By adulthood, much of your ideological foundation has been laid but significant adult experiences may continue to shape it.

In the summer after sixth grade, I shared a tent at church camp with two girls from a Chicago housing project and a girl from an Indian reservation in South Dakota. The Chicago girls hated the bugs, the primitive conditions, and complained that it was so quiet they couldn't sleep. Backpacking was torture to them. Even at our young age, each of us already had established a relationship and comfort level with the natural world that would continue to mold our developing ideologies, regardless of the same direct experience with nature that we shared at camp.

Understanding environmental belief systems and how they form is essential to understanding and analyzing environmental messages. This chapter explores some of the factors that influence ideology formation:

> Childhood experiences
> A sense of place
> Historical and cultural contexts

## Childhood and Nature

Almost everyone can remember a special outdoor place from childhood. Mine was the woods and fields of my rural midwestern neighborhood. On three sides of our house was a strip of woods with basswood trees for climbing, shagbark hickory trees with nuts to shell, and an assortment of tree limbs for building forts. The woods had squirrels, rabbits, raccoons, deer, blue jays, and owls, and for our summertime delight, fireflies. Across the road in the "park," an undeveloped parcel held in common by all the families on our road, we played Capture the Flag and held important meetings among the trees. Beyond the next road to the west was "the crick," a steep, wooded gully that held a small stream where we explored every inch, catching crawdads in summer and attempting to ice skate its crooked course in winter.

Even if I never saw this place again, I could draw a map of it in magnificent detail as if it were yesterday. Without intellectualizing or categorizing the experience, I could label the neighbors' houses, the paths through the woods, even a few favorite trees and landmarks. When I remember this place, a flood of senses—smells, sounds, colors, features, sizes, and shapes—returns. A person's childhood memory map can just as easily be an urban vacant lot or an abandoned building as a grandparents' farm or a family cottage on the lake.

Author, poet, and naturalist Gary Snyder reminds us, "The childhood landscape is learned on foot, and a map is inscribed in the mind—trails and pathways and groves—the mean dog, the cranky old man's house, the pasture with the bull in it—going out wider and farther. All of us carry within us a picture of the terrain that was learned roughly between the ages of 6 and 9."[2]

It is well documented that the experiences we gain from special outdoor haunts as children are carried through—with knowledge added and reinterpretations made—to adulthood. Even decades ago, psychologists knew that children's experiences with nature had crucial and irreplaceable effects on their physical, cognitive, and emotional development.[3] As one noted, "The non-human environment, far from being of little or no account to human personality development, constitutes one of the most basically important ingredients of human psychological existence."[4] Earlier forms of a child's knowledge are not lost as the child develops but are embedded, reworked, and transformed into more comprehensive ways of understanding the natural world and acting upon it.[5]

Experiences with nature are like baggage a child carries that help shape the present and future. One researcher found that childhood experiences indeed helped direct future careers. The two most common attributes among a diverse group of environmental activists were the many hours spent outdoors in a keenly remembered natural place in childhood or adolescence, and an adult who taught respect for nature.[6] The adults were parents, grandparents, other relatives, camp counselors, and neighbors. In another study, over 95 percent of people reported that the outdoors was the most significant physical environment in their childhood.[7]

There are, of course, different ways to experience nature. A *direct* experience involves actual physical contact with natural settings and nonhuman species, and activities associated with this type of experience are largely nonplanned and nondirected.[8] Building forts in a wooded area, wading streams, and exploring an overgrown city gully are direct experiences with the natural world.

*Indirect* experiences also involve physical contact with nature but in more restricted, programmed, and managed contexts. Here, contact with natural settings and species is the result of regulated and/or contrived human activity, and nature is often the product of deliberate and extensive human manipulation. Indirect experiences include visits to zoos, aquariums, botanical gardens, and contact with domesticated animals and habitats such as pets, gardens, and manicured parks. Although some indirect experiences may seem "wild" on the surface (like a wooded nature center), the experience qualifies as indirect if the children's activities are largely directed and controlled by adults.

A *vicarious* or *symbolic* experience lacks any physical contact with nature and instead takes place via representations that are sometimes realistic, sometimes not. TV specials, books, and movies about nature are vicarious experiences, which can be metaphorical, stylized, and symbolic. In this sense, an animated Disney movie is just as much a vicarious experience as is an ancient cave painting of bison.

All of these types of experiences with the natural world are important and have their place, particularly at different times of development. A toddler is more captivated by the vicarious experience of a book about a family of talking bears than by a solo jaunt through the woods. But what concerns child development specialists is the explosion of vicarious experiences and the dramatic decline of available, authentic, and unprogrammed direct experiences. They have noted an erosion of direct and spontaneous experiences with relatively undisturbed nature, especially by urban and suburban kids, and the corresponding substitution of more artificial and symbolic encounters. There has been a very real decline in children's direct experiences, particularly with healthy and abundant natural systems.

Scholars know that overall, childhood today is more structured, more indoors, and more fearful.[9] One study noted a sharp decline in the amount of time kids age three to twelve spent outdoors—from eighty-six minutes per day in 1981 to just forty-two minutes in 1997.[10] Another researcher concluded that childhood experiences with nature were diverging from direct contact with nature and animals, to more contact with symbolic nature, virtual reality, and "things."[11] The changes in the outdoor lives of children are profound enough for one to warn of "the extinction of experience" for future generations as landscapes and habitats continue to erode and degrade.[12]

There is no substitute for direct one-on-one experiences with authentic nature and the role such experiences play in child development: "direct experience of nature plays a significant, vital, and perhaps irreplaceable role in affective, cognitive, and evaluative development"[13] of children.

## Sense of Place

A friend once told me that she knew she'd grown attached to a place when she landed at the airport one day and subconsciously—but strongly—knew she was "home." Some people feel that at-home-ness in the mountains, some feel it near a body of water, and some feel strongly at home in a small rural town where they know every back road and change of the season. Urban environments also can evoke strong attachments to place. That at-home feeling has to do with the attachment to a physical landscape or space, not just to the people living there. It's a location that gives you a feeling of security, belonging, and stability. It's a feeling of living in an environment that has both boundaries and identity. The physical place is a source of rootedness, belonging, and comfort.

Attachment to place can mean fierce emotional struggles over the most appropriate use of that place, and at times, an inability to see one's own place as degraded. Studies have shown that people have the tendency to believe that the next city up the road has more pollution and environmental problems than their own city.

Sense of place has been described as the "rich and often powerfully emotional sentiments that influence how people perceive, experience, and value the environment."[14] The place is a physical space imbued with meaning and special significance and represents a highly subjective encounter. The meanings that individuals associate with a place may have purely instrumental or utilitarian values (what the land "is good for") as well as intangible ones like belonging, beauty, and spirituality.

"Places have a way of claiming people."[15] However, some of that strong attachment no doubt exists at the subconscious level. In the context of our everyday lives, we are familiar enough with "place" that we tend to relate to it in a largely unconscious way.[16] Because our regular routine is part of being in the world, we're not always conscious of our feelings for place.[17] Yet we very much associate comfort and security with places we "know" and feel a sense of place attachment.

For many people, the relationship they have with a particular place also becomes the means by which they grapple with issues like identity and self-development. If you feel troubled, you might go for a walk in the park or woods. If you need time to think, you go to a favorite fishing hole. Children likewise need undirected time alone in a favorite place. The restorative effects of natural environments are well documented: people seek out nature as a temporary escape and to reduce mental fatigue, and also gain self-esteem and a sense of competence from being in nature.[18]

Our relation to a physical place helps us make sense of the world and know how to act within it.[19] In other words, "Places inform who we are and therefore how we are to behave; in short, to be some-*where* is to be some*one* . . . [P]laces are also imbued with socially constructed (and often politically defined) expectations of appropriate behavior."[20]

For example, if you see a deer in a forest, you observe the animal at a distance. Yet if you see a deer in a petting zoo, you would approach the animal, perhaps with food. So place is not just the biophysical characteristics of woods or zoo, but also the social and political processes (rules and norms) and cultural meanings that define a space, give it value, and help determine how we are to use it. (Chapter 3 contains more detail about rules and norms.) The meaning of a place (not just the physical characteristics of it) is what holds power over people.[21]

People with different social roles and identities can view the same physical place through very different lenses. For example, imagine a developer, a farmer, and a hunter all looking at an open field.[22] Each will conceptualize the place (and its potential) according to who they are and how they define themselves. The values and importance they attach to that field and the way each of them views it is fundamentally an expression of their self-identity. "Not only do places affect how individuals look out on the world, they influence how they look at themselves. How one understands, evaluates, and acts in a geographic setting directly reflects one's self-identity. Like a tinted window, place is at once reflective and transparent, allowing one to look on oneself while looking on others."[23]

At the same time, the physical landscape affects the social role you see for yourself. In other words, how you interact in a place shapes your identity relative to that place. In your office, your identity is wrapped around your role as a manager, an employee. When walking through the desert, your social role may shift to that of a naturalist or a recreationist. Your perceptions and evaluations of the environment in those places are expressions of place-based self-identity.[24]

It makes sense that conflict over the use of public lands is "as much a contest over place meanings as it is a competition over the allocation and distribution of scarce resources among interest groups."[25] Relationships to place and self-identity become very wrapped up in collectively shared, conscious, and contested political natures.[26] Places then become important to group identity as well; anglers or ranchers or hikers will identify strongly with their group's values and interests as well as their own individual ones.

If sense of place is so important—both in the development of our belief systems and to the protection of places to which we are attached—are there ways to better "know" the natural world and to connect with it? Environmental education programs maintain that when children know a place intimately, they are more likely to care for it, respect it, and safeguard it. Learning about the species that live in a natural system, the plants that rely on it, and the cycles of precipitation and growth that unfold, helps children in their psychological development and in their sense of themselves in a particular place. Some states and municipalities have institutionalized environmental education programs in their school systems, though the reach is far from encompassing.

For adults, environmental education may take place in natural history classes or field trips. Others have looked to something called "bioregionalism," a practice which calls for restructuring everyday life (urban and rural) to allow people to live more harmoniously "in place." For example, a bioregionalist would strive for more regionally based self-sufficiency in obtaining basic supplies and in food production and consumption. The bioregionalist might turn toward Community Supported Agriculture (CSA), a cooperative partnership between an organic farmer and members who buy a "share" of the farm's produce, which is then delivered weekly to a convenient (and often urban) location. The buy-in removes a great deal of the risk from organic farming and reduces the time and attention required for marketing. Many CSAs also involve members and children in activities on the farm (such as spring transplanting or pumpkin harvesting). After all, many adults and kids alike don't realize that perfectly shaped mini carrots don't come out of the ground that way!

To see how well you know and understand the natural environment in which you live, take the Bioregional Quiz, Box 1.1.

## Box 1.1
Bioregional Quiz

> Trace the water you drink from its source to your faucet.
> What stage is the moon in right now?
> What was the total precipitation in your area last year?
> Name two native, edible plants in your region. Name two native grasses in this area.
> From what direction do winter storms generally come in your region?
> Where does your garbage go?
> How long is the growing season where you live?
> When do the deer (or other ungulates) rut here, and when are their young born?
> Name five resident birds in this area. Name five birds that migrate from this area.
> What primary ecological event or process influenced the landform here? What's the evidence?
> From where you are sitting right now, which direction is north?
> What spring wildflowers (not human planted) are consistently among the first to bloom here?

Source: Adapted from Charles, Dodge, Milliman, and Stockley "Where You At?" *CoEvolution Quarterly,* Winter 1981.

### *Historical and Cultural Context*

The environmental belief systems of most Americans have been significantly influenced by the history of colonization of the country, as well as the religious traditions brought by its settlers. Before colonization, a vastly different environmental ideology was held by Native Americans. The next chapter discusses their beliefs in more detail, but the environmental ideology of these original inhabitants has played little role in the formation of the country's dominant beliefs about humans in relation to the natural world.

When Columbus landed in 1492, the land was not pristine;[27] it was lived in. Indians sometimes killed large numbers of animals, though their actions, unlike the white settlers, rarely endangered or exterminated species.[28] Overall, Indian food gathering and farming procedures can said to be environmentally "smart" for they used the land competently without spoiling it.[29] At least part of this relationship must be attributed to their ideologies regarding the natural world, which encouraged living within natural ecosystem limits.[30] The use of low-impact technology (in construction of dwellings, harvesting, and agriculture) and the lack of mass-scale development were consistent with a harmonious relationship with nature. Many tribes in North America had semi-nomadic lifestyles, traveling with the seasons for reasons of climate and food availability. In addition, most tribes relied on a series of "ecological safety nets"[31] to sustain their subsistence way of life. For example, if a drought or other disaster harmed an agricultural crop, the tribe could rely on hunting and gathering. Even with the introduction of the horse (which preceded the arrival of significant numbers of settlers), with few exceptions, few tribes willingly gave up agriculture to rely solely on the buffalo.[32]

At the time Columbus arrived on the Atlantic coast, there were an estimated 100 million Indians living on the continent.[33] By the time European settlers arrived in North America, there were only 10 to 12 million, their populations ravaged by waves of European diseases against which they had no immunity: smallpox, influenza, diphtheria, measles, tuberculosis, and chicken pox. One scholar said, "It was the greatest mortality in history."[34]

The clash between Indians and settlers was also ideological in terms of relationship to the natural world. Until the Age of Enlightenment and the scientific revolution, the prevailing viewpoint of the peoples on earth—nature-based cultures like the Indians but also the Greeks, Romans, and Sumerians—was that the earth was a living thing.[35] If the Earth is a living, conscious being, it must be treated with respect and loving care. Many native peoples (not just Indians) speak of the planet as "mother"—a mother who nurtures plants, animals, and all life, and from whom humans germinate and burst into life and back into whom they eventually dissolve.

The first Europeans who arrived in this country brought with them a dramatically different view of the natural world. As one scholar put it, "It wasn't so much that Europe *discovered* America as that it *incorporated* it and made it part of its own special, long-held and recently ratified, view of nature."[36] The record of medieval Europe was one of massive deforestation, erosion, siltation, exhaustion, pollution, and extermination. Animals were subject to severe exploitation and cruel treatment. Hunting was "far more than a fashion and only slightly less than a sacrament,"[37] and flesh played a larger role in the diet of medieval Europe than anywhere else in world. It could be said that warring against species and predators was Europe's preoccupation as a culture.

Some have argued that Europeans' regard for nature was more hostile and antagonistic than any other developed civilization. Although other cultures certainly had effects on the environment, "nowhere else was the essential reverence for nature seriously challenged, nowhere did there emerge the idea that human achievement and material betterment were to be won by *opposing* nature, nowhere any equivalent to that frenzy of defiance and destruction that we find on the Western record."[38]

With rampant utilization of the natural world also came an estrangement, a distancing of humans from creation, and, a fear of it. It wasn't until fairly recently (the eighteenth century) that most Europeans viewed wilderness and mountains in their own countries with anything but horror and dread.[39] Nature was seen as antagonistic and mountains were places of dread, full of diabolic creatures, and just plain hideous. This viewpoint is reflected in words such as "wilderness," from an old English word meaning "of or about wild beasts." Wilderness was the place where covenant-breakers and the cursed were sent. "Be*wild*ered" indicates one who is lost, confused, and where nothing is predictable. It is a very short step from having a fear of the "wild" and love of the "tamed" to an imperative of human domination and control of the natural world.[40]

The ideology that shaped the actions of the first settlers also allowed colonizers to justify their east to west march across the wilds over the next centuries. Nature was seen as a storehouse of commodities, there for the taking. Restraint was remarkably absent in the use of nature, as was appreciation of it. Instead, eyes were firmly focused on what the settlers perceived as their "manifest destiny" to conquer and tame the wilderness. As the Frenchman de Tocqueville wrote two centuries after the conquest began: "In Europe, people talk a great deal about the wilds of America, but the Americans themselves never think about them; they are insensible to the wonders of inanimate nature and they may be said not to perceive the mighty forests that surround them till they fall beneath the hatchet. Their eyes are fixed upon another sight: the American people views its own march across these wilds, draining swamps, turning the course of rivers, peopling solitudes, and subduing nature."[41]

There are numerous historical accounts of the centuries-long westward expansion and the toll it took on natural resources. The land underwent inconceivable transformation—60 million beavers killed, and game birds, herbivores, and fur-bearers vastly depleted. Deciduous forests were similarly exploited, with states in the upper Midwest harvesting over 90 percent of their trees by 1900.

Many settlers believed it was their Christian duty to impose control, civilize, tame, subdue, and in essence, denature nature. Christian and non-Christians are familiar with passages from the Bible's book of Genesis that say God created man to have "dominion over the fish of the sea, and over the fowl of the air . . . and over all the earth, and over every creeping thing that creepeth upon the earth" (1:26). Man was commanded to "be fruitful, and multiply, and replenish the earth, and subdue it" (1:28). One historian concluded that the New Testament "places man at the center of the universe,"[42] obviously a human-centered relationship to the natural world.

Some religious scholars point out that some Old Testament passages set limits to human's dealings with nature and urges respect for creation. But the Bible made clear that nature was man's to use (and even to use responsibly), but not to worship. A strict interpretation would be that God transcends nature: "God is wholly other: He cannot be revealed through nature."[43] Humans were admonished to remember that the Creator and creation are "radically distinct . . . it is idolatrous to worship creation, and so there is certainly nothing sacrilegious about treating nature as a resource for human benefit."[44] In addition, man exclusively is created in the image of God and is, thus, segregated from the rest of nature.[45] Thus, the Judeo-Christian view of nature is hierarchical: God over man, and man over nature.

Since the first European settlers, there has been ongoing debate over interpretations of the Bible and what those mean for environmental ideology. Like any ancient text, Biblical passages have been translated and interpreted repeatedly. The debate has been particularly vociferous since the 1960s. In 1967, Lynn White, Jr. began a firestorm of discussion about the role of Christianity in environmental problems when he published "The Historical Roots of Our Ecologic Crisis" in *Science*. White argued that these roots could be tied directly to the "Christian dogma of creation."[46] White called for a resurrection of the teachings of St. Francis of Assisi, who he said "tried to depose man from his monarchy over creation and set up a democracy for all God's creatures, for all creatures have souls, and all is reflected in the glory of the Creator."[47]

White's essay touched a chord with the growing environmental awareness of Americans, but it also touched a nerve with many Christians. Attacks and rebuttals flew. Some argued that science and technology and cultural forces had more to do with the ecological crisis than Christianity. Still others used the essay to contemplate and further articulate what they saw as "Christian stewardship."

Today, the historical and cultural context set largely by the European colonizers remains one of the most dominant influences on the environmental belief systems (and resultant messages) of a large number of Americans. Meanwhile, history has left us with a very different context for Native American culture and its effect on our environmental belief systems. In pop-culture depictions, Native Americans are portrayed as "ecologically noble savages" who are at one with nature. Indians' affinity for nature is viewed as quaint but impractical. White culture also tends to present what is "native" as synonymous with "nature." In movies, advertisements, and even news portrayals, Indians are shown as timeless beings who have grown little historically and remain primitive, uncivilized, and "wild"—part of a once-great but essentially dead or dying culture. Though Indian ideology survives today, it has contributed far less to the formation our dominant environmental ideologies than that of our European ancestors.

## Conclusion

Our current belief systems about the natural world owe much to the historical and cultural context in which we live. Over time, we have been schooled to view resources as ours for the taking and creatures as justifiably below us in the pecking order. Our organizations, leaders, authors, laws, and cultural practices reflect our human-dominated belief system. Our cultural place in time seems a far more potent influence than our childhood experiences and geographical rootedness in determining our relationships to the natural world.

Yet, we can't dismiss the importance of the individual and the contributions that individual experience makes to environmental beliefs. Research has found that the direct experiences we have as children with undeveloped natural places and through the guidance of significant adults do indeed shape us profoundly and even affect career paths. I know firsthand the powerful influence of a childhood and adolescence immersed in creeks and critters and open woodlands. It was an indelible stamp on my future beliefs about where humans "fit" in relation to the rest of the nonhuman world.

As any natural resources professional knows, geography plays an undeniable role in every environmental issue. At a public hearing about land use alternatives, what shapes the communication is far more than the discrete physical characteristics. Places have a way of claiming us. It is not just the physical features but the meaning of a place that holds power over us and helps us determine what a piece of ground "is good for"—development, preservation, and everything in-between. Our sense of place—in addition to childhood experiences and historical and cultural contexts—influences how we perceive, experience, and value the natural world and ultimately, influences all our entire belief systems.

# 2

# A Spectrum of Environmental Ideologies

In communication about the environment, we often hear words like "preservation" and "conservation." Most of us have at least vague notions of their meanings, but perhaps don't connect them to the ideologies they represent.

As noted in the last chapter, our environmental belief systems are formed and shaped by childhood experiences, a sense of place, and historical and cultural contexts. A fully formed belief system concerning the natural world is an environmental ideology. By adulthood, a fairly well-formed ideology informs our communication and helps us interpret the communication of others. This chapter examines the full range of contemporary environmental ideologies.

The *Oxford Dictionary* defines an ideology as "A system of ideas or way of thinking pertaining to a class or individual, especially as a basis of some economic or political theory or system, regarded as justifying actions and especially to be maintained irrespective of events." To extend this definition, an environmental ideology is a way of thinking about the natural world that a person uses to justify actions toward it. Ideology articulates a relationship to the land and its creatures, and to some extent, guides the way we act toward it. An ideology is deepseated and not easily swayed by external events (as opinions are). If someone defines himself as a "preservationist" (desiring to preserve and protect the natural world), a downturn in the economy, a divorce, an earthquake, or a change in the political make-up of Congress won't change his underlying environmental ideology.

A practical way to order a discussion of environmental ideologies is on a spectrum that represents the range of human relationships with and beliefs about the natural world (see Box 2.1). Although a variety of labels might be used to anchor the endpoints of such a spectrum, a useful and descriptive labeling is "anthropocentric" and "ecocentric." It is important to note that everyone falls somewhere in this spectrum, whether she regards herself as an "environmentalist" or not. It's also important to note that even though some belief systems attract far more adherents than others, all of the ideologies mentioned here can be found today.

*Anthro*pocentric is human-centered. Humans are superior to and dominate the rest of creation, and the natural world is ranked hierarchically with humans at the top. Natural resources exist only to serve human welfare. Humans consider themselves separate from nature, if not alienated from and fearful of it. If a shape represented anthropocentricism, it would be a pyramid with humans at the top and the rest of the natural world beneath. Most Americans' ideologies lie on this end of the spectrum.

According to some, anthropocentrism has been a "detour" of thousands of years,[1] preceded by primitive earth-based cultures. Historians have pondered what factors led cultures to become so highly anthropocentric. Some point to the replacement of hunting and gathering by large-scale agriculture.[2] Others cite the growth of "civilized" cultures (from the Latin word "civitas" meaning cities) and the rise of science and technology as key reasons for an anthropocentric shift. Still others claim that Christian theology insisted on a human-centered focus.

The ecocentric (sometimes called *biocentric*) end of the spectrum can be represented by a circle, a nonhierarchical mix of interdependent relationships or a web of all life. According to ecocentrism, no single species (like humans) rules—heterarchy as opposed to the hierarchy. Humans are an interdependent, integral part of the biological world but no more or no less important than other portions of it. All living and nonliving elements of the nonhuman world—animals, fish, birds, insects, water, air, soil, rocks, trees, plants, and so on—are intrinsically valuable and important.

Some scholars consider the dualism of anthropocentrism and ecocentrism to be only one dimension of environmental belief systems.[3] Here, the terms are used in the broadest possible way to denote the overall relationship humans have with the natural world, a

## Box 2.1
### A Spectrum of Environmental Ideologies

The figure on the opposite page roughly locates some environmental ideologies on a spectrum of anthropocentrism to ecocentrism—roughly because the relative positioning is a subjective best guess. Even within a single ideology, adherents disagree on definitions and core beliefs and have staked out subunits within the same perspective. Because ideology ultimately rests at the individual level, interpretations naturally vary.

This spectrum is adapted and expanded from previous taxonomies of environmental thought.[1] What this spectrum attempts to make clear is that these ideological perspectives are not historical and linear in their development, and that all ideologies are present in American society today.

Unrestrained instrumentalism: The natural world and all its resources exist solely for human use, use that need not be restrained or limited in any way. Extremely anthropocentric, instrumentalism decides how to treat and use resources with only immediate human desires and wants in mind.

Conservationism: "Wise use" and the "greatest use [of natural resources] for the greatest number" of people. Nonhuman entities have only utilitarian value, that is they are valuable only in their potential as resources for human use.

Preservationism: Conserving resources for humans to use and enjoy for reasons that go beyond their purely instrumental value to include scientific or ecological, aesthetic, and religious worth.

Ethics and values-driven ideologies: Nonhuman entities have value that goes beyond utilitarian, scientific, aesthetic, or religious worth to possessing intrinsic value. Humans have moral and ethical duties to (some) nonhuman entities, which have a "right" to exist. Humans are members of a biotic community but traditional hierarchy is modified only slightly. Includes land-based ethics and animal rights.

Transformative ideologies: Seek to transform anthropocentric relations and extensionism of "rights" into more ecocentric relationships. These ideologies are more radical because they attempt to move beyond reformist "shallow ecology" to a deeper questioning of the root causes of anti-environmental attitudes and behavior. Some transformative ideologies seek new or drastically revised social institutions and recognize the effect of power and dominance on treatment of the natural world. These ideologies include ecological sensibility, deep ecology, social ecology, ecofeminism, Native American ideologies, and Eastern religious traditions.

1. John Rodman, "Four Forms of Ecological Consciousness Reconsidered," in *Ethics and the Environment*, eds. D. Scherer and T. Attig (Englewood Cliffs, NJ: Prentice-Hall, 1983), 82–92; Warwick Fox, "A Critical Overview of Environmental Ethics," *World Futures* 46 (1996):1–21; Peter Hay, *Main Currents in Environmental Thought* (Bloomington: Indiana University Press, 2002).

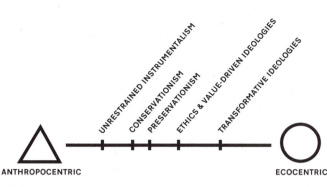

**Figure 2.1**

relationship that includes perspectives on growth and progress, on how other entities (living and nonliving) are valued, and the ethical perspectives that arise from each.

Although the distinctions may appear minor at first, the ideological differences are tremendous and call for very different ways of relating to and communicating about the natural world. At its most extreme anthropocentric end, the natural world is merely a storehouse of commodities for humans to use without restraint. Pure ecocentrism is harder to imagine. First, despite the presence of "environmentally friendly" ideologies, the dominant paradigm of American (and European) culture is still decidedly human-centered in its relationship to the natural world. Second, some scholars adopt a fairly postmodern interpretation that it's impossible for us to escape anthropocentric ideology simply because we are humans and cannot remove "the human face" from our perspective. Third, still others argue that more pure forms of ecocentrism are no longer historically open to us given the current state of global technology and culture.[4] Nevertheless, ecocentric ideology is a vital perspective to understand. Native American and Eastern belief systems clearly articulate a way of being in the natural world that differs dramatically from traditional Western ideologies and perhaps offer lessons to modern-day environmentalism.

It's important to emphasize that a person's belief system informs and guides behavior, but may not be entirely consistent with it. The reason for the disconnect may lie at the individual level; I may believe that all living creatures are valuable, but my words or actions might contradict that. At the cultural level, a variety of factors may reinforce a gap between belief and practice. It is very difficult to fully act upon an ideology that differs from the dominant ideology in a particular culture. Just as a person with a political ideology of socialism would find it difficult to fully practice that ideology in the United States, a person with an environmental ideology of ecofeminism may not be able to fully act upon that ideology. The existing social structure (and the dominant institutions in it) work as social controls upon individual choices and actions, whether through energy use, landscaping, or basic land ownership. Religious doctrines throughout the world attempt to shape or restrict the actions and beliefs of its adherents. The American legal system has determined that certain actions are illegal (e.g., killing protected species), regardless of whether those actions are consonant with someone's ideology. Thus, even if an individual possesses a strong ecocentric ideology, supportive lifestyle choices might be very limited. The dominant power institutions within a social system regulate or encourage conformity to a set of norms through socialization, the threat of coercion, or both.[5]

## Unrestrained Instrumentalism

"There is no 'democracy' of all creatures; a single human soul is worth more than the entire material creation. Just as man is here to serve God, so nature is here to serve man."

—R.V. Young, Jr.

At the heart of this ideology is a belief that humans are the most important and dominant entity in the natural world and resources exist entirely for humans' unlimited use. This belief system holds that decisions about resource use should be made only according to immediate human desires and wants. Because resources exist just for humans, their use need not be restrained or limited in any way. Of all environmental ideologies, it is unmistakably the most human-centered and anti-environmental, for the decision of how to treat and use resources is made with only immediate human desires and wants in mind. Natural resources of all kinds are "instruments" whose essential purpose is to serve human ends.

It's fairly easy to find communication and actions that fit this ideology, including the quote above. We could argue that typical American beliefs and practices regarding oil and gas (despite the increasing impacts from global warming) represent this ideology. The quote by President Reagan at the beginning of the last chapter—"If you've seen one redwood, you've seen them all."—expresses an instrumental belief. Typical land use practices often exemplify unrestrained instrumentalism, for human wants trump existing undeveloped habitat or watershed.

Fundamentalist Christians also believe in human superiority in relation to the nonhuman world. As one philosopher noted, "Fundamentalism's theology focuses on the relationship between God and the unique soul, to the exclusion of any relationship between humans and God's creation. . . . To devote one's life to reaching a paradise far superior to the world of earthly substance readily leads to apathy concerning the fate and condition of the physical world—especially when it is destined for the destruction of Armageddon in any case."[7] President Reagan's fundamentalist secretary of the interior, James Watt, stated that "My responsibility [as secretary of the interior] is to follow the Scriptures which call upon us to occupy the land until Jesus returns."[8]

Another avenue for unrestrained instrumentalism ideology was the "Wise Use Movement," a counter-environmental movement born out of the 1980s Sagebrush Rebellion, a movement of largely rural Western landowners who believed that environmentalists were out to destroy free enterprise, private property rights, and jobs, and were responsible for forcing entire industries out of business because of environmental regulations. In this century, President George W. Bush has made very clear his philosophy of instrumentalism and his desire to change and loosen environmental restraints, to the point of overriding laws and opposing public comment.

## Conservationism

"Building a just society requires that we develop and conserve the land's resources, because conservation without economic growth is morally untenable, while economic growth without conservation is unsustainable."[9]

—Pat Shea

Conservationism is less human-centered than instrumentalism but more so than preservationism. A conservationist ideology recognizes that there should be some restraints on humans' use of natural resources. However, the aim is to use those resources in a way that doesn't deplete or permanently damage them. Hence, good "conservation" means that people will have rivers for boating or swimming and clean water to drink. A conservationist ideology is not concerned about conserving water for fish—unless humans want to use those fish themselves. Thus, the focus of this ideology is still very much on humans and their needs and desires, but it is concerned with using natural resources "wisely."

In this country, the greatest growth in a conservationist ideology came about in the early 1900s, when the first sportsmen groups and environmental groups were founded, and the framework of governmental conservation was put into place to manage the nation's first national parks and national forests. After witnessing rampant and reckless exploitation across the continent, the belief was that the country's resources should be used wisely "for the greatest good of the greatest number" of humans, a phrase used by Gifford Pinchot, a forester for President Theodore Roosevelt.

Conservationism is an ideology not confined to "environmentalists" or members of an environmental group. Pinchot and President Roosevelt were examples of early conservationists, believing that the way forests were "managed" ensured a healthy supply of trees to cut in the future. A farmer who practices contour plowing and other techniques to protect topsoil has a conservation philosophy. A city dweller who believes in wise energy use by lowering thermostats and using mass transit demonstrates conservationism. Legislators who set hunting limits do so to ensure there will be sufficient animals for people to hunt in the future.

In all of these examples of conservationist practice, the focus is nevertheless on human benefit, not other species or entities. If fishing limits were set because of a belief that the fish had a right to exist—regardless of their value or benefit to humans—that would be a more ecocentric ideology. Conservationism holds that nonhuman entities (fish, plants, rocks) have only *utilitarian* value and are valuable only in their use-potential as resources for humans. The ideology is committed to maximizing the value of resources through maximizing their human use. It's an ideology, however "wise," of human chauvinism and human imperialism.[10]

Conservation (and preservation) describes much of the hundred-plus-year history of the environmental social movement and the current dominant ideology of the movement. Indeed, these two ideologies constitute what most Americans think of as environmentalism. The political struggle of the last several decades over environmentalism is a classic example of the tensions between the ideologies of conservationism and preservationism and the opposing instrumentalism that is embedded in the social structure and its history.

Despite how some people attempt to paint the discourse surrounding it, conservationism is not a radical ideology, but a reformist one. Conservationism can be thought of as a very conservative ideology for it attempts to be cautious and ensure resources for future generations of humans. Compared to unrestrained instrumentalism, conservationism calls for prudent or enlightened self-interest when making decisions about resource use. But taking conservation actions requires no drastic reformulating of institutions within the existing social system—economic, political, social, or cultural—or even in individual lifestyles. For example, to conserve air quality, "tinkering" within existing institutions of government and industry has brought about improvements in car emissions and gas mileage. But it hasn't meant changing individual or institutional lifestyles centered around automobiles or highway use. Likewise, recycling encourages a fairly minor action to ensure future resources; recycling doesn't say don't consume resources in the first place, but it actually supports their continued consumption.

The current worldwide buzz around *sustainable development* is also an example of a conservationist philosophy, attempting to ensure adequate arable land, water, and other resources to sustain human populations and economic growth well into the future. In the language of the Brundtland Report, one of the first ratified worldwide statements on the subject, sustainable development is "development that meets the needs of the present without compromising the ability of future generations to meet their own needs." Activists throughout the world have worked to ensure that people's lives are indeed sustainable at a very basic level—food, water, and shelter—but the word "sustainability" has been subverted by its association with economic growth and trade liberalization, which often includes widespread environmental degradation.

Depending on its use, "stewardship" can be considered part of a conservationist ideology. Although the original definition of the word concerned the responsible use of resources (especially money, time, and talents) given in the service of God, stewardship in an environmental sense concerns responsible use of natural resources. Indeed, some Protestant denominations have tried to articulate a stewardship philosophy as part of their doctrine, attempting to distance themselves from the no-holds-barred resource use advocated by some fundamentalist Christians. At the 1992 Earth Summit in Rio de Janeiro, the World Council of Churches held a major ecumenical meeting to discuss a Christian stewardship position. The group noted that "anthropocentric, hierarchical, and patriarchal understandings of creation lead to the alienation of human beings from each other, from nature, and from God" and recommended that traditional hierarchical views be replaced with a more relational view where "human beings are created for the purpose of communion with God and all the living and non-living things."[11]

This recommendation (which was adopted formally by some denominations) moved Christianity only slightly on the spectrum. Humans nevertheless remained stewards of creation, knowing how to best care for (and manipulate) nature for human ends. While some stewardship proponents have stressed the value of nonhuman nature (a tenant in preservationist ideology), the belief overall remained in the utilitarian value of nature, particularly to future generations of humans. The status of nonhuman life continually trips up the meshing of Christianity and more ecocentric ideologies; many theologians and believers still think it a sin to treat nature as if it has the same type of value or "spirit" as humans.

Some religious pronouncements have equated environmental degradation with sin, but left intrinsic value unaddressed. In 1997, the head of the Greek Orthodox Church stated that "to commit a crime against the natural world is a sin." His All Holiness Bartholomew I said: "For humans to cause species to become extinct and to destroy the biological diversity of God's creation, for humans to degrade the integrity of the Earth by causing changes in its climate, stripping the Earth of its natural forests, or destroying its wetlands . . . for human to contaminate the Earth's waters, its land, air, and its life with poisonous substances—these are sins."[12]

Regardless of religious beliefs, many people consider a conservationist approach a pragmatic, realistic environmental ideology because it recognizes limits to resource use and the need for restraint; it also recognizes that good-quality resources contribute to human quality of life. However, others label conservationism as "shallow ecology" for its goal to protect nature for human welfare and enjoyment, believing that as an environmental ideology it is ultimately incapable of protecting the natural world. This charge also is directed at preservationism.

## Preservationism

"If the desert is holy, it is because it is a forgotten place that allows us to remember the sacred. Perhaps that is why every pilgrimage to the desert is a pilgrimage to the self. There is no place to hide and so we are found."[13]

—*Terry Tempest Williams*

As an environmental ideology, preservationism stands only a brief distance from conservationism, although current debates around preservation issues would lead one to think them miles apart. Preservationism supports conserving resources for humans to use and enjoy in the present and future, but it also believes in preserving resources for reasons that go beyond their purely instrumental value —that is, the utilitarian and economic value they hold for humans. In preservationism, this "value" is articulated in different ways, such as scientific or ecological, aesthetic, and religious terms.

An ongoing preservationist issue is formally designated wilderness with a capital "W." Scientific arguments made to preserve wilderness include its value as a storehouse of data, gene pools, and undiscovered medicines, as well as its value as ecosystems that protect water and watersheds, produce game and nongame animals, and regulate climate.

Aesthetic arguments for wilderness preservation are its value as a place of wonder, awe, and beauty. Wilderness is seen as having therapeutic value as a place of escape, solitude, and renewal. Sierra Club founder John Muir touted the ability of wilderness to aid "thousands of tired, nerve-shaken, over-civilized people." Aesthetic appreciation of nature can be traced to writers like Ralph Waldo Emerson and Henry David Thoreau, as well as to early painters who captured the sublime in natural landscapes and felt awe "in the presence of overwhelming power, magnitude, or antiquity."[14] This is not to say that such awe was felt equally for all landscapes, for preservationists' efforts have been biased toward "more-or-less pristine wilderness at the expense of disturbed areas"[15] and for rocks-and-ice, high-elevation mountainous areas. Of course, evaluation of the aesthetic is a subjective act, but arguing preservation on aesthetic terms is very different from arguing to protect healthy and intact ecosystems. In current-day wilderness fights, preservationists continue to tap the powerful feelings and rhetoric of the romantic aesthetic to make their case for preserving the natural world.

Religious references about wilderness note its sacred value or its status as a temple or cathedral, which is "a very ancient and widespread notion that certain natural areas were sacred places where human beings could encounter the holy."[16] When the government announced plans to dam Hetch Hetchy Valley to provide water for San Francisco, John Muir called the act desecration by "temple destroyers." Over sixty years later, the Sierra Club mocked the Bureau of Reclamation's plan to dam the Grand Canyon, saying "Should we also flood the Sistene Chapel so tourists can get nearer the ceiling?" Current preservationists and nature writers continue to invoke religious terms about wild lands, such as writer Terry Tempest Williams's frequent references to wilderness as "sacred" and "holy."

What keeps preservationism on the anthropocentric side of the spectrum is that the "value" of nature is still determined by either a subjective human experience (such as aesthetic or scientific) or because of an alleged "objective deity that is manifested in nature."[17] Although defining value in this way may sound supportive of the intrinsic and inherent worth of nature, it still is very human-centered in its arguments. Despite charges by wilderness-opponents of land being "locked up," no wilderness has ever prohibited human use; in fact, some wilderness areas permit not only recreation but also grazing and mining. Therefore, preservationist ideology is vulnerable to the same trap of reductionism as conservationist ideology: reducing the value of the natural world to what it affords humans, either directly or through some deity that is manifested in nature. What separates these two ideologies from the next two is that value is granted to the nonhuman world with human strings attached.

## Ethics and Values-Driven Ideologies

"A thing is right when it tends to preserve the integrity, stability, and beauty of the biotic community. It is wrong when it tends otherwise."[18]

—*Aldo Leopold*

The next logical step along the ideology spectrum is to grant non-human entities "value" that goes beyond utilitarian, scientific, aesthetic or religious worth to possessing intrinsic value or an inherent worth. In other words, a bear or a wilderness or a earthworm is valuable—regardless of its benefits (or costs) to humans. As living entities, each holds a place in the biotic community and is therefore unique, important, and valued.

Values-driven ideologies add a moral and ethical dimension to human behavior by believing that humans have duties to (some) nonhuman natural entities and even that these entities have a "right" to exist. These ideologies recognize that humans share and are members of a biotic community (which is closer to being ecocentric than the previous ones), but are still closer to the traditional hierarchy (with humans at the top). Humans accord more rights to some entities (such as animals) and less to others (rocks, fungi, ecosystems, and so on). For instance, some might attribute intrinsic moral worth only to living beings that possess "sentience," or a capacity to feel sensations and to seek pleasurable (and avoid unpleasurable) states of being. Therefore, if a creature can feel pain (and seeks to avoid pain), it should be considered a moral subject.[19]

While values-driven belief systems do look beyond traditional human-centered concerns to the well-being of the rest of creation, they nevertheless engage in "moral extensionism"[20] by applying morals and ethics to the nonhuman world that were developed to work in human society. By relying on existing institutions in the social system (such as legal and political) to ensure that nonhuman entities are valued, these ideologies are more reformist than radical, although they do call for a rethinking (if not reordering) of the value of the natural world and how humans see themselves in relation to it.

A good example of an environmental issue whose discussion falls under this framework is the protection of endangered species, generally under the auspices of the 1973 Endangered Species Act. One of the first battles to protect an endangered species was the big fight over the little snail darter, which was thought to live only in the river that would be flooded by the proposed Tellico Dam in Tennessee. Those opposed to stopping the dam to protect this creature argued that it had little utilitarian value in the grand scheme of things. Supporters said the snail darter had a right to exist and was important to preserve. Some of the arguments relied on preservationist values such as scientific importance (even if unknown or uncertain), but overall the argument was that humans had a moral obligation not to extirpate the last known remaining individuals of this species. In a way, this viewpoint imbues traditional stewardship with a moral and ethical duty: humans *should* do everything possible to protect living entities.

There are numerous ideologies that fit under this ethics and values-driven framework, of which only two will be described briefly: animal rights and land-based ethics.

### Animal Rights

Animal rights ideology holds that nonhuman animals are "another aggrieved group being subjected to unjustifiable discrimination by a privileged group (humans) with the power to indulge their urge to discriminate."[21] Thinking that humans are somehow superior in their sentience, according to this ideology, is "species-ism."

Critics of animal rights ideology say it is only in some senses "environmental" for it pays scant attention to nonanimal nature. Habitat has primarily instrumental value for its role in preserving individual animals. The ideology also falls short on changing human relationships to the natural world in a holistic or ecological sense for it is most concerned with animal-human relationships. One scholar called animal rights ideology "zoo-centric,"[22] for it assumes that the sole value of a rainforest community, for example, is the sentient beings within it, not the entire ecosystem of both living and nonliving entities.

Another limitation to rights-based ideologies like animal rights is that rights are primarily individualistic and legalistic, and involve matters of who has the power and/or desire to grant rights to some and not others.[23] To return to the example of endangered species, which has more right to exist and be protected, tuna or dolphins, wolves or sheep? This is still moral extensionism because it merely extends conventional anthropocentric ethics to decide which animals are more valued than others. It also is reductionist because it focuses on saving or protecting individual animals or species but not ecosystems and communities.

### Land-based Ethics

Many people are familiar with the classic *A Sand County Almanac* by Aldo Leopold, first published in 1948. In this book, Leopold makes a case for a "land ethic," saying that humans have duties and obligations in their treatment of the natural world. By the late 1970s, people recognized the modern potential for Leopold's philosophy: human actions should not damage the "holistic integrity" and healthy functioning of entire ecosystems.[24]

Leopold's land ethic most successfully moves beyond the limited criteria of sentience, which can be possessed only by living and breathing beings. Leopold attributed value to an entire functioning ecosystem—animals, and also all the elements that were a part of a biotic community and contributed to its functioning. This perspective embraces two additional criteria: possessing cell-based life, and the intrinsic value of all biological life. Cell-based life includes not just animals but all live carbon-containing plants—trees, grasses, and flowers, and the tiniest lichens and living elements in the soil. The second additional criterion goes much further toward ecocentrism by granting intrinsic value to all biological life—plants, species (not just individual animals), gene pools, minerals, elements like air and water, and entire communities and ecosystems. In ascribing value and worth to these elements, there is a recognition that these natural elements have a *telos*, or an end of their own, an autonomy in the sense of "having a capacity for internal self-direction and self-regulation."[25] It is an essential feature of living systems to continually produce and sustain themselves, their activities, and their structures. A coastal forest will continue to exist as a coastal forest—producing new trees to replace dying ones, providing habitat for other creatures, providing nutrients to make soil, and so on—in perpetuity, unless disturbed by some other force. The tide will continue to rise and fall ceaselessly, and its actions sustain tidal life, estuaries, and many other creatures. According to this criterion, an entire desert or prairie is an entity in its own right and should have the freedom to unfold in its own way.

Thinking of the entire nonhuman world as autonomous in its potential to unfold requires quite a leap in typical human thinking. Our usual reasoning is that we humans are needed to manage natural communities. The shift from humans-as-integral to humans-as-nonessential in the functioning of the natural world is a significant one. Seeing ourselves as nonessential is a far humbler and less hierarchical position. We are not needed for the successful unfolding and ongoing existence of the natural world, and undoubtedly often impede and interfere with that process. Leopold describes this shift as being able to think of a muskrat not as a *subject* of human interest, but as an *object*, as a being that has its own purposes, activities, and unique muskrat-perspectives on the natural world around.

The criterion of telos puts this ideology much closer to the ecocentric end of the spectrum than rights-based ideologies. But all ethics and value-based ideologies fail to connect human beliefs about the natural world to systems of power that are integral in either maintaining or changing relationships. In other words, it's one thing to say humans "should" morally treat the natural world and it's another to find the root causes or needed social change to support those relationships. Identifying the root causes of our current treatment of and relationship with the natural world is the goal of the final set of environmental ideologies, which attempt to seriously question or radically change the human-dominated hierarchy.

## Transformative Ideologies

When the modern-day environmental movement began, there was hope that it would transform the way people related to the earth and to each other.[26] The final set of ideologies to examine are called transformative ideologies because they question the dominant environmental ideologies and call for extensive social change. Current Western environmental ideologies of instrumentalism, conservationism, and preservationism are held responsible for the current ecological crisis and are seen as ineffective within an unsustainable system of increasing deterioration. Transformative ideologies claim that reformist environmentalism is inadequate to salvage the environmental life of the planet.

In everyday use, people equate the word "radical" with leftist politics. However, "radical" means going to the root to discover what affects something's fundamental origins, and here concerns the root causes of humans' current relationship to the natural world, such as systems of domination and exploitation. These ideologies seek to transform a language and practice that constructs nature as a set of passive, inert resources for human benefit, and all of these ideologies focus on the problem of hierarchical ordering of the biological world.

Some people call them "still emergent."[27] Others label them utopian and unfathomable. Perhaps. But that is unavoidable when attempting to look beyond one's own dominant paradigm and envision an entirely different way of "being" in the natural world. It may help to remember that at one time in human history, there was no Christian doctrine about having dominion over the earth. And until very recently, there was no American tradition of preservation. If you expand the timeline of history, anything is possible.

## Ecological Sensibility

Ecological sensibility recognizes the importance of relationships, systems, and individuals. Its ethic is one of noninterference and a knowledgeable, respectful, and restrained use of nature.[28] It moves beyond Leopold's land ethic by integrating values with systems of land management. The first component of this ideology (developed by political philosopher John Rodman) is a "theory of value" that recognizes intrinsic value without moral extensionism: "one ought not to treat with disrespect or use as a mere means anything that has a telos or end of its own" or has an autonomous capacity for self-direction and self-regulation. Telos—as in the previous example of the coastal forest—is important, but insufficient to guide human behavior.

The second key component to ecological sensibility is "a cluster of value-giving characteristics that apply both to natural entities and natural systems: diversity, complexity, integrity, harmony, stability, scarcity, etc."[29] These values-giving characteristics are guidelines to evaluate alternative courses of permissible action toward the natural world. That is, the action that optimizes the characteristics in the cluster is the better action to take and will do a better job of respecting the telos. Obviously, these are quite different from frequently used economic criteria and from the aesthetic, pristine criteria used to judge wilderness areas or scenic rivers.

An example of this cluster-principle is how the environmental group The Nature Conservancy decides which lands to buy and preserve. The Conservancy compiles extensive databases of landforms, plants, birds, and animals in need of protection, which are used to help the group decide which lands to purchase. That means the Conservancy would purchase prairie land, a bog, or a desert dune if safeguarding it will optimize values like diversity, scarcity, and so on. In more recent years, the Conservancy has shifted its focus to regional ecosystem preservation, but the guiding ideology remains.

An example of a typical "land management" decision that does not maximize these cluster-values (nor recognize telos) is the elimination of predators. A decision to protect domestic livestock but not predators is a hierarchical ranking of which animal is more valued, and of course it denies the predator its telos, or autonomy in directing its own life. According to the principle of cluster-values, so-called predator control does not maximize the stability, diversity, and complexity of the area because it takes away the area's capacity for self-regulation of other animal populations (such as small mammals) that the predators kept in check.

A third component of ecological sensibility is "a metaphysics that takes account of the reality and importance of relationships and systems as well as individuals."[30] In other words, saving one polar bear or one herd of caribou or a vast expanse of tundra is of little consequence if the root causes of their demise are not addressed. In this example, that may be as simple as local land use patterns or as complex and intractable as global climate change.

The fourth and final component spells out a variety of ethical duties:

> Noninterference with natural processes
> Resistance to human acts and policies that violate noninterference
> Limited intervention to repair environmental damage in extreme circumstances
> Cohabitation that promotes the knowledgeable, respectful, and restrained use of nature

Think of the typical construction of a new house. First, a large earth-moving machine removes ground-cover, which may include mature trees and which displaces innumerable species. When a large housing development is planned, the surface is essentially undeveloped ecologically; it's razed and leveled. Finally, typical landscaping means a host of nonnative, water-loving grasses and plants, often not the types preferred by the original nonhuman inhabitants. If you were to "rebuild" this house following the cluster-values and ethical duties of ecological sensibility, what would the process look like?

A strength of this ideology is that it provides both a set of core environmental values and some social criteria for better directing human actions toward the natural world. What is perhaps less "transformative" is that it does not account for social system constraints that prevent its widespread application. For instance, an individual landowner could employ the cluster-values, telos principle, and ethical duties for decision-making on her own land, but might find numerous building codes (minimum house size, required or prohibited landscaping materials, and so on) that foil the principle. At the level of watershed or biome, innumerable restrictions would stand in the way of implementation.

## Deep Ecology

Deep ecology has in common with ideologies previously discussed a desire to transform human interactions with the natural world from anthropocentric to ecocentric, and a recognition that all life on earth possesses equal intrinsic value, value that exists independently of human needs and desires.[31] As the name implies, it attempts to break with what it sees as the "shallow ecology" of conservationism and preservationism to deal with the root causes of environmental breakdown. As Earth First! proclaims, "No compromise in defense of Mother Earth!"

Deep ecology emerged during a critical moment in the U.S. environmental social movement. After major successes and widespread public awareness of environmental problems during the 1960s and '70s, some activists began to question whether the mainstream movement could truly transform the instrumental mindset of Americans. Radical groups formed and splintered from mainstream groups, convinced that there was a need to drastically shift and rethink human relationships to the natural world. One such group was Earth First!, which was viewed as the direct action (i.e., protests, tree-sitting, and boycotts) branch of deep ecology.

Deep ecology was first articulated by Norweigan Arne Naess and brought to prominence in the late 1970s by two California academics, philosopher George Sessions and sociologist Bill Devall. It espoused a radical transformation of human society and a need for deep questioning (philosophical, religious, and other) of human life, society, and nature.[32] The platform of deep ecology recognized the intrinsic value of the nonhuman world and declared that "humans have no right" to reduce the diversity and richness of the natural world except to satisfy vital needs. Current human interference with the natural world was excessive, and a decrease in human population was necessary for human life and nonhuman life to flourish. Finally, individuals had an obligation to implement the necessary changes.[33]

The two ultimate norms of deep ecology are "biocentric equality" (intrinsic worth of all life) and "self-realization." The traditional Western self sought gratification and enjoyment. But through personal growth, an enlightened Self could see her/himself as part of something larger and see the interrelatedness of all life. An individual must develop an enlarged frame of reference and see all life as one—human and nonhuman, living and not-living. This notion of growth and enlightenment has great resonance with Eastern philosophies like Buddhism and Taoism.

A general criticism is that deep ecology is misanthropic, largely from its association with Earth First! but also for its support of population control. Another criticism is that deep ecology has not moved beyond rights-based ideologies, and that rights remain focused on the individual and within the legal system with no real recognition of the privileged position of some to hold power over others.[34] The deep ecology norm of biocentric equality still relies on rights granted to individual species and ignores relationships between larger biotic entities (the essence of ecology and ecocentrism). Deep ecology also has received criticism for its use of war as a metaphor for environmental activism. (Much of this stems from Earth First! and its use of a raised, clenched fist as its symbol.) Critics question the means-ends of war as the best route for achieving peace and see the war-peace dualism as a harmful but inevitable outcome when the focus is placed on individual rights.

### Social Ecology

Social ecology has two rather distinct forms that both recognize the role of power in environmental relationships. One form is Eco-Marxism, which emphasizes the inherent contradiction within capitalism: ever-increasing production and limited natural conditions. An important tenet of Marxism is that capitalism is responsible for a massive "externalization" of social and economic costs. What this means is that the costs of producing something with natural resources (such as lumber, paper, or gasoline) do not include the costs and impacts to health, quality of life, environment, ruptured social and family structures, and so on. When these costs are externalized, they are not borne by the owners of that production, but by the workers—and the environment.

The second form of social ecology (championed by Murray Bookchin) strays from Marxism. It doesn't critique capitalism per se but points to the hierarchy both in capitalism and within the social system as the source of ecological crisis. Bookchin replaced the Marxist concept of class exploitation with a broad conception of human hierarchy.[35] The solution, therefore, is to radically transform the social system and put an end to the hierarchy within it, which would lead to nonhierarchical, egalitarian relationships between humans and nature. The type of "social justice" envisioned by this ideology is one of decentralization, alternative technology, and a fairly libertarian form of governance based on "loose federations of self-governing municipalities,"[36] direct democracy, and direct action for social change. Like the interdependencies of ecology, the keys (and solutions) lie at multiple levels—local, regional, or even global.[37]

Bookchin's social ecology details a framework of "first nature" (the ecosystem) and "second nature" (a reformulated human culture) as existing in a dialectal relationship where neither can determine the other. Some have charged that this nature-culture relationship is idealistic in the way it views harmonious freedom.[38] Another critic argued that Bookchin's social ecology allows no voice for nonhuman nature nor does it fully explore the power dynamic between humans and nonhuman nature.[39] In the end, social ecology sometimes seems progressive and modern, yet at other times, reverts to historic notions of the rise and fall of hierarchical cultures.


## Ecofeminism

A good starting point for discussing ecofeminism is the far-too-common perception of what a "feminist" is. Many undergraduate students (men and women) tell me they picture a feminist as a woman who is loud, hairy, dowdy, and angry, and wants to become just like a man. A handful of feminists have supported such masculinizing of feminism, such as Simone de Beauvoir who wanted to rid feminism of its ecological concerns and to radically distance women from nature because she felt the association kept women imprisoned.[40] But for most feminists, feminism is about valuing the female and what is feminine. A feminist does not want women to be discriminated against in multiple realms: political representation, property rights, pay (U.S. women make seventy-three cents for every dollar that men make), legal treatment, social rights, and control over their destinies and bodies.

The common thread among various strains of ecofeminism is that the oppression of women (and races and classes) and nonhuman nature are an interconnected part of same dynamic. Deep ecology identifies anthropocentrism as the primary factor in environmental degradation, and ecofeminism identifies androcentricism (male centeredness) as responsible. Ecofeminism believes that society is gendered in ways that subordinate, exploit, and oppress women and the natural world.[41] Ecofeminism is very much a theory of power relations and political action focused on social change at the level of human relationship and individual voices. Social change regarding the environment must address the systems of power and domination and how they subdue and dominate the natural world. Ecofeminists maintain that patriarchy is embedded in daily life within all dominant social structures. This patriarchal framework is used to subordinate through "a logic of domination" that has been used historically to justify the domination of women and nature.

Ecofeminists argue that differences between genders and species should be honored equally—heterarchy instead of hierarchy. Hierarchical thinking places what is female and feminine as "lower" and silences subordinate voices. The dominant Western worldview values reason (masculine-associated) over emotion (feminine-associated), rationality over intuition, civilized over primitive, knowing over feeling, mind over body, and culture over nature. Ecofeminists believe that these dualisms are political and cultural artifacts rather than the natural order of biology. Whereas traditional Western ethics is rights based, ecofeminism supports "relational ethics" that utilize humility and respect in dealing with nonhuman nature. As one scholar put it, "an ecofeminist perspective about women and nature involves this shift in attitude from 'arrogant perception' to 'loving perception' of the nonhuman world. . . . Any environmental movement or ethic based on arrogant perceptions builds a moral hierarchy of beings."[42]

Two challenges to ecofeminist ideology continue to spur discussion: reductionism and essentialism. Reductionism questions to what degree we can reduce the causes of nature exploitation and domination to patriarchy. Could it be possible that the emancipation of women would not lead to the emancipation of the nonhuman world, and vice versa?[43] Essentialism holds that *biologically* females are closer to nature than men. Throughout history, nature has been more identified with the feminine (i.e., Mother Nature, Mother Earth) than the masculine. But essentialism takes it one step further, arguing that there are innate qualities of being female that make females more identified with or even closer to nature.

There is one segment of ecofeminism—earth-based ecofeminist spirituality—that supports biological essentialism, saying that women and nature share a common essential power. Some who follow this spiritualism worship Gaia (the Great Mother in Greek mythology) as a Goddess.[44] More traditional ecofeminists scoff at the Mother Earth metaphor as perpetuating domination and seeing the earth as generous, nurturing, and full of limitless bounty—but all without tangible economic worth (like "women's work").[45] They also criticize the cultural appropriation of Native American spiritual traditions for Mother Earth "worship."[46] As one ecofeminist put it: "The earth is not our mother. There is no warm, nurturing, anthropomorphized earth that will take care of us if only we treat her nicely. The complex, emotion-laden, conflict-laden, quasi-sexualized, quasi-dependent mother relationship . . . is not an effective metaphor for environmental action."[47]

Unlike deep ecologists, ecofeminists say there is not a single path of enlightenment and no centralized rule for transcendence: "Ecofeminists insist on a contextualized, relational, and changing understanding of self. For example, ecofeminists in the 'first world' may adopt a 'self' that embraces vegetarianism in honor of animals, because of . . . the availability of a multitude of choices in food in the first world and their desire to reduce their impact on the Earth. Yet an ecofeminist 'self' in Africa works for better management of cattle, facilitating meat-eating as an aspect of regional development."[48]

### Native American Ideologies

"So this land of the Great Plains is claimed by the Lakota as their very own. We are of the soil and the soil is of us. We love the birds and beasts that grew with us on this soil. They drank the same water as we did and breathed the same air. We are all one in nature. Believing so, there was in our hearts a great peace and a welling kindness for all living, growing things."[49]

—*Luther Standing Bear*

A continuing debate in the last half century has often confused and confounded historical Native American environmental practice with their contemporary ideology. The debate has at times rendered Native American environmental beliefs wholly historical and therefore irrelevant. Yes, it would be impossible for Indians to fully practice their ideologies in a populous country with extensive private land ownership. The Indian way of life probably could not support the large human population in North America today.[50] However, this does not obviate their ideologies, only the full practice of them.

Although there are variations in Native American environmental ideologies by tribes and regions, there is an "essential sameness"[51] that allows a generalized discussion: belief in a living planet. This ideology maintains that the entire world is alive—not just plants and animals but rocks, air, water, land, minerals—and humans hold an reciprocal and equal (not superior) relationship with all of it. These relationships are integrated with all aspects of daily life, governing not only how the earth is treated, but also how Indians treat each other, how they govern themselves and view power, and the kind of subsistence economics they practice. Native Americans rarely distinguish between religious and secular life; there is nothing in life that is not religious and spiritual. Nature is viewed as *hierophanic*, as a source of spiritual revelation.[52] All activities are infused with the dimension of the sacredness of the earth, and every action is opportunity for reflection and contemplation.[53] In the words of one Native American, the task of tribal religion "is to determine the proper relationship that the people of the tribe must have with other living things."[54]

A basic universal symbol of great importance to many tribes is that of the circle or "sacred hoop."[55] The circle signifies the family, the clan or tribe, and eventually, all of creation. "Because a circle has no beginning and no end, all parts of the circle are of equal value, and all have their own roles and parts to play . . . if the circle is to be whole, healthy, and unbroken."[56] Tribal meetings are held in a circle; the tepee and the igloo form a circle. The circle represents interdependence and connectedness with each other and all of creation.

Native beliefs for the most part adhere to pantheism, the belief that a God (or supreme being) is identifiable with the forces of nature or that God and universe are identical. Pantheism admits or tolerates all gods, not one single God. Because of the interrelatedness of living things, all life constitutes a community whose individual components are in a sense anthropomorphized. "Wolves weren't just wolves, but wolf people. Salmon constituted a nation that had rights and stature equal to that of human nations."[57] There is an integration of the past and present, in which the dead are present, not gone. Native American relationships with the natural world tended: "to preserve biological integrity within natural communities and did so over a significant period of historical time. These cultures engaged in relationships of mutual respect, reciprocity, and caring with an Earth and fellow beings as alive and self-conscious as human beings. Such relationships were reflected and perpetuated by cultural elements including religious belief and ceremonial ritual."[58]

There is a great deal of ritual in Indian interactions with animals to demonstrate reciprocity and balance in human-animal relationships. For anything taken, something has to be offered in return, as a matter of fair exchange and respect. The ecological consciousness of Indians is due in part to the kinship and knowledge that was codified and passed on through legends and myths, many involving animals.[59] According to many tribes, animals once shared a common language with humans and continued to understand humans after humans lost their ability to understand the animals. Animals assumed a fleshy body in the physical world but lived in a spiritual world, which made them mediators in all things. It is a common Native American belief that animals are very much aware, sensate, and feeling beings who can be offended and must be treated with respect. According to this view, animals are never viewed in strictly quantitative terms as resources, but as an equal part of the web of living systems and with whom humans have relationships.[60]

Indians revere the land as a bountiful community of living beings. In the Cherokee language, the word for land is "eloheh"; the same word also means history, culture, and religion. Indians consider land to literally be a part of them, a living body with spirit and power; "sense of place" is inextricably bound to Indian identity.[61] Without knowing the land deeply, it is impossible to know the self. The existence of holy places on the land confirms native peoples' connectedness to all life.[62]

Native American author Paula Gunn Allen explains their connection to the land: "We are the land. To the best of my understanding, that is the fundamental idea embedded in Native American life and culture. . . . More than remembered, the earth is the mind of the people as we are the mind of the earth. The land is not really the place (separate from ourselves) where we act out the drama of our isolated destinies. It is not a means of survival, a setting for our affairs, a resource on which we draw in order to keep our own art functioning. It is not the ever-present 'Other' which supplies us with a sense of 'I.'

It is rather a part of our being, dynamic, significant, real. It is ourself, in as real a sense as our notions of 'ego,' 'libido,' or social network, in a sense more real than any conceptualization or abstraction about the nature of the human being can ever be."[63]

Native beliefs about animals and land are apt examples of an eco-centric, nonhierarchical relationship with the natural world: "In the Native American system, there is no idea that nature is somewhere over there while man is over here, nor that there is a great hierar-chical ladder of being on which ground and trees occupy a very low rung, animals a slightly higher one, and man a very high one indeed. . . . All are seen to be brothers or relatives . . . , all are offspring of the Great Mystery, children of our mother, and necessary parts of an ordered, balanced, and living whole."[64]

## Eastern Traditions

At various points in recent history, people have looked to Eastern tra-ditions and Asian-based philosophies as a panacea for environmen-tal ills.[65] Many view the dominant religions of East Asia—Buddhism, Taoism, and Shintoism—as more "ecologically benign"[66] than domi-nant Western religious views. Yet despite the ecocentrism of most Eastern religions, the countries of East Asia have been some of "the world's most aggressive plunderers of their own and other's environ-ments."[67] But caution is needed in making cause-effect judgments for contradictions between ideology and action exist in Eastern reli-gious traditions as in Western ones.

What makes these Eastern traditions instructive in terms of envi-ronmental ideology and communication is how they articulate key concepts of ecocentrism in a way that allows us to envision a dif-ferent relationship with the nonhuman world on earth and with the entire cosmos. Though little practiced or known to Americans, Eastern traditions have an essential sameness in their more equalized and humble position of humans in nature, compared to the hierar-chy so evident in Western relationships. In ecocentric terms, Eastern philosophies view humans as an integral, interdependent entity in the cosmos, neither essentially nor morally segregated from nature.

What follows is a brief sketch of several Eastern religious tradi-tions and their views toward nature, a sketch that is bound to oversimplify what are complex and rich philosophies. It is impossible to isolate religious traditions from the countries in which they are practiced, because multiple philosophical influences have led to unique "blends" of practice; for example, Japan is heir to three distinct traditions, Buddhism, Confucian philosophy, and the indigenous Shinto mythology.[68]

The teachings of Buddhism stress contemplation and worldly inaction, rather than activity and intervention. The focus of human life is not on material acquisition and possession, which would trap a person in a cycle of reincarnation. A person needs to dissolve desires, recognize that permanence is an illusion, and understand that the individual is part of the universal whole. Because all beings (humans and nonhumans) come from and seek to return to nirvana (a state of nothingness or nonexistence), they essentially have the same cosmic purpose.

The centerpiece of the Buddha's teaching—the "dependent co-arising of all phenomena"—supports a cosmos without species hierarchy or any species' claim to privileged interests.[69] Instead, Buddhism teaches interspecies empathy and compassion for all living things; humans and all of nature are inseparable and entwined. One of the more difficult and misunderstood concepts of Buddhism is that there is no independent self. The individual is "one of the Western world's most cherished beliefs and greatest source of suffering. . . . In Buddhist thinking, to be enlightened is to awaken from this delusion."[70]

"Buddhism holds that the universe and all creatures in it are intrinsically in a state of complete wisdom, love and compassion, acting in natural response and mutual interdependence."[71] As environmental ideology, this means that there are no dualisms like human-nonhuman, mind-body, or even sacred-profane.

As noted, deep ecologists have borrowed from Taoism for its unique reverence for the natural world, the place of humans in the web of life,[72] and its concept of the "enlarged Self." As the founders of deep ecology note, "The Taoist way of life is based on compassion, respect, and love for all things. This compassion arises from self-love, but as part of the larger Self, not egotistical self-love."[73]

The Tao or "the Way" is all that is, was, and is yet to come—a single flow of becoming. Some see the main recipe of the Tao as following nature as the basis of practice and acting in accordance with the nature of things. The Taoist philosophy is a nonexploitive "letting be," which doesn't imply doing nothing and inactivity, but rather seeing the essentialness of work and sustenance as treading lightly and having a nonaggressive relationship with nonhuman nature. "Real work should therefore go with and not against the grain of things."[74]

Shintoism developed as an indigenous religious mythology from the ancient people of Japan who cultivated crops high in the mountains. This belief system is pantheistic and animistic, and all entities (living and nonliving) are believed to participate equally in a seamless web of divine presence.[75] It was in the mountains where the gods (or "kami") were in attendance. Kami were embodied within forests, streams, rocks, wind, and mountains and were offspring of the mythical creators of the universe. Some regard Shintoism as a nature-worshipping religion for its shrines to gods of the mountains, forests, and decoration of sacred rocks.[76]

#### SHARED CONCEPTS IN EASTERN TRADITIONS

Three concepts found in Eastern traditions help explicate the connections to ecocentric ideology: connectedness and continuity, emotional engagement, and interdependence.

*Connectedness and Continuity*

In Chinese cultural history, there is no creation myth, such as "God created the world." Instead, the fundamental assumption about reality is that all modalities of being are organically connected. This "continuity of being" is a basic motif in the Chinese philosophy of reality that sees nature as the all-enfolding harmony of cosmos.[77] This is obviously a foreign notion to the Westerners who believe in a willful God who created the world out of nothing.

In Chinese thought, spirit and matter are undifferentiated parts of the whole. That is, spirit is not reducible to matter and is of a more enduring value. Within every entity is ch'i, translated as life-force or matter-energy. All beings (living and not) are made of ch'i and share the same consanguinity (relationship by descent from a common ancestor) with humans. "The continuous presence of ch'i in all modalities of being [rock, heaven, human] makes everything flow as the unfolding of a single process. Nothing, not even an almighty creator, is external to this process."[78]

There is a similar concept in Taoism that expresses the notion of connectedness and continuity called "self-so." The phrase (used in modern Chinese to translate the English word "nature") views nature as all-inclusive, the spontaneously self-generating life process which excludes nothing.[79] The inclusiveness and connectedness of "self-so" is similar to "telos" or the natural unfolding of processes.[80]

### Emotional Engagement

Many Eastern religious traditions consider an intimate knowing and emotional engagement with the natural world as crucial for knowing oneself and others. Shintoism and Buddhism desire to "see" nature in an undistorted fashion, like a polished mirror that reflects all things clearly. To be truly aware of nature, one must be good listener. Experiences with the natural world teach, explain, and expound dharma (the "truth" in Buddhism) by manifesting itself within each and every experience and thing. Dharma permeates all sentient and nonsentient beings.

In the Japanese tradition, the development of character "depends upon an emotional engagement with nature and others,"[81] a development borne both from a sense of ethos and ethic and from an intimate and emotionally charged relationship with the natural world. Such a cultivated "love of nature" is characterized by a sensitive, feeling-filled interaction that "provides the necessary and sufficient condition for an intimate interaction with our natural surroundings."

### Interdependence

A typical American worldview treats humans as autonomous and rather separate from the natural world. In contrast, Eastern philosophies view all modalities of being as organically connected, making it impossible to place humans on a different plane than the rest of the cosmos. What a Westerner might think of as an "identity" to an Easterner is more appropriately "interdependence." Obviously, this is not easy to picture for Westerners who define the universe in terms of a divine plan with respect to its beginning and end. It's easier to think of isolated beings within a hierarchy than of one Being with total intercausality—"a unity of existence in which separate entities are all interrelated in a profound manner."[82]

A metaphor for intercausality might help clarify. When I participate in a square dance, what I am and what I do are completely defined by my inclusion in the dance. Just as I "am" the square dance, each individual "is" the square dance, and the relationship would change if any individual were removed. In other words, "that I am, and that I am defined in a certain way, is completely dependent on the other individuals who compose the dance, but this dance itself has no existence apart from the dancer. The Buddhist, in viewing things as being interdependent in this manner, comes to have, ideally, a profound feeling of gratitude and respect for things, however humble they may appear to people who do not share his understanding, for . . . he is aware that what he is, depends utterly upon them."[83]

## Conclusion

When I worked for the Bureau of Land Management (BLM) in the 1980s, I helped analyze "public participation" comments we received on proposed management plans. Almost all of the comments fit the first three ideologies discussed: unrestrained instrumentalism, conservationism, and preservationism. On the rare occasion we got a more ecocentric comment, I was stupefied by what to do with it. An argument for intrinsic value didn't fit the comment categories, and a plea for telos over tinkering didn't support any management alternative. The same thing happened when I worked for the Idaho Governor's office; I remember listening to a Native American give testimony about anadromous fish runs and not understanding how he viewed fish as "brothers" and the land as living.

In virtually all environmental communication in this country, we hear messages only from the anthropocentric side of spectrum. Our daily dialogue about the environment is fairly limited and one-sided in terms of the ideologies typically expressed. Our dominant social paradigm—and the laws and regulations that emanate from it—is designed to accommodate viewpoints on the anthropocentric end and is poorly equipped to understand other ideologies and ways of relating to the natural world.

Knowledge of the full spectrum of environmental ideologies is prerequisite for understanding where environmental messages are "coming from." You can even typify organizations by the ideology they most closely embody. The BLM operates under a different ideology than the National Park Service. The Sierra Club adheres to a different ideology than Earth First!, the Izaak Walton League, or PETA (People for the Ethical Treatment of Animals). Even environmental laws—the National Environmental Policy Act, Endangered Species Act, Superfund, and Clean Water Act—represent different ideological viewpoints. Cultural practices like parks, xeriscaping, mass transit, and litter cleanup all spring from ideological relationships with the natural world.

Indeed, what many people simply lump together as "environmentalism" is more accurately a diverse spectrum of beliefs. And most of what gets painted as "environmental" is nevertheless fairly anthropocentric and reformist, not "radical." American conservationism and preservationism, the hallmark ideologies of the environmental movement, propose little to alter basic, long-standing relationships with the natural world.

It's important to notice that there is a place for humans in all of these ideologies. A sentiment often expressed about "environmentalists" is that they want to "lock up" nature and remove people from the natural world. Some of my students think that environmentalists are in a sense antihuman and want people to suffer and to do without, which is a misreading of the fundamental difference between anthropocentric and ecocentric ideologies. There is plenty of room for humans in ecocentric ideologies; it is the relative role of humans that shifts. Ecocentric ideologies recognize humans as an interdependent part of a larger biotic community and with a desire to behave more humbly toward the life systems that sustain them.

# 3

## The Links between Environmental Attitudes
## and Behaviors

In its attitude to the land, and the creatures thereof, a culture
reveals the truest part of its soul.

—*Kirkpatrick Sale*

I headed to graduate school after ten years as an environmental communicator to learn whether there were any surefire ingredients, any
magic recipes for good communication. My communication successes and failures seemed a jumble of luck, creativity, and mystery.
But the more research I read, the more I understood that communicating about the environment involved far more than crafting persuasive messages. Although a message is received by an individual,
the "room" is very crowded. Messages are designed and launched
from a social and cultural stage full of actors. Even if one little message manages to best the competition and reach the ears or eyes of
one individual, that person must understand, believe, weigh, and
interpret the words and images in the context of her own personal,
complex psychology.

The more I studied the multifaceted theories of individual attitudes and behaviors, the more I wanted to look *beyond* the individual
for explanations. Okay, researchers found that this one message was
effective in this one instance with this group of people, but did they
watch the news last night? What movie or advertisement did those
people last see? What did Congress do that day? Was air pollution
lingering in the valley and irritating everyone? Surely, stepping back

to study the bigger societal picture would be just as informative—
wouldn't it?

But the fact remains that day to day, we live life as individuals
with our own beliefs and opinions, and sometimes they are translated into behaviors. We need to understand the psychological context if we are to understand how environmental messages are received. Although significant social change involves masses of people
and institutions, by necessity it must begin with one person and
another person and another. Thus, for all the flaws and pitfalls, it
makes sense to study individuals and how they come to express their
attitudes about the environment and sometimes change them.

This chapter seeks to explore the links between environmental
belief systems introduced in the last chapter and the opinions, attitudes, and behaviors derived from them. The linkages can be messy;
sometimes we can predict when people will be persuaded by environmental messages, but oftentimes not. But a clearer understanding
nevertheless gives us the grounding necessary to understand in later
chapters how environmental issues are crafted by different actors
and institutions. The study of attitudes and behaviors is more accurately psychological research than simple public opinion measurement. In particular, this chapter discusses the attitudinal, personal,
contextual, and habitual factors that affect individual behaviors, and
well as approaches to changing behavior.

First, some terms. *Beliefs* are assumptions by which we understand things and live our lives, such as, "Humans are more valuable than other animals." *Values* are statements about the way things
"should" be: "Humans should not be cruel to animals." *Attitudes* express a positive or negative evaluation of another person, idea, or entity: "I like elephants." *Opinions* are a publicly expressed preference:
such as "I don't support the proposed highway," usually concerning
a controversial social or public issue.

## Environmental Attitudes and the People Who Hold Them

For as long as people have had sentiments about the environment,
researchers have tried to measure, understand, and influence them.
But it wasn't until the late 1960s that the American public gained a
vocabulary of environmental awareness that included concepts of

ecology, resource scarcity, balance of nature, and human impact on the natural world. Pollsters, policy makers, and others soon wanted to get a handle on these sentiments and what were known as "environmentalists."

Nowadays, the word "environmentalist" tends to be a loaded, emotional label, often used to stereotype what is an extremely diverse set of beliefs. At a series of focus groups I held last year, a variety of environmental professionals and resource managers referred to the "e-words" (environmentalist, environmentalism, environmental) as "dirty words" and admitted that they avoided using them. For some, an environmentalist is a "tree-hugger," or someone who wants to restrict freedom and harm people and their livelihoods. Yet, under certain circumstances and certain contexts, virtually everyone is ready to proclaim herself or himself one. Even the presidents who were least protective of natural resources (such as President Ronald Reagan in the 1980s) have proudly claimed themselves to be environmentalists. The evolution of this word and its broadbased yet conflicting definitions are part of what makes measuring environmental attitudes so tricky and interpreting their results so difficult.

So what really is an "environmentalist" and this thing called "environmentalism"? According to the *New Oxford English Dictionary,* an environmentalist is "a person who is concerned about or seeks to protect the environment, especially from pollution." This fairly benign definition helps to explain why a majority of Americans align themselves with this definition. If thought of in terms of behavior rather than attitude, environmentalism is the propensity to take actions with pro-environmental intent.[1] While that could mean joining an environmental group, it also could mean simply cleaning up your campsite and recycling newspapers.

For quite some time, pollsters and professors have tried to find similarities among those who hold pro-environmental attitudes. Demographic information (the discrete facts collected as part of the study of human populations) is often obtained to better understand environmental attitudes. Typical demographic data include age, sex, education, race and ethnicity, income, political and religious affiliations, and place of residence. Researchers have tried to discover whether some factors are more or less associated with environmental concern. This is not to say that a certain factor like age *causes* environmental concern, only that the two are related or correlated in some way.

Overall, concern for the environment is much more broadbased among Americans than previously thought, and it's not strongly tied to those whom sociologists call "social elites."[2] Since the 1980s, the demographic factor most strongly and consistently associated with environmental concern is age, though new research has found female-male differences as well. The relationships between all other demographic factors and environmental concern are weak or inconclusive (see Box 3.1).

What remains contested is whether these relationships (both the consistent and inconsistent ones) are due to psychological factors—such as, women tend to be more nurturing and other-oriented—or stem from elements in the social structure. For example, some suggest that environmental beliefs are influenced by the experience of race. One study found that white men perceive less risk from environmental conditions (and therefore less concern) because of their privileged position in society, while women and people of color feel more vulnerable to risk because they possess less power and control.[3]

### Opinions and the Environment

From decades of public opinion research, we now have a good picture of what Americans—both those who fit the demographic profile and those who don't—value and believe when it comes to the natural world. Because some questions have been asked repeatedly over the last several decades, we can track stability as well as changes in opinions about the natural world.

However, a key measurement problem in such surveys is how "environment" is treated as an attitude object, in other words, how "environment" is defined and presented as a "thing" about which people have beliefs and feelings. In its most global sense, environment is a very broad and abstract thing, potentially as big as the earth itself. Yet in its most personal sense, environment may be the outdoor spaces you encounter each day. In reality, we don't directly experience the environment as a whole but instead encounter specific aspects or specific places. If a pollster asks whether you agree or disagree that "Humans are severely abusing the environment," your response may represent what you see and experience around you every day, or may instead be based on environment in a far larger sense.

Some researchers argue that environmental attitudes are largely synonymous with "environmental concern," itself a broad concept that refers to a wide range of things, from awareness of environmental problems to support for protection. According to one definition, environmental concern refers "to the degree to which people are aware of problems regarding the environment and support efforts to solve them and/or a willingness to contribute personally to their solution."[4] To break down "environmental concern" even further, it's possible to isolate two components: the environmental component (concern about a particular environmental issue such as global warming or water pollution) and the concern component (the way the concern is expressed and measured).[5]

The concern component deserves a little more discussion. One way to measure concern is with a policy survey that asks people to say how serious environmental problems are, their major causes, who is responsible for solving them, and how they think we should solve them. This approach is often used in public opinion surveys about environmental issues.[6] Another way to tap the concern component is by asking about people's cognitions (thoughts and knowledge), affective expressions (personal feelings or evaluations), or behaviors or behavioral intentions. Here are examples of survey questions that measure these concern components.

*Policy*: Would you say that the amount of money we spend as a nation to protect the environment is too much, too little, or about the right amount?

*Cognition*: I think it is important to protect water resources (agree/disagree scale).

*Affective*: I'm worried about storing radioactive waste so close to our city (agree/disagree scale).

*Behavior*: In the last month, have you made any changes in your energy consumption?

For decades, behavioral scientists have worked to create an overall measure of environmental concern that is more stable and reliable than single questions yet can accurately assess respondents' overall levels of environmental concern. One of the more widely

## Box 3.1

### Demographics and Environmental Concern

*Age*: Of all the demographic variables, age is the most strongly associated with environmental concern, with younger adults more concerned than their counterparts.[1] Perhaps this is because young adults are less fully integrated into the existing social order and therefore don't view environmental solutions as threatening to that order.

*Sex*: While some studies have found stronger intentions for environmental action and stronger beliefs in women,[2] other studies have failed to find a gender connection. A recent comparison across ten years of research found that women report stronger environmental attitudes and behaviors than men.[3]

*Race*: Increasingly, research has found fairly consistent levels of environmental concern across race and ethnicity, though differences may exist between priority of issues and types of environmental groups joined. One study found that nonwhites were generally more concerned than whites.[4] A recent comprehensive comparison of environmental concerns discovered that African Americans were just as concerned about the same kinds of environmental issues as were white Americans.[5]

*Education*: The well educated tend to have moderately higher levels of environmental concern than their counterparts.[6]

*Social class*: The relationship between income and environmental concern has not been widely investigated,[7] but on occasion researchers have created a measure of social class based on both education level and income. The higher the social class, the greater the level of environmental concern. A possible explanation may be that only after a person's basic material needs are met will that person be able to demonstrate greater concern for the environment, though at the same time, living in poorer conditions may spur a greater concern over environmental risks.

*Political ideology*: Those who consider themselves more liberal politically are more likely to demonstrate higher levels of environmental concern. Possible reasons for this are that business and industry (which are typically more conservative) are often opposed to environmental reforms, and some environmental solutions entail extending government action and regulation (to which conservatives are more likely to be opposed).[8]

used is the New Environmental Paradigm Scale developed in the 1970s by two Washington State University professors and revised in 2000 and renamed the New Ecological Paradigm Scale (see Box 3.2).[7] From years of testing and refining the scale, researchers now believe that the composite score of answers to these fifteen questions gives a

## Box 3.1 continued

*Residence*: Once again, the picture is mixed. Some studies have found that urban residents express higher levels of environmental concern than their nonurban counterparts. Some have concluded that this may be due to the fact that urban residents' orientation is less utilitarian, and urbanites may be exposed to more signs of environmental degradation.[9] However, other studies have concluded that residence has little relationship to environmental concern, and that rural-urban differences are better explained by factors such as income, education, and age.[10]

1. Robert E. Jones and Riley E. Dunlap, "The Social Bases of Environmental Concern: Have They Changed Over Time?" in *The Environment and Society Reader*, ed. R. Scott Frey (Needham Heights, MA: Allyn & Bacon, 2001), 164–79; Kent D. Van Liere and Riley E. Dunlap, "Environmental Concern: Does It Make a Difference How It's Measured?" *Environment and Behavior* 13 (1981):651–76; Susan E. Howell and Shirley B. Laska, "The Changing Face of the Environmental Coalition: A Research Note," *Environment and Behavior* 24 (1992):134–44; Thomas A. Arcury and Eric H. Christianson, "Environmental Worldview in Response to Environmental Knowledge: Kentucky 1984 and 1998 Compared," *Environment and Behavior* 22 (1990):387–407.

2. Paul C. Stern, Thomas Dietz, Linda Kalof, and Gregory A. Guagnano, "Values, Beliefs, and Proenvironmental Attitude Formation toward Emergent Attitude Objects," *Journal of Applied Social Psychology* 25 (1995):1611–1636.

3. Lynnette C. Zelezny, Poh-Pheng Chua, and Christina Aldrich, "Elaborating on Gender Differences in Environmentalism," *Journal of Social Issues* 56(3) (2000):443–57.

4. Jones and Dunlap, "The Social Bases of Environmental Concern."

5. Paul Mohai, "Dispelling Old Myths: African American Concern for the Environment," *Environment* 45(5) (2003):11–26.

6. Jones and Dunlap, "The Social Bases of Environmental Concern."

7. Niklas Fransson and Tommy Garling, "Environmental Concern: Conceptual Definitions, Measurement Methods, and Research Findings," *Journal of Environmental Psychology* 19 (1999):369–82.

8. Fransson and Garling, "Environmental Concern."

9. Arcury and Christianson, "Environmental Worldview in Response to Environmental Knowledge"; Howell and Laska, "The Changing Face of the Environmental Coalition."

10. Thomas A. Arcury and Eric Howard Christianson, "Rural-Urban Differences in Environmental Knowledge and Actions," *Journal of Environmental Education* 25(1) (1993):19–25.

good indication of an individual's ecological worldview. Though the researchers do not tie their scale to the anthro-eco ideology scale, you can see some similarities in the role of humans in relationship to the environment.

## Box 3.2

The New Ecological Paradigm Scale

Listed below are statements about the relationship between humans and the environment. For each one, indicate whether you *strongly agree* (SA), *mildly agree* (MA), are *unsure* (U), *mildly disagree* (MD), or *strongly disagree* (SD).

| Statement | SA | MA | U | MD | SD |
|---|---|---|---|---|---|
| 1. We are approaching the limit of the number of people the earth can support. | — | — | — | — | — |
| 2. Humans have the right to modify the natural environment to suit their needs. | — | — | — | — | — |
| 3. When humans interfere with nature, it often produces disastrous consequences. | — | — | — | — | — |
| 4. Human ingenuity will insure that we do *not* make the earth unlivable. | — | — | — | — | — |
| 5. Humans are severely abusing the environment. | — | — | — | — | — |
| 6. The earth has plenty of natural resources if we just learn how to develop them. | — | — | — | — | — |
| 7. Plants and animals have as much right as humans to exist. | — | — | — | — | — |
| 8. The balance of nature is strong enough to cope with the impacts of modern industrial nations. | — | — | — | — | — |
| 9. Despite our special abilities, humans are still subject to the laws of nature. | — | — | — | — | — |
| 10. The so-called ecological crisis facing humankind has been greatly exaggerated. | — | — | — | — | — |
| 11. The earth is like a spaceship with very limited room and resources. | — | — | — | — | — |
| 12. Humans were meant to rule over the rest of nature. | — | — | — | — | — |
| 13. The balance of nature is very delicate and easily upset. | — | — | — | — | — |
| 14. Humans will eventually learn enough about how nature works to be able to control it. | — | — | — | — | — |
| 15. If things continue on their present course, we will soon experience a major ecological catastrophe. | — | — | — | — | — |

Source: Scale developed by Riley E. Dunlap, Kent D. Van Liere, Angela G. Mertig, and Robert Emmet Jones, "Measuring Endorsement of the New Ecological Paradigm: A Revised NEP Scale," *Journal of Social Issues* 56(3)(2000):425–42.

Additional questions to tap environmental attitudes have been developed by major polling organizations like Gallup and Roper. Environmental questions also are asked as part of the General Social Survey, a near-annual survey of the American public designed to gauge opinion on a wide range of issues facing the country and conducted by the National Opinion Research Center.

*Environmental Concern over Time*

Public opinion polls have consistently found that the majority of Americans support environmental protection and many are even willing to pay more to protect it. A comprehensive review of public opinion toward environmental issues since 1965 discovered several trends.[8] First, environmental concern increased dramatically in the late 1960s and reached a peak with the first Earth Day in 1970. Second, this concern declined quite a bit in the early 1970s and continued to decline more gradually for the rest of the decade, but nevertheless remained substantial. Third, during the 1980s, there was a "significant and steady increase in both public awareness of the seriousness of environmental problems and in support of environmental protection."[9] By Earth Day 1990, public concern for environmental quality had reached "unprecedented levels."

The shifts in pro-environmental public opinion between the 1970s and 1990s were dramatic. Responses to the Roper Organization question "Environmental protection laws and regulations have gone too far, not far enough, or have struck the right balance" had increased from 34 percent believing "not far enough" in 1972 to 54 percent in 1990.[10] When Cambridge Reports asked whether people agreed that "We must sacrifice economic growth in order to preserve and protect the environment," those choosing environmental protection grew from 38 percent in 1976 to 64 percent in 1990.[11]

When the Gallup poll asked Americans in 1990 "Do you consider yourself to be an environmentalist or not?" a remarkable 73 percent said "yes." Clearly, by this decade Americans overall had become significantly more environmentally oriented and their environmentalism had gone deeper than merely attitudes and opinions and affected their core values and beliefs.[12]

**Figure 3.1**

However, by the next decade, some pollsters had reported environmental attitudes slipping and blamed the weakening economy, war in Iraq, and concern over terrorism. Gallup's annual Earth Day poll in 2003 found that even though Americans grew more negative about the state of the environment, they were less likely than in years past to favor aggressive action to address environmental problems.[13] Gallup also discovered that just 47 percent of Americans choose environmental protection over economic growth. In contrast, throughout the 1990s, people sided with the environment over the economy by a two to one margin. While each poll represents just a snapshot of opinion at a particular time—opinion which is highly influenced by current events—the trends are worth noting. Even when Gallup asked respondents to name the most important problem our nation will face twenty-five years from now, mentions of "the environment" had typically led mentions of "the economy" by significant margins—until 2003.

### Environmental Knowledge

When the pollster calls, it's possible to participate without *knowing* anything about the issues. Polls can include questions that filter out individuals who lack sufficient knowledge, but space and time concerns limit their use. Does this mean that measures of attitudes and behaviors are similarly suspect? Not necessarily, in part because the relationship between knowledge, attitude, and behavior is complex and not particularly strong.

First, it's important to distinguish between types of knowledge.[14] Many an environmental campaign struggles to raise awareness, or simple familiarity with a subject or issue and a low level of knowledge. By itself, awareness has little long-term effect on pro-environmental attitudes or behavior. And depending on the topic, the majority of Americans have "heard of" major environmental topics like air pollution and climate change. A second and slightly deeper form is "personal conduct" knowledge, an immediate and fairly simple step such as buying a "green" product or turning off lights. It goes beyond awareness because it involves personal action, but it usually doesn't require specific knowledge of causal sequences, ecological systems, and so on. A significantly higher level of knowledge is "environmental literacy," which is equated with more in-depth information and an understanding of underlying principles, consequences, and applications.

As you might guess, very few Americans can be considered environmentally literate. Roper polling estimates just 2 percent of adults qualify, though the percentage increases with education level. Interestingly, despite their poor performance on such literacy measures, Americans believe they are pretty knowledgeable: 11 percent said they knew "a lot" and 59 percent said they knew "a fair amount" about the environment.[15]

Although it may be logical to assume that knowledge affects attitude, and attitude affects behavior, researchers have concluded that such a knowledge-attitude-behavior model is too linear and simplistic.[16] These three factors may be associated in some form but don't necessarily "cause" one another. In most cases, the relationship between knowledge, attitude, and behavior tends to be positive but not very strong.[17] When the behaviors are simple (recycling newspapers or avoiding the use of yard chemicals), increased knowledge increases the likelihood of the behavior. But the reverse can be true for a behavior such as the use of alternative transportation. However, a study in Minnesota found that the most environmentally knowledgeable group was from 8 to 25 percentage points more likely to engage in pro-environmental actions than the least knowledgeable group.[18] It's also heartening to hear that 56 percent of Americans say they want to help the environment but don't know how.[19]

## The Links between Attitudes and Behaviors

We tend to assume that attitudes (broadly defined to include beliefs and values) are strongly related to behavior; that is, people typically behave in a way that's consistent with their attitudes. If you profess to have pro-environmental values, you will strive to act accordingly in daily life. But the relationship is not that simple. It is, of course, quite different to tell a pollster that you strongly favor a bottle bill than it is to actually collect and return bottles for your deposit. And despite poll numbers that show fairly consistent, widespread environmental concern, Americans are using more energy, building ever larger houses, driving more miles, and buying more stuff.

Why the disconnect? Some of it may stem from the fact that it's pretty easy for us humans to say one thing and do another; consistency in all areas of human endeavor is difficult. The disconnect may also be a symptom of how the goals and terms of environmentalism have been co-opted by institutions and individuals who do not support significant pro-environmental change. It's also difficult for an individual to enact numerous pro-environmental behaviors in a culture governed by a paradigm based on continual growth and consumption. That said, it remains important for those seeking to effect pro-environmental behaviors to understand the link between attitude and behavior, and the very real constraints and barriers on individual action imposed by the social structure.

The general conclusion from decades of psychological research is that attitudes are only moderately good predictors of how people will act,[20] and depend to a great degree on a whole host of factors. Individual factors (such as resources, knowledge, experience, values, and skills) and social factors (such as the political and cultural environment, obstacles, dominant environmental values, and public and legal policy) all come into play.

The most common way that attitudes and behaviors are measured is through self-report, that is, an individual telling a researcher.

Research has come a long way in question-writing and survey administration in order to make these measures more accurate, but a self-report is still subjective and subject to error. However for attitudes, it's nevertheless the most accurate way to find out how a person thinks or feels. When it comes to behavior, it is preferable to collect verifiable reports if possible. To ascertain whether a campaign to promote recycling is working, measure pounds collected in addition to self-reports of behavior (which can be subject to a "social desirability response").

*Influences upon Attitude*

Consider "Sue," a fictitious (but entirely realistic) twenty-nine-year-old white college student, a single mom who lives in a first-tier suburb of a medium-sized city and works part-time in a bank. Sue is not politically active, but she generally votes for Democrats. Although she doesn't call herself an "environmentalist," she is worried about environmental quality, in particular about environmental health effects on her child who has asthma. Lately, Sue has noticed that it costs more to fill her gas tank. At dinner last week, she listened to her boyfriend discuss the prospect of drilling in the Arctic National Wildlife Refuge. Recently, she noticed on TV some public service ads criticizing SUVs. Last week, she rode for the first time the city's new electric rail car system up to the university from a meeting she had downtown. And, she read the little newsletter that came with her gas bill about possible price increases. In the last month, it seems that Sue has been exposed to lots of messages about energy and has been thinking more about it.

Given what we know of "Sue," what can we say about her environmental attitudes and what might influence them? We already know, just based on her demographics, that Sue is more likely to have higher levels of environmental concern: she is young, educated, Democrat, female, and urban. But those factors (with the exception of age) are fairly weak predictors and aren't sufficient to explain what might influence her attitudes (and subsequent behavior).

Obviously, *events* and *personal experience* are part of the reason that Sue has been thinking more about energy issues lately. She has been paying more at the gas station and has become aware of current events that have the potential to affect gas prices. Depending on her past, even experiences in childhood could contribute to her beliefs about energy. Perhaps one winter her parents lacked money to pay the heating bill. Or, perhaps her family relied on woodstoves for heat and a windmill to fill the stock water tanks on the farm.

Sue also is being influenced by the *opinions of others*. Significant friends, family, and colleagues have the potential to greatly influence opinions, and depending on the topic, may exert more significant influence than mass media news or so-called experts.

Sue also has been receiving and processing a variety of *messages*. She paid attention to and remembered a public service ad about SUVs, and she took the time to read the newsletter from the gas company. Perhaps in her college classes, related messages from economics or public policy have prompted her to connect this information with energy use. Every single day, we are literally bombarded by messages, only a small portion of which we actively process and remember. Some messages come from so-called objective sources like the news media, but many more come from sources advocating a certain opinion or behavior.

Sue's *value orientation* also may be influencing her attitude toward the environment and energy. According to psychology research, value orientation is a cluster of prioritized values that a person adopts and relies upon to help make decisions and inform action. If Sue has an *egoistic value orientation*, she would consider only the costs and benefits to herself when forming her attitudes. If Sue has a *social-altruistic value orientation*, she would consider the costs and benefits to human beings more generally and in a way that transcends purely individual concerns. And if Sue possesses a *biocentric* or *ecocentric value orientation*, she would consider the costs and benefits to the entire ecosystem or biosphere.[21] When trying to evaluate the rhetoric of messages, Sue may rely on value orientations, her environmental ideology, or a variety of other personal norms and values.

## Types of Pro-environmental Behavior

A lot of people who might express particular pro-environmental attitudes would never identify themselves as environmentalists nor join an environmental group. Does that mean there is no kind of environmentally significant behavior available? Hardly! Because the definition of environmentalism is the propensity to take actions with pro-environmental intent, there are many ways to demonstrate environmental concern.

*Environmental activism,* or the active involvement in environmental organizations and their activities, is an extremely committed type of environmental behavior. Although membership in national environmental groups runs into the millions, the majority of members are "paper members," members who donate money but not time or participation. Still, a monetary donation is a type of activist behavior.

Another type of environmental behavior is *nonactivist behavior in the public sphere.* Nonactivist individuals may support the goals of environmental groups, but express that support in the public sphere, perhaps by testifying at hearings, attending rallies or meetings, writing letters, or making phone calls to political leaders. Institutions in the public sphere include government, public education, the legal system, and other publicly funded organizations.

*Private sphere environmentalism* concerns behaviors that take place in the private sphere and demonstrate pro-environmental intent. The collective purchase, use, and disposal of personal and household goods have a great deal of environmental impact. Infrequent purchases such as major household products (cars and appliances), and installing and maintaining heating and cooling systems can have far more significance than other decisions. So-called green consumerism, purchasing practices that consider product features such as recycled and organic, has significant impact only when many individuals independently make the same green choices.

Finally, individuals may significantly affect the environment by influencing *actions within organizations* to which they belong.[22] Such behavior changes can result in significant environmental change because organizational actions are a large, direct source of many environmental problems.[23] "For example, engineers may design manufactured products in more or less environmental benign ways, bankers and developers may use or ignore environmental criteria in their decisions, and maintenance workers' actions may reduce or increase the pollution produced by manufacturing plants or commercial buildings."[24]

Although it's unlikely that the average person would engage in environmental activism, it's possible that under the right circumstances, she might engage in nonactivist behavior in the public sphere. It's perhaps most likely for such an individual to undertake private sphere environmentalism—not just in purchasing, but also in energy awareness at home, at work, and in transportation. Given the relationships an adult has with coworkers, she might eventually feel comfortable enough to bring up work practices that have environmental impacts.

### Predicting Behavior

A whole lot of people would just love to be able to predict how you'll behave—advertisers, politicians, coworkers, special interest groups, and no doubt your mother. But you know from past experience that even if you have a lot of information and good instincts, it's no guarantee you'll be able to predict someone's behavior.

"Bob" is a forty-five-year-old husband and father of two sons who owns a small landscaping business. He's never been particularly active politically and considers himself only somewhat religious. Bob reads the newspaper when he can and listens to the radio at work. In the summer, his family goes car camping in the mountains. Once an avid fly fisherman, Bob says he lacks time to indulge in the pastime nowadays.

Although we have some demographic information about Bob, we don't have a clear picture of his environmental attitudes or how they might guide his behavior. We also don't know what personal skills or external factors impinge on what he believes his behavior choices to be. We don't even know how his daily habits and routines affect his behavior. In other words, we need to consider these pieces together as an entire process or linked chain of events that work together to influence behavior. We'll consider each in turn:

> Attitudinal factors
> Personal factors
> Contextual factors
> Habit and routine

#### ATTITUDINAL FACTORS

First, consider the following four statements.

"I distrust big corporations."
"I support the new open-space initiative."

"People should treat the natural world with respect."
"Humans can solve environmental problems with technology."

A casual observer might label all these statements as "attitudes." But on closer inspection, important differences exist that have implications for their measurement, and for how closely they may be linked to behavior.

"I distrust big corporations" is indeed an *attitude* because it expresses a positive or negative feeling toward something. Attitudes are learned, enduring, emotional evaluations of another person, idea, or entity. An attitude focuses on feelings about an object, not about the characteristics of the object.

The second statement is an *opinion*. While attitudes are predispositions to respond or lean in a certain way, opinions are the responses themselves.[25] Another way to think about the distinction is that attitudes are complex structures, and opinions are simple or even singular expressions. The opinion "I support the new open-space initiative," is a single expression of a larger attitude, perhaps about likes or preferences toward outdoor activities.

The third statement expresses a *value*. "People should treat the natural world with respect," is an expression of an ideal, the way things should be, or an overarching goal that people should strive to obtain. Values tend to be more general and global than attitudes.

The last statement, "Humans can solve environmental problems with technology," is the expression of a *belief*, a thought that an individual has about an object or action. Beliefs are assumptions by which we understand things and live our lives.

In different ways, each of these attitudinal statements might provide clues as to relevant behaviors a person could take. But if you had to guess, which of those four statements do you think provides the strongest standards of conduct? That is, which of the four seems to be the most stable across contexts, or even predictive in terms of what behaviors might follow? The best guess is values. Values are relatively stable across person's life span and function as prescriptive standards of conduct;[26] thus, values can be important determinants of environmentally oriented behavior.[27]

If you think of a value as an ideal or overarching goal, you can see how the consequences for behavior can likewise be overarching.

Let's say that Bob has strong altruistic values and believes that people need to think about future generations when it comes to open space. His values serve as a blueprint in deciding what the salient consequences of particular behaviors are and may also influence whether he seeks out more knowledge and information. For example, if Bob comes across an advertisement that lauds a new housing development on five-acre lots, his altruistic values might be activated in a way that leads him to interpret the ad's rhetoric as encouraging selfish land use that has harmful consequences for future generations.[28] When faced with a behavior choice down the road—perhaps involving his own landscaping business—his values may once again serve as a blueprint in evaluating consequences and choices. These values also may influence his knowledge acquisition or perception of the responsibility of the political system.

As you might expect, altruistic values (along with ecocentric values) are those that most strongly activate pro-environmental personal behavior. (Egoistic values and "traditional" values such as obedience, self-discipline, and family security are associated with anti-environmental behavior.)

A final piece of the attitudinal puzzle is to examine the role of norms, for norms provide a framework for translating values and beliefs into possible behaviors performed in a social context. A *norm* is an expectation held by an individual about how she or he ought to act in a particular social situation or context. Norms recognize that we are social beings, and that our personal values interact with social environments to guide our behaviors. That is, I am aware that there are social expectations (not just legal ones) about how I ought to behave in a forest, which I internalize. My norm is informed by my values and beliefs about forests and how someone "should" behave in them, such as, "People should treat forests with respect." If someone else held a value such as "People should utilize forests for their enjoyment," that value will support different behaviors.

Norms may be internalized differently, depending on the "social power" that the norm expectation has over us. A *social norm* is enforced by the threat of punishment or promise of reward by others around us; that is, a person perceives a great degree of peer pressure to act a certain way. A *personal norm* is internalized as a guiding principle for how to act and doesn't need to be "enforced" by others. A *moral norm* is a person's perception of the moral correctness or incorrectness of performing a behavior or having personal feelings of a responsibility to perform. For environmental issues, survey questions have tapped the role of all three types of norms:[29]

> "People I know believe that good stewardship of water resources is very important." (social norm)
> "I try to do my part to conserve energy." (personal norm)
> "It is my moral responsibility to protect natural resources for future generations." (moral norm)

At times, personal norms clash with social norms. If part of your ecocentric value orientation is that it's wrong to confine and slaughter animals for food, you may act this out by not eating meat. Your personal norm comes with a high awareness of consequences, not only of limits you face when eating out, but also in a broader sense of land use and health issues. However, you may be very reluctant to speak out when you see others eating meat or raising animals for food. The social norms of others are strong enough that you might fear the reaction—punishment in the form of rebuke or ostracism— if you said something. In this case, despite a fairly strong attitude about meat eating, the sanctions of a social norm are strong enough to prevent your behavior.

We all know people who depend far more on cues and expectations from the external social world than from their own internal principles for guides for their behavior. We might conclude that these people are very concerned about what other people think, or that they are like chameleons, adapting their behavior or persona according to the situation at hand. *Self-monitoring* is the extent to which a person monitors (that is, how the person observes, regulates, and controls) the "self" displayed in social situations. "High self-monitors" are adept at controlling the images of themselves that they present in social settings and are highly sensitive to social cues and expectations about appropriate behavior.[30] In contrast, "low self-monitors" rely less on situational cues and more on internal feelings and values to help them decide how to act in particular situations. What does all this mean for measuring environmental concern? Low self-monitors are more likely to say what they really think in a public opinion survey and are less likely to answer the way they think the surveyor wants or the context calls for. There also is a much stronger link between attitudes and behaviors for low self-monitors than for high self-monitors.[31]

### PERSONAL FACTORS

All of us at some time feel limited in our personal ability to take action on our environmental beliefs. We may lack the knowledge or skill required for particular actions, such as installing weather proofing or evaluating the cost effectiveness of energy-efficient appliances. Or, we might have very limited available time to act, whether arranging our schedule to drop off used paint or chemicals or getting involved politically in energy issues. Resources—not just monetary, but also resources such as literacy, social power, or status—are lacking for some people.

A theory called the "theory of planned behavior"[32] maintains that two specific attitudinal factors (a person's attitude toward a behavior and social norms related to the behavior) combined with personal capability factors can predict the intention to undertake a specific behavior. One personal factor is *perceived behavioral control* or the extent to which performing a target behavior is considered easy or difficult. These perceived "controls" can come from both external and internal forces. An internal factor may be inadequate knowledge of how to conserve energy or where to dispose of a worn-out fluorescent bulb (which contains mercury). External factors may be perceived as constraints to performing the behavior that lie outside the control of the individual, such as the cost of energy-efficient appliances. Perceived external barriers (i.e., "The city recycling drop-off center is too far away for me to use") may reflect an individual's perceived personal limitations, but also may point to very real social system constraints (i.e., the city has far too few recycling drop-off centers). Such real-world constraints aside, this theory has demonstrated that the more control a person believes she has over a behavior, the stronger the person's intention to engage in that behavior.

People are more likely to engage in behaviors for which they possess *self-efficacy* or feel they are capable and empowered. Researchers investigating environmental behaviors have defined self-efficacy as the belief that an individual's actions make a difference in overall environmental quality (i.e., "Conserving energy in my own home makes a difference").[33]

Of course, it's easy to see your own pro-environmental behaviors as pretty inconsequential in the grand scheme of things: "What difference does it make if I take the bus when everyone else drives?" This kind of thinking is reinforced when the timeframe is short-term and the perspective is self-oriented. Several decades ago, the metaphor of "the tragedy of the commons"[34] expressed this predicament:

> . . . a herdsman can realize a substantial personal benefit at little personal cost by adding an animal to his herd grazing on common [or publicly owned] land. The benefit that comes from having an additional animal is his alone, whereas the cost, in terms of slightly less grazing land per animal, is shared by all, so the herdsman with the additional animal realizes a net gain. The problem, of course, is that every herdsman sees the situation the same way, so collectively, with each person working in what appears to be his own best short-term interest, they ruin the land.[35]

For environmentally responsible behaviors, it's important for attitudes and social factors to join forces in an attempt to overcome the "tragedy of the commons." If, for example, peer pressure supports the purchase of a high-mileage vehicle, or city government supports walkable neighborhoods (both in attitude and practice), a more supportive environment will be created for individual action in a way that reinforces self-efficacy and the belief of one person's ability to make a difference.

*Information factors* such as the degree of information seeking, information processing, or exposure to information also can be important links to behavior and behavioral intention.[36] It makes sense that if a person is actively seeking or reading information on something like energy-efficient appliances, that information seeking could be a good indicator of the person's future behaviors. One study found that an individual's seeking of information and exposure and attention to it (in addition to attitudes and norms) predicted the individual's intention to conserve water.[37]

## CONTEXTUAL FACTORS

A person's attitudes, norms, and personal capabilities might be good predictors for behaviors that are strictly voluntary and fairly simple, like recycling or turning off lights. However, behavior may be harder to predict when it requires skills or resources outside an individual's control.[38]

I often hear from students who say they would like to use the bus more often to travel to campus, but several contextual factors work against this choice. The last bus for some routes leaves campus at eight P.M., but some night classes end at nine P.M. In addition, many students have part-time and even full-time jobs, making it difficult to travel from work to campus and back again in a timely way. Hence the *availability of public services* doesn't make mass transit a good behavior choice for many. To address the availability of recycling services, many communities have provided curbside recycling and immediately experienced great increases in recycling behavior.

Let's say it's time to buy a new refrigerator that won't freeze your lettuce. If you live in some states, the purchase of an energy-efficient appliance is rewarded with a state tax rebate, an example of a *government regulation* or *policy* that supports environmental behaviors. If such *monetary incentives* are not available in your state, you may feel compelled to purchase a cheaper but less efficient model, despite the fact that your belief system strongly supports the energy efficient choice.

In many realms, individuals feel constrained by *community expectations* regarding appropriate environmental behaviors. Green, weed-free lawns are an expectation in many cities. Last year, residents on my block were lobbying the city to install old-fashioned-looking "acorn" streetlights. Some of my neighbors argued that more streetlights were vital to prevent crime, but others opposed these types of lights because they contribute to "light pollution" of the nighttime sky by sending light up, not down.

The *message environment* also can create a supportive or nonsupportive context for environmental behavior. Every day, we are bombarded by advertisements that encourage consumption—of goods, energy, food, whatever we want. But we are exposed to very few messages promoting nonconsumption and conservation. Good information resources may exist on Web sites and through government agencies and private businesses, but seeking out conservation messages may require time, effort, and even special knowledge.

Constraints to environmental behavior also may be imposed by *technology* and the *built environment*. Classrooms in older buildings on my campus are notoriously too hot or too cold. The building's heating and cooling system is old and lacks individual room controls. To make the room temperature comfortable, students open the windows. Modern solutions to such constraints include individual thermostats, room lights controlled by motion sensors, and building (and landscape) designs that incorporate passive solar heating and cooling. Even a bike path is an example of how the built environment can accommodate and promote environmentally friendly behavior.

*Legal* and *institutional factors* also serve as contextual factors in environmental behavior. Recently, a newspaper story told about a man who received a citation for replacing the vegetation on his parking strip with desert plants and landscaping rocks. The man was trying to save water and energy, but the city had codified into law what was considerable acceptable as a "lawn." (Following a public uproar, the city backed down.)

Finally, a broad array of *economic* and *political features* provide contexts for behavior that exist outside of our control. Interest rates, the price of oil and gas, and political policies that reward and support energy development and use over energy conservation all provide real constraints to individual behavior options. If the price of gas in the United States were less subsidized and as expensive as it is in many parts of the world, it's more likely that fuel efficiency would drive car design and many more mass transit options would be available.

"ABC theory" considers contextual factors such as these just as important as attitudes in determining behavior.[39] According to this theory, behavior (B) is the interactive product of personal-sphere attitudinal factors (A) and contextual factors (C). In other words, behavior is a function of an "organism" and its interaction with its environment: "The attitude-behavior association is strongest when contextual factors are neutral and [the association] approaches zero when contextual forces are strongly positive or negative, effectively compelling or prohibiting the behavior in question."[40] So, when personal behaviors are not strongly favored by context, and the more difficult, time-consuming, or expensive the behavior, the less the behavior depends on attitudinal factors alone.

### HABIT AND ROUTINE

Much of our daily behavior is influenced by habit and routine. We tend to drive the same route home and buy the same brand of peanut butter. We have a set temperature for the thermostat and a way we wash the dishes.

Although past behavior does not cause subsequent behavior, frequent or repeated performance may help turn the behavior into a habit. For habitual acts such as recycling, past recycling may play a dominant role in predicting future recycling behavior.[41] Part of the reasoning may be that when a behavior becomes habitual, a person may be more likely to use simplified decision rules and to use the past behavior almost as a source of information in decision making.[42] Information possessed because of past behavior is then capable of being automatically activated by the context in which the behavior occurs.[43]

In order to break a habit or routine, a person needs to decide that the past behavior pattern no longer "works" for some reason. Perhaps the habit is becoming too expensive, such as buying large cars with low gas mileage, or keeping the thermostat temperature at seventy degrees during the winter. Or maybe new information is received that activates a person's norms or sense of responsibility. Maybe you see a news story about car-pooling and car-sharing and decide to call for more information.

It should be obvious from this discussion that the link between attitudes and behaviors is indeed messy and not easy to understand or predict. And of course, there are a lot of "depends." It depends whether the behavior is easy or whether formidable constraints exist. It depends on whether social norms support the behavior. It depends on the influence of external or contextual factors beyond an individual's control. It depends on whether a deeply rooted habit overrides the best of intentions. And of course it depends on whether a person knows the effects and consequences of different behaviors, behaviors that are both familiar and unfamiliar. For example, do you suppose that environmentally minded people would continue to buy bottled water if they knew the enormous environmental consequences— resource use, energy use, waste created—of that behavior choice?

## Approaches to Changing Behavior

There are a host of organizations and individuals who are interested in changing your attitudes and behavior on environmental issues— especially if you fit the demographics most associated with pro-environmental attitudes (young, educated, female), possess social-altruistic values toward the environment, and have a minimal level of awareness but have been actively processing information. You could be a target of a behavior change campaign.

Attempts to intervene and change individual behavior in a pro-social or pro-environmental way are most successful when they involve a combination of appeals.[44] Campaigns with an *educational* appeal seek to change attitudes and behavior by providing information. *Moral* and *worldview* approaches appeal to underlying values and norms in order to change broad beliefs. *Material incentives* can be used to intervene in existing behavior by providing monetary or other rewards or penalties. A *community management* appeal involves the establishment of shared rules and expectations; this approach has been used successfully for a variety of land or watershed management campaigns based at the community level. Some of these appeals interact, most notably those using information and incentives.

No matter the appeals, research has found that campaigns must address multiple spheres: the information environment and context of individuals, as well as the social and community context and barriers. If a community appears supportive of environmental changes, individuals may feel that they are not acting alone and find motivation in their peers.[45] If an individual feels that she or he is acting alone, it's more difficult to feel that the individual action is making a difference. One researcher found that one of the more important determinants of behavior change was people's beliefs about the pro-environmental behaviors of *others*.[46]

Over the decades, literally thousands of campaigns have tried to promote so-called environmentally responsible behavior (ERB), such as recycling, water conservation, or even noxious weed control. Oftentimes, the appeal is altruistic—doing something for the good of the environment or the good of the entire community—for example, drive less to help the air quality in the valley. But if I really have no suitable alternatives to driving (at least to work), how is this campaign likely to make me feel? Guilty, lacking control over the situation, or at the very least, helpless. In this case, acting altruistically would require a great deal of sacrifice on my part. I might think, here's another "dour environmentalist"[47] who's calling for sacrifice that I believe will reduce my quality of life. Most likely, I will resist making this behavior change.

In this case, an altruistic appeal might not be a good motivator of environmentally responsible behavior. "A central failing of the altruistic position is that it attempts to put aside the issue of gain, of self-interest, in human behavior. . . . The requirement of receiving no benefit from one's action and the inclination to enshrine sacrifice as a paradigmatic environmental virtue communicate a powerful, if unintended message, namely that ERB inherently leads to a reduction in the quality of life."[48]

One possible lesson to draw from this is that it is necessary to position the desired behavior as a route to a better life—for me, not just for others. For many years, self-interest was seen as a major *source* of environmental problems[49] because it implied that people were focusing solely on short-term individual or familial gain to the exclusion of long-term societal or environmental benefits.[50] Now, some scholars are suggesting that self-interest may be a potential *solution* to environmental problems, but it also must coincide with altruism.[51]

How could a drive-less campaign shift its appeal to include both altruism and self-interest? According to one model,[52] the campaign should move beyond telling people what to do, to helping people understand the issues and inviting them to explore possible solutions they find desirable. For example, campaign messages could help me understand how poor air quality directly affects my health (self-interest) and how it affects the health of all residents (altruism), as well as the health benefits of walking instead of driving for very short trips (self-interest). Messages could also explain that vehicle emissions are the worst in the first five minutes of driving, and then provide a wide array of "desirable choices" that I might choose to reduce my contribution to air pollution.[53] For example, I might not be willing to give up my use of the drive-through window, but I might choose to walk to errands and use fuel in the evening. These choices don't greatly reduce my quality of life, and I feel in control and not helpless. Such participatory problem solving and the joining of altruism and self-interest holds great promise in making behavior changes more sustainable and satisfying. It may be that "people prefer making the environmentally responsible choice when they are not seriously disadvantaged by doing so."[54]

Any intervention or campaign to change environmental behaviors is doomed to fail if it does little to address or remove barriers to change. In the case of driving less, if my city lacks safe, walkable neighborhoods, bike paths, or workable mass transit, I may feel constrained from making changes in my driving habits. Or if a campaign promotes drought-tolerant landscaping but local nurseries don't stock water-wise plants and shrubs, behavior change is less likely. Language, literacy, and finances may be barriers in a campaign to remove lead-based paint from homes. In a campaign promoting investments in home insulation, participation might face several potential barriers—financial, informational, and operational (locating a contractor).[55]

## Conclusion

The strong support expressed each year by Americans for environmental protection is often not carried through to behavior. How can those positive sentiments be translated into action?

Anyone interested in changing individual attitudes and/or behaviors (in themselves or in others) must remember that there is no top-down, "magic bullet" message that will cause people to "see the (environmental) light." We are far too complex social and psychological beings for such a simple fix. It does indeed matter what we saw on TV last night, the behavior we witnessed in coworkers, the question our child asked, the price we pay at the pump—though it all matters in infinitesimal and often unknown ways. It's impossible to fathom the number of events, messages, and experiences that contribute to your beliefs about global warming or predators or forests. In the phenomenally crowded and complex communication environment, it's a wonder that any one message "works" at all.

Achieving social change in small or large ways must cross and include all levels: individual, societal, cultural, even global. Any attempt to change attitude and behavior that puts the entire responsibility on the individual will not succeed. Even if a person believes in a certain environmental behavior, a variety of contextual factors may thwart its exercise: social norms, government regulation, community expectations, monetary resources, and time.

# 4

## Work and Consumer Culture

Think of a typical day in your life and its routines and patterns. What connection does it have with the natural world? Perhaps you drove through the rain to work. Maybe you jogged or walked the dog. You might have mowed the yard or shoveled the sidewalk. If you're observant, perhaps you heard birdsong or saw the sunset.

But chances are you spent the vast majority of the hours in your typical day inside. Most of us live indoor lives, and the natural world is very much in the background of—if not divorced from—daily life. We think of "nature" as something to which we must travel to leave that daily life behind. You might fill your indoor life with reminders of the one outside: computer screensavers of mountains or beaches, house plants, and paintings or photos of natural places. If you're athletic or outdoorsy, you might head outside when you get off work.

For those of us who don't work outside, there's a strong tendency to compartmentalize our work lives. Work seems separate from consumption and the ubiquitous consumer culture. Work seems unrelated to environment and devoid of nature. Despite the seeming gulf, the economic lives made possible by our work and the daily activities of consumption and leisure couldn't be more intertwined.

This chapter tackles the realm of work and consumer culture and the environmental communication that takes place there. It is paid work, after all, that drives our consumer culture, which is the backdrop and context for so much of modern life. And there is no other act that says as much about your relationship with the environment as your consumption.

## Work versus Leisure

If you had to say which part of your life was most connected to nature—work or leisure—most of us would say leisure. But is the separation—between work and leisure, and even between nature and work and nature and leisure—really that distinct?

The Greek and Roman words for "leisure" were *schole* and *otium*; the words for business and employment were *a-scholia* and *neg-otium*. In other words, a job meant a *lack* of leisure. "For the Greeks and Romans, work was the time or condition when one lacked leisure. For us nowadays, the definition seems reversed: leisure is a time or condition when one is not working."[1] In many senses, we still understand leisure in opposition to work; work is what we *have* to do and leisure is what's left over. This differs greatly from primitive societies when work and leisure were entirely linked and fused.[2]

If work is the realm of necessity, leisure is the realm of freedom and the one we fill with voluntary or chosen activities; we call it "free time." Think of the stereotypes and expectations from work versus leisure:

> Work involves strain, effort, exertion, pay; leisure, on the contrary, is effortless, easy, pleasurable. Work is done through compulsion or necessity; leisure is not forced upon one, nor is it necessary for subsistence. Work is thought to be a means to an end; leisure is thought to be an end in itself. . . . Work is time spent for others; leisure is one's own time. Work is thought to be socially useful; leisure is individually enjoyable but not necessarily of service to anyone else. Work is rewarded; leisure is its own reward. Work is likely to be routine or monotonous whereas leisure is a holiday or a liberation from the everyday . . .[3]

Since most of our work hours are spent inside, it follows that most indoor workers might consider their work as largely irrelevant to or at least unconnected with nature. Typically, we think about nature most—if at all—during nonworking hours, meaning that leisure bears the burden of reconnecting us with nature and perhaps also providing the satisfactions we lack in work. (Leisure is the focus of the next chapter.) But that doesn't mean that work is not re-

**Figure 4.1**

lated to leisure or to nature. After all, in our highly industrialized and consumer-driven society, our work is what "buys" our leisure and the toys we use in it. And as argued here, *all* work intersects with nature though in very different ways.

## This Thing Called "Work"

To begin with the basics, employment describes a relationship between buyers and sellers of labor, not just the distinct activity engaged in. A particular job describes how the relationship between employer and employee is organized and the circumstances under which it occurs. As we all know, the degree of discretion and control of the employer varies greatly.

Work is infused with political and moral values. Paid work establishes a right to respect, a feeling of self-worth (some would say an identity), especially when compared with typical evaluations of unpaid work ("I'm just a housewife").[4] Work not only produces wealth, it produces and enables a social life.[5] Increasingly, those at the top of the employment and income scale (shall we say, upper class) own and control far more property, resources, and information than those further down.

Individuals who find satisfaction in their work point to characteristics such as creating something, using a skill, working wholeheartedly (not being slowed down), using initiative and having responsibility, social contact, and working with competent people. Dissatisfaction from work may be due to a repetitive job, making only a small part of the larger whole, doing useless tasks, feeling insecure, and being supervised too closely.[6]

But even if a worker finds a job satisfying overall, that doesn't mean that all desires are fulfilled. My friend Barb is fifty years old and has worked as a midlevel manager for the same corporation since she graduated from college, surviving innumerable mergers and acquisitions. She plans to retire early and "follow her bliss." She spends her weekends walking her dog along the river, riding her horse, and sailing with friends. Barb's job, like the vast number of jobs in a capitalist society, is "instrumental" in that it provides her a paycheck and allows her to buy commodities that will provide her the satisfaction that her job does not. Some would even say that the quest for material possessions has replaced intrinsic personal satisfaction as the prime goal of paid labor, if not the very goal of life itself.[7]

If paychecks are merely instruments to find satisfaction, it appears that we are easily deceived about how much happiness those paychecks will provide: "Most people believe that a 25 percent pay increase would make them much more satisfied with their lives—but those whose incomes are now at that higher level are not, in fact, happier or more satisfied with their lives."[8] If someone is above the poverty line, more money quickly loses its power to make him or her happy: "The rich are no more satisfied with their lives than the merely comfortable, who in turn are only slightly, if at all, more satisfied with their lives than the lower middle classes."[9]

Though there is now a higher percentage of the U.S. population in the workforce (about 60 percent), with earlier retirements and longer life expectancy, the total percentage of all of life's hours devoted to work has declined from 23 percent in 1900 to 15 percent in 1960, and continues to decline.[10] But for those from their twenties to their sixties, the work-pace and hours during those years may be intense.

In their productive working years, a great many people find precious little meaning and satisfaction in their jobs. In one study, the number one satisfaction that people derived from their paid employment was the ability to "stay busy"; the number one satisfaction that people gained from their leisure was "escape."[11] If that's the case, why don't we work less and escape more?

### Working . . . to Shop

In her popular book *The Overworked American,* Harvard economist-turned-sociologist Juliet Shor says that since 1948, the productivity of U.S. workers has more than doubled, meaning that we could produce a 1948 standard of living now in about half the time: "We actually could have chosen the four-hour day. Or a working year of six months. Or, every worker in the United States could now be taking every other year off from work—with pay. Incredible as it may sound, this is just the simple arithmetic of productivity growth in operation."[12]

So what happened to all that "extra" money? We went shopping. Shor says that by the 1990s, the average American owned and consumed more than *twice* as much as he or she did in 1948, but also had *less* free time.[13]

To get an idea of how Americans have up-sized, look at housing. In the 1950s, a standard house for a *family* was 750 square feet. That had doubled by 1963 to 1,500 square feet and by 2003 it was

2,330 square feet. Fifty years ago, only 20 percent of houses had more rooms than people living in them, but by 1970, over 90 percent of homes had more than one room per person. According to Shor, "The size and quality of American housing stock has not been replicated anywhere else on earth."[14] Of course, there are domino effects for desiring spacious houses; residents who sold small houses in core urban areas to buy larger ones in suburbs essentially traded for a far longer commute.

To fill big houses, we "shop 'til we drop." We spend far more time shopping—three to four times as many hours as people in Western Europe[15]—and spend a higher fraction of the money we earn. Of course with credit cards and instant cash, many people spend much more than they earn.

Think of the last time your income rose. Did it mean more savings or more money left in the checking account at the end of the month? For many, the answer is no. What Shor calls the "work-and-spend cycle" becomes a treadmill that is hard to get off. When income rises, consumption rises, which creates a "need" for yet more income. Yet many of us say we reject materialist values. The Gallup Poll asked people to rate how much they valued nine discrete things and materialism came in last.[16] People say they would like to spend more time with their spouses and kids, have more time for themselves, to exercise, to cook meals and eat together, and they recognize that stress and work is harming their health. Yet, they work and spend more and more.

The work-and-spend cycle has obvious, detrimental implications for the natural world. The United States has only 5 percent of the world's population but consumes an astonishing 20 percent of its natural resources and 25 percent of its energy supply. The footprint of our country is larger and heavier than any other country on earth. As Shor asks, "In an era when the connections between perpetual growth and environmental deterioration are becoming more apparent, with the quality of public life declining in many areas (public safety, decline of community, failing education system), shouldn't we at least step back and re-examine our commitment to ever-greater quantities of consumer goods? Do Americans need high-definition television, increasingly exotic vacations, and climate control in their autos? How about hundred-dollar inflatable sneakers, fifty-dollar

wrinkle cream, or the ever-present (but rarely used) stationary bi-
cycle?"[17]

### Working . . . toward Leisure

Let's say you boldly decide to step off the work-and-spend cycle,
dramatically cut your consumption, cut back work hours, and make
more room for leisure. You decide to pursue the Zen path to happiness, reducing your desires rather than continually increasing them,
and shunning hedonistic pleasures that are shallow and addictive.
You renounce materialism and believe that you can enjoy material
plenty without lowering your standard of living. Although you've
always known the exact price of time, now you want to fully appreciate the value of time.

After all, in many centuries and cultures, leisure made up a much
bigger portion of the week, if not the year. In the old Roman calen-
dar, 109 of 355 days were designated as "nefasti," or days when it was
"unlawful for judicial and political business."[18] By the mid-fourth
century, the number of public festival days reached 175. Early Native
Americans labored for only three to four hours per day, which was
all that was needed to sustain livelihoods in an economy that wasn't
geared toward profit and productivity.

In current times, the workplace and the marketplace may not
be of much help in your efforts to reduce work. In the eyes of some
critics, "Today's corporate philosophy values leanness and mean-
ness, and views workers at all levels as little more than a small part
of the entire production process. . . . Workers are looked upon as a
support to the economy rather than the object which the economy
serves."[19] In addition, employers generally don't offer—and employees don't demand—trading income gains for leisure. Built into capitalist economies and their incentive structures is a bias toward long-
hour jobs,[20] meaning professional jobs organized by tasks and not a
time-clock. A long-hour job requires that you put in enough hours
to get the job done, regardless of whether that stretches well beyond
a forty-hour week.

According to some studies, the result of increased time at work
is less time spent not only on leisure, but also on basics like sleep-
ing and eating (especially cooking) and less time spent with family

members. With more and more women employed full-time,"second-shift" work (unpaid household labor such as child-rearing, cooking, and cleaning that must be completed after the long-hour job) also creates a squeeze in time.[21]

Part-time employment may not be a viable option either. Very few such opportunities exist with benefits and at pay-scales similar to full-time work. Sadly, unaffordable private health insurance keeps millions of workers stuck in full-time jobs just to hold on to the employer-supported health insurance.

Every now and then, we read about a family who chucked it all—the high-paying sixty-hour-per-week job, the big house, the grand lifestyle—and drastically downsized. Perhaps they moved to a plot of land "off the grid" (no connections for utilities like water, electricity, and phone), or maybe they just did without and "simplified" their existing life. Since the 1970s, various so-called simple living movements have emerged. But generally, they appeal to white, upper-middle-class individuals who are able to retain health insurance coverage! In the eyes of our culture, these sacrifice-scenarios just don't sell; anticonsumption is not vogue or upbeat. There are still occasional calls for "voluntary simplicity" and "conscientious consumption." But achieving life satisfaction with less faces the constraints of the economic and social system, which values consumption and disposal over thrift.

## Consumption and Daily Life

*We can't even do the simple rituals that bind us together without purchasing paraphernalia.*[22]

There is no other act—period—that communicates as much about your relationship with the environment as your consumption. Obviously, we must consume food and water, and in most climates, we require shelter and heat. On the simplest level, these basic requirements account for extremely little of our daily diet of consumption. So how did the United States turn into world's "best"—or at least biggest—consumer paradise? Why is the urge to shop so strong, even for those with strong environmental values? How does consumption contribute—not just to the obvious depletion of resources and mounds of waste—but also to heightened ecological illiteracy?

In case you're thinking that consumerism isn't a problem for environmentally responsible people, think again. "Lifestyle" to the marketplace is a consumer package, a collection of things and practices; "One's body, clothes, speech, leisure pastimes, eating and drinking preferences, home, car, choice of holidays, and so on are to be regarded as indicators of the individuality of taste and sense of style of the owner/consumer."[23] How is an "environmental lifestyle" communicated and marketed? What do the clothing and footwear look like? What stores sell these products? What leisure activities or vacation destinations are associated with an outdoorsy lifestyle? What kind of car matches this lifestyle? Not hard to picture, is it? Yet when the *market* defines this lifestyle, there doesn't need to be any relationship to environmental ideology or practice. The environmental lifestyle being promoted and communicated by the marketplace is hedonistic and narcissistic—it's all about your enjoyment, your pleasure and comfort, about your looking good and having the latest toys. A recurring theme of the environmental lifestyle is escape; escape into nature and rejuvenate, leave civilization and its stressors behind. We also create such lifestyles in our homes, purchase by purchase: soothing water fountains, "natural" fabrics and materials, paintings and photographs, and so on.

We are inundated with messages encouraging consumption; messages encouraging conservation or nonconsumption are rare. We are also surrounded with the consumptive practices of others. The next section takes a closer look at the substance of messages from the marketplace and the consequences they have on our psyches and the physical world.

### Development of the "Buyosphere"

In a book aptly titled, *I Want That!*, the author concluded that we live much of our lives in the "buyosphere," a place that is as much a state of mind as it is a physical and virtual place: "We come into the buyosphere with a mixture of attitudes and emotions. We are serious and lighthearted, sensitive and greedy, thrifty and competitive. The buyosphere is not a civic space, but it is our chief arena for expression, the place where we learn most about who we are, both as a people and as individuals."[24]

**Figure 4.2**

The author is correct in asserting that this "buyosphere" is not a civic space, for individuals in a society with an all-powerful marketplace behave more like a nation of consumers than a nation of citizens. But it is misleading to state that this is an area we "come into" from some space that is utterly divorced from our lives as consumers. One could even claim that in modern society, we are so enmeshed in consumer culture that it is virtually impossible to *leave* this space.

While it is true that consumerism is a culture in itself, it is a sad commentary to assert that we express and come to know ourselves best through shopping. Ubiquitous consumerism is arguably *the* religion of the late twentieth century[25] for it has reached far beyond the mere provision of material goods to the fulfillment of a pseudo-spiritual life; we look to the marketplace to provide answers to our problems and a sense of fulfillment. More and more, the primary way we construct our life experiences is through consumption, not the everyday experiences of work and social relationships.

Consumer culture governs many of the relations we have—personal, professional, social, and even political—and affects our words and practices in these realms. Some call modern-day consumerism not just a way of life, but the "master logic" of social relations:

Consumer culture is a culture of men and women integrated into society as, above all, consumers. . . . Thus every item of culture becomes a commodity and is subordinated to the logic of the market either through a direct, economic mechanism, or an indirect psychological one. All perceptions and expectations, as well as life-rhythm, qualities of memory, attention, motivational and topical relevance are molded inside the new "foundational" institution—that of the market.[26]

According to communication professor Arthur Asa Berger, "Consumer cultures are cultures in which the personal consumption of goods and services becomes an all-powerful force. This force dominates other matters, such as the need for investment in the public sector to take care of the education, housing, health, and other needs of the general public. In these cultures, advertising and marketing play all-important roles, and privatism—a focus on one's personal interest and desires, in contrast to a sense of public responsibility for others and for one's society—tends to dominate most people's thinking and behavior."[27]

But the bounty of consumer culture is not heaped equally on buyers in the marketplace. Seemingly endless consumer choice and freedom are available just to those with money, and a great many Americans (and citizens across the globe) are effectively disenfranchised from consumer culture: "The consumer culture we live in is more remarkable for the way in which it divides than for the ways in which it provides."[28] The top 1 percent of Americans own 33 percent of the nation's total wealth, and the next 9 percent own another 33 percent. That's right: the bottom *90 percent* of the population shares the remaining 33 percent. And news reports tell us that the middle class is shrinking. Some critics say our own country is becoming a "banana republic" (no, not the trendy clothing store) with a very small group of people owning almost everything and living high on hog, and a very large group owning extremely little and scraping by.[29]

Certainly we weren't always such big consumers, were we? In the 1500s, Protestant theologian John Calvin cautioned against the extremes of excess and intemperance, but also against austerity and asceticism. We should make use of God's blessings, he said, but we need to draw a line between the extremes. Both Calvin and the early

1900s German sociologist Max Weber suggested that there is an important religious or sacred dimension to our passion to consume.[30] Weber maintained that "the Protestant [work] ethic" was behind the development of capitalism: "What the Protestant ethic did, in essence, was loosen the grip on people's minds of medieval notions about the value of poverty and justify consumption as something that God wants people to do, that has a divine significance."[31] As a result, "it provided a diligent, hard-working workforce, and it explained to people that their place in the scheme of things was settled by God." At the same time, Weber lamented that our insatiable desire for material goods had become an "iron cage" with an inexorable amount of power over human lives.

About the same time as Weber's *The Protestant Ethic and the Spirit of Capitalism* appeared, a series of theorists issued rather remarkable prognostications about the development of the marketplace and its strategies for continually increasing the passion to purchase. In 1892, Simon Patten's vision of the future embraced waste and saw human gratification as the result of the continual obsolescence of products: "The standard of life is determined, not so much by what a man has to enjoy, as by the rapidity with which he tires of the pleasure. To have a high standard means to enjoy a pleasure intensely and to tire of it quickly."[32] By early 1920s, the advertising industry had publicly defined itself as both "the destroyer and creator in the process of the ever-evolving new."[33]

By this time, the marketing industry had realized that its selling strategies had to revolve around making the customer discontented with the product in hand, and to desire instead the new one in the store. Forget consumer satisfaction; dissatisfaction with "obsolete" products had to be nurtured instead: "Obsoletism . . . sought to erect a visible environment of change in which the profit margins of business would neatly mesh with a *nurtured condition of consumer dissatisfaction*, perpetual feelings of disorientation and self-doubt."[34]

After World War II, the ideal of suburban prosperity contributed nicely to built-in obsolescence. But on the heels of wartime, marketers knew they still needed to combat thrift-oriented thought. In 1947, industrial designer J. Gordon Lippincott wrote, "Our willingness to part with something before it is completely worn out is . . . truly an American habit, and it is soundly based on our economy of abundance. It must be further nurtured even though it is contrary to one of the oldest inbred laws of humanity—the law of thrift—of providing for the unknown and often-feared day of scarcity."[35]

The bigger (and more expensive) the product, the longer it is designed to last, hence the term "durable goods." So marketers sought to make durable cars and appliances "dynamic" products, with ever-changing styles, colors, and features. By the 1950s, the auto market perfected "dynamic obsolescence"[36] with a goal of shrinking the average length of car ownership from five years to one. If you remember the "hip" colors of kitchen appliances in the 1970s (avocado, burnt orange, and harvest gold) you know how color creates an "in" and then an out-dated look and stimulates the desire for new goods.

Ever-changing products add pressure to continue buying by making older versions inherently less satisfying. Think of the telephone; rotary dialing was a significant improvement over switchboards, and Touch-Tone was an even bigger improvement. Long telephone cords increased freedom, and portable phones did away with cords entirely. Now, dialing itself is passé with voice-recognition dialing features, and portability is at a new level with cell and wireless phone connections. A current craze is buying ring-tones and jingles. Each iteration becomes a powerful "need" and requires more raw resources, and creates more consumption and more waste.

The marketing strategies of built-in obsolescence and nurtured dissatisfaction contribute to the trend that one author called "premeditated waste."[37] One way to nurture dissatisfaction is to appeal to an individual's fears of being "less than" without the product: without X, Y, and Z, you'll miss out on sex and love, get passed over for promotion, and raise bad children. Ads for outdoor gear communicate fears, too—survival against the elements, discomfort, danger, and even social isolation. When qualities we value like simplicity, honesty, and compassion are associated with a product, what was once the product's simple "use value" is transformed into "exchange value."[38] If I buy this four-season tent, in the exchange I'm also buying safety, serenity, comfort, and family togetherness.

Even alternative or oppositional cultures and lifestyles are targeted by marketers. At first, counterculture youths typically catch industry by surprise, but industry eventually seeks to appropriate and commodify their idioms and ideals. When the idiom of sub-culture enters the marketplace of style, its meaning is lost and it is reduced to the status of an ordinary commodity. Even the word "environment" was so appropriated by marketers in the 1970s and its meaning turned upside down: "Ironically, a term that was gain-ing currency as part of a growing awareness of the pollution and waste intrinsic to the consumer economy was . . . seen as a 'hook' that could help to promote more and more consumption, more and more waste."[39]

### Why We Buy

Think of the language of consumption: "I'm going to get that." "Let's order that." "It was a real steal." "Look what I found." "We need to book a room."[40] Notice how there is no talk of "buying" here, which takes consumption out of the picture and perhaps assuages some guilt. I have several girlfriends who are geniuses at relieving guilt and helping justify whatever purchase I might ponder. "It's on sale." "You deserve it." "It looks great on you." "It's so you." "It's the last one."

Whatever the reason, and whether the conversation is internal or external, why we buy is essentially a dramatic narrative—it's the story we tell ourselves about ourselves. It may be one of insecurity, reward, imagination, or success. We use shopping to get noticed, to show the world the kind of creative and successful people we are. And if we're not all that successful, at least we can imitate others who are. Advertisements play upon this "mimetic desire" by show-ing people using the products who are skinny, attractive, cool, and famous. For example, take the Uggs boots fad. These boots with the furry tops had been staples of ski communities for decades, but it wasn't until Oprah and actress Gwyneth Paltrow wore them that they became urban-chic and a must-have.[41]

Regardless of the stories we tell ourselves, they're just stories and they live in our heads. To understand it in terms of Sigmund Freud's structural model of the psyche,[42] shopping expresses the conflict between your emotional sphere which says, "I want it now" (the id) and your conscience which evaluates the need and responds, "I can't afford it." Holding the middle ground is your seat of rationality, which says "I should think about it some more." Marketing messages, as you might guess, appeal entirely to the emotionally driven id (which also houses your base fears of inadequacy), and try to overcome the strictures of conscience and rationality. The goal of the message is to create discontent, dissatisfaction, and a powerful emotion-based desire to buy.

When human *needs* are translated into *wants*, the wants become infinitely insatiable. So the language of marketers must persuade consumers to buy things they most certainly do not need, yet portray the product as an absolute *necessity*. In the view of one scholar, they have succeeded: "The modern world is now one where free-enterprise market capitalism has triumphed, where the passion to consume things now dominates most people. Desire is infinite; there is not a point, is seems, at which people say 'enough' and lose their desire to make more money and buy more things."[43]

The entire "logic of desire"[44] operating in the marketplace speaks not just to individual desires, but also to the product's value in the social realm: "The consumption of goods and services is therefore important not so much for the intrinsic satisfaction it might generate but for the way in which it functions to mark social differences and act as a communicator."[45] In this way, our "needs" are not so much needs for objects as they are needs for social meaning and differentiation.[46]

Fifty years ago, Thorstein Veblen discussed the identity-value of goods in his classic *The Theory of the Leisure Class*.[47] Veblen wrote that the "conspicuous consumption" of the leisure class functioned as a primary index of its social status and prestige. Although Veblen focused on how the leisure class distanced themselves from the world of necessity and paid employment with their consumption, Veblen suggested that no social group was entirely exempt from the practice: "No class of society, not even the most abjectly poor, forgoes all customary conspicuous consumption. The last items of this category of consumption are not given up except under the stress of direct necessity."[48] So, no matter how poor, consumption by the poorest individuals has identity-value, not just use-value.

In this light, consumption is primarily based on cultural alignments and the social groups to which a person belongs, rather than on individual wants or desires. The British social anthropologist Mary

Douglas argued that shopping is the struggle to define not what one is, but what one is not. Douglas said that to differing degrees, a person's life is shaped and sustained by membership in a group, groups that have either few or many rules and prescriptions for their members to obey. If you identify strongly with the social group of wilderness advocates, the unstated "rules" of that group hold that you will own backpacks but not dirt bikes. Perhaps the widespread ownership of SUVs (as much in urban as in rural settings) indicates that many people feel "membership" with the lifestyle of rugged, outdoorsy individualists, whether or not the vehicle ever leaves the pavement.

Every social class has different "habitus" or differences in taste.[49] A French scholar defined this as the unconscious tendencies and taken-for-granted preferences that are evident in a person's sense of the appropriateness and validity of cultural goods and practices. For instance, imagine the "members" in two social groups of recreationists: hunters and bird-watchers. Each group has preferences and tastes (unspoken and at the level of everyday knowledge) that are readily apparent in what its members consider appropriate material goods and practices. In this case, is it possible to separate all of the goods purchased as the result of individual desires from those resulting from group preferences?

### Consumption as Process, Not Purchase

The purchase and initial use of a product is the fun part and generally the only one we think about. But consumerism is more accurately a process, not a single product, and needs to be considered "cradle to grave." At the cradle end, "where things come from" is abstract and insignificant to most consumers. We see "Made in China" on a tennis shoe or a shirt and don't think twice about the meaning of this message, that is unless we've recently heard of yet another sweatshop and the lives of the people who make tennis shoes and shirts. We don't ponder while lacing up that shoe where the raw materials came from or how its production contributed to air pollution. The most meaningful translation of "Made in China" is that the shoe is inexpensive.

The "where things go" point in the process has been normalized to such an extent that we consider it of little consequence. Lacking knowledge and understanding of these basic processes of consumer product life cycles has contributed greatly to our ecological illiteracy.[50] Other than the occasional news story revealing industrial practices in a distant country or a leaking landfill, the cradle and grave portions of the consumer cycle are not really communicated at all—especially when compared with the excess of communication surrounding purchasing.

As an entire process, consumerism obviously has a profound effect on our local environment and landscapes (not to mention distant ones). We have all witnessed these effects when retail centers move from city to suburbs or edge-of-town strip malls. Urban diversity is displaced by retail mono-economies resulting in the exact same stores in every city and that are accessible primarily by private automobile.

If you want to get an idea of your personal contribution to the "grave" portion of the formula, carry a five-pound sack of potatoes each day for a week. That's roughly the pounds of municipal solid waste (4.6 lbs) that the EPA says each person generated per day in the United States in 2005, which is almost 25 percent more pounds than was generated in 1970. When we "take out the garbage," we're not thinking about the space required for the 1,600-plus pounds that each one of us generates each year. It may not be just a garbage truck that handles your waste; your city may be forced to ship its waste via rail or ship. Remember the garbage scow *Mobro* that in 1987 ferried 6.2 million tons of garbage from Long Island up and down the East Coast (all way to Mexico) in search of someone to let it dump its load at sea.

Imagine how much of your yearly waste poundage is composed of "needs" and how much is "wants." How much was designed to be short-term and "disposable"? From a marketer's point of view, "disposability is the golden goose."[51] Even goods that were once considered fairly durable are now designed not to be—razors, mops, kitchen containers, cameras, wash-cloths, toilet brushes . . .

How much of your waste is packaging? Product packaging is all about design, style, and persuasiveness: "The most visible and unremitting aestheticization of waste . . . is seen in the continually changing styles and packing that, in order to stimulate sales, affects nearly every commodity. Here the principle of waste is not embedded in any particular image, but rather in the incessant spectacle that envelops the marketing of merchandise."[52]

The effect of our country's consumer culture has enormous effects beyond our borders: "Third World countries find themselves in situations where they are forced to develop markets that will do little to help their long-term economic cause but, rather, merely serve to prop up the major economies of the world while increasing dependence upon them."[53] Environmental degradation and human rights violations in the production of consumer goods are frequently reported, but the production is distant and divorced from the products.

Other countries are far outpacing the United States when it comes to viewing consumption as a cradle-to-grave process, even making manufacturers bear responsibility for the safe and environmentally friendly disposal or part-by-part recycling of its components. Our country's attachment to recycling is only one piece of the consumption process, not a panacea for it (see Box 4.1).

## Working or Playing in Nature

The modern workplace tends to divorce us from the natural world—perhaps most of all through indoor jobs. Yet, a good many environmentalists and others look down their noses at "work in nature." Logging, mining, fishing, farming, herding—all of these kinds of resource-dependent or -extractive labor are routinely labeled as destructive and bad for the environment. But the stereotype speaks to the estrangement from nature of so-called white-collar work and an ignorance of the environmental impacts of all work. In a provocative essay, historian Richard White urges us to examine how all work intersects with nature, and he suggests that environmentalists focus on work as well as leisure.[54]

The title of White's essay comes from a bumper sticker he saw in Forks, Washington, a small town on the west side of the Olympic Peninsula that relies heavily on logging: "Are You an Environmentalist or Do You Work for a Living?" From the standpoint of Forks residents, environmentalism appears very much opposed to work and readily condemns work in nature as destructive.

The dualism that some environmentalists seem to be promoting is that "productive work in nature" is *destructive* while all other

## Box 4.1
### That '70s Triangle Revisited

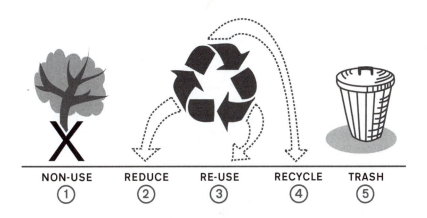

| NON-USE | REDUCE | RE-USE | RECYCLE | TRASH |
|:---:|:---:|:---:|:---:|:---:|
| ① | ② | ③ | ④ | ⑤ |

The "reduce, reuse, recycle" triangle appeared decades ago as the symbol of an environmental approach to waste reduction. It was a good idea, but it needs some revision. First, it implies that when executed, consumption is a closed loop. It ignores the fact that raw materials enter the loop and trash exits it. Even a product that's recycled once or reused numerous times eventually must be tossed. And just because the "recycle this" triangle appears on the bottom of a container doesn't mean it will be or can be recycled. Some communities lack any recycling, some types of plastics can never be effectively recycled, and there are limits to recycling some kinds of paper. Here, the triangle is flattened and endpoints are added, which communicates something quite different.

1. ***Non**-use*—With the ever-increasing array of products designed for one-time use and the proliferation of to-go food and drink containers, we should think about *non*-use as the beginning of the process. Non-use is often a far superior choice to reduce or reuse, especially when it comes to the popular "use-and-toss" products. In the name of convenience and a market-bred fear of germs, North Americans consumed eighty-three thousand tons of "disposable wipes" in 2005.[1] Other good targets for non-use are food and drinks in nonrecyclable containers, paper *or* plastic shopping bags, paper towels, and paper napkins.

2. *Reduce*: An obvious place to start reducing is your consumption of energy, water, and waste. Buying in your "village" helps to reduce packaging and resources used in transportation. Reduce purchases like clothing and home furnishings, and perhaps even gifts. Purchase goods in bulk or with minimal packaging. Swear off buying bottled water and buy a sturdy, refillable water bottle.

**Box 4.1 continued**

3. **RE**-*use:* Many people can claim a grandparent or great-grandparent who practiced the fine art of reuse, perhaps out of necessity during the Depression or a sense of thrift. Keep a supply of cloth shopping bags handy. Use dishes and glasses for food and drink. Turn old T-shirts and pajamas into rags and dustcloths. Use every piece of paper on both sides, if not for printing, as note paper. Consider using "gray water" from your home on plants and lawn. Send your kitchen scraps to the compost pile, not the disposal or garbage. Buy *durable* furniture, appliances, and kitchenware, and repair them.

4. *Recycle*: Although recycling has greatly freed up landfill space, any recycled product still represents a commitment of resources, such as the transportation, energy, and water used in its remanufacture. A large percentage of goods either escape recycling or cannot be recycled efficiently.

5. *Trash*: See how close "recycle" lies in proximity to trash? Only by seriously practicing non-use, re-use, and recycling can we achieve a significant reduction in consumption and its attendant trash.

1. Karen Klages, "Wipe Out: Helpers Can Clean, But Aren't So Green," *Chicago Tribune* (appeared in *Salt Lake Tribune* May 9, 2005, D1).

---

work is *constructive*. White says that this frames the choice as between humans and nature (as if humans are somehow outside of nature), which means that nature seems safest when shielded from human labor. But does "pure nature," separate from our work, exist? White argues that all labor embeds us in nature, but the environmental consequences of white-collar labor are far less obvious. As White types at his computer, he observes that "Nature, altered and changed, is in this room. But this is masked. . . . My separation is an illusion. What is disguised is that I—unlike loggers, farmers, fishers, or herders—do not have to face what I alter, and so I learn nothing from it."[55]

My workplace, a college campus, is a good place to examine the environmental consequences of white-collar work. Paper is used copiously—for tests and assignments, research, readings, and administration—yet professors don't fell or mill the logs themselves. According to the EPA, paper products account for a whopping 40 percent of our municipal solid waste. Many campuses have the ability to recycle office paper and cardboard, though on my campus, it's hardly an institutional ethic. Far more sheets land in the wastebasket than the recycling bin. Like many campuses, mine uses great amounts of energy. Individuals prop open doors and windows while heat or air conditioning is on. In the 1990s-vintage building where I work, it's literally impossible to turn the hallway lights off; when you flip the switch, only half the lights go dark, ostensibly for safety. Yet students and staff don't mine the coal and see the effects of that work-in-nature. The lawns of my campus are lush and rolling, but in this semi-desert clime they require thousands of gallons of water each day during summer. The faucets in older buildings invariably drip and leak, and the older toilets are gallons away from low-flow. Yet when walking across the luxurious lawns, you don't see the dams and diversions that took the water away from streams and fish, and you don't see the results of chemical manufacturing for herbicides and fertilizers that keep those lawns lovely and green. Food in the cafeteria is, well, cafeteria food and therefore gets wasted, and it is served entirely on disposable plates, utensils, and cups. Yet, most folks are relatively immune from the operation of the county landfill and what happens after they "take out the garbage."

Then there are the computers, thousands on my campus alone. But most of us are entirely ignorant about the resources used to make one, particularly the metals. The basic desktop computer is 25 percent silica (by weight), 23 percent plastics, 20 percent iron, and 14 percent aluminum.[56] Lead and copper each contribute about 6 percent of its weight. After that are literally dozens of metals, some with high "recycling efficiency," many with virtually no ability to recycle. There's silver and gold, nickel, tin, and zinc, but also beryllium, titanium, cobalt, manganese, tantalum, mercury, and arsenic. Yet for all the messages about consuming computers and other electronics, next to nothing is communicated about the end-of-life of electronics. Only recently have a few states begun to institute computer drop-off and recycling.

No job, no matter the color of its collar, escapes the environmental consequences of its labor. But distance allows the white-collar worker to think that others bear the burden of environmental harm.

Work once bore the burden of connecting us with nature, providing knowledge both of nature and of the body. Digging in soil, working with wood, catching fish—all gave humans a chance to know something intimately through their labor. But of course labor, either archaic or modern, is not necessarily kind to the land. As White acknowledges, "A connection with the land through work creates knowledge, but it does not necessarily grant protection to the land itself. There is a modern romanticism of place that says that those who live and depend on a place will not harm it."[57]

If environmentalists do not view nature as a place for work, how do they view it? As a place for human play! Just as work once connected us to nature, for many this burden has now shifted to leisure. It's curious that the most intense moments of play in nature—such as "extreme" outdoor sports—are when it seems to matter as much as work! You take risks and make decisions as if your life (or livelihood) depended on it. There's a certain irony to the fact that "the play we feel brings us closest to nature is play that mimics work."[58]

From this perspective, the sentiment in the Forks bumper sticker is less surprising and makes nature-players seem like a privileged, sanctimonious leisure class: "Environmentalists so often seem self-righteous, privileged, and arrogant because they so readily consent to identifying nature with play and making it by definition a place where leisured humans come only to visit and not to work, stay, or live."[59] Intense, physical play in nature may also provide bodily knowledge, and "It is admirable; it yields lessons and insights, but it does not yield a living."[60]

White argues that a powerful, long-standing myth in this country is that the original human relation with nature was really one of leisure. Both in the Garden of Eden and for this country's first white colonizers, it seemed as though there was no human mark on the landscape; nature was an untouched paradise full of harmony. The most popular first white men—Lewis and Clark and Daniel Boone—got to go places that were supposedly unchanged by humans (though Native Americans had long occupied and changed the land). Although modern accounts of the Lewis and Clark expedition have treated their exploration as one long backpack across the West, "What most deeply engaged these first white men with nature, what they wrote about most vividly, was work. . . . Environmental writers have edited this out; they have replaced it with a story of first white men at strenuous play or in respectful observation. We have equated their work with our play."[61]

The focus of environmentalists on pristine nature as a place for play is troubling to White, who believes it will only widen the gap between environmentalists and others: "If environmentalists segregate work from nature, if they create a set of dualisms where work can only mean the absence of nature and nature can only mean human leisure, then both humans and non-humans will ultimately be the poorer. For without an ability to recognize the connections between work and nature, environmentalists will eventually reach a point where they seem trivial and extraneous and their issues politically expendable."[62] He argues that environmentalism should focus on our *work*, not just our leisure.

## Conclusion

Bill is a professor in another department on my campus, an avid hiker, mountain climber, and wilderness advocate. He chides me to get involved in his wilderness group, as though it is the litmus test for my environmental stripes. Bill, a bachelor, lives in a gigantic house with multiple bathrooms and even more bedrooms. He lives a mile or two from his office (and near a bus-line), and drives there every day in his SUV.

The disconnects we make between work, lifestyle, consumption, and environment are some of the more pernicious ones we make. It's impossible to compartmentalize nature or environment in a separate box from other pieces of your life, including your white-collar job. White-collar, blue-collar, and work-in-nature jobs all create significant environmental impacts, though in many types of work we do not face what we alter. Virtually all jobs use paper, electricity, water, and other resources, and in far greater amounts than individuals. All of us—including environmentalists—need to recognize that nature is not just a place for play, but is a place for work that provides us the resources of daily life.

Therefore work, both in substance and of necessity, is linked to our play and our consumption. At the workplace, we strive to earn more ostensibly to be "more comfortable," to get what we want, to buy more. Yet we often remain unconscious of the work-and-spend cycle and how our consumption expands to fit the size of the paycheck.

"But I recycle," someone tells me. Well, that's wonderful, but recycling says very little, actually, about your overall environmental impacts or even your ideology. And recycling doesn't change the fact that it's your consumption that communicates the most about your relationship with the environment. The domination of the marketplace promotes a preoccupation with private, personal concerns. Desires for material goods threaten us with an iron cage of consumption than can seem impossible, even in the middle of nature, to escape.

Recently I saw a young woman with a T-shirt that declared "Born to Shop!" It was interesting (and frankly discouraging) that the identity that she had chosen above all others to proclaim publicly was that of a consumer. The buyosphere she so enjoys is not a civic space of and for citizens, but an all-powerful marketplace full of consumers. Thinking that we can find solutions to our individual problems by buying products can only serve to detract from community life and broader public concerns, not the least of which is the environment.

# 5

## Leisure in Nature as Commodity and Entertainment

As discussed in the last chapter, we tend to think of work as what we must do, and leisure as the time that remains after the practical necessities of life are taken care of. However, that doesn't mean that leisure takes place far from the economic realm. Far from it, modern-day leisure has been swallowed, in many respects, by the marketplace. Leisure and entertainment in nature (or related to it) are increasingly promoted as a consumption opportunity. When leisure in the natural world is packaged and promoted, it mitigates and clouds our experience with it.

This chapter delves into the communication of leisure and how our consumer orientation has changed the way we view leisure time and the way we understand the environment. Outdoor recreation is a multi-billion-dollar industry that sells lifestyle as much as it sells goods. Simple leisure pastimes like visiting city parks and spending time in backyards are often linked to the products that culture (in particular, consumer culture) communicates are necessary to enjoyment. In addition, the landscapes of parks and yards communicate much about ideal nature and its function. The chapter also looks at nature-related entertainment and movies and their depiction of human-environment relationships. Finally, when leisure leaves home we call it tourism. The development and current practice of tourism tends to manage and direct our experiences with the natural world.

## Leisure: Busy and Commodified

If you spend much time outdoors, you have undoubtedly noticed that many outdoor enthusiasts seem to work pretty hard on their leisure. Joggers and trail runners speed by, hikers set their stopwatches at the trailhead, mountain bikers and skiers fly down hillsides. Advertisements for outdoor gear and autos reinforce this hard-driving outdoor athleticism. Such recreationists are what researchers describe as "more-more" types—those who work longer hours who also tend to be more active in their leisure lives.[1] They might find their work boring and dull, and long to escape that everyday pattern, believing they can find excitement in their outdoor leisure.

But leisure is more than simply time away from work; it is a condition of being or state of mind. According to one scholar, "True leisure, for Aristotle, is the self-sufficient activity of the mind, a mind which is its own best company, one which is not dependent on external stimuli for its action."[2] That is, leisure does not depend on consumption and external goods. "Leisure, for Aristotle, is the love and contemplation of what is; it is a thanking and a thinking. It is an affirmation of the world and an attempt to comprehend, not to change it. . . . Leisure is the end of existence, the cessation of striving."[3]

In this Aristotelian view, leisure is expansive and gives the individual time for growing and true restoration. Leisure implies a bit of distance—no matter the activity—from the realm of necessity. It is not just time from, it is time for. "Leisure activities are those which are intrinsically choice-worthy rather than instrumental; they are the activities of freedom rather than of necessity."[4] Leisure has a mental attitude of nonactivity and inner calm, of silence. It's not being busy, but letting things happen.

In this framework, leisure is not merely idleness or spare time but the true basis of culture: ". . . . the use of leisure exhibits the essence of a particular society's relationship to the universe. The greatest contributions to civilization are made principally in leisure, not by intellectual work; but by contemplative, intuitive, religious, or romantic orientation stemming from a release from travail."[5]

In his 1862 essay "Walking," Henry David Thoreau described a manner of walking he called "sauntering." The original definition of a "saunterer" was someone on a crusade to the Holy Land, but in Thoreau's case, the goal was to reach "a holy or sacred space in mind or spirit through walking."[6] One needed to remove oneself from civilized society and become immersed in and sensitized to nature, walking at a slow, methodical pace and without a prescribed timeframe or destination. One should not be sauntering for fitness purposes in order to truly connect, "part and parcel," to the natural world.[7] Thoreau explained that sauntering can help preserve and feed health and spirit, inspire intellect through this daily connection, and bring us back into what we naturally are: wild, free, and independent.[8]

Though Thoreau was satisfied to go sauntering with little more than a walking stick, today's marketplace encourages us to think of free time as yet another consumption opportunity and recreation as just another market. Commodifying leisure means convincing you that successful, enjoyable leisure requires a lot of material goods, and that you can purchase things which are ultimately incapable of being bought or sold. Outdoor-related leisure has become highly commodity intensive; the outdoor recreation equipment industry rakes in close to $5 billion annually and is growing at about 7 percent a year.[9] Obviously, we spend a great deal of discretionary income on leisure-time toys.

Thumb through any outdoor equipment or clothing catalog and you can see the line walked between "green" and "goods." The models are thin, handsome, and happy; the nature backdrops are sublime. REI donates to environmental causes, and Patagonia touts its fair and equitable working conditions. In their communication, such businesses try to address ecological issues but without challenging capitalism (or alienating customers); this position doesn't pose any uncomfortable questions about the accumulation of capital[10]—that is, the latest and greatest outdoor stuff.

Patagonia uses short narratives and stories interspersed through the catalog to work around any guilt related to consumerism. A message in many of the catalog essays is that you must leave the domestic life behind before you can personally transcend and receive all that wilderness has to offer (with the right gear, of course). Although the company grossed over $220 million in 2001, one catalog essay advocated rediscovering "the dirtbag within." The author talked about his early climbing days when he lived on ramen noodles and sold aluminum cans collected from dumpsters. Yet the catalog sells a "Patagucci" lifestyle of economic privilege "in which SUVs and conspicuous consumption are par for the course, even if the backcountry is never reached."[11] Patagonia's focus on wilderness preservation fits its customer demographic of young, fit, white men.

Fly-fishing is a highly commodified and popular outdoor pastime. Its boom in the western United States in the 1970s is attributed to increasing leisure time and disposable income, more interest in outdoor recreation, and technological innovations (such as monofilament line) that made the sport more accessible for beginners.[12] Of course, the novel and movie *A River Runs Through It* interpreted fly-fishing as an historically authentic Western experience.[13]

The Sundance Catalog is another example of the commodification of leisure pursuits, this time tied to a rustic yet elegant home base. By purchasing an Appalachian twig table or Indian rug, you can reconnect to an earlier and less corrupted version of society. Sundance clothing features leather and fringe, but also fleece and cotton. Products fetishize what is "western" and "rather ingeniously harmonizes the conflicting meanings given the West by cowboys and environmental recreationists, Sioux Indians, and wealthy second home owners."[14]

The Sundance Catalog, the brainchild of actor and director Robert Redford, emulates the philosophy of the arts and crafts movement, stressing simplicity, utility, and the democratization of art, and serving as a reaction to urbanization and the growth of corporate structures. To the arts and crafts movement and to Redford, rural life represents the path to moral regeneration and a rejuvenating work ethic.[15] Nature has great moral value, and Indians become alternatives to modern industrial life. Whereas the arts and crafts movement stood as a *critic* of consumer culture and capitalist society, "Sundance Catalog accomplishes just the opposite: it commodifies artisans' wares for a global urban consumer and turns its featured artisans into a sort of endangered species, remnants of a lost world. . . . And unlike the Craft reformers' solution, regeneration in Redford's West is accomplished not through work but through leisure, recreation, and consumption. . . . Redford reconciles western symbols but not the relationships implicit in them: work and play, the natural and the artificial."[16] Through catalog products—such as a $119 old-time hayfork to hang on your wall—rural life operates mainly as scenery, ignoring the reality of rural work and its relationship to nature.[17] The West of Sundance is ultimately a place of play, escape, and relaxation, not a place of work.

The Nature Company cashes in on the *idea* of nature sold as a consumable experience. While one might like to believe that nature somehow counters consumption and materialism, nature stores like these recognize that even nature lovers buy things to define themselves. The Nature Company allows you to donate to good causes— put a quarter in the Rainforest Meter—and to "reiterate, enjoy, and share one's commitments to nature"[18] as a consumer. As a successful and expanding business found in the most up-scale malls, it has been able to capitalize on the seeming contradiction of nature as commodity: "The Nature Company markets twelve thousand products that, on the one hand, sustain American middle-class ideas of nature that mitigate the materialism and artifice of modern capitalist society and, on the other hand, sustain, through the creation of artifice the capitalist overconsumption of resources that underpins American middle-class life."[19]

## Local Landscapes

Although we associate much outdoor recreation with places beyond the city, we also spend our leisure time in places close to home. The city streets, neighborhood park, and backyard may not feel like "escape" or "nature" in any sense of the imagination; nevertheless, local landscapes are where you communicate in word and practice your "ordinary" relationship with the natural world. (Undoubtedly, the most ordinary encounter with the natural world is the continuous encounter with the weather; see Box 5.1.) These everyday, lived-in landscapes are very much the stuff of environmental communication, for it is here that "The confrontation with the nonhuman occurs every second. Every breath is an encounter with nature. . . . We have been conditioned to reserve feeling and thoughtfulness and attention to the nonhuman for our visits to [more] scenic enclaves . . . "[20]

When you fly or drive into many cities, you may notice that the city landscape varies greatly from the undeveloped portion beyond

## Box 5.1
### The Weather Doesn't Give a Damn!

Ever find yourself conversing with strangers about the weather? No surprise: the weather is the universal environmental connection we share. But weather forecasts don't emphasize the scientific and ecological conditions of weather; forecasts present weather as a phenomenon that's anthropocentric, to be controlled, and with which we connect most strongly though consumption and leisure.

When they "put the weather maps into motion," nature's clouds, jet stream, and atmospheric stability become dramatic "weathertainment."[1] Weather reporters are both "priests" and "bards."[2] Weather priests are elite authority figures who translate scientific discourse to a lay public. They are heroes who sacrifice their comfort in "live weather updates" in the eyes of storms that remind us of nature's moodiness.[3] TV anchors grant the weather priests special power over the weather, cajoling, "see what you can do" about that gloomy forecast, or "we want more of the same." As bards, weather reporters are tribal storytellers, passing on salient messages of our cultural identity[4] and using symbols with broad legitimacy (sunshine is good, rain is bad).

Weather forecasts help us feel prepared and in control, even though they are based on rough probabilities. Much attention is paid to how the weather is "supposed" to be—"normal" high and low temperatures and precipitation. Yet a key characteristic of weather is its variability, its mercurial progression. A focus on "normal" interprets the weather as knowable and controllable.

To appeal to audience self-interest, weather reports connect weather to our social and economic lives. The weather person says stay tuned to learn whether weather will "ruin your weekend" or "wreak havoc" with your morning commute.

---

its border. City roads bisect and define land and its value. There often is a dramatic difference in vegetation from city to country. This is especially striking in much of the West where cities are green, tree-filled oases surrounded by dry scrub. Common features in suburbs are the domination of the private auto and the strip-malls that such development spawns. You have no doubt noticed that much of suburbia is not pedestrian-friendly.

What you're witnessing is the effect of what we call landscaping, or the planned manipulation of natural systems. The profession of landscape architecture developed as a response to people's desires to remake outdoor landscapes according to their own ideals and moral and creative imperatives. Landscaping can transform a piece of ground into something completely different and in complete indifference to what grew there "naturally." A typical practice in a new

**Box 5.1 continued**

The weather map orients you with an overlay of the freeway system or human-constructed boundaries of city and state. On the Weather Channel, a cold snap is brought to you by Wigwam socks; Afrin Nasal Spray sponsors the allergy report. "Consequently, the earth's atmosphere becomes a commodity, effective for the way it provides an effective background for sponsorship."[5] Weather becomes a reflective billboard: "What is reflected back to weather watchers is a constant reminder of the economic and social realities that dictate consumer life. Thus, visual representations of the earth's atmosphere . . . are aimed at consumers who use meteorological information for health, safety, and . . . leisure activities, while companies use the weather for short-term profits."[6]

The fact remains that . . . the weather doesn't give a damn! "Mother" nature doesn't care whether you want warm sunshine on Saturday, or snow at Christmas. What the weather "is" has absolutely nothing to do with you (global climate change notwithstanding). The weather simply has no ability to discern human desires or to deliver them. In today's vernacular, "it's not about you!"

1. Mark Meister, "Meteorology and the Rhetoric of Nature's Cultural Display," *Quarterly Journal of Speech* 87(4) (2001):415–428.

2. Ibid.

3. Ibid., 423.

4. Ibid.

5. Ibid., 424.

6. Ibid., 424.

housing development is to bulldoze the area down to the soil and start over with a clean slate.

## A Long Affair with Lawns and Landscapes

Walk into any art museum and look at the paintings. In them, the natural world is distorted, exaggerated, and made sublime to communicate a feeling and a sentiment toward nature. The term "landscape" came into being in the sixteenth century to represent these pictorial abstractions of ecosystems. "Such pictures were at first imaginary scenes composed from literary images and were soon formulated by aesthetic theory."[21]

"Landscape" then is the pivotal word: "It is not a synonym for habitat or place, certainly not for a natural community or ecosystem. A landscape is a representation of a certain kind of visual experience.

... The earliest ... 'landskip' paintings (in the West) were imaginary scenes inspired by biblical and classical themes—that is, literary images. 'Scenery' ... was originally a Greek term for stage props. Thus landscape is a way of tangibly representing a dramatic moment by using terrain and sky and plants as stage props, eventually as actors. Gardens made to be seen, or which are designed around viewpoints, are another tangible expression of the idea. . . . A place that looked good as a picture was regarded as 'picturesque.'"[22]

Influenced by imagination and aesthetic, landscapes are therefore symbols—not just of what we value, but of who we are and the social roles we play in that landscape. "'Landscapes' are the symbolic environments created by human acts of conferring meaning to nature and the environment, of giving the environment definition and form from a particular angle of vision and through a special filter of values and beliefs. Every landscape is a symbolic environment."[23]

If humans attach symbolic meanings to landscapes that are not inherent in the nature of a place, does that imply a person has to continually say, "hmmm, what meaning will I construct today?" Obviously not. How we view (and treat) landscapes reflects not just individual sentiment, but values of the entire social and cultural system in which the sentiment lies. Think of how these values are communicated. Many cities and towns have legal ordinances as to how local landscapes (private and public) "should" look. Regulations may require green grass, define some native plants as weeds, and dictate how tall plants should be allowed to grow. Some cities have special rules for what may be planted in the parking strip, that piece of ground between the sidewalk and street that is often owned by the city. Consider how lawn care and lawn products are communicated. In ads for lawn products, common themes are the battle or war waged, that love of family dictates an impeccable green lawn, or that peer pressure from neighbors is a legitimate motive for your actions and purchases. The message in any garden store is that a lush Garden of Eden is desirable and attainable with the right purchases. (See Box 5.2 for more discussion of lawns.)

The living landscape that dominates any area—whether green grass or woods or weeds—is the one preferred by those with the greatest degree of power (political or social) to define and impose a certain landscape reality onto the physical environment. If we think

## Box 5.2
## A Long Lawn Love Affair

Nothing says "summer" more than the smell of freshly cut grass. But Americans' love affair with lawns requires great commitments of time, resources, and equipment. According to a grounds-keeping magazine, sales of lawn and garden "consumables" (fertilizers, pesticides, mulch, seeds, and growing mediums) approach $7 billion annually.[1] Lawns increasingly get pegged for environmental pollutants, noise, and water use.

Gas-powered equipment—mowers, blowers, wackers, trimmers, and so on—releases noise and pollutants. Lawnmowers and leaf blowers emit almost one hundred decibels, the amount of noise that risks permanent hearing loss with regular exposure of more than a minute. Mowing with a typical gasoline-powered lawnmower for one hour produces as much air pollution as driving about two hundred miles in a typical car.[2] The two-stroke engine of a leaf blower is even worse, causing as much smog as seventeen cars. In response, numerous cities across North America have banned or restricted some yard equipment.

Concern has been mounting about the effect of lawn chemicals on humans, pets, wildlife, and the environment. Far heavier amounts of chemicals are applied per acre to lawns and gardens (about 67 million pounds) than on agricultural lands.[3] In 2004, an analysis of 250 epidemiological studies concluded that there were consistent, positive relationships between lawn chemicals and cancer, birth defects, reproductive disease, neuro-toxic effects, and other serious illnesses.[4]

Predictably, the lawn industry has fought back. The industry, which now dubs itself "the green industry" (a rhetorically interesting use of the word "green"), created a lobbying organization called Project Evergreen.[5] Members include Dow AgroSciences, the Scotts Company, Perma-Green Supreme, TruGreen ChemLawn, John Deere, Lawn Doctor, and a variety of landscaping, irrigation, nursery, and golf course companies. Project Evergreen's goal is to support traditional grass lawns and the ways we care for them, and communicate awareness of lawns' "lifestyle benefits." Their Web site says your lawn is "more than a landscape—it's a lifescape." In an ad titled "The Gloves Are Off," Project Evergreen announced it was going to fight back against "activists, extremists, and misinformed politicians" for leading consumers to question the health and safety of lawn products and practices.

In a countering ad campaign, the activist nonprofit group Beyond Pesticides printed an ad titled, "Get a Grip," which cited the dangers of lawn pesticides and urged the use of nontoxic lawn care. Activists predict that pesticides will become the next tobacco because pesticides are a bit like secondhand smoke; that is, you don't have to use them to be exposed to them.[6]

1. Grounds Magazine Web site: http://grounds-mag.com/news/lawns-garden-sales.

2. Louisville, KY, Metro Air Pollution Web site: www.apcd.org.

3. Beyond Pesticides Web site: www.beyondpesticides.org/lawn (National Coalition Against the Misuse of Pesticides).

**Box 5.2 continued**

4. Joan Lowry, "U.S. Lawn-care Industry Fighting Back against Pesticide Bans," Scripps Howard News Service (Jan. 17, 2005).

5. Project Evergreen Web site: www.projectevergreen.com.

6. Lowry, "U.S. Lawn-care Industry Fighting Back."

of power as the ability to construct and control knowledge, what entities most shape our visions of local landscapes? Perhaps it's real estate developers, government planners, the construction industry, city councils, or even the lawn-care industry.

A decade or two ago, the term used to describe the rapid, unchecked expansion of developed landscapes was "urban sprawl." Such development was entirely dependent on—if not driven by—private vehicle use. The concept has been supplanted by the current moniker "smart growth." The shift is not entirely rhetorical. There is a now a greater recognition that some types of development are more congruent with quality of life—both for humans and nonhumans. If private lots are smaller and clustered, neighborhoods are more walkable and lawns smaller. With higher density housing, travel and commute times are more reasonable. And in such neighborhoods, small businesses can be interspersed with housing in a walkable, friendly, and safe manner.

But smart growth has not necessarily altered our attitude that growth is good and inevitable. In addition, city planners advocating smart growth inevitably find that such social change is fought by many who are vested in the current system and patterns of development. So even a seemingly positive term like smart growth represents a conservative ideology—not a strong challenge to the basic growth and consumption paradigm.

Another term now in vogue in local landscapes is "open space," meaning the undeveloped pieces of land, often adjacent to or interspersed with developed lands. Open space can be used as greenbelts along waterways, traditional parks, or even mixed habitat supporting wildlife and low-impact human use. "Islands" of natural habitat can be a welcome and peaceful oasis for humans and can help ensure that development doesn't eat up all remaining undeveloped lands.

Across the nation, citizen ballot initiatives, government actions, and private conservation groups are trying to protect the best remaining open spaces. However, isolated parcels may have questionable value as nonhuman habitat and even if "saved," important ecosystems may still be fragmented and incapable of sustaining populations, a principle biologists call "island biogeography."

The local landscapes in which we spend so much time fit handily within the dominant social paradigm. They are designed and operated almost entirely for human use and enjoyment. They often represent a total reconstruction of the environment, transforming what biology and ecology put there naturally into landscapes that reflect exclusively human meaning and desires. Despite the occasional push to attract "backyard birds," landscaping remains the manipulation of natural systems into "monocultures," habitats that best support humans and only a narrow range of other plant and animal species. But as an institution more widespread than apple pie and more enduring than baseball, traditional landscapes and American's love affair with lawns are bound to survive.

## Local Parks

In the introduction to this book you read about City Creek Park. Its landscaping is entirely different from the brushy, wild habitat surrounding the creek farther upstream and is a good example of how people remake natural landscapes according to their own ideals. City Creek Park conforms to a long tradition of valuing manicured, tamed nature that serves humans.

The majority of city parks are landscaped in the same manner as private yards, with grass and plantings and manipulated natural systems. Like national and state parks, local parks are public spaces. But how local parks developed as part of the local landscape and how they communicate the manner in which humans should come together and experience the outdoors is quite distinct. Designers of urban parks have manipulated the same elements (water, trees, flowers, paths, architecture) across the country, but over time have emphasized different elements in order to advance social goals.

One of the first types of parks was the *pleasure garden*.[24] In the last half of the 1800s, the spread of cities meant it was increasingly hard to travel to the countryside. Urban reformers agitated for large, open, green places to offer relief from the rigors of work and pace of factory production. Following the cholera epidemic in New York City in 1852, officials noticed that epidemics were worse in congested areas and suggested that parks might be an antidote. The pleasure garden was an idealized agrarian scene. Woods opened and closed around grass-defined meadows, and large sheets of water suggested the placidness of a pastoral setting. Buildings were kept to a minimum and paths were curved to contrast city streets and separate pedestrians from vehicles. These parks were justified as a "wedge for introducing culture" and as a reinforcement of the family. As one scholar said, "Ultimately parks are mechanisms of social control. Park promoters hoped to create a shared civic culture by getting users to internalize and carry Anglo-Saxon rules and behavior back to the streets."[25] Some pleasure gardens had museums, exhibit halls, and concerts and were a place where all social classes could interact, at least visually.

In the first thirty years of the 1900s came the *reform park*, essentially an inner-city, multi-purpose park and playground. Elites thought that these parks should be oriented toward the needs of the working class and would go a long way toward reform of inner cities. "Progressives interested in neighborhood reform argued that recreational needs should be met daily at nearby sites, rather than occasional outings to the city's outskirts."[26] A typical reform park occupied a square city block, sometimes separated from city traffic and noise by a berm planted with trees and flowers. A new type of building, the fieldhouse, exemplified a new focus on physical education and could be utilized in the evening. Some reform parks also had swimming pools—foremost for public health reasons and secondly for recreation.

In the middle third of the 1900s, "Parks no longer had to justify their existence as accomplishing needed social change. Recreation was established as a municipal function, an established institution, rather than a zealous reform movement."[27] Thus, a third type of park, the *recreational facility*, came into favor. The programs and facilities of recreational parks—bandshells, stadiums, checkerboards, and swimming pools—sustained morale during wartime and kept people busy. These parks paid less attention to landscaping and more to active recreation. To serve a new class of white-collar workers who were professionals and suburbanites, recreational parks with gym equipment extended into the suburbs. By the 1950s, recreational parks accommodated the handicapped and elderly.

Since 1965, urban park development focused on disparate bits of vacant land as potentially valuable gems. *Open space parks* could be developed into a tot-lot, a nontraditional adventure playground (using cement culverts and railroad ties), or an urban plaza. Citizens and professionals viewed all unbuilt space as potential sources of psychic relief. What we think of as "open space" today is somewhat more "wild," with a less-heavy hand of landscape manipulation than the 1960s planners.

## Entertainment

Sometimes we want our leisure to leave the familiar landscapes of parks and yards and simply to be about entertainment, including entertainment that in some sense "connects" us with nature. Of all the various and sundry ways to be entertained, this section will focus on two that have had a significant effect on how we view the natural world and our relationship with it: Disney theme parks, and the environment in films and television. Perhaps the most profound effects of these entertainment industries are their representation and commodification of nature.

### What Disney Has Given Us

One author, upon visiting the Swiss Family Robinson treehouse in Florida's Disney World asks, "So we have a fake tree holding a fake treehouse, representing a fake story told in a different medium from, but alluding to, a classic piece of literature, in an amusement park visited by 30 million people a year, most of whom are, like myself, enchanted. What is going on here?"[28]

Disney creations captivate us! In a world of fantastical Disney images, it's hard not to get carried away and be discerning, to tell what's real and what's fake. Even when we can distinguish the fake leaves from the real ones, we often don't care which is which and are likely to think that the simulations are fine.[29]

Every element of a Disney theme park communicates its messages in a highly controlled environment. Through the architecture, language, and the continuous performances, the goal is to leave no doubt as to how visitors should feel about and interpret the place. Venues are called attractions, visitors are guests, and workers are referred to as cast members or hosts. Additional Disney-speak provides many metaphors for performance: backstage (a restricted area), audition (a job interview), audience (a crowd), casting (hiring for a job), and costume (a uniform).

All the Disney literature and advertisements emphasize the "magical"—and not just at the Magic Kingdom. Everything is exhilarating, wonderful, and amazing: "We are told what is whimsical: 'You don't want to miss X'; 'everybody loves Y'; 'we all become children at Z.' Walt Disney World literature is the retirement home of the inflationary descriptive adjective. We are ordered about by language that is constantly performative and directive. We are drained of interpretive autonomy. The rhetoric is so overexuberant that we stop noticing its intent: It is just normal Disneytalk."[30] This sublime talk fully immerses "guests" in the market experience that is Disney.

Stephen M. Fjellman, author of *Vinyl Leaves: Walt Disney World and America*, takes readers through some of the pavilions at EPCOT in Florida, pointing out how natural settings like land, garden, and sea are commodified and performed. The first pavilion at EPCOT (the Experimental Prototype Community of Tomorrow) is "land" and is sponsored by Kraft Foods, one of the world's largest producer of processed foods. Visitors can ride through the exhibit or view it from above at a rotating restaurant. Small planters on the tables have seedlings of economically important U.S. crops like corn, wheat, and soybeans, and provide blurbs about the productivity of U.S. farms. The menu contains a list of Kraft products and an ad for "free enterprise."[31]

The land pavilion also features robotic bison and prairie dogs, and a soundtrack of birds and monkeys. "Rain" falls on the roof of the boat that visitors ride. The "smellitzer" aroma cannon disperses smells to create atmosphere, and everything looks quite real. But the trees are "flexible, lightweight plastic that simulates the cellulose found in real trees. The trunks and branches were molded from live specimens. . . . Hundreds of thousands of polyethylene leaves, made in Hong Kong, were snapped on. They are fire retardant, as are the blades of grass, which are made of glass fibers implanted into rubber mats. In the South American rain forest scene, the water on the leaves and trunks is supplied by a special drip system that provides a constant flow of moisture."[32]

What does the land pavilion communicate about the environment? The primary value of land is as a commodity that serves human interests. Courtesy of Kraft, visitors learn about cash crops and how science and technology are vital to the productivity (for humans) of that land. Nature is controllable and exists to fulfill human needs. And of course, the natural world exists to entertain us. It also communicates that nothing exists in nature that humans cannot recreate and control—the rain, the birdsong, a particular tree. And of course, the fake tree is more predictable than a real one for it will never lose its leaves or die.

Okay, you say, Disney is Disney. We expect everything to be contrived and fake, and hey, it's all just for fun, it's good entertainment. True. But what Disney represents in its typical grandiose fashion is how commodification and the marketplace have crept into every cell of our lives and become the overarching message of our time. Fjellman concludes that commodification has spread into perhaps the last two domains—the unconscious and nature—and pronounced that everything is for sale: "As consumers we are now convinced not only of the justifiable insatiability of our desires but of new, unexpected needs, symbolically set before us and symbolically solved."[33]

Disney is not an isolated exception in the world of commodity entertainment. One scholar makes a strong case that the Disney principles are being transported, transferred, and relocated to other places by more and more sectors of society, here and around the world:[34]

> The employees—smiling and helpful, transformed into hosts and performers
> The architecture—a blending and blurring of artifice and real
> "Hybrid consumption"—fusing consumption items (food, drink, merchandise, entertainment, lodging) in one location so people will stay longer and spend more. Creating a "destination" has been utilized by casinos, cruises, other theme parks, and shopping malls
> Blurring and transforming "shopping" into "play"
> Merchandising—promoting goods with copyright images or logos in order to extend the value of a well-known image
> Theming

The last principle of *theming* deserves a closer look, for it has been used extensively in representations of the natural world. Adopting and carrying out a theme—whether in a restaurant or retail store—is based on the idea that people don't consume solely for "use value."[35] Instead, the themed setting communicates an identity or lifestyle and gives the consumer the chance to be entertained with something novel, even if the main focus is just one activity like eating. Theming can highlight taken-for-granted features, particularly if a place lacks an obvious must-see quality. A theme also gives the visitor a short-course in how a place should be gazed upon.[36]

Theming in outdoor stores has "turned themed shopping into an art form."[37] Bass Pro shops have indoor waterfalls, archery and shooting ranges, and outdoor decks for fly fishermen. The new REI-Seattle store (with 1.5 million visitors in its first year) is a hundred thousand square foot warehouse-like structure that sports a sixty-five-foot-high freestanding artificial rock-climbing wall, a glass-enclosed wet stall to test rain gear, a vented area to test stoves, and an outdoor trail to try out mountain bikes. Cabela's in Owatonna, Minnesota, features a thirty-five-foot-high mountain with a waterfall. It also boasts two big dioramas of African scenes with the Big Five safari animals, three aquariums with lots of prized fish, and almost seven hundred different kinds of animals mounted all around the store. Is this shopping or entertainment?

Traditional shopping malls also construct their spaces to feel more like the outdoors. The 4.2-million-square-foot Mall of America in Minnesota—built in 1992 for $650 million and with more than five hundred stores—has four hundred trees, thirty thousand plants, an artificial mountain, a waterfall four-stories high, and a gigantic indoor amusement park.[38]

Theming represents a substantial investment. It also can rachet up people's expectations. The extra features in these stores' "servicescapes" supply multiple cues to consumers about how to enjoy and experience the service. One scholar sees theming as a powerful, ongoing trend: "Themed malls, heritage shopping and themed shopping are clearly becoming more and more prevalent. . . . [T]hey constitute a major approach to combating shopping from home in its various forms: television shopping, catalogue shopping and above all internet shopping. [T]hemed environments . . . supply reasons for getting out of the house in order to shop. They also provide alternatives to the pile-'em-high and sell-'em-cheap strategy of discount shops and warehouse by giving the customer additional value in the form of memorable experiences and entertainment as part of the shopping transaction."[39]

If you think that artificial re-creations of the natural world are found only in Disney parks and shops and restaurants in this country, think again. A project in the United Arab Emirates entails the total creation of three hundred islands that are being built and positioned to form the shape of the world's land masses.[40] The "new" pieces of land are being constructed from scratch right in the middle of the ocean. On top of the new islands will be ultra-luxury condos, hotels, and private residences. The World Project, developed by the government-controlled developer Nakheel, lies two miles offshore from Dubai. Some of the islands are already under construction; completion of the entire $14 billion project is set for 2008. Needless to say, building up land to form islands has been very harmful to gulf marine life, damaging coral reefs, oyster beds, and sea grasses. The silt produced by construction has made diving impossible—not to mention what it's rendered impossible for nonhuman marine life. Project developers say that once finished, sea life will thrive in the islands' artificial reefs. Regardless of what sea life might return, the project represents the total transformation of a vibrant, wild landscape into an essentially artificial, urban one with entirely different species of plants and animals—all for the pleasure (and profit) of humans. The World Project's creation and commodification of three hundred new islands makes Disney's representations of "land" and "sea" seem meek and mild in comparison.

### Television and Films

Watching television is the most popular form of entertainment in this country (even though it's rarely mentioned as a favorite activity).[41] If we accept what pollsters have found—that a majority of the American public values the environment and supports protection of it—we might assume that TV programs would to some extent reflect environmental issues or values. Because TV is such a ubiquitous cultural force, TV content might give us an indication of how integrated environmental values are in our everyday lives.

But researchers have found barely a whisper coming from TV about the environment. In a six-year study of nonnews programming on network TV (ABC, CBS, NBC, and FOX), there was actually a decreasing amount of attention paid within programs to environmental topics.[42] In a sample of 410 hours of entertainment programming, the total time allotted to environmental issues was 2 hours and 22 minutes—about 0.5 percent of the total hours.

When environmental topics were present in TV shows, they appeared more frequently "during programs with nature themes, which are relatively infrequent, than during programs having home and family or law enforcement themes, which are much more common." When characters appeared in environmental episodes, they were predominately white, middle class, middle-aged, and male— which does not match the demographics of those favoring environmental protection.[43] The researchers concluded that "despite some noteworthy exceptions, environmental topics are largely absent from U.S. television's prime-time network non-news entertainment and fictional programs."[44]

Another study found that heavier consumers of TV were less likely to support environmental positions or engage in pro-environmental behaviors; they also possessed less environmental knowledge.[45] One study found that entertainment TV use was not linked to environmental concern or behaviors, though watching TV news and nature documentaries was linked to these environmental measures.[46]

If we journey beyond prime-time network programming to TV movies and films in movie theaters, does the same lack of attention to the environment hold true? In terms of overall proportion, yes. One generalized statement we can make about portrayal of the natural world in this type of entertainment is an obvious one: nature is most often kept in the background and its features are used as a form of cultural shorthand for movie-makers. Although movies have a far longer timeframe than an advertisement in which to communicate, they nevertheless rely on similar agreed-upon stereotypes of the natural world and what it represents. For example, the call of a great-horned owl communicates that the wild is a bit threatening and omnious.

Unless the movie was created as a nature documentary, the movie isn't about nature per se, even though the natural world is front and center. Instead, nature *serves* the movie's plot and characters. Nature becomes the battleground for good and evil, a place where humans can demonstrate their smarts and bravado for conquering and/or saving nature, or for defeating bad guys intent on harming nature. In movies where nature functions in the foreground, its prominent role is part of an ongoing cultural effort to interact with and better understand the natural world:

> Humans have always invented ways to form an interactive relationship with the Earth, often by endowing that Earth with the qualities of the only subjects we know—ourselves. Nature and wildlife movies . . . are thus one expression of a long human tradition of investing the natural world with meaning. Those meanings are often as not laden with sexism, colonialism, and species hierarchy—witness the number of cars, tractors, and military machines named after animals. Still, the anthropomorphic gesture is a means of making the world beyond the garden wall intelligible to us, and of breaking down the ideology of "humanity vs. nature."[47]

A second generalization is that many nature-oriented movies revolve around animals. As discussed in a later chapter, animals are a handy Hollywood shorthand with the ability to stand for all of nature and its values. The downside of such a focus is the simplistic understanding of ecological systems. It seems to viewers that "saving" an individual bear or wolf magically saves an entire ecosystem, and that saving only the big, dramatic, top-of-the-food-chain animals saves everything else.

It's true that most Americans see wildlife on TV or in movies long before they see them live, if they ever do. Most of us are not likely to get as close to a whale as we are to Willy (in *Free Willy*), nor nose-to-nose with a gorilla (*Gorillas in the Mist*). Does the source of knowing—celluloid versus captive versus wild—affect our perceptions and the values we place on these animals, or the degree to which we anthropormophize them?

When we watch gorillas in their forest "home," we're tempted to say that we "know" gorillas because we saw them in their habitat doing their own thing. But in reality, the camera has presented us with an unnatural, atypical view. Every few years, a tourist in Yellowstone National Park is hurt (or killed) by a bison. Typically, the tourist walks right up to a bison with the intent of taking its photo, or having another person take his or her picture with the bison. Of course, when bison are viewed in films (or zoos), they look pretty docile, fuzzy, lethargic, and perhaps even friendly. It's a mistake to assume that every individual bison fits this stereotype, or that any film has really allowed you to understand and know that species and its "natural" behavior.

Movies featuring wildlife give us photographic intimacy with nature, making the encounter look "real," not contrived and staged. What is more accurately an animal performance in front of a camera crew is presented as natural, authentic animal behavior. Wildlife movies also promise that we can view nature without becoming involved in it—as if the bison will stand politely for its photo and not "interact" with you. Detachment from nature is possible in movies because the viewer doesn't see the behind-the-scenes activities needed to create it: "This detachment is an illusion that nature movies at least partly promote. Many of them don't reveal the deep involvement with nature necessary to their making: large crews, helicopters, camera blinds, sets, telescopic lenses, remote sound, and trained animals flown in from another part of the continent. In other words, nature films traffic in images that are ordinarily invisible. Our ability to produce these films of 'life in the wild' is an index not only of our power over nature but also of our distance from it."[48]

A third generalization is that the camera-as-narrator gives us a distorted sense of reality. When you read a book, you are aware of the narrator—perhaps the viewpoint of the lead character, or the omniscient narrator who is able to observe everything said and done, and get into the thoughts and hearts of each and every character. In a movie, an added narrator is the camera. Viewers get the sense that the lens is an impartial observer who was really there and accurately "captured" the essence of the wild scene or animal. But the camera-as-narrator has several consequences[49] that are as true for the PBS nature documentary as for the blockbuster about tornados.

First, the camera distorts and separates the visual from the rest of our senses. The camera exaggerates the eye's tendency to fragment, objectify, and estrange in a way that makes us feel like neutral observers. However, at same time that we *gain* objectivity, we *lose* the notion of interrelation and being there. As the camera's eye closes in on a slug on the forest floor, we get a seemingly objective visual but one that is divorced from smell and touch and that becomes separated from the entire forest system and its constant unfolding.

Second, the camera facilely provides a false intimacy with what are actually exceedingly rare moments. If you spend a great deal of time outdoors, you know how rare the encounters with skunks or cougars or floods or record snowfall really are. With multiple cameras and skillful edits, we watch hurricanes and animal mating rituals, missing out on the weeks of waiting for these events. What may actually be a once-in-a-lifetime performance is presented by the camera as normal and everyday. The powerful camera narrator can even convince us that it is natural and commonplace for animals to return our gaze.

Finally, a fourth consequence of the camera as narrator is its ability to reinforce human dominance. Naturally, because a human is operating the camera, the viewpoint is limited to a human one. The phrases of photographing (you take a shot, shoot a picture) are metaphors of the hunt and of conquering. There is an element of "bagging" and capturing a scene in the natural world and presenting the trophy to the human audience.

Although the sophistication of nature-based movies has increased greatly, the overall message has been updated only somewhat. Disney movies, documentaries, and even the modern *Crocodile Hunter* present a similar message: the natural world should be used wisely or it won't last, and when necessary, humans should step in to save nature or conquer it.

## THEMES FOR ENVIRONMENTAL MOVIES

Quite a few categorizations of movie themes and genre exist (action-adventure, romantic-comedy, and the Western) but few apply well to nature-based movies. Presented here is an adaptation and expansion of themes of nature-based movies presented by Alexander Wilson in *The Culture of Nature*. Naturally, some movies fit in multiple themes. (For simplicity, examples here do not include made-for-TV movies.)

### Humans as Both Destroyers and Saviors of Nature

The two predominant roles for humans are either as destroyers of nature or as scientists and conservationists intervening to save it. This is also a partial theme in numerous animal movies, often coupled with a theme about the bonds between humans and animals. In both *Erin Brockovich* (2000) and *A Civil Action* (1998), heroine Julia Roberts and hero John Travolta respectively battle corporate greed and environmental wrongdoing. *Sahara* (2005) and *On Deadly Ground* (1994) are environmental-action-adventure movies whose heroes battle envirodestroyers.

### Science Can Solve and Can Save

Human expertise in the form of authoritative science is necessary for the survival of wildlife and the natural world. This theme can be used to justify human dominance and paternalism, or to justify that humans know what's best for other species and need to "manage" them. TV shows such as *Nova* and *Nature* also employ this theme.

Scientists are often lead characters who use their knowledge to "save" the environment. In *Twister* (1996), the lead characters are tornado researchers who intentionally put themselves in harm's way to better predict tornadoes. They are battling both the elements and a rival team of storm trackers. *Medicine Man* (1992) stars Sean Connery as an eccentric scientist working for a large drug company in the Amazon rainforest; he is close to finding a cure for cancer, as the bulldozers come ever closer.

In some science-themed movies, officials fail to heed scientists' warnings. In *Dante's Peak* (1997), a USGS volcanologist (Pierce Brosnan) urges the mayor and city council to put the city on alert about the nearby volcano, arguing that economic interests are being put ahead of people's safety. Calls for "scientific proof" delay action, resulting in the town's destruction.

### Nature as a Human Test

The natural world and natural phenomena play a starring role in these movies, though the heroes are people. Wild nature is an exciting setting for men and women to demonstrate their courage, strength, tenacity, and bravery in battling the elements. There is often a dual focus in these movies: struggling with nature, and battling with other humans.

*Fly Away Home* (1998) is about a fourteen-year-old girl (played by Anna Paquin) who wants to help a family of orphaned Canada geese. She and her father guide the geese south on their first migration with an ultra-light airplane. The journey is fraught with trials and tribulations, not the least of which is the relationship between the girl and her father. In *The River Wild* (1994), Glenn Close stars as a professional river rafter who takes her family on a river trip, only to befriend two men they later learn to be armed, escaped robbers. Thus the river trip involves a battle with the bad guys as well as with the river, both of who become increasingly dangerous.

*Natural Events as Demonic Other*

Though movies in this category may likewise emphasize human scientific smarts or sheer bravado, what distinguishes this grouping is that natural disasters are fingered for the catastrophe. Virtually every possible "natural" disaster is featured: the iceberg in *Titanic* (1997), the sea in *The Perfect Storm* (2000), the obvious events in *Volcano* (1997) and *Earthquake* (1974), asteroids and comets in *Armageddon* (1998) and *Deep Impact* (1998), and forest fires in *Always* (1989).

*Boundaries between Animals and Humans Are Important and Should Be Enforced*

If nature remains "out there," separate from humans and behaving itself, it can be revered from afar and left alone. However, when that boundary is crossed—such as, lions eating humans in *The Ghost and the Darkness* (1996)—the natural system is at fault and must be put back into it proper (nonhuman) place. Our fear of marauding sharks, snakes, and spiders have been featured in *Jaws* (four versions from 1975 to 1987), *Anaconda* (1997), *Arachnid* (2001), and *Arachnophobia* (1990). The message in *Jurassic Park* (1993) and *The Land that Time Forgot* (1975) is that dinosaurs are cool, but they need to behave and stay where we confine them.

*Nature Battles as Allegories of Progress*

Although a movie may focus on the survival of a species or place in the face of industrialization, it is often left unspoken whether or not humans will ultimately survive such continued "progress." The separation of humans from the effects of industrialization tends to legitimize our metaphors about the inevitability of our current path of growth.

In *The Emerald Forest* (1985) (based on a true story), an engineer is sent to Brazil to oversee construction of a dam. The engineer's young son is kidnapped by a native tribe and raised as their own. As the father searches the Amazon rainforest for his son, he begins to understand the damage that the dam project is causing to the forest and its people. Development is a threat to both the environment and a way-of-life in several movies. In *The Milagro Beanfield War* (1988), for example, a developer plans to build a major new resort in a small town in the Southwest, which will displace the local Hispanic farmers.

Several films feature the lives of white settlers in Africa. Nature (and the natives) are still wild and present dangers but can be loved and appreciated from a safe distance. *Out of Africa* (1985) and *I Dreamed of Africa* (2000) feature women who accompany their husbands to Kenya to start colonizing enterprises (coffee and cattle, respectively). The women must learn to live among the local tribes and face natural elements like fierce storms, roving lions, and venomous snakes. By the movie's end the whites have a better appreciation for the local environment and native peoples, but their presence—and the progress that it represents—is not questioned but presented as normal and inevitable.

### It's How the West Was Won

The exploration and settlement of the West remain one of the more powerful narratives of our country. Brave, courageous men (and a few women) battled nature, settled the land, conquered the elements, but seemed to live in harmony with it. As the Western landscape became peopled, the same myths of freedom and space were transported elsewhere—first to Alaska, and then to "undiscovered" lands around the world. Movies with this theme tend to portray nature as "contested terrain" where those with the more righteous, moral stand prevail.

In *Legends of the Fall* (1994), a discharged colonel decides to raise his three sons in the wilds of Montana, where they can grow up away from the government and society he has learned to despise. Amidst breath-taking scenery, their lives are affected by nature, history, war, and love. The lesson is that men like these are what tamed the West and contributed to its unique character.

### The Tribal Is Synonymous with the Natural

The message is that tribal ways have much to teach us and it's enviable to return to "simpler times" when people had archaic connections to the natural world and could communicate with creatures. Though there are elements of truth regarding the relationship of native people to the natural world, the film representation is one gigantic, tribal stereotype of sameness. Most movies in this category creatively make whites the focal characters, not the natives.

More than a few of the movies in this theme also depict the "Wild West" as an allegory of the clash between tribal and "civilized" cultures. In *Dances with Wolves* (1990), Kevin Costner is the white Lt. John Dunbar, who chooses a remote western Civil War outpost. He befriends wolves and Indians, gradually earning the respect of the Sioux, shedding his white-man's ways, and falling in love with a white woman who was raised by the tribe. *The Last of the Mohicans* (1992) takes place during the French and Indian War in the 1800s. A white man adopted by the last two members of a dying Mohican tribe unwittingly becomes the protector of two daughters of a British colonel.

### Animals Starring as Humans

There are quite a few movies starring animals that aren't really about animals at all. In these movies, the animals essentially play humans, which is made easier when the movies are animated and the animal characters speak English. The father-son relationship in *Finding Nemo* (2003) could just as easily have taken place in a human setting and not the sea. *Antz* (1998) stars a worker-ant (the voice of Woody Allen) trying to reconcile his own individuality with the communal work-ethic of the ant colony, who falls in love with an "ant-princess." Animals also take on human roles and titles, whether father and son, or prince and princess. In the classic *Bambi* (1942), a deer fawn is hailed as "Prince of the Forest" and must use bravery and intelligence to lead the other deer to safety when the hunters come.

Two movies endeavor to tell a less anthropocentric tale and weave in ecosystem lessons. *FernGully: The Last Rainforest* (1992) features "fairy people" living in a spectacular and unpeopled rainforest. When the curious tree fairy Crysta ignores friends' warnings and explores the world beyond FernGully, she meets Zak, a human who is there to log the forest. Crysta accidentally shrinks Zak to fairy-size, and from this perspective, Zak sees the beauty and magic of the place and vows to save it . . . but it may be too late. A young lion "prince" Simba is born in *The Lion King* (1994), and is led to believe by evil uncle Scar that the death of his father was Simba's fault. Only after years of exile does Simba return to claim the kingdom and thus complete the "circle of life." Though the lesson of ecosystem balance is a valid one, the creatures in *The Lion King* basically present human motives and actions. The viewer does not see life in the jungle from a nonhuman perspective.

Hollywood, by appealing to our deeply held beliefs and cultural myths, has sold us a depiction of nature that supports a starring role for humans with nature as an idealized and often dangerous backdrop. With extremely few exceptions, "nature" movies support the dominant social paradigm: humans are superior to the rest of creation and are necessary to save, manage, or study the natural world.

Imagine, then, the expectations that people have when they enter "real" nature as tourists with their wild-nature movie myths. Anthropologist Colin Turnbull found that many American tourists are actually disappointed by their African safaris![50] He found that the average tourist on safari perceives that there's too much distance between humans and nature. In most African game parks, tourists get only structured, supervised access to wildlife (for obvious reasons) and say they don't get the sense of oneness and participation with the natural world.

## Tourism

Vacationing in nature is popular with Americans; over three-quarters of travelers have taken a trip involving the outdoors.[51] Tourism of all kinds is a enormous business, widely estimated to be world's largest industry and employing (directly and indirectly) almost 200 million people. It accounts for one in twelve jobs globally and 10.2 percent of the world's gross domestic product. "If tourism were a country, it would have the world's second-largest economy, surpassed only by the United States."[52]

U.S. tourists often travel outside its borders in search of nature-centered places, particularly to Mexico and its coastal resorts, a fairly inexpensive and close destination that fits our search for the primitive and remote. Much global tourism is organized on such axes of centers (developed countries, like the United States) and peripheries (less developed ones, like Mexico). "Tourism is one of the engines which manufacture and structure relationships between centers and peripheries. . . . Much of tourist activity reflects a world in which one segment—affluent, civilized and industrial—projects its desires onto another segment—poorer, more primitive, less developed."[53] This has significant ramifications for resource use and distribution in peripheral countries. In traveling from the airport to the hotel, a tourist to Mexico can't help but notice that fresh water, fresh food, and access to resources like beachfronts are not equally available to native residents of modest means. As such, "tourism is defined by (and helps itself to define) global consumer culture"[54] as well as environmental resource use.

## Pilgrims and Pilgrimages

Think back to your last vacation. What defined it as a vacation and not just a weekend? Although dictionaries define vacations as leisure for a specific purpose or freedom and respite from work, we associate a vacation with "vacating," leaving for some place distant from our everyday lives. A vacation is "there," not "here" and thus we "go on vacation." We also think of vacations as occupying an extended amount of time, often more than a two- or three-day weekend. Another defining characteristic of a vacation is behaving differently than you do at home, engaging in different activities and routines or purchasing different things.

Of course, one additional element seems to define most vacations: a desire to "get away," to escape to someplace different, foreign, exotic, or even familiar and beloved. A vacation that involves the natural world fits that definition for many people, particularly for those who live far from pristine nature and make a strong distinction between culture and nature. Vacations to natural areas also fit our notion of nature as a refuge and sublime landscape, worthy of Kodak moments. Our national parks are good examples of our aesthetic and social preconceptions of what's beautiful and awe inspiring. One author called nature tourism the temporary migration of people to what they understand to be a different and usually more "pure" environment.[55]

In a sense, a vacation resembles a pilgrimage, in which tourists are seeking things from which they have been alienated by daily life in the modern world. It may be about tradition (the annual vacation at the lake or yearly trip to the grandparents' farm) or a reinvention of tradition. ". . . [T]he tourist, like a pilgrim, is searching for a sense . . .of the authentically social in order to reclaim that which has been lost by an essentially isolating and fracturing post-modern life."[56] It may be that the greater the alienation of the tourist, the greater the search for authenticity.

What is being sought is probably a combination of some "authentic Other" as well as one's "authentic Self." The "authentic Other" is the local culture and its inhabitants, which are imagined to be more whole, structured, and authentic (or premodern) than the everyday world you inhabit the rest of the year. Thus, the authentic Other may be a tropical island, a primitive village in Nepal, an Amish settlement just off the Interstate, or just the nonhuman in general. One feature that makes a tourist destination attractive is the belief that it has a special characteristic or spirit, derived from the sociability of the residents. In other words, the natives are friendly.[57]

The tourist's "authentic Self" is the "true" person thought to be lying deep within, perhaps a person free of stress and at peace, detached from the normal conveniences of everyday life, or surviving only with what is carried in a backpack or suitcase. Obviously, this search often leads people to the natural world. Given the separation of daily life from nature that many people feel, and the connection between leisure and nature, we may plan vacations that we hope will reconnect us.

### The Visual, Consumable Vacation

It's safe to bet that TV and movies played a part in the high expectations we have for close encounters, active participation with nature, and escape. Another source of our expectations is the publicity of tourism: advertisements, brochures, and postcards. All of these communication pieces seek to render culture consumable by tourists; for the right price, you can buy (or at least, buy into) that Costa Rican experience and bring back postcards as proof.

Thumb through a magazine and examine the ads for tourism. What do they encourage you to expect? Good weather, no bugs, incredible sunsets, uncrowded venues, friendly natives, even sex. Also, notice who is shown (or not shown) in these ads.

One scholar concluded that tourists play the role of myth-makers, and tourist brochures are the myths whose function is to present images of destinations that have ideologically potent meanings for tourists.[58] In a study of 5,172 pictures in global tourist brochures, the researcher concluded that brochure images of a destination and its native people are couched in the language and imagery of social (and political) control—not in a sense of greater democracy. The emphasis was on tourists getting away and leaving their unsatisfying home routine behind in some exotic place.

In the pictures he analyzed, about 60 percent showed tourists only (and no local residents), "emphasizing advertisers' support for normative segregation of hosts from guests."[59] The researcher concluded that these photos conveyed a *paradise confined*, where small numbers of tourists were shown dining or poolside as one, large, happy family, and where distinctions of wealth and class were obliterated. Almost a quarter of the brochure photos had virtually no people, highlighting the importance of "getting away from it all." These photos showed a *paradise contrived*, emphasizing how people could escape the humdrum world of the masses to a serene and seemingly unpeopled place. Hotels were empty palaces and beaches were deserted. The natural was sublime, without bugs or heat. In the remaining photos, local residents were shown in only 7 percent, and combinations of locals and tourists were in 9 percent; in many of these, locals were servants or entertainers. This highlights a curious contradiction; you may really desire to know the authentic Other, yet you don't want to get too close to the natives.

Postcards are a powerful tourism myth-maker. Of course, we know that cameras can't lie, so a postcard must be an authentic representation of available sights. However, postcard images are dislocated

**Figure 5.1**

in space and time; you were not present during their creation and have only an indirect reference to the scene. After all, all of us have bought a postcard of some scene that we never saw, but we felt was somehow representative. In addition, a postcard is removed from

any recognizable present and separated from any tangible social context—a kind of gift-wrapped, contrived authenticity. Postcards (for
both the buyer and receiver) make places exotic and moored in a
vicarious but unreal past experience.[60]

Of course most of us also take our own "postcards," photos for
the vacation album. With your camera, you are able to "capture"
and consume scenery and preserve vacation memories. But long before digital and Polaroid cameras, cameras were important vacation
equipment for communicating and sharing the vacation experience.
In the first half of the 1900s, the practice spawned its own special
term, "kodaking." Taking your own images allows you to, in a sense,
take possession of a strange or foreign landscape and help feel more
secure in it: "Photography was one way visitors could control this
imposing and at times aggressive theatricality. Certainly, photography gave tourists a language through which they could describe and
appreciate the environment surrounding them. Photographs and
the albums in which they were assembled also gave visitors a way to
recollect stories and adventures—to explain, even justify, how and
why they visited a particular place."[61]

### The Development of Tourism

The development of tourism and vacationing in this country has
had a direct impact on the natural world and how we experience and
communicate about it. After all, "Tourism locates us in space as well
as time. It has redefined the land in terms of leisure and reorganized
our relations to it."[62]

In this country, the reorganization of our relations to the land
in terms of leisure has taken place over the last couple of centuries.
Historically, less leisure time and less wealth made vacationing an
activity primarily of the very well-to-do. Before the migration to cities, one's everyday life was likely already rural or had some connection to nature, thus an individual had no need to "get back to." With
industrialization and urbanization, more Americans wanted to leave
the industrial cities and an increasingly popular destination was nature parks. "By the late nineteenth century, almost half of North
Americans lived in cities. . . . [P]rogress was measured by how far
nature . . . had been pushed back, and the feeling at the close of the

nineteenth century . . . was that the job was nearly done. It became possible to argue then that the wilderness had to be preserved."[63]

By the 1900s, wealthy city dwellers were traveling to Rocky Mountain spas and seaside resorts. The growing urban middle class was attracted to hunting, fishing, canoeing, and going to the country on holidays. Church and youth organizations established their own outdoor education programs, such as Woodcraft Indians and Boy Scouts. By the end of World War II, increasing general affluence meant that outdoor recreation and the automobile vacation had become mass phenomena—though mainly phenomena of white Americans.

Until the spread of private automobiles, visiting distant, pristine nature was reserved for those with the time and the money to travel by train. The designation of America's earliest national parks corresponded with the completion of rail lines to their borders: Yellowstone in 1872, Yosemite and Sequoia in 1890, and Mt. Rainier in 1899. By 1916, the year the National Park Service itself was created, 365,000 visitors had entered the new national parks. In just seven years, visitation was 3.5 million.

Once trains traveled to these distant landscapes, nature and wilderness enjoyment was easily delivered to tourists in a safe, convenient package. Spending time in western wilderness was no longer limited to virile, courageous men; now an entire family could enjoy natural wonders in a way that was safe, fun, and stimulating. In the most remote locations, modern yet rustic conveniences were supplied: lodges, dining facilities, and plumbing.[64] Long before tourists arrived at the park gates, sublime images of these areas had been communicated to them in paintings and photographs:

> The story of the development of the national parks is the story of people who saw such perfect pictures of wilderness and then wanted to go and see the real thing. The more that photographs were reproduced in nature magazines and railroad brochures, the more people wanted to buy train tickets and experience the parks for themselves. In a deeply democratic move, national parks had been set aside for "the enjoyment of the people." And as people began to vacation in them, they became giant playgrounds for urbanites who desired contact with wilderness—a contact that was

expected to take place within a safe, controlled and protected set-ting. Nowhere was this truer than in the western states.[65]

Yellowstone National Park, the nation's first national park, was a powerful template that guided the development, architecture, com-munication, and even type of employee in all national parks that followed. Yellowstone was developed as a joint venture between the federal government and capitalist enterprises, particularly railroads and concessionaires. Early park architects helped to develop "an ar-chitectural language that spoke of the conservation of nature and at the same time constructed wilderness as a place of leisure."[66]

The grand Old Faithful Inn in Yellowstone is a massive structure built from local materials, yet it has a general aesthetic of simplicity, hand-crafted design, and uncluttered details: "By taking the *image* of the log cabin, the Old Faithful Inn celebrates the final conquest of the West, and because it is a very large building, it reaffirms the validity of the conquest. But it turns inside out the metaphor of the pioneer hard at work to transform 'wilderness' into productive land. Because the national park has been legally pulled out of a productive relation to the land—because it cannot be farmed, logged, or mined—the im-age of the log cabin is left to signify nothing but leisure, or in other words, non-productive and recreational activities."[67]

The first people to staff national parks were generally soldiers, there to provide safety from wild animals and Indians and to guard forest reserves and resources. When park rangers replaced the sol-diers, they retained some aspects that resembled military: a uniform, badge, and the entrance requirements to be fit and a "good shot." "But unlike the solider, the park ranger was encouraged to educate the tourist 'to make them understand what they see.' It was assumed that park visitors came from urban environments and had little knowledge of nature or the local region and therefore required in-struction in the form of evening lectures and guided walks."[68] More and more, the National Park Service turned to the word and concept of "interpretation."

When transportation to national parks shifted from railroads to motor cars, the parks adapted to people who wanted to drive and camp. Magazines of the early 1900s communicated the restorative effects of camping. Campgrounds became a standard, controlled experience of wilderness; in exchange for drinking water, a latrine, and garbage pick-up, visitors obeyed rules, contained their fires, and so on.

After the original inhabitants of national parks were forced out, the parks commodified Indian culture and made Indian crafts part of the park experience. Indians were enlisted to give demonstrations and their goods could be purchased in the gift shop. "As a rule though, the place for Native Americans in the representations of conservation was very restricted—generally taking the form of 'bygone' cultures or folk entertainment and craft."[69] Indians also were exploited; the concessionaire for Glacier National Park stationed members of the Blackfoot tribe as bait along roadways to the park to lure tourists.

National parks remain complex cultural landscapes. The representation of parks as sublime nature has endured for generations, now communicated through standardized brochure-maps. Though many parks are severely crowded, face traffic jams and air pollution, and lack money to repair badly eroding infrastructure, the landscape communicated is pristine, people-less, and available for visitor consumption. In 2004, roughly 277 million visits were made to U.S. national parks and monuments.

## The Management of Tourists and Their Experiences

"Getting away" from it all—whether at a national park or nearby reservoir—remains an important feature for a vacation today. But it's important to note that a great many (if not most) tourism experiences really aren't escapes at all, but are instead highly managed and directed experiences. Take, for example, how roads manage the movement of tourists. A freeway is designed for expedience, to whisk you through what might be considered insignificant landscapes, while a "parkway" or "scenic byway" denotes important landscapes worthy of time and attention. Scenic view pull-outs, overlooks, historical markers, and rest stops are all attempts to manage your tourist experience. This management encourages a similar, preplanned experience, not necessarily a personal one. The communication of tourism organizes the relations between humans and the natural world, and in doing so, has consequences for the natural world. There is an inherent (some would say necessary) contradiction in directing tourists to natural places: a desire to protect natural resources versus allowing maximum enjoyment (and attendant development) by all. Lake Powell is fouled by human sewage, there is smog over the Grand Canyon, traffic jams in Yellowstone, and stop lights in Yosemite.

In his book *The Culture of Nature*, Canadian Alexander Wilson examines how one parkway was designed and built as a complete managed tourist experience.[70] The Blue Ridge Parkway stretches 470 miles through five mountain ranges in Virginia and North Carolina. The parkway was a Depression-era job-creation project that is now managed by the National Park Service. The entire parkway is restricted to leisure traffic (no commercial vehicles allowed) and like many such roads, it has its own logo on road signs. Land use along the parkway is restricted to things considered compatible with the parkway aesthetic. Vistas were planned, the roadways planted to screen out undesirable views, and curves constructed to keep speeds down. All such actions made the parkway organized entirely around the private car and the private consumption and enjoyment of nature.

Have changes in transportation meant better vacations and better escapes? They have perhaps made for more insulated experiences, though not necessarily better ones. As one author argues, "Everyone is aware that improved transportation has not reduced the haste of the vacation. . . . [F]ew of us hear a landscape any more. Taste and smell are likewise handicapped. The day is here when the air-conditioned automobile carries us across Death Valley without discomfort, without disturbance to our heat receptors, and without any experience worth mentioning. We do not touch the burning sand."[71]

If vacationing once had a pastoral aura about it, the shift has been made to a consumer-oriented, automotive one. Since many parks were not created until transit was available to them, much of the infrastructure of tourism has sprung up as a direct domino effect of the automobile: roads, motels, campgrounds, mini-marts and strip developments, the RV and trailer industry, highway signs, billboards, and later the snowmobile, ORV, and dirt bike. As a sign of how consumerism has entered the campground, a firm in Boise, Idaho is now offering high-speed Internet access to campgrounds via satellite. The service has so far been tested in twenty-five Forest Service campgrounds in the Northwest.[72]

*Ecotourism*

At some level, driving through Death Valley or the Blue Ridge Parkway is tourism involving nature. So is bungee-jumping off a river bridge. Tourism also can involve nature in a more integral way. "Nature-based tourism" is defined as traveling to relatively undisturbed or un-contaminated natural areas with the specific objective of studying, admiring, and enjoying the scenery and its wild plants and animals, as well as any existing cultural manifestation found in these areas.[73]

If you have participated in nature-based tourism to ecologically fragile or undeveloped areas, you may have felt firsthand the impact of your presence. You might have recognized that you used more resources and lived more luxuriously than the people who call that place home. You also might have known that much of the money you spent did not grace the palms of the local people or help protect the natural resources that made the place so desirable, but was de-posited in the accounts of global hotel chains, restaurants, and tour operators.

In response to deepening concerns about the negative effects of conventional and some forms of nature-based tourism (abroad and at home), the concept of "ecotourism" appeared in the 1970s—de-fined by the International Ecotourism Society as "responsible travel to natural areas that conserves the environment and improves the welfare of local people."

Ecotourism strives to show how both environmentally responsi-ble and socially useful tourism can work in tandem; natural resources are considered an integral part of the economic base and are linked to the local social and economic sectors. Ecotourism hopes to provide economic justification for protecting natural areas and also preserv-ing cultural and social values. The focus of ecotourism shifts from the tourist to the tourist *in conjunction* with the local community: "While nature tourism and adventure tourism focus on what the tour-ist is seeking or doing, ecotourism focuses on the impact of this travel on the traveler, the environment, and the people in the host country—and posits that this impact must be positive. As such, ecotourism is closely linked to the concept of sustainable development."[74]

By the 1990s, ecotourism was fastest growing sector of travel in-dustry, growing at a rate of 10 to 15 percent annually, much of it to developing countries.[75] Tourists were willing to pay two to three thousand dollars for an authentic ecotour. But ecotourism is not likely to appeal to all tourists. One study identified two basic groups of ecotourists: one group was wealthy, healthy, in their thirties and forties, liberal, and middle class; the other group was twenty-something individuals who were sensitive to environmental issues and wanted an alternative vacation experience.

Businesses can participate in environmentally conscious business practices, yet not fit the definition of ecotourism. You may have stayed in a hotel where they communicated their efforts to reduce resource use, such as not washing sheets daily, using energy efficient lighting, and recycling. The actions of such a "green hotel" are commendable, but do not alone meet the requirement of social and economic responsibility if hotel profits benefit distant economies more than the local economy or do not contribute to the preservation of the natural area people came to see.

In addition, some business operations adopt the moniker of "green" or "ecotourism" without committing to the actions. "There is ample evidence that, in many places, ecotourism's principles and core practices are being corrupted and watered down, hijacked and perverted. Indeed, what is currently being served up as ecotourism includes a mixed grill with three rather distinct varieties: ecotourism 'lite' businesses . . . , 'greenwashing' scams . . . , and genuine ecotourism."[76] The fact that there are almost sixty certification schemes for ecotourism ventures shows the difficulty of defining and regulating authentic ecotourism. Nevertheless, many tourism experts see certification programs as key to separating the authentic from the rest.

One researcher studied tourism in parts of Belize and found that depending on who is running the ecotourism, it can still exploit and displace residents.[77] Her case study demonstrated "how the politics of class, gender, and patronage inequities limit the co-management of ecotourism associations, equitable distribution of ecotourism income, and support for conservation regulations across the community."[78]

## Conclusion

As strange as it might sound, there seem to be few opportunities to experience leisure in the natural world on its own simple terms.

Much of outdoor leisure seems swallowed by the marketplace and/ or altered by the shovel and bulldozer, which repositions our perception and relationship to nature. The messages in many leisure realms: products are needed to enjoy leisure, artifice is preferable, and humans are in control of nature. We don't need to cite Disney or the World Project in Dubai as extreme examples of the intentional creation of artifice for our leisure enjoyment, for plenty of examples exist in our daily environs.

The most significant and potentially damaging trend lies in the commodification of leisure activities in nature. The marketing of outdoor "lifestyles" make environmental concern seem available with the right gear, not through belief or practice. Commodifying leisure means convincing you that leisure requires a lot of material goods, and that you can purchase things which are ultimately incapable of being bought or sold: peace, relaxation, spirituality. Leisure increasingly is being fused to shopping in various forms, blurring the natural and artificial, confusing what is shopping and entertainment and nature. Commodification of nature is a theft of value from the natural world that cheapens it and does nothing to clarify or deepen our relationships to it. Even our vacations, where we hope to escape and reconnect the most, can be highly managed and commodified leisure experiences.

# 6

## Faint-Green: Advertising and the Natural World

A young boy works through the pages of a coloring book. He reads aloud, "Help the knight reach the castle," and with his crayon follows the winding path around the dragon to the castle. Next he reads, "Help the Jeep Wrangler reach the fishing hole." "Hmm," he says, grins, and makes a noise like a truck revving up. He draws a line straight across the coloring book landscape, across two mountain ranges, a deep valley, and a patch of quicksand, ignoring the cleared path. As he smiles smugly, the announcer tells us that a Jeep is "more fun than you imagine."

It is virtually impossible to think of any other message that is as pervasive, invasive, and ubiquitous as the advertisement. Ads are sandwiched between news and entertainment programming in the mass media, but there is also the ad on the bus bench and on the bus, on the telephone pole and billboard, on the sweatshirt, before the movie and on the popcorn bag, on "commercial free" radio, on cars and trucks, on Web sites, stuffed in bills and mailboxes, and on classroom walls. According to the American Association of Advertising Agencies, we are exposed to three thousand advertisements each day (if that seems impossible, think of the ad logos you see just on clothing). Of those three thousand ads each day, we notice only eighty, and have some sort of reaction to only twelve.[1] But with daily repetition through multiple channels, the jingles and slogans move quickly to the lips of young and old, setting the trends for cars, clothes, and consumption. The advertisement is, without a doubt, the ultimate pop culture message.

The TV ad described above is typical because it's not really *about* the natural world. No one is hawking a product as "recyclable" or a company as "caring for the environment." You probably wouldn't even think of the ad as a green message. Nevertheless, it speaks volumes about a relationship with the natural world as a central part of its message. We see the environment and elements of it featured in commercials for allergy medicines, lawn care products, orange juice, tennis shoes, and Jeep Wranglers. In them, nature is a backdrop for selling, a useful symbol for communicating what are ostensibly shared cultural values, thus promoting a certain viewpoint as widely held and appropriate.

Nature-as-backdrop ads, even though they represent the most widespread depiction of the natural world in advertising, are the least studied. The bulk of research on "green advertisements" has focused on ads that promote environmental sensitivity toward some aspect of the biophysical world,[2] or promote a "green lifestyle," or present a corporate image of environmental responsibility.[3]

Advertising's overall depiction of the environment idealizes and materializes a way of experiencing the natural world. In advertising depictions, nature is pristine, not endangered, and holds simple solutions to what are essentially complex dilemmas, lifestyles, and choices. Advertising taps into our dissatisfactions and desires for qualities like solitude and health, but does so by linking those nonsaleable qualities with material goods. Such commodification is a process in which nonsaleable objects, activities, and images are purposely placed in a material context.[4] By mixing the artificial with the natural, the environment becomes a commodity whose value is primarily economic.

Ads are not the root cause of environmental evil. Advertising and marketing have evolved during the past century with numerous other social and structural changes, such as the mass production of consumer goods, unprecedented scientific advancements, and a host of inventions from the automobile and color TV to the computer. Advertisements are not alone in attempting to influence our thoughts and behaviors. However, there is enough evidence to suggest that advertising has a "special cultural power"[5] and sends particular, powerful messages about the natural world and our relationship with it.

This chapter first describes how the environment is used in different types of ads, from those touting product attributes to those promoting a green image or issue. Next, the chapter considers the powerful and ubiquitous business of advertising and its development. Finally, it explores the psychology of advertising and how ads "work" on us.

First, some definitions. *Advertising* is the task of producing discrete promotional messages about products, services, or organizations and paying to display them through mass media channels like newspapers and televisions and in public venues, typically billboards, bus placards, and so on. (Logos and product names also appear on items such as caps and T-shirts, although you indirectly pay for such "advertising" in the purchase price.) *Marketing* is concerned with the entire process of selling a product or service through pricing, distribution, positioning, and promotion. Obviously, marketers often use ads to help "create a need" for a product. Marketing tools, such as point-of-purchase displays and product packaging, also "advertise" the product and may repeat the graphics and text used in formal media ads.

## Four Types of Ads Featuring the Environment

Consider the following four types of ads that "use" the natural world in different ways:

> Nature-as-backdrop
> Green product attributes
> Green image
> Environmental advocacy

### Nature-as-Backdrop

In a TV commercial, two raccoons peer inside a brightly lit living room window, "singing" a song from *My Fair Lady*. As the camera moves beyond the raccoons into the living room (where it appears the residents aren't home) it focuses on the Lazy Boy rocker. The raccoons sing from the musical, "All I want is a room somewhere, far away from the cold night air. Warm hands, warm feet . . ."

In this ad, you are not being asked to buy something that has a direct or obvious connection to the natural world, but nonhuman icons are very much part of the overall persuasive message, playing the role of nature as backdrop. Animals, as popular symbols of the nonhuman environment, are a way for viewers to link the personality and cultural meaning of the animal to the product.[6] From what we know about the habits and behaviors of raccoons, we could interpret the ad's message this way: these cute, mischievous "bandits" would like to break in to this warm room "far away from the cold night air" and maybe even snooze in that rocker. Of course we know that raccoons can't sing, but their actions are designed to demonstrate how comfortable and desirable a certain brand of chair is. (When we give human characteristics or emotions to animals, like singing, we *anthropormorphize* them.)

Using nature merely as a backdrop—whether in the form of wild animals, mountain vistas, or sparkling rivers—is the most common use of the natural world in advertisements. For all but the most critical media consumers, the environment blends into the background. We know that an advertisement for an SUV shows the vehicle outdoors and that ads for allergy medications feature flowers and "weeds." In them, the environment per se is not for sale, but advertisers are depending on qualities and features of the nonhuman world to help in the selling message. Although this intentional but seemingly casual use of the environment in advertising is by far the most common, it is the least studied by researchers.

### Green Product Attributes

On a package of paper towels, there is a graphic of an evergreen forest. The text reads: "Soft, strong and absorbent Green Forest products work just like other paper products but they're better for the environment. Green Forest is made from 100 percent recycled paper, including at least 10 percent post-consumer paper. . . . By purchasing these products you help to 'close the loop'—paper that was bound for crowded landfills is expertly recycled to make Green Forest. Green Forest bath tissue, paper towels, napkins and facial tissue—the right thing to do for the Environment."

**Figure 6.1**

In this example, the ad highlights the green attributes of the product. Consumers are encouraged to believe that if they buy this brand of paper towels, they are contributing to a green lifestyle—using recycled products, keeping waste out of landfills, and so on. Consumers are persuaded to think that there is a less harmful relationship between the product and the environment than one without green qualities, and they also are supporting what appears to be an environmentally responsible manufacturer. Even the product's name, Green Forest, is designed to evoke positive environmental images. Other examples of products positioned on the basis of their environmental appeal are Rainforest Crunch and "dolphin-safe" tuna.

But as discussed later in this chapter, making claims about environmental attributes means negotiating a slippery slope. In Green Forest paper towels, only 10 percent of the content was used previously and recycled—so-called post-consumer waste. The other 90 percent is preconsumer waste, most likely "cutting room floor" scraps in a manufacturing plant. While it's true that both pre- and postconsumer waste might otherwise have been dumped in a landfill, it's not clear what the Green Forest claim really means. Does it mean that the company supports community paper recycling programs? Even a general claim such as "better for the environment" is vague. Does it mean that manufacture of the product did not harm the environment in any way? Does it imply "friendliness" at all stages of a product's production, consumption, and disposal? Such green claims appeal to buyers' sense of doing the right thing, but tell buyers little about the true environmental costs of the products they buy.

### Green Image

In the center of a magazine ad is a color photograph of two bald eagles and a bold, red headline: "Bringing couples together before there's only a couple left." At the bottom of the page, also in red, is "Budweiser, Brewing solutions for a better environment." The text of the ad tells how Budweiser is "proud to help the Conservation Fund provide a safe breeding habitat for hundreds of bald eagles on Kodiak Island in Alaska," as well as helping the World Bird Sanctuary, Ducks Unlimited, and the Rocky Mountain Elk Foundation.

This green image ad says nothing directly about Budweiser beer and doesn't even ask you to buy it. Instead, it presents the beer maker as an environmentally responsible corporate citizen. Of course, if you are concerned about the environment (and you drink beer), Budweiser hopes that you'll be encouraged to buy their product as part of your green lifestyle—not that beer drinking helps the planet, but that supporting a pro-environment company might. The ad's imagery also relies on a powerful American symbol, a symbol both of freedom and of the environmental success story of the bald eagle's comeback.

Compare the image created with the Budweiser ad with another ad that also uses a bald eagle. Underneath a photo of a bald eagle frozen in flight, the ad explains that when you donate fifty dollars to the National Park Foundation, you'll earn miles on American Airline's frequent flyer plan. This ad is not purely a green image ad because it's tied to the airline's service. If American Airlines had donated money to the group without strings, it would be a true image ad.

Image advertising is also called "institutional advertising" because it focuses on the institution rather than on a discrete product or service. A green image ad tries to draw attention to actions of the organization that could be seen as pro-environment. The Budweiser ad is a typical example of an image ad that says "look what we're doing" for the environment. Another type of image ad is instructional, urging consumers to join the company in recycling efforts or teaching kids about oceans. According to some, image advertising offers companies an opportunity to spruce up their images at relatively low cost,[7] sometimes with minimal substantive action or organizational change.[8]

Of the four kinds of green ads, image ads are most subject to "greenwashing," when corporations pose as friends to the environment but their performance doesn't match the image.[9] Advertising is a controlled message, therefore whoever forks over the money (which is substantial!) to print or air an ad dictates the exact message without control or input. As you'll see in the next example, many types of ads remain unregulated.

*Environmental Advocacy*

The headline in a magazine advertisement by the U.S. Council for Energy Awareness says, "Trees aren't the only plants that are good for the atmosphere." In the photo above this headline sits a nuclear power plant in a tree-covered bucolic setting on the shores of a body of water. The text states: "Because nuclear plants don't burn anything to make electricity, nuclear plants don't pollute the air." It later says, "But more plants are needed—to help satisfy the nation's growing need for electricity without sacrificing the quality of our environment."

This is an example of the fourth way to communicate about the environment through advertising: encouraging environmental action, or advocating a particular stance on an environmental issue. Environmental advocacy ads are purchased by corporations, environmental groups like Greenpeace, and interest groups interested in affecting public policy or environmental decisions. Although the U.S. Council for Energy Awareness might sound like a government-sponsored entity, it is a lobbying group for the nuclear power industry.

Advocacy ads express ideas on controversial social issues of public importance[10] and have tackled virtually every environmental issue including energy use, air and water pollution, animals, wilderness designation, and other land use matters. An advocacy ad might deny or downgrade arguments from opponents in an attempt to change public perception from skepticism and hostility to trust and acceptance. Advocacy ads are not subject to "truth in advertising" laws because they are considered expressions of political beliefs and are therefore not regulated.

### Ads with Combined Appeals

Of course, there are endless variations and combinations of these four basic types of ads. For example, a magazine ad for Nature Valley granola bars combines product attributes and a green corporate image: In a distance, we see a woman jogging across a verdant, green, rolling hillside. A cutline points to the green hillside and labels it "Mother Nature's Treadmill"; another cutline at the bottom points to a photo of a granola bar and labels it "Mother Nature's Energy Bar. The Energy Bar Nature Intended." In fine print at the bottom of the ad, it says "Nature Valley is proud to have donated $240,000 to The Nature Conservancy since 1998."

The green corporate image part of the ad is obvious, highlighting the corporate largess to an environmental group. The product attributes, however, don't mention any environmental benefits such as "recyclable" or "biodegradable," and make only indirect and less explicit connections to responsible environmental behavior. Instead, this ad features "nature" and qualities associated with nature, indirectly linking the health of nature to the health of individual consumer. "Nature" and "Mother Nature" are powerful symbols with the ability to evoke feelings of goodness, purity, and naturalness.

## How "Green" Is the Appeal of Ads?

Each advertisement, green or otherwise, is designed to appeal to a target audience who is most likely to buy the product or be sympathetic to the message. In the case of green ads, the target is often the "green consumer," a socially constructed market segment composed generally of maturing "baby boomers" who are educated, middle-class or affluent, and more politically liberal. In 1992, the Roper

Organization identified five levels of environmental commitment, which were readily adopted by marketers.[11] True-Blue Greens (20 percent of the population) were recyclers, members of environmental groups, and supporters of environmental regulations, while Greenback Greens (5 percent) lacked the same level of commitment but were willing to buy green products. Sprouts (31 percent) were considered a swing group, supporting pro-environment legislation but not believing they could make a difference by their behavior. Grousers (9 percent) and Basic Browns (35 percent) were not environmentalists. Other market studies revealed that three out of ten consumers buy products because of green advertisements, green labeling, or other environmental endorsements.[12]

Research into the particular types of appeals made by green product or image ads to green consumers is fairly limited. "Preservation of the planet" was the focus in three-quarters of the print ads in one study,[13] while promotion of a green corporate image was the most common theme in both TV and print ads in another study.[14] In these same studies, three types of appeals were the most common. "Zeitgeist" (defined as a general green climate or joining the green bandwagon) was the appeal in 32 percent of the print ads. Emotional appeals (fear, guilt, or self-esteem) accounted for 21 percent of the appeals, while corporate appeals (proactive corporate involvement) were used 22 percent of the time.[15] TV ads used emotional appeals 27 percent of the time and corporate appeals 34 percent.[16]

As you might expect, the depth of green-ness in green ads is relatively shallow. Adapting the deep and shallow ecology concepts of environmental philosopher Arne Naess[17] to advertisements, researchers found that about 40 percent of the TV and print ads were "shallow" or vague in their environmental appeals, like "earth-friendly." Even more ads were labeled "moderate," mentioning slightly more specific actions such as recycling but perhaps not discussing related environmental issues. Very few ads were "deep"—2 percent of TV and 9 percent of print—defined by the researchers as discussing environmental issues in depth and mentioning actions requiring more commitment like backyard composting.[18] Of course, "deep" is relative. An ad by its very nature is designed to appeal to human desires and needs and to sell products that benefit humans—a decidedly anthropocentric and shallow philosophy.

Beyond categorizing appeals as emotional or corporate and deep or shallow, do green advertising appeals differ according to the salience of the environmental issue or the involvement of the recipient? One researcher found that when an environmental problem is considered relatively unimportant, a "sick baby" advertising appeal is advantageous.[19] In other words, when existing concern is low, it's important for the message to increase concern, and focusing on the severity or "sickness" is one way to do that. However, when concern is already high for an issue, focusing on its severity might make the problem seem too large to be solved. In such cases, the researcher argued, an alternative "well baby" appeal could stress the significance of individual action. Of course, this depends on the audience. If a person is highly involved with the environment, it made no difference whether an ad used a green or nongreen appeal.[20]

By the late-1990s, there was a decline in green product advertising, perhaps ironically due to widespread acceptance of environmentalism, or due to the commodification of environmentalism generally[21] and a decline in controversy over antigreen products such as disposable diapers and SUVs. Two researchers found that green ads in prime-time TV never amounted to more than a blip, with only 1 percent of ads making environmental claims in 1991, increasing slightly to 1.5 percent in 1993, but virtually disappearing (0.01 percent) by 1995.[22] In the eyes of these scholars, TV was not the best-fitting medium for green consumers, and "reflected the television tendency to get off the environmental bandwagon after it had lost its trendiness."[23] Despite the ups and downs of green product ads, green image and advocacy ads continue to increase, and nature-as-backdrop ads remain as prevalent as ever.

## The Phenomenon—and Oxymoron—of "Green" Advertising

At the most basic level, is it an oxymoron to label marginally useful or necessary products as somehow "good" for the environment? Can an advertisement that encourages consumption of a product (or patronage of a company that produces the product) ever be green with a capital "G"? One scholar tackled this question by identifying three levels of green. At the lowest level, if an advertisement promotes a small "techno-fix" such as biodegradability or recycling, it is "green" in the weakest sense, not "Green": "It requires no political or social reform, and even the responsibility for the behavior is shifted from the producer, who should be responsible, to the consumer."[24] The hidden message is still that "consuming is good, more is better, and the ecological cost is minimal." If the company goes a step further, advocating conserving or preserving resources for the future, that represents a second level. But even though such an ad recognizes finite resources and the needs of future generations, it still views the environment purely as a resource, not as possessing intrinsic, non-economic value. The researcher concluded that from a purely eco-logical position, a truly Green ad is indeed an oxymoron: "the only Green product is the one that is not produced."[25] Others have argued that a truly green economy would require all products to be audited and analyzed from cradle to grave for their environmental effects.[26]

Another problematic piece of the green phenomenon is the abil-ity of consumers to separate the hype and hyperbole from the genu-ine and interpret the environmental claims. An advertiser can pro-claim "now no animal testing" in its laundry detergent, when in fact there never has been. A label on a plastic container can say "recy-clable," yet fail to mention that virtually no sites in the country can recycle that particular form of plastic. A manufacturer can boast in an advertisement that it reduced smokestack emissions by 80 per-cent, when actually it took steps only after being fined and forced to comply by law. When Mobil claimed that its Hefty trash bags were biodegradable, did that mean the bags would turn into soil in a landfill? If an ad for aerosol cleaner says it's "ozone friendly," does that mean there's nothing in it that will hurt the ozone layer? When Standard Oil of California boasted that a Chevron gasoline additive produced "pollution free" exhaust, does that imply that cars using this gas emit nothing harmful? This is why regulatory agencies and the courts get involved in green ads.

The green claims made in advertising range from the general ("environmentally friendly" and "safe for the environment") to the specific ("biodegradable," "recyclable" or "recycled," and "energy ef-ficient"). The products challenged most frequently for their claims are aerosol and plastic products. In the case of Hefty and other trash bags, the FTC was concerned that the claim of "biodegradable" was not adequately qualified. A biodegradable material can be broken down by natural processes into pieces small enough to be consumed by micro-organisms in soil. Even if such a plastic were developed, it is extremely unlikely that it would so degrade when buried in a landfill. The FTC and other regulatory bodies have also objected to claims about ozone. Labeling a product "CFC free" implies that this is unique, when in fact the use of CFCs has been banned since 1982. Calling a product "ozone friendly" does not mean it does not contain some other ozone-depleting chemicals.

Despite the involvement of regulatory and legal bodies, deception and errors of omission are still present in the majority of green ads.[27] There also is evidence of hype and half-truths in green advertising. In one study, researchers concluded that only 40 percent of the ads were unambiguously true, while 42 percent of the claims were vague and ambiguous, and 18 percent were either outright lies or errors of omission.[28] In the Chevron example, the gas additive did reduce *visible* pollutants, but the pollutants that are *invisible* to human eye are the more harmful ones,[29] so the claim of "pollution free" exhaust could be considered deceptive and misleading.

Green advertising will never be free of misleading statements. As mentioned earlier, "truth in advertising" does not apply to advocacy ads because they are classified as expressions of political beliefs and are considered free speech and remain totally unregulated. Green image ads are particularly subject to half-truths. For example, Arco launched a "clean" gas campaign in California with the slogan "Let's drive away smog."[30] (Advocacy ads are discussed further in chapter 9.)

The final piece of green ad claims has to do with the fine line between what we consider "persuasion" and "propaganda" (See Box 6.1).

## The Business of Advertising

Advertisements are nothing new to this century or previous ones. There are plentiful examples in literature, including the works of Shakespeare, that peddlers and sellers have long enticed buyers by advertising (in print or orally) a good's attributes and associated meanings. But it was after World War II that advertising found a firm place in the worldview of Americans. Corporate capital, big government, and professional experts pushed practices of a throwaway affluent society onto consumers after 1945 as a purposely political strategy to sustain economic growth, forestall mass discontent, and empower scientific authority.[31] Revitalized mass production needed a mass market, and a burgeoning advertising industry was ready to let consumers know what goods were available. To help in the dissemination of consumer information, a new type of daytime entertainment called the "soap opera" was created for the relatively recent phenomenon of television. These daytime dramas were created for the sole purpose of delivering an audience of homemakers to eager manufacturers of soap and other household products. Advertisers realized that advertising on soap operas would help to establish "branding," or creating differing values for what are essentially common, interchangeable goods like soap.

Essentially, advertising was viewed as fuel that would help keep a capitalist economy burning. Capitalism is a market system that measures its success by constant growth, such as the gross national product and housing starts. You might even say that advertising developed as the culture that would help solve what some economists view as the central problem of capitalism: the distribution of surplus goods.[32] One sociologist concluded that "Advertising is capitalism's way of saying 'I love you' to itself."[33] In a capitalist economy, advertising is a vital handmaiden to consumption and materialism. In the words of the author of *Adcult*, Americans ". . . are not too materialistic. We are not materialistic enough."[34]

The development of mass media, particularly radio and TV, played an important role in delivering audiences to advertisers. By the mid-1980s, half of U.S. homes had cable, and the drastically increased number of channels allowed advertisers to target more specific audience segments. Today, the Internet has great potential to further fragment and change the media audience. Since the widespread adoption of TV, societal patterns also have changed dramatically, with increasingly mobile households, greater numbers of working women and single-parent households, and a fading middle class as the rich-poor income gap grows wider.

In the face of such change, advertisers and media programmers engage in a dance to fill each other's needs, each having a vested interest in constructing certain versions of the world and not others. According to one media scholar, "the ad industry affects not just the content of its own campaigns but the very structure and content

## Box 6.1

## Propaganda or Religious Redemption Story?

Say the word "propaganda" and people think bad, evil, even Hitler. But actually, there's a rather fine line between propaganda and the seemingly neutral "persuasion."

> *Persuasion*: An interactive attempt between one known party who is trying to influence or evoke a change in the attitude or behavior of another person or audience. Any changed attitude or action on the part of the recipient is strictly voluntary and is undertaken with the recognition that he/she has access to other information.
>
> *Propaganda*: A deliberate, systematic attempt to shape perceptions and thoughts, and control or change behavior in a way that benefits the propagandist. The desired response is one that furthers the interest of the propagandist, not necessarily the receiver. The propagandist may conceal his/her identity and may try to contain information or discourage the receiver from seeking outside information.

So, propaganda is a one-sided message (like advertising) that may conceal identity (like some kinds of ads), is repetitive (certainly like advertising), is presented in closed environments that lack competing or additional information (generally how ads are presented), and may selectively withhold important information (like an ad that promotes an insecticide's effectiveness without acknowledging its risks). If we take away its label, it's easier to see that propaganda is nothing new; Machiavelli realized centuries ago the importance of withholding some information and selectively combining information.

Without too much of a stretch, the storyline of advertising can be compared to religion. Both invoke themes of sin, guilt, redemption, and rescue, and both present a clear process of transformation. In ads, people testify, give witness, confess

---

of the rest of the media system."[35] At the same time, media decide whether formats and tones of their outlets and programming are acceptable to the audiences that they hope marketers find most attractive. What this means for programming is that the upscale twenty-something audience—the most appealing segment to advertisers but not the most environmentally committed—is represented in more media outlets than older men and women to whom only a small number of highly targeted formats are aimed.

It is precisely the ability of advertisers and media programmers to tell some stories and not others that gives these entities power. "When people read a magazine, watch a TV show, or use any other ad-sponsored medium, they are entering a world that was constructed as

**Box 6.1 continued**

their guilt and shame (about using paper plates or their desires for an expensive car), and the disembodied voice of a narrator delivers redemption . . . in the form of a product.

**Propaganda Devices**

*Testimonial*: Having someone respected (or reviled) say that a product, idea, person, etc. is good or bad, endorsing it. Testimony may be offered by a "common person" or celebrity.

*Bandwagon*: Maintaining that "everybody has one" or "everyone thinks this." This is a compelling device to convince a person to follow the crowd and accept the inevitable.

*Transfer*: Relying on a person of authority or respect to express approval (or disapproval) of something. It is similar to testimonial, but the hope is that the recipient will transfer the qualities of the authority onto the product or company. This device can include a "plain folk" appeal—the authority is "just like you."

*Name calling*: Labeling a product, idea, person, etc. as good or bad in order to make us reject, condemn, or support—without examining the evidence. This device is often emotional and relies on stereotypes.

*Card stacking*: Selecting and using certain facts or falsehoods, or logical or illogical statements in order to present the best or worst possible case. Includes telling just one side of the story or representing one point of view while obscuring or distorting relevant facts.

*Glittering generalities*: Associating something with a "virtue word," which is used to make someone accept or approve of something without examining the evidence. Virtue words include "free speech" and "patriotic."

---

a result of close cooperation between advertisers and media firms."[36] Because all such encounters provide people with insights into parts of their world with which they have little direct contact, media representations of the natural world to a largely urbanized population are highly significant. If we are to believe the worlds portrayed by advertisers, the environment is valued for its use as a pristine playground by the young, but it's not in any danger. Even if a stream is churned to mud by a vehicle in one ad, the following ad returns us to sparkling water for drinking, bathing, or fishing. The idealized environment of advertising and programming is uncomplicated, uncrowded, and uncompromised.

By sheer dollars alone, advertising and programming have more power than other institutions like school and church to promote particular images about our place in society—where we belong, why, how we should act toward others, and how we should treat the natural world. For newspapers and some magazines, at least 50 percent of their revenue is from advertising, and ad support approaches 100 percent for much of radio and television. By some estimates, advertisers spent $27 billion to support TV, $9 billion on radio, $46 billion on daily newspapers, and about $7 billion on consumer magazines.[37]

## Advertising and Education

The business of advertising also has entered the hallowed halls of education. Captive youngsters are a tempting market: more than 43 million kids attend schools and even elementary-age children exert tremendous spending power, about $15 billion a year.[38] Ads cover school buses, book covers, and scoreboards, and corporate flags fly next to school flags. Consumers Union particularly criticized "supplemental educational materials" (SEMs) that are produced by commercial interests, provided free to schools, and often contain biased, self-serving, and promotional information.[39] Another critic noted that in a classroom with SEMs, "American students are introduced to environmental issues as they use materials supplied by corporations who pollute the soil, air, and water. They have good eating habits explained to them by purveyors of junk food."[40] The National Education Association, the National PTA, and Consumers Union argue that commercialism in schools cedes control to those outside education and blurs the lines between education and propaganda.

Consumers Union studied seventy-seven SEMs on a variety of topics, including twenty-one about ecology, environment, and energy. Although these materials are not advertising in the traditional sense, Consumers Union found that half the packets were commercial or highly commercial, and nearly 80 percent contained biased or incomplete information.

So blatantly commercial and biased was one sponsored educational packet—Decision: Earth from Procter & Gamble—that a coalition of environmentalists . . . asked attorneys general in 11 states to investigate the kit's truthfulness. Decision: Earth taught that clear-cut logging is good for the environment ("It mimics nature's way of getting rid of trees") and that disposable diapers are better for the environment than cloth ones. It did not mention that P&G, the country's largest manufacturer of disposable diapers, had financed the study that produced those favorable results.[41]

Consumers Union said of the six SEMs that discussed solid waste issues, five bypassed serious discussion of reducing consumption or reusing products and presented recycling as the main solution to waste disposal. For example, a teacher resource guide from the Aseptic Packaging Council called *Waste Wise* teaches that "drink boxes are easily recycled, but fails to mention that few communities have recycling programs to handle them."[42]

The bulk of in-school commercialism involves products like snack-foods, soft drinks, health and beauty items, and sporting goods. Although pushing such products may seem a step removed from green advertising, it nevertheless reinforces a consumptive-based mentality from a very early age. According to some experts, efforts by advertisers to inculcate consumerism begins as early as age four. Ads encourage kids to become materialistic, giving them a desire for expensive products and teaching them to equate consumption with happiness. While similar appeals are made to adults, experts argue that kids are impressionable and even less capable of sorting fact from fiction. Just like all ads appeal to our anxieties, ads aimed at children play on their insecurities, telling them that if they lack certain products, they're losers.

## The Psychology of Advertising

Because ads appeal to our emotions more than our rational minds, their messages communicate to us at the level of our individual psychological selves. Here we'll discuss how ads use nature to sell products, how ads appeal to our narcissism, how ads depict nature as idealized and sublime, and how the result is a disconnection from nature.

## Nature as a Selling Tool

Have you ever viewed a single advertisement and then rushed out to buy that product? Probably not. That's not the way that advertising generally works on us, especially not for national consumer goods. Advertising scholars argue that ads cannot create, invent, or even satisfy our desires but instead channel and express our desires with the hope of exploiting them.

You may disagree that ads cannot create desires, particularly if you've ever found yourself yearning for a product that six months ago you didn't know existed or that you "needed." But even if ads don't greatly corrupt our immediate buying habits, they can gradually shape our values. As we become increasingly detached from traditional cultural influences, ads become our social guides for what is important and valued.[43] "Advertising works not by its impact on specific individuals but by influencing the social climate in which action takes place. Advertising affects the shared ideas, common understandings and the social meaning of acts."[44] The prominent (though not monopolistic) role of advertising in the symbolic marketplace is what gives advertising "a special cultural power."[45]

In the words of one scholar, "Advertising is simply one of a number of attempts to load objects with meaning . . . it is an ongoing conversation within a culture about the meaning of objects."[46] The rhetorical challenge for an advertiser, then, is to load one particular product (even though numerous similar ones exist) with sufficient meaning so that the product appears able to express a desire. The natural world is full of cultural meaning with which to associate products. By borrowing and adapting well-known, stereotypical portrayals of nature, advertising is able to associate water with freshness and purity, and weather as fraught with danger. If, for example, an ad wants to attach the value of "safety" to one particular car, it might demonstrate the car's ability to dodge "dangerous" elements of nature, such as falling rocks. On the other hand, if the ad wants to convey a truck's durability, it could just as easily attach a very different meaning to the same resource and say the truck is "like a rock." Neither product guarantees that you can buy safety or durability; both product ads merely expressed a consumer desire for them by associating a nonmaterial good with a material one.

Animals in particular provide cultural shorthand for advertising. Animals, as popular symbols of the nonhuman environment, are a way for advertisers to link the perceived "personality" and stereotyped cultural value of the animal to the product.[47] In car advertising alone, ads compare vehicles to rams, eagles, wolves, cougars, falcons, and panthers. Some ads go so far as to portray the vehicle as an animal itself. An individual needs no direct experience with untamed environs to know what an eagle or cougar represents and is valued for. (Animals in advertisements are considered in more depth in the next chapter.)

Even if the original function of advertising was to market simple products like soap, it functions now to market feelings, sensations, and lifestyles.[48] Discrete objects—whether SUVs or detergents—are easier to sell if they're associated with social and personal meaning. The purpose of an ad is not to stress that the product functions properly, but that consumption of it will cure problems,[49] whether loneliness, age, or even a desire to connect with the natural world. Advertising channels our psychological needs and ambitions into consumptive behaviors.[50] The success of the store The Nature Company depends "not so much what nature *is* as what nature *means* to us."[51]

Take for example a series of print and TV ads for a particular SUV that label the vehicle as "the answering machine for the call of wild." The print ad tells us that "nature calls out for us" but with the vehicle's leather-trimmed seats, "civilization's never really that far away." In TV versions, we see the vehicle traveling over rugged terrain (but cannot see the woman driving it) while an answering machine plays numerous messages from a worried mother and boyfriend to this woman driver who has escaped into the wild. The ads give us no reason to believe that the repair record, gas mileage, price, or other important product attributes are somehow superior. Instead, a rugged environment (yet one somehow made safer and more civilized by this SUV) is portrayed as the best place to find peace, and by the way, this vehicle is a good way to get there.

Some scholars insist that advertising appeals primarily to personal dissatisfactions in our lives and insecurities over the ways and pace in which we live, not to our personal needs. In doing so, ads are carriers of anxiety that only serve to alienate us further.[52] In the SUV ads, the driver isn't portrayed as using the vehicle for personal need, but for escape from relationship problems to an environment that is depicted as being free of all problems. The intent of advertising, says one critic,[53] is to preoccupy society with material concerns and to see goods as a path to happiness and a solution to problems.

In many of the appeals of green advertising—particularly in image and nature-as-backdrop ads—the advertisements attempt to associate material goods with nonmaterial qualities that have disappeared from many people's lives, qualities like solitude, wilderness, lush landscapes, free-flowing water, and clean air. In the ad for L.L. Bean in Chapter 4, a man wades across calm, milky blue waters to a small sailboat in early morning light. The caption reads, "Don't mistake a street address for where you actually live." Apparently this man cannot "live" in his everyday life—which we assume takes place is a far less serene setting—but must leave it to achieve qualities it lacks.

### Narcissism in Ads

Another common feature in advertising appeals that employ the natural world is narcissism. The word derives from Narcissus, a youth in Greek mythology who fell in love with his own reflection in a pool. The way in which media portray this universal emotional type is as self-absorbed, self-righteous, and dependent on momentary pleasures of assertion. Narcissism in green advertising often takes the form of outdoor adventure, as in this print ad: two bright red pick-up trucks are parked on an expansive, rolling sand dune. In the open bed of each truck, a young man in a wet suit (through the manipulation of computer graphics) appears to be wind-surfing. Water splashes around them in the air and onto the sand. The caption says the trucks are "built fun tough" and have "gallons of attitude." Of course we know this picture to be "fake" (although a similar juxtaposition of unlikely elements exists in human-made Lake Powell in the middle of the desert), but it tells us that these men are in it for the fun, for the adventure.

A narcissist is most concerned with pleasing his- or herself and may be so self-absorbed as to be oblivious to the harm caused to others, and if we extend the analogy, to the environment. In terms of environmental ideology, a narcissist would be anthropocentric, believing that his or her own outdoor pleasure comes before that of other species and their needs. Ads that show people "conquering" natural elements are expressing me-first anthropocentrism. Our culture is now marked by an exaggerated form of self-awareness and mass narcissism, finely attuned (with the help of advertising) to the many demands of the narcissistic self.[54]

Narcissism in nature-as-backdrop ads is particularly common. The ad described at the beginning of this chapter with the boy taking a crayon short-cut is one example. Yet another truck TV commercial begins in a deserted mountain valley at twilight. Next, a gigantic booted foot with a spur crashes to the ground, reverberating all in sight. We then see that the foot belongs to a cowboy the size of Paul Bunyon. The message is that the human is essentially larger than life, dominating the entire landscape and all within it, as Bunyon did. Such exaggerated domination intentionally positions humans at the top of a pyramid, instead of belonging equally to a biotic community.

## Nature as Sublime

As much as ads intentionally distort reality (like wind-surfing in a pickup in the desert), they also present reality as it should be, a reality that is worth desiring and emulating (and "owning"). If you've ever backpacked or camped, you know that slapping mosquitos, dirty clothes, hiking in the rain, and the smell of sweat are often part of the package. Do you see that kind of "real" outdoor experience depicted in advertisements? Instead, ads subordinate reality to a romanticized past, present, or even future. "Real" in advertising is a cultural construct: "The makers of commercials do not want what is real but what will seem real on film. Artificial rain is better than 'God's rain' because it shows up better on film or tape."[55] There is no intent by advertisers to capture life as it really is, but instead to portray the "ideal" life and to present as normal and everyday what are actually relatively rare moments, such as a phenomenal sunset, a flower-filled alpine meadow, or a mosquito-less lake.

A great many nature-as-backdrop ads present the natural world as sublime, a noble place inspiring awe and admiration. The sublime is a literary and artistic convention that uses a prescribed form

**Figure 6.2**

of language and pictorial elements to describe nature, and which in turn encourages a specific pattern of responses to nature.[56] Artistically, sublime representations can include blurring, exaggeration of detail, and compositional elements such as a foreground, middle ground, and frame. Settings are frequently pastoral or wild with varying amounts of human presence. There is a self-reflexive nature to the positioning, with the observer feeling both within a scene and also outside of it, viewing the scene (and reflexively, the self) from a higher or more distant (and morally outstanding) perspective.

The sublime has been called the founding trope in the rhetoric of environmentalism: "Sublimity has remained a touchstone or grounding for our public conception of nature and, through nature, of the environment."[57] As a conventional linguistic device, the sublime represents our understanding of the natural world. Because the sublime is associated with what is "natural," "the sublime connotes an authenticity and originality that is part of its very meaning; yet like rhetoric itself, it has a long-standing reputation for exaggeration and even falsehood."[58]

In sublime nature, the artificial seamlessly approximates the real. What appears as real rain is artificial, what looks like a natural wildlife encounter is contrived, and what appears entirely wild was created with computer animation and digital manipulation.

The sublime is as much a part of advertising as it is the artistic and literary realms. A host of pharmaceutical ads, for example, enlist nature backdrops as rhetoric for the sublime. One ad for an arthritis medication takes place in a pastoral setting assumed to be a park. The sun is shining, the park is empty except for the actors, there is no litter or noise, and even the dogs are exceedingly friendly and behaved. In another ad for what is presumed to be a mood-enhancer, a woman strolls slowly along a pristine, deserted beach in soft light, a contented smile on her face. In these instances, the sublime backdrop doubly represents the sublime state the person will achieve with the medication. Many of these ads rely so heavily on the power of sublime meaning that the actual type of drug is not stated.

Other commercials depict the ability of products to transform problematic nature into idealized nature. Numerous ads for lawn care products and allergy medications first portray nature in a state of chaos or war, needing to be tamed and brought under control. One TV ad for lawn chemicals literally showed a small army of men and supplies descending from the sky to tame and tackle nature. Some allergy commercials depict the flowers and weeds physically attacking people. But ah, after the product is introduced, unproblematic and peaceful nature returns.

**Figure 6.3**

When humans are introduced into sublime scenes, their representation is also idealized. Just as nature is presented as reality-as-it-should-be, people are presented as-they-should-be in a limited number of social roles. Therefore, people in ads are primarily attractive, young or middle-aged, vibrant, thin, or they are celebrities with those qualities. The environments in which they live, whether inside or outside, are also limited to idealized conditions; no one has dirty houses or unkempt lawns, and no one travels through dirty city streets, encounters polluted rivers, or finds abused landscapes. In the world of advertising, there are no poor people, sick people, few unattractive people, and sometimes no people at all. Most car ads do not show anyone actually driving the vehicle through the tinted windows, and you hear only the disembodied voice of the announcer. The social roles played by advertising actors are easily identifiable—the businessperson, the grandmother, the teenager—but the actors are anonymous as individual people and portray only social roles tailored to specific demographic categories. The flat, abstract, idealized, and sometimes anonymous world of advertising, "is part of a deliberate effort to connect specific products in people's imagination with certain demographic groupings or needs or occasions."[59]

Of course we recognize pieces of this idealized presentation of people and their environments, just like we recognize the utterly impossible pieces—a car parked on a inaccessible cliff or polar bears drinking Coke. We are not stupefied by such depictions of the natural world. In fact we expect it.

## Disconnecting from Nature

Some critics believe that advertising may be more powerful the less people believe it and the less it is acknowledged. According to one sociologist, ads don't ask to be taken literally and don't mean what they say, but "this may be the very center of their power."[60] While we're being exposed to those three thousand ads a day, we may carry an illusion of detachment and think them trivial and unimportant. But according to some theories, it is very possible to "learn" without active involvement, a so-called sleeper effect. This myth of immunity from persuasion may do more to protect our self-respect than help us comprehend the subtleties and implications of their influence.[61] Although we may not think an ad speaks to us, its slogan may suddenly pop into our vocabulary—Where's the beef, Just do it, It does a body good . . . We may be unaware and uninvolved in front of the TV, but the message of the ad may prove important at purchase time, or in gradually changing our habits.

Take the habit of drying your clothes, an activity that for many people throughout the world involves pinning clothes to a line in the backyard or between buildings. Ever since childhood, I've loved sliding between clean sheets dried outside on the clothesline and drinking in the smell. How do many people get that same outside-smell nowadays? With detergents and fabric softeners with names like "mountain air" and "springtime fresh" or similarly scented dryer sheets. Although perceived convenience and affordable dryers no doubt helped change our clothes-drying habits, where did we learn to associate the smell of outdoors with purchased products? Advertising.

The message in these product ads is that the artificial smell is somehow easier or superior or even just equivalent to the real smell in the natural world. It not only appropriates something of value from the natural world, it gradually disconnects us from that thing of value. The more successfully ads teach us to associate natural qualities like fresh air with products, the more disconnected we become from what was originally valued. If advertising tells us that nonsaleable qualities of the outdoors like fresh air and natural smells are easy to bring inside, need we worry about the condition of the real world? Advertising does more than merely stimulate wants; it plays a subtle role in changing habits.[62]

Just as advertising can change habits, it can help create rituals and taboos. A good example of a taboo largely created by advertising is litter. Through national advertising campaigns begun decades ago, litter was labeled as an environmental no-no. While cleaning up litter makes for a visually appealing environment, the automobiles from which the trash is generally tossed cause far more environmental harm than most all types of litter.

Advertising also works to create rituals. A ritual begins when we make inert, prosaic objects meaningful and give them symbolic significance. Mistletoe means little to us as a parasitic evergreen, but it is loaded with significance as a holiday ritual about kissing. Whales mean more to us as communicative, spiritual symbols of the deep than for their inherent value and place in ocean ecosystems. Native American fetishes and baskets, which have been ritualized by nonnative populations (and appropriated by advertising), "associate nature nearly interchangeably with indigenous peoples."[63] In a similar way, once a species or animal has been so ritualized, it precludes a more complete and accurate knowing of it.

Advertising, directly and subtly, idealizes and materializes a way of experiencing the world, including the natural world. It promotes products as the simple solutions to complex dilemmas by tapping into our dissatisfactions and desires. If you feel disconnected from the natural world, you can "solve" that with mountain-scented laundry products, bear fetishes, and whale audiotapes, but these purchases only increase the estrangement. If you need to escape modern life yet want to feel safe and civilized while doing so, you can simply solve that by taking a rugged SUV into "wilderness."

Yet environmental dilemmas are anything but simple, and water is a good example. We see it babbling down brooks in beverage commercials, refreshing someone in a soap commercial, quenching thirst in ads for water filters and bottled water. Pure, clean, healthy—but simple? More than half the world's rivers are polluted or drying up. Political and legal fights are waged over dams, diversions, and water rights.

### Psychological Elements Working Together

Here is a TV ad that is a great example of how these elements come together in a seamless and powerful way. First, the visual: a waterfall flows over the driver's seat of a car and a tiny kayaker spills down the face of the falls. The scene quickly shifts to the kayaker (full-sized now and paddling away from us) amid glaciers. The next scene takes us into the car's back cargo area—still covered with water—and two orca whales breach in front of the kayaker, who pauses midstroke. (In all of these shots, we have never seen the kayaker's face; when he paddles away, his head is covered by a fur-lined parka hood that looks "native.") The next shot is a close-up of a paddle dipping into sunset-filled water above the words "Discover Chevy Tahoe." The last scene shows the unoccupied vehicle parked on the edge of a stream in front of snow-covered mountain peaks. The accompanying audio includes Native American drum beats and a mixed chorus singing a chantlike, non-English song. Over this audio, we hear the voice of a male announcer who quotes a passage from John Muir about how one needs silence to get into the heart of the wilderness, away from dust, hotels, baggage, and chatter.

The meanings that these elements convey are multiple: peace, serenity, at-one with nature, and a return to a simple "native" existence are part of the promise of this vehicle. Native drums, whales, glaciers, paddling through still waters, and even the deep ecologist

Muir are powerful, idealized, and ritualized symbols that are employed to market a feeling and a sensation. The seamless juxtaposition of scenes both inside and outside the vehicle conveys that nature is transported effortlessly for you to experience these things directly, without leaving the safety and luxury of your car. The vehicle is the commodity enabling your escape to this sublime place, a place depicted as both real yet entirely contrived, with kayakers spilling over car seats. The entire promise is one of self-gratification, helping the driver/kayaker travel to this idealized wilderness. Yet, if you truly want to heed John Muir's advice, silence is needed to get into the heart of the wilderness, not a noisy car. Hence if you "buy into" the vehicle being the solution, the result is further estrangement from the very thing desired and valued.

## Conclusion

Advertising, as a primary support system for a capitalist economy, can only transfer meaning and express latent desires—not deliver on any of these promises. Ads may invoke public values of family, friendship, and a common planet, but these values are put to work to sell private goods, a very capitalist principle. The satisfaction derived from these goods, even those that seem inherently collective like water, is invariably private. What this encourages is "the promotion of a social order in which people are encouraged to think of themselves and their private worlds,"[64] a very anthropocentric and narcissistic perspective. The environment, in many respects, doesn't work well as private space.

For advertising to wield power, it must exist in concert with other social institutions in a way that is mutually reinforcing. Advertising is layered within our culture and bound up with other institutions, from news media and popular culture to corporate America and manufacturing. Each element continually leaks into each other (referred to as *heteroglossic*), with advertising slogans showing up in casual conversation and political speeches. The very ubiquitousness of advertising—extending beyond regular media buys to include placing products in movies, sponsoring sporting events, and the full-length "infomercial"—ensures its power and influence in numerous places and institutions.

Advertising has played an enormous role in instilling a materialistic, consumer way of life (beginning as early as age four). Although we have a sense that "nature" somehow *counters* consumerism and is able to function as antonym and antidote to materialism,[65] it functions quite differently in advertising. Like the old ad slogan of Prudential Insurance, we're told that we *can* indeed own a piece of the rock—if we have the right vehicle and the right shoe to get us there, and the right lip balm and Global Positioning System. As one academic asked, "Is it possible that people in our culture have become so estranged from nature that their only avenue to it is consumerism?"[66]

As scholars argue, ads never intend solely to sell a product, but to sell you a *meaning* associated with it. The meaning conveyed by ads for antigreen products like throw-away plastic containers is likewise anthropocentric and narcissistic; human convenience is the most important factor, and resource use is trivial. Even ads with obviously surreal or fictitious elements that don't ask to be taken literally still convey meaning about the natural world, which may be the very center of their power.

If we're exposed to three thousand ads per day—even if we only react to a dozen—a lifetime of exposure means that it's virtually impossible to remain detached, immune, and oblivious to the portrayal of a nature from which we're increasingly detached.

# 7

# Communicating the Meaning of Animals

In southern Utah, the gift shops are full of animal symbols: howling coyotes on kerchiefs, lizards on key chains, roadrunners on T-shirts, and rubber rattlesnakes. Shops in western Wyoming sell elk refrigerator magnets and belt buckles, bear light-switch plates, moose coffee mugs, lamps with antelope dancing around the base. Area restaurants and businesses, too, sport animal themes. Although physical features sometimes represent these states (the red-rock Delicate Arch is pictured on a Utah state license plate and the Teton Mountains frequently symbolize western Wyoming), animals are more frequent and prominent place-markers.

So why do lizards "mean" southern Utah and elk western Wyoming? These particular animals are not geographically endemic to these states; elk and bears live in Utah and lizards, rattlesnakes, and coyotes are found in Wyoming. How it is that select animals have been chosen to serve as symbols of these locations? What do these products communicate—not just about the animals, but about certain natural environments and how we live in them?

These animal messages were brought to you by the pop culture industry, whose job it is to create, disseminate, and sell meaning. In this case, they are not selling you a moose, but what a moose means to you—the characteristics and qualities that you and most people associate with the species *Alces alces*.

If you think your attitudes about animals are free from pop culture influences, look around your house for animal images in artwork, clothing, jewelry, even the name of your car or favorite sports team. Look through your books and videos—or better yet, through

**Figure 7.1**

some kids' books and videos—to see what animals are featured. Next, complete the following phrases:

Sly as a _____
Eyes like an _____
An eager _____

Wiley _____
Stubborn as a _____

It's impossible to divorce pop culture messages from your preconceived notions of what animals are like, especially if you don't have sufficient personal experience and knowledge to bring to the table. Many a person expects the lion at the zoo to act more like the "king of the jungle" than the lethargic beast dozing in its cage. Every year, tourists get injured while approaching wild animals, expecting them to be as tame or at least as harmless as they've observed in nonwild settings. As a child, I loved roadrunner cartoons; twenty years later I saw my first wild roadrunner and he didn't give what I thought was his characteristic "beep beep!" before zooming away. I was, frankly, a bit disappointed.

Of course, many animal representations we put into our houses and on our clothes we've never seen in their native wild habitat. So where did we first become acquainted with them? It's likely that you saw the movie *Bambi* before you ever saw a deer in the wild. Like most children, you also read about the Big Bad Wolf and about that little blonde girl's encounter with a "family" of three bears. Most likely the only place you've encountered the animals from the movie *The Lion King* was at the zoo. As an adult, you continue to encounter pop culture animal representations, whether it's while shopping, at the movies, or from that frog croaking in the beer commercial.

Much as we might want to understand animals at a level deeper than pop culture, we can only understand them in terms of our own experiences, language, and emotions, and interpreted within our social, historical, and cultural contexts. The only way we have of understanding animals is to recognize that "when we gaze at animals, we hold up a mirror to ourselves."[1] This chapter attempts to be that mirror and investigate how the images we see and words we read influence the way we talk, think, and communicate about animals and what they mean to us.

For centuries, the lives of animals and humans have been inextricably intertwined. Until fairly recently, animals were at the center of our world.[2] Our language is saturated with their presence and continues to employ them for expression. Animals have been captured figuratively in paintings (including on the earliest cave walls) and captured literally in zoos. Throughout history, we have struggled against animals, but at the same time, they have helped us survive, worked for us, protected us, and fed us. Animals have been deities for us to worship, demons to fear, and our teachers in myths and fables. And of course, they have been our friends and companions. Today, animals remain a fundamental part of our emotional lives and everyday existence. The human-animal relationship is like no other.

In the broadest possible sense, "animal" can include insects, reptiles, birds, amphibians, and of course mammals. Although there are several million species on earth, most of us can name only a few dozen mammals or birds, and probably even fewer insects. Yet, unglamorous invertebrates (lacking vertebrae or backbones) account for about 98 percent of all animal life.

Likewise, "wild" animals comprise the largest category of animals and are far more numerous than the kinds of domesticated animals and pets living near us. We think of a "wild" animal as the opposite of tamed or domesticated. But "wild" is a *cultural* label, not a zoological classification, just as "weed" is a cultural label for a plant that we don't like and consider invasive.

"Wild" also implies location; that is, wild animals don't (or shouldn't) live where we do. At least for urban dwellers, there are invisible boundaries between where we live and where wild animals are "supposed" to live.

"Wild" also implies character. When an animal is not closely linked to humans or subject to their control, "wild" is often taken to mean "dangerous."[3] Even if a wild animal poses no significant threat, the sort of killing that animal engages in might lead us to think it wild or dangerous. One zookeeper called this the "bite-sized theory of eating live food";[4] people are okay seeing an animal kill another creature if the prey can be eaten quickly in one small bite, such as an insect, mouse, or small fish.

## Animals as Symbols and Shorthand

If an environmental group wanted to visually depict the untamed and pristine nature of a threatened Canadian forest, what animal might the group choose to represent that? If a car maker wanted to represent the toughness of its cars, what animal's characteristics say that? Based on common meanings presented to us from an early age, animals are the perfect shorthand communication symbol. We use animals as devices, metaphors, and symbols for a great deal of our expression and ideas.[5]

Advertising very much appreciates the symbolic power of different species. The car is named Jaguar because this creature is viewed as sleek, dark, fast, mysterious, exotic, and sensual. Sports teams called Cougars, Badgers, Timberwolves, Rams, and Colts strive to perform like the best of these species. As an advertising icon, the bald eagle must perform double-duty, serving as both a symbol of American freedom and pride, and representing the natural beauty and abundance of the habitat in which it resides. American Airlines and the U.S. Postal Service (which have both used our national bird as their symbol) also want us to equate soaring and speed with the eagle.

In addition to relying on animals' physical characteristics or abilities, we attribute certain feelings and motives to certain animals. According to some, the wolf is a dark, malevolent sexual symbol,[6] and some cats (tiger, cheetah, and even house cats) are considered female sexual symbols. We assume that coyotes are chicanery personified and raccoons have thievery in mind.

Animals also serve as symbolic messengers for human values. In a random sample of 150 preschool books, over 91 percent had animal characters.[7] These animals were essentially disguised humans who expressed a variety of psycho-social issues and dilemmas that humans face. In a book my nephew enjoys, two small chimps stray from their mother at the town market, only to be carried away by elephants and then left adrift in a basket floating down a river. The very human message: don't stray from your mom at the store or bad things will happen to you.

Animals are equally important symbolic shorthand for environmental issues. Over the decades, environmental groups have used grizzly bears, wolves, spotted owls, and other critters to represent pristine places in need of protection, and to raise funds to use in that protection. Symbols of marine protection have included whales ("Save the Whale"), harp seal pups, dolphins, and manatees. International conservation symbols are the panda, tiger, and the megafauna of Africa, such as the elephant, lion, giraffe, and others. Even the little snail darter was a symbol of the Endangered Species Act and the value of all creatures, no matter the size.

For many people, animals are the most tangible element of the larger environment and environmental issues; they may not care what happens to faraway forests, but they seem to care about the lynx living there. It makes sense that we tend to identify most closely with the living, breathing components of the natural world. Visually, animals are concrete, picturable, and evoking of emotion. It's easier to reduce a complex environmental issue—such as climate change in the Arctic—to a story about the polar bears living there.

According to professor Stephen Kellert, who has studied public perceptions of animals for decades, "animals may represent a metaphorical device for people to express basic perceptions and feelings about the nonhuman world. As the most sentient and evident characteristic of the natural world, animals often function as a symbolic barometer of people's fundamental beliefs and valuations of nature. Additionally, most discussions of animal species lead to considerations of natural habitat and, as a consequence, wildlife issues often become basic land-use questions."[8] For decades, land managers have recognized that "wildlife management" is more accurately a problem of human management and the negotiation of human values.

### Why Do Animals Matter to Us?

Since the average person's daily contact with animals is minimal (outside of a household pet), why do animals matter so much to us and play such an important role in our culture? It may be as simple as our need for "the other,"[9] the need for some creature that is a counter to human culture, something beyond the domain of our own activities, things, and lives. Perhaps we need a sense of wonder or astonishment that our own products and culture cannot supply.

Think of how thrilling it is to see an animal up close in the wild. Whether it is a moose in a national park, an eagle alongside a river, or a beautiful bird at the backyard feeder, it's exhilarating to feel as though you share space with this creature, that there is little separating you from it. For a moment, there is no gulf between nature and culture. If you're like many people, you may have tried to "capture" the creature on film to try and preserve that moment with the other.

Close contact with animals is also meaningful as a chance to move into the animals' environment, a domain in which they move confidently and "know their way about." In their natural habitat, animals have a place that has meaning for them. According to one scholar, the ties that people have to our own "field of significance" have eroded in modern times, and we often lack an environment where we similarly move confidently and which holds meaning for us.[10] When place-differences are leveled out and we encounter the same supermarkets, the same TV programs, and the same restaurants no matter where we are, it's all just a domain that's interchangeable and not tied to the landscape or its particular creatures. It's as though we are adrift in standardized physical spaces where we feel out-of-place, superfluous, nonintegral, like foreign visitors. Perhaps this is part of what we admire or envy about animals, particularly wild ones—their complete possession of an environment and the ease of movement and activity within it:

> As a living symbol of possession of an environment, the animal represents the antithesis of the technological artificiality of our present condition. More often than not, it belongs in a small and simple community where each creature has a natural place and role; absorbed in its environment, it is incapable of that ironic distance which we are increasingly incapable of closing; it fits itself into the rhythms of its life and the seasons, instead of endeavoring as we do to level them out; and its world is one, unlike our own, where things and other creatures have a consolingly stable significance and value.[11]

For all their symbolic value, animals do indeed possess enviable skills and abilities that greatly surpass our own. The eyes of the eagle are many times more powerful than ours, and the grasp of a hawk's talons is stronger than a human's grip. Elephants are able to hear (and make) sounds far below the audible hearing range of humans. True hibernators are able to slow their bodily functions to a near-deathlike state. "Animals, indeed, afford us symbols, reminders, of something worthwhile—of a life congruent with the ancient ideal of integration with the environment. . . . [T]he lives they symbolize—lead, indeed—are to be admired."[12]

## Predators

There are some animals, however, that historically have not evoked our admiration. Consider these phrases:

*Wolf down your food.*
*Cry wolf.*
*Thrown to the wolves.*
*A wolf at the door.*
*Wolf whistle.*
*A wolf in sheep's clothing.*

These phrases do not communicate flattering things when used to describe humans. A person called one of these things could be gluttonous, not credible, condemned, a debtor, manipulative, and preylike if so whistled at. When a murderer or rapist is called "an animal," the picture evoked is usually a predator (such as a wolf) with despicable or sadistic behavior, even when the offending behavior is distinctly human.

Canis lupus carries with it the cultural baggage of centuries of ill treatment at the hands of humans, and much of it is based on the erroneous notion that wolves harm humans. In most cases, it's just the *idea* of a predator that's terrifying, an idea not warranted by the verified habits of actual animals.[13] The research on wild North American wolves strongly suggests that they simply do not attack humans, even when provoked.[14]

So why do wolves and other predators get such a bad rap? Is it just an overreaction to or misunderstanding of predators? Is it a historical perception that we're competing with them for the same resources? Or do predators evoke our most deeply held myths that the "wilds" are dangerous and animals within them must be controlled?

As you might imagine, there is a telling history of our attitudes toward predators. In medieval Europe, a belief in werewolves was widespread, and the wolf was a symbol of greed and evil. The wolf in the German folk tale Little Red Riding Hood is sinister and conniving. Even after the evolutionary link between animals and humans was established, some species were still considered unmoral and degenerate, and "guilty" animals needed to be brought to justice. "Because ethics were defined in terms of man, those animals who did not live by human principles were condemned."[15]

William T. Hornaday, an early director of the New York Zoological Park, proclaimed that no wild creatures were "more despicable than wolves" which were black-hearted murderers and criminals.[16] Even Theodore Roosevelt—ardent conservationist and big game hunter—said the wolf was "the beast of waste and desolation" and a vicious, bloodthirsty creature.

Competition for resources was part of the ascription of such evil, though early in the 1900s the abundance of deer and other prey was undeniable. The attitudes of competition held by white settlers were not held by Native Americans and Eskimos who didn't mind sharing game and who attributed the wolf with many positive qualities, such as intelligence, boldness, and skill.[17]

Wolves were not the only predators who received condemnation. Coyotes and cougars were similarly despised. General popular sentiment was that coyotes were slinking, sneaking, skulking, crafty, cowardly, piratical, cruel, and cunning; Native Americans, however, thought of coyote as a good-natured trickster. In 1915, the respected journal *Scientific American* called the cougar "a brutal murderer" that victimizes "harmless, beautiful animals." Director Hornaday called the cougar an "intolerable pest."[18]

Even small predators didn't escape disdain. Weasels were called cruel, remorseless, and wicked; wolverines were devilish; and snakes were deserving of death. Meat-eating birds were viewed with derision; Hornaday said all hawks should be "at once put under sentence of death for their destructiveness of useful birds."[19]

By calling predators wicked and devilish, these animals were judged according to human standards for something that humans do as well: kill prey. Some early humanitarians and vegetarians linked base savagery (in people as well as in animals) to a meat diet. They believed that people needed to "work out the beast" within them. The ethical relations they sought favored the rights of individual animals and utilized religious justification: "Humanitarians had retained the religious conviction that strife in nature was the result of human sin and would one day be amended. Eventually, the lion and the lamb could live side-by-side in peace, as prophesied in Isaiah 11:6–10. . . . Whether condemning predators or attempting to reform them, animal lovers of the late 19th and early 20th centuries were constructing their version of the peaceable kingdom."[20]

Whether based on a German fairy tale or religious doctrine, these stories about predators make up what author and journalist Mark

Trahant calls "master narratives," the stories that make up the human version of our software code. He wrote, "These stories are recorded deep in our brains, our souls, teaching us how to think, act,
and participate in society."[21] It also appears that our environmental
ideology in general influences our sentiments toward predators and
the master narratives we carry. In one study, there was a positive association between anthropocentrism and negative attitudes toward
carnivores, and conversely between ecocentrism and positive attitudes toward carnivores.[22]

How these master narratives played out in the United States was
as a full-scale war against predators. The Bureau of Biological Survey
was established in 1905; in its first two years alone, it killed 1,800
wolves and 23,000 coyotes on national forest land. At first, the public was either indifferent or very supportive of the program. During
the 1920s, the Bureau was poisoning 35,000 coyotes *per year*. The
National Park Service participated as well, killing bears, wolves, coyotes, and cougars on its lands. The policy, which wasn't questioned
by the Park Service until the 1930s, assumed that the protection of
desirable wildlife involved control of carnivores. Even the Audubon
Society killed predatory birds (such as hawks and owls) in its sanctu-
aries. Private citizens also were encouraged by the Biological Survey
to participate in predator killing with the sentiment that you could
enjoy hunting and help your country at the same time.

Killing predators was financially lucrative because of government
bounties paid for predators' hides. Part of the reason for highly exaggerated bad deeds of wolves was the bounty system: "Wolves did take
their share of livestock, especially when human activities displaced
or destroyed their natural prey, but because they were the most easily identified cause of the losses, they got more than their share of
the blame. The clamor to compensate livestock owners gave rise to
a bounty system, and the need to rally political support for such a
system led to exaggerations of danger and losses."[23]

People very much believed that survival, particularly in the West,
was an either-or proposition regarding predators: "Either wolves or
cows. Either civilization or nature. Either a frontier West or a new
West. These narratives surface again and again in Western history."[24]

It wasn't until the late 1930s and '40s that any real critics of predator policies came forth. Well-known biologists Olaus and Adolph

Murie, who had studied the wolves of Mt. McKinley (now called Denali), argued that predators were necessary to well-functioning natural systems.

Gradually, some predators were remade in a human image, an image that any predator could be tamed and made accessible to humans if the animals followed human standards for good behavior. One such predator was the bear. The myth of Grizzly Adams (who was a real person by the name of John Capen who lived in the mid-1800s) was that even the most dangerous animal could be tamed and made into a pet. The Forest Service icon Smokey Bear was dressed up in human clothes and spoke English. Bear policies in national parks followed a similar bear-friendly philosophy; Yellowstone rangers used garbage to lure black bears to gathering points for the amusement of tourists. The tourists loved the bears, with their humanlike features and humorous antics. The Yellowstone bear dumps were eventually closed, and federal land managers now "dispose of" problem bears; animals are still required to act peaceably by human standards, and in the case of a conflict, the interests of humans come first.

Additional scientific studies and pop culture messages increased public understanding of wolves. Studies of Lake Superior's Isle Royal wolves began in 1957, followed by the comprehensive ecological and behavioral book *The Wolf* by renowned wolf researcher David Mech.[25] *Never Cry Wolf* was written by Canadian government biologist Farley Mowat about his stay in the Canadian wilderness.[26] He was sent to find out whether the decline of caribou herds was due to wolves; he found instead that wanton caribou slaughter by humans was to blame for their decline. In his book, which was later made into a popular movie, Mowat humanized wolves and depicted them as gentle, compassionate creatures. Biologist Aldo Leopold (*Sand County Almanac*) advocated the return of wolves. Barry Lopez's *Of Wolves and Men* also became a popular book. (Of course later, the movie *Dances with Wolves* starring Kevin Costner and various TV documentaries contributed to the wolf's shifting image.)

Most of these writers, however, still "found it necessary to impart human qualities to animals" in their attempts to remake attitudes. In essence, they argued that wolves deserved protection *because* they were useful, good, and compassionate. Many predators still "could not be defended on their own terms; to avoid condemnation they were required to act like well-behaved humans."[27]

Urbanization may have been one factor in changing attitudes toward wolves: "A century ago, when we wanted all wolves gone forever, seven out of 10 Americans lived in rural areas; now, 80 percent of all Americans live in or near metropolitan areas."[28] By the early 1970s, the Endangered Species Act was passed and the Nixon administration banned the use of poison for predator control (although to this day, ranchers and farmers can obtain it with restrictions). But, for the next twenty-five years, efforts by the U.S. Fish and Wildlife Service to study and bring back wolves were thwarted by politics, ranchers, sportsmen's groups, and others.

Since the 1970s, more and more Americans have been seeking to preserve places that reflect what they perceive as once "perfect" states of nature, a perfect state that includes the presence of free-roaming wolves. While the idea appeals to urban dwellers who want the chance to see or hear wolves, the idea is very threatening for those still living the Old West story of ranching and farming and who fear wolves will endanger their lifestyles and hurt them economically.[29]

In 1993 under President Bill Clinton and Interior Secretary Bruce Babbitt, an environmental impact statement for wolf reintroduction was finally prepared. Two years later, wolves captured in Canada were released, thirty-one in Yellowstone and thirty-five in central Idaho. Parallel restoration was underway in Minnesota, and wolf packs eventually spread to Michigan and Wisconsin. The reintroduction has surpassed expectations: four thousand wolves now live in lower forty-eight states, seven hundred of them in Idaho, Montana, and Wyoming.[30]

But more favorable attitudes toward animals can nevertheless lead to significant misperceptions of them, and this may be contributing to the a new mythology about wolves. According to some, this mythology holds that wolves can do no wrong and even denies that wolves kill and eat livestock.

But lest you think that predators are now beloved and appreciated or at least protected, the federal government still engages in a significant predator control program. The killing of predators once undertaken by the Biological Survey was handed in 1931 to a new division in the U.S. Department of Agriculture, Animal Damage Control (ADC), which recently changed its name to the more politically acceptable Wildlife Services and still kills thousands of predators each year.

## Box 7.1

### "Kill a Varmint, Help a Kid"

In a southern, conservative Utah county, the first Varmint Hunt was held Thanksgiving weekend in 2003 to benefit the "Shop with a Cop" program. The program, which provides Christmas presents for needy children, sent out this public service announcement: "Hey all you hunters!!!! Wiley Coyote's family, Rusty Raccoon's friends, and Pepe and Suzie LePew's young'uns have taken over our domain." The entry fee for the hunt was $15 (or two people for $25) and the targeted species were coyotes, red foxes, raccoons, and skunks, none of them protected species in Utah (meaning they can be shot without any sort of license and without bag limits). Official sponsors were the Utah Farm Bureau, the Cattlemen's Association, the Woolgrower's Association, and Sportsmen for Fish & Wildlife. In a newspaper article in the *Salt Lake Tribune* in northern Utah, one critic said the hunt demonstrated a crude and troubling mentality. She said we should teach people to coexist peacefully, and said instead of killing raccoons in her garden, she put up fence and planted things not attractive to animals.

The results of the Varmint Hunt: one coyote killed, and $2,500 raised. About one hundred people registered. Wildlife officials also reported thirteen violations: spotlighting (using artificial light to locate animals at night), shooting across a road, and carrying loaded guns in vehicles.

Sources: Brent Prettyman, "Kill a Varmint, Help a Kid," *Salt Lake Tribune* (Nov. 11, 2003), A1; Brent Prettyman, "Coyote Dropped, $2,500 Raised," *Salt Lake Tribune* (Dec. 3, 2003), C1.

As the "Kill a Varmint" article demonstrates (Box 7.1), negative sentiments toward predators very much remain. The editorial "Killing Cougar for Deer" (Box 7.2) shows that even if significant public sentiment questions current predator control policies and values the place of predators in the natural cycle, state game departments still hold the upper hand in decision-making regarding the populations of animals that happen to eat other animals.

### Attitudes toward Animals

The way people feel about animals is naturally a subjective evaluation, one that often bears little relation to actual contact or experience. We like elephants and dislike weasels though we've never "met" them. Why then are these feelings important? Because "the destiny of many animals will depend on people's subjective feelings toward particular species."[31]

**Box 7.2**

**"Killing Cougar for Deer"**

An editorial appeared in the *Salt Lake Tribune* on August 17, 2003, after the Utah Department of Wildlife Resources increased the number of cougar permits from four to five hundred, of a roughly estimated statewide population of three thousand. It said in part:

> Utah deer herds are declining, and cougars are taking the rap. . . . This sacrifice of a magnificent predator is misguided, particularly because so little is known about the cougar, its numbers in Utah, and its direct effect on the deer population. . . . [T]his debate is about financial resources as much as wildlife resources. The DWR derives much of its revenue from deer hunting licenses. . . . The trouble with all this is that humankind is not very good at playing God. When deer are managed as a cash crop—there are more mule deer in Utah now than when the pioneers arrived—this skews the way other critters are treated. . . . If more cougars are killed, coyotes and other predators will be affected, too. The whole ecosystem gets nudged in one direction or the other.

*Perceptions of Animals*

For several decades, professor Stephen Kellert at Yale University has studied public attitudes and perceptions of animals.[32] Through extensive public surveys, he has identified the most common ways we feel about animals, and how that differs by demographic factors. Table 7.1 presents the attitude categories he developed.

In a national sample of over three thousand adults, by far the most prevalent attitude orientations toward animals were the first four: humanistic, neutralistic/negativistic, moralistic, and utilitarian. Interestingly, we either like individual animals such as pets and are concerned with the way they're treated, or we avoid them, or we see them for their usefulness. The least common perceptions were scientistic and dominionistic. Overall, there was a relative disinterest in and lack of affection for animals among the least educated. College-educated respondents were more protective, emotionally attached, actively involved, and factually informed about animals.

The survey also found interesting regional differences. Alaska residents expressed the strongest wildlife interest, concern, and appreciation. Individuals in Western states generally had greater wildlife appreciation and knowledge. Respondents from the South had

**Table 7.1**

**Value Orientations toward Animals**

| | |
|---|---|
| 1. Humanistic | Interest and strong affection for individual animals, especially pets |
| 2. Neutralistic / negativistic | Passive avoidance of animals due to indifference, or active avoidance of animals due to dislike or fear |
| 3. Moralistic | Concern for right/wrong treatment, oppose cruelty and exploitation |
| 4. Utilitarian | Practical and material value of animals or animal's habitat |
| 5. Naturalistic | Interest and affection for wildlife and the outdoors |
| 6. Ecologistic | Concern for environment as system, interrelationships between wildlife and habitats |
| 7. Dominionistic | Interest in mastery, control of wildlife primarily in sporting situations |
| 8. Scientistic | Interest in physical attributes and biological functioning of animals |

Source: Adapted from Kellert, "Affective, Cognitive, and Evaluative Perceptions of Animals," in *Behavior and the Natural Environment*, eds. Irwin Altman and Joachim Wohlwill (New York: Plenum Press, 1983).

the least interest and concern for animals and the most utilitarian attitudes.

Those who rated the naturalistic, ecologistic, and moralistic attitude orientations highest had a college education or beyond, lived along the Pacific Coast, and were less than thirty-five years old. People identifying with the humanistic attitude were less than twenty-five, Pacific Coast residents, and included more females; those rating humanistic the lowest were farmers, rural residents, and those older than sixty-five. Scientistic orientations belonged most to the highly educated, young, and Alaska residents. A utilitarian orientation toward animals was mentioned most often by farmers, the elderly, and Southern residents; also identifying with this orientation were livestock producers, meat hunters, fishermen, and animal-activity group members. Those choosing "dominionistic" were farmers, males, individuals with high incomes, trappers, and hunters. Finally, respondents who most identified with the negativistic orientation were elderly, had limited income, and were females.

Professor Kellert also has studied children's attitudes toward animals. Children overall possess very similar orientations as adults.[33] However, there was positive value in direct, participatory contact with animals; children who bird-watched, were in animal-related clubs, and who hunted were more appreciative, concerned, and knowledgeable. Not surprisingly, rural children were more interested in and knowledgeable about animals than urban kids. White children had a far greater knowledge of animals and the natural environment, and black children expressed a greater willingness to subordinate animals.

Kellert's study also found that attitudes toward animals change as children grow. Younger children placed the needs of people over animals and expressed minimal concern for animal protection and little interest in animals, particularly wildlife. According to Kellert, "These results were somewhat surprising, perhaps due to our society's idealization of young children's perceptions of animals. The tendency is to believe that young children have some natural affinity for living creatures, regarding them as little friends or kindred spirits. The results suggest otherwise, as young children were the most exploitive, unfeeling, and uninformed of all children in their attitudes toward animals. . . . These results suggest education efforts among children six to ten years of age might best focus on the affective realm, mainly emphasizing emotional concern and sympathy for animals."[34] By the eleventh grade, children were the ideal age for developing ethical concerns about animals and were more interested in direct contact and recreational enjoyment of wildlife.

### Animal Knowledge

In an opinion poll, you can state your feelings about animals or your fear and dislike of them without knowing much about them. And the general public doesn't know a lot about animals.

In a national sample of adults, Professor Kellert found that respondents were most knowledgeable about animals that harmed people and about domestic wildlife issues that were highly emotional or hazardous to humans.[35] Although people expressed a "bedrock of affection and concern," the American public had an extremely limited knowledge of animals:

> [O]nly 26 percent knew the manatee is not an insect. . . . [J]ust 13 percent knew that raptors are not small rodents. . . . A better but still distressingly low 54 percent knew that veal does not come from lamb, and just 57 percent knew that insects do not have backbones. . . . The public was most knowledgeable on questions concerning animals implicated in human injury, pets, basic characteristics of animals (e.g., "All adult birds have feathers") and domestic animals in general. On the other hand, they were least knowledgeable about invertebrates, taxonomic distinctions (e.g., "Koala bears are not really bears"), and predators.[36]

Those least knowledgeable were people with less than a high school education, respondents older than seventy-five and younger than twenty-five, and those living in cities with more than 1 million residents. Members of animal activity groups scored higher in animal knowledge than the general public. Birdwatchers, nature buffs, and all types of conservation group members had significantly higher scores than did livestock producers, antihunters, and sport and recreational hunters and anglers. Zoo visitors score no higher than nonvisitors in their knowledge of animals.[37] However, another study found that children learned little from visits to the zoo.[38]

The vast gulf between humans and animals is certainly not just American, but it can be considered Western. In contrast, other cultural perspectives (from Native Americans to Australian Aborigines and beyond) perceive continuity between humans and animals, and possess an essential concept of oneness and close alliance. As an example, the well-known totem carving defines and delineates social relationships (between humans and animals) and illustrates a mystical union with animals through common descent. Contrast that with our culture where there exists a strong separation between nature and culture and animals are a distant other.[39]

### Good Animal, Bad Animal

We may feel a "need for the other" on some level, but it seems that we have a very short list of what creatures we want on it. As a class exercise, my students put animals (including insects, birds, amphibians, and reptiles) on two blackboards—one labeled "good" and one "bad." Quickly and with relatively little disagreement, they are able to fill both boards.

In the same national study mentioned above, Professor Kellert asked respondents to rank animals on a seven-point scale, with one representing the animals most liked and seven those most disliked.[40] The rankings (Table 7.2) are similar to what my students create. The two most preferred animals are the dog and horse, and the most liked predator is the eagle. The most favored wild animal is the elephant. People dislike insect pests and animals implicated in physical injury or disease (like rattlesnakes and rats). People generally hold negative views about the coyote and wolf.

Is there more than just a gut reaction that determines what we like and don't? Researchers have identified a variety of factors that may influence public preference for different species—some of which have to do with their perceived physical similarity to humans. Box 7.3 lists possible factors.

According to these factors, how would insects fare? They are small, reproduce like crazy, lack a skeleton, are not physically similar to hu-

**Table 7.2**
**Humans' Animal Preferences**

| | | | |
|---|---|---|---|
| Dog | 1.70 | Wolf | 3.98 |
| Horse | 1.79 | Coyote | 4.02 |
| Swan | 1.97 | Crow | 4.06 |
| Robin | 1.99 | Lizard | 4.13 |
| Butterfly | 2.04 | Skunk | 4.42 |
| Trout | 2.12 | Shark | 4.82 |
| Salmon | 2.26 | Vulture | 4.91 |
| Eagle | 2.29 | Bat | 5.35 |
| Elephant | 2.63 | Rattlesnake | 5.66 |
| Turtle | 2.69 | Wasp | 5.68 |
| Cat | 2.74 | Rat | 6.26 |
| Ladybug | 2.78 | Mosquito | 6.27 |
| Raccoon | 2.80 | Cockroach | 6.45 |

Mean scores based on people's rating animals on a 7-point scale, with 1=most liked and 7=least liked.

## Box 7.3
Factors for Liking or Disliking Animals

> Size   *(larger animals preferred)*

> Aesthetics   *(considered attractive, graceful)*

> Intelligence   *(thought to have capacity to reason and for feeling, emotion)*

> Danger or competition to humans

> Likelihood of inflicting property damage

> Predatory tendencies

> Phylogenic relatedness to humans   *(evolutionary closeness)*

> Cultural and historical relationship to humans

> Relationship to human society   *(domestic farm, pet, game, pest, native or exotic)*

> Texture   *(more like humans' bodily appearance and structure)*

> Mode of locomotion   *(prefer one similar to humans)*

> Economic value of species to humans   *(cost or benefit, use value)*

> Neoteny   *(retention of youthful traits into adulthood)*

> Zoomorphism   *(an animal bonds to person, exhibits "friendly" behavior)*

> Individual variability   *(exhibit individual "personalities")*

> Communication method   *(reliance on vision, hearing, smell, touch)*

> Social habits   *(parenting, loyal to pack, rescue each other)*

> Lifespan and reproductive rate   *(prefer longer-lived and less reproduction)*

> Population size   *(often prefer rare to common)*

> Geographic distribution   *(found in exotic, faraway locations)*

Source: Adapted from Stephen R. Kellert, "Affective, Cognitive, and Evaluative Perceptions of Animals," in *Behavior and the Natural Environment,* eds. Irwin Altman and Joachim Wohlwill (New York: Plenum Press, 1983); Elizabeth A. Lawrence, "Neoteny in American Perceptions of Animals," in *Perceptions of Animals in American Culture,* ed. R. J. Hoage (Washington, D. C.: Smithsonian Institution Press, 1989), 57–75; and Gordon M. Burghardt and Harold A. Herzog, "Animals, Evolution, and Ethics," in *Perceptions of Animals in American Culture,* ed. R. J. Hoage (Washington, D. C.: Smithsonian Institution Press, 1989), 129–151.

mans, and we tend to lump them together and consider them harmful and damaging. Quite a few people have entomophobia, a fear of insects that is often irrational and leads to the overuse and misuse of insecticides, which often carry the cultural label of "pesticides." We associate some insects with disease or even poverty (cockroaches, fleas, bed bugs, flies, mosquitos) but treat even beneficial insects like wasps, bees, and spiders with disdain and dispatch them. Some entomologists consider the aversion to insects "germ theory gone astray."[41] Although a few insects evoke fondness—ladybugs and butterflies, for example—the vast majority of insects are treated with animosity.

Also consider these factors in terms of what we do to either protect or eliminate certain animals. Not only do our attitude preferences govern much of our country's "wildlife management" practices, such attitudes also are portrayed in pop culture representations. How are rattlesnakes portrayed in modern-day movies? How are eagles depicted in advertisements? In contrast, Lassie, Old Yeller, and a passel of current-day pooches receive a great deal of good press.

*Neoteny*

Perhaps you once participated in a contest that required you to guess who's-who from a collection of unidentified baby pictures. By analyzing the eyes, shape of the face, and nose, you tried to match the freckle-faced toddler to a coworker. The reason we can do this is that humans are one species that more-or-less retains our youthful features into adulthood. If you compare the youth and adult profiles of humans and chimpanzees, the human head remains more domed and the face less protruding into adulthood. Neoteny, or the retention of youthful traits into adulthood, is one of the factors that may be at work in our perceptions of animals.[42]

Picture a mouse, an ordinary house mouse. Now picture Mickey Mouse. Nobody really thinks of Mickey as a *mouse* because he doesn't really look like one. Instead, he fits what has been called a "child schema":[43]

1. Prominent forehead with eyes positioned below center of the head
2. Relatively large eyes
3. Generally rounded form of head and body

4.  Short extremities (i.e., arms and legs)
5.  Soft elasticity of body surface

Mickey has been juvenilized in form and behavior, in part so visitors can relate to him as a child. Over the years, Disney artists have progressively made Mickey look younger and younger.[44] Mickey tells us nothing about mice, but lots about ourselves.

One zoo animal is a good example of the child schema and our preferences for animals: pandas. The authors of *The Giant Panda* say the panda "appears sexless and thus harmless, as opposed for example to the essentially male gorilla."[45] Ever since President Nixon's visit to China, pandas—either on loan or as gifts—have been attendance boosters at every zoo they inhabit. Other reasons why we have such a strong anthropomorphic appreciation of the panda include its ability to sit up vertically and manipulate small objects, its rounded and soft-appearing form, and its seemingly playful and clumsy nature.

According to Elizabeth Lawrence, a veterinary surgeon and anthropologist, consciously or not, people have selectively neotenized cartoon animals and real animals.[46] Many of pop culture's animal representations—in stuffed animals and storybooks—exaggerate the big head and big eyes of infancy. We first learn about neoteny in childhood from crib animals, as well as in stories like the Three Little Kittens and the Three Little Pigs. In contrast to the rounded, youthful features of these threesomes, "villains" have low foreheads, long snouts, and small, narrow—shall we say "beady"—eyes. Even some dog breeds (Chihuahua, Pekingese, and Boston terriers, to name just a few) have the big head and big eyes of infants and are similar in size to a human newborn.

While it may seem harmless enough to juvenilize animals, Lawrence maintains that we do so because we need to have control over them: It is a "short leap indeed from perceiving nonhuman life as different, separate, and inferior to perceiving them as juvenile. . . . Juvenilized creatures offer people no competition, and relieve us of the responsibility to understand and respect them for qualities intrinsic to their species. . . . By anthropomorphizing and especially by neotenizing selected species of animals, we are able to impute moral qualities to them in differing measure and to suit our own purposes. Through these mechanisms, species can be assigned varying rank and status according to their usefulness or lack of it in the human scheme."[47]

## Anthropomorphism

It's easy to think of examples of how we talk about animals in human terms. We say that the cat was angry when we returned from vacation. At the zoo, we comment that the fish are kissing or that the primates are playing. In ads and movies, animals even speak English, from crows commenting on sparkling clean windows, to entire English-speaking casts in *Babe* and *Finding Nemo*.

Attributing human qualities—whether emotions, motives, behaviors, or language—to nonhuman animals is called anthropomorphism. It puts a human-centered focus or interpretation on animal lives and behaviors. We're most likely to anthropomorphize animals we know best, such as pets. The rather circular question then becomes, how can we *not*? How can we speak about animals in anything other than human terms and language? Is it possible to understand "the other" on its own terms?

In an essay titled "Anthropomorphism is Not a Four-letter Word," psychologist Randall Lockwood explains that the negative view of anthropomorphism was developed in part by those who first studied animal behavior.[48] C. Lloyd Morgan in his *Introduction to Comparative Psychology* (1894) instructed that, "In no case may we interpret an action as the outcome of the exercise of a higher psychical faculty if it can be interpreted as the outcome of the exercise of one that stands lower in the psychological scale." In other words, "Don't talk about intelligence when instinct will do; don't discuss 'mind' when 'reflex' will do."[49] Morgan's Cannon, as it came to be known, was embraced well into the 1950s by biologists and others who were convinced that anthropomorphism was bad science, and it prohibited humans from being objective and measurable when it came to understanding animal behavior.

It's true that most forms of anthropomorphism in which we engage "make no attempt to understand the animal in its own world or

. . . verify that our explanation of a behavior is correct."[50] Lockwood says four different kinds of anthropomorphism use this simplistic kind of human projection and therefore have scientific shortcomings.

*Allegorical anthropomorphism* consists of descriptions that use animals to make something more appealing or to conceal true identities (such as fables) or to present literary allegories in works such as *Alice in Wonderland*. The animals' behavior is not intended to be interpreted as biological fact or reality, and as such is essentially harmless.

*Personification* is when people superimpose their own desires onto animals, such as dressing pets or chimpanzees in human clothes. Personification does not recognize the true biological needs and adaptations of the animal, but in this case, animals are essentially being used to portray some symbolic human message and may suffer in the process.

*Superficial anthropomorphism* is the interpretation of an animal's behavior on the basis of surface qualities that are unrelated to what actually produced the behavior. Lockwood gives the example of the chimpanzee that returned from an early U.S. space flight and "smiled" when the cockpit door was opened. The media interpreted the "smile" behavior to mean he really enjoyed his trip. Actually, the chimp was giving a "fear grimace," a behavior that often accompanies something unsettling that a chimp experiences. Other examples would be to say that an owl's wide-eyed stare showed great intelligence, or two tropical fish are "kissing" as if the mouth-touching behavior is intended to show affection.

Finally, *explanatory anthropomorphism* is a circular explanation of an animal's behavior, believing that by naming something we've actually explained it. If the dog tears apart garbage when left alone, we call it "spite." How do we know? Because the behavior seems spiteful!

By contrast, there is a constructive way to anthropomorphize animals that uses human powers of observation and knowledge of the entire context of the behavior. Lockwood calls this *applied anthropomorphism*, or "the use of our own personal perspective on what it's like to be a living being to suggest ideas about what it is like to be some other being of either our own or another species. . . . But the essence of consciousness is using self-knowledge to predict the behavior of others."[51] A person must first study and understand the biological elements that are linked to pain, stress, and so on that are remarkably widespread in the animal world. A person also must pay close attention to the context in which the behavior occurs, which necessitates understanding the animal's ecological, evolutionary, and individual history. Only then are we able to use our empathy to make a prediction and evaluate it. In the case of the chimp in space, knowing the animal's responses to stress, and understanding the context of being placed in a wholly foreign environment and subject to terrific noise and physical discomfort or pain, would have helped people to understand that the chimp's display of teeth was anything but a smile.

These distinctions may seem fine or even picky. But it's so very easy for us humans to apply our will and projections onto animals and perhaps misuse animals in the process. Engaging in applied anthropomorphism helps us view animals as autonomous creatures with lives separate from our own.

## Ethical Relations and Animal "Rights"

You no doubt already have an opinion about "animal rights activists" and perhaps consider them violent whackos, passionate animal-protectors, or somewhere in-between. Regardless of your stance, your moral values provide clues as to the way you believe animals should be treated and the ethical relations that humans should have with them.

Some of what forms our ethical evaluations include those same factors that make up our perceptions and attitudes about animals, such as human benefit or cost, aesthetics, and so on. Knowledge and factual information play a role. In addition, there is reason to suggest that part of what forms our ethical relations may be part cultural and part biological. Whatever the source, some philosophical orientations maintain that humans have only *indirect duties* toward animals.[52] This view holds that we should limit human freedom because human cruelty to animals will cause us to treat other humans cruelly. A contrasting philosophy is that humans have *direct duties* toward animals, which stemmed in part from the changing perceptions of human distance from animals.

Charles Darwin's *Origin of the Species* fundamentally changed our notion of a great evolutionary gulf between humans and animals: "By breaking down the barriers between man and the rest of the animal kingdom, Darwin cast doubt on the idea that there was a clear dividing line between reason and instinct, between the forces that shape our behavior and those that guide animals. Although his ideas were, and sometimes still are, met with resistance and ridicule, it gradually became less and less plausible to act on the assumption that there exists an unbridgeable chasm between animals and humans. As the assumption became discredited, so too did the moral arguments based on them; it became possible to entertain the hypothesis that some duties might be owed directly to animals."[53] Darwin and others posited that humans and animals shared numerous common qualities: the ability to feel pain and suffering, an interest in living, self-awareness, desires, kinship awareness, a sense of the past and future, a concern for and ability to relate to others, an ability to communicate, and a sense of curiosity. People then entertained the idea that humans might have some direct duties to animals—that animals, too, might have "rights." Having direct duties means that we should limit human freedom because animals are entitled to certain kinds of treatment and humans owe something directly to them.

In a series of studies, acceptance of evolution was indeed a powerful factor in human perceptions about animals.[54] Individuals who accepted evolution were much more likely to see connections and essential similarities between humans and animals (such as in emotions and feelings, intellectual capabilities, and normal behavior patterns) than those who did not accept evolution. A belief in animal-human similarities means a person is more accepting of direct duties toward animals.

Biologist Edward O. Wilson claims that our values toward animals may be under the influence of our own evolutionary heritage. Some of the strong feelings we have about animals may have been influenced by natural selection. For example, a fear of snakes may be an unlearned phenomenon because it also occurs in other primates when direct learning has been excluded.[55] The reasoning is that possessing an intrinsic (rather than learned) fear of snakes may have provided a slight evolutionary advantage in some human and animal populations. It's possible that "many of our apparently value-laden attitudes toward animals may be based on innate biological predispositions. These may derive from our genetically evolved responses to fellow humans, or from the survival value that certain attitudes toward animals had for humans."[56]

Believing that humans have direct duties toward animals is essentially an "animal rights" view. We owe certain things to animals, apart from how humans will be affected. Animals are not reducible to instrumental value to humans but have independent, intrinsic value. Does that mean that someone who believes in some consideration for animals must be a vegetarian who doesn't wear leather shoes or utilize animals in any way? Not necessarily, for it is the *degree* of direct duties toward animals that define various animal rights perspectives.

Scholar Tom Regan argues that there are three options for our ethical relations toward animals.[57] A *status quo* position would accept our current institutions and practices toward animals (such as meat-raising and consumption, animal control and removal, and zoos) and would not recognize any need to improve them. A *reformist* position, though accepting of these basic institutions, would seek to improve them in practice. Reform could involve anything from limits on predator control and an end to factory farms, to ensuring that animals in captivity do not suffer unduly. Another term that fits under the reformist umbrella is "animal welfare," whose adherents support good, reasonable, and humane treatment of animals in all circumstances.

It is only an *abolitionist* position that seeks to end all human practices that utilize animals in some way, as food or fiber, in scientific research, and for entertainment. In practice, abolitionists have taken two different directions. An animal rights abolitionist wishes to abolish the exploitation of animals and grant them legal rights. In contrast, animal liberationists support physical confrontation against animal exploiters in order to liberate animals. Much media attention has been given to liberationists and their stealth actions, such as freeing mink at mink farms and attacking labs that conduct animal research.

Both the reformist and abolitionist positions recognize direct duties toward animals but vary in the scope and amount of those duties. Obviously, all three positions differ according to how animal suffering is judged to be necessary to fulfill human needs or desires.

Moral controversies don't seem to erupt over the treatment of animals that are universally disliked, such as cockroaches or mice. But the wide middle ground of a reformist position can contain numerous inconsistencies. People might not mind killing rodents that eat grain, but will throw up their hands when "bunnies" are killed. Wildlife management actions, even when intended to restore balance to an ecosystem, can be sharply criticized if one animal is harmed in order to benefit others. Removing nonnative mountain goats from Olympic National Park and burros from the Grand Canyon were met with heated public protests. Attempts to reduce an overpopulation of deer or black bears often generate a public uproar. (Of course, management actions may be thought necessary as a result of human tinkering, habitat destruction, or predator removal.) It's worth noting that no matter how strongly held the direct duties toward animals, ". . . an ethical system for animals will only be successfully implemented by any human group to the extent that it does not deter human survival."[58]

In 1988, three gray whales were trapped in the fall's advancing ice in Alaska, which according to nature's way meant eventual death. However, for the next two weeks, a multinational effort to rescue the whales captured the hearts and minds of people around the world—thanks to the barrage of media coverage that brought the whales' plight into living rooms and "mesmerized an anxious world."[59] But local Alaskans viewed this event much differently than those in the Lower 48 and were willing to let the natural event unfold rather than intervene.

Locals and nonlocals used very different systems of reasoning regarding "rights" to determine the most appropriate way to act toward the trapped whales.[60] The nonlocals were concerned primarily over the *rights of individual animals*—the right of these particular whales to exist, to their autonomy, unfolding of life, and chance to have offspring. Under this system of reasoning, the only course deemed ethical was to "save" these animals. In contrast, many Alaskans were guided by a *right of the species to exist and flourish*. According to this ethical reasoning, these three animals were not as important as the vitality of the entire population of gray whales and were a natural part of the "survival of the fittest." Belief in the right of species to exist and flourish may be based on either benefits for the whole ecosystem or benefits to humans.

It's possible for passionate concern for an individual animal to interfere with the normal functioning of an ecosystem's predator-prey relations. As one example, a friend of mine gets extremely upset at the small hawks that approach her bird feeders, and she will chase off the predators and even remove the bird-seed temporarily. She has created a feeding ground for both songbirds and raptors, but her concern for individual songbirds usurps the right of the predators to exist and flourish.

From a legal standpoint, only beings that can possess things or objects have rights and only those who have "interests" can have rights—in order words, not animals. Nevertheless, this country has passed a lot of laws protecting certain kinds of animals, beginning nearly a hundred years ago. One of the earliest was the Migratory Bird Treaty Act of 1918 which made it unlawful to capture, kill, possess migratory birds. In 1940, the Eagle Protection Act made it illegal to kill or possess a bald eagle, and later, a golden eagle. The Animal Welfare Act of 1966 insured humane treatment for animals used in research or exhibition and prevented the use of stolen pets for research. Of course the most controversial animal protection act is the 1973 Endangered Species Act, passed to aid in the survival and increase of animal (and plant) species threatened with extinction.

Though the role of animal rights might seem better suited to the courts, the news media, and the philosophers, it is in the realm of popular culture communication because as a society we dole out unequal protections and sentiments toward particular animals. The popularity of Dalmatian puppies soared after the release of the movie *101 Dalmatians* (followed, sadly, by a glut of young Dalmatians in animal shelters). Through news and entertainment exposés of animal cruelty, we have granted special protections to some species. Pets have risen to star status in this country. And through zoos, the circus, and TV documentaries, we've acquired a fondness for elephants. Pop culture attention to animals continues to raise the reformist position of direct duties toward (some) animals and the protection of (some) individual ones.

## Mass Media Messages and Animals

Although people generally recognize advertising as a pop culture industry, most people regard the news media as more of a social institution. Nevertheless, it's impossible to divorce the two. Not only does ad revenue support the news media, ad and news messages are interspersed and mutually reinforcing. Journalists occasionally find ads themselves newsworthy, and news media overall reflect the cultural values portrayed in advertising. Pop culture reflects the values of numerous social institutions and cultural trends. Because there are separate chapters on news media and advertising, this discussion will focus narrowly on how these two message channels portray animals.

### News and Animals

A wide variety of animals come to our attention via the morning newspaper or the evening newscast: the bear who bites the hiker, sea otters threatened by an oil spill, elk suffering from a severe winter.[61] Aside from an occasional TV documentary or recreational contact, a frequent source of information about wildlife is news coverage in the mass media. Through news, people are exposed to a great deal of scientific and management information about animals, the ecosystems in which they live, and the human actions that affect them.

But not all animals are equally likely to get news coverage. Domestic or farm animals rarely are considered newsworthy. Animals occasionally receive news coverage in human interest stories: a dog rescues a toddler or a raven steals golf balls from the greens. Also newsworthy are the rare but sensational instances of a dog (or other animal) biting or attacking a person.

News about wildlife actually makes up a large part of environmental news coverage. In a daily environmental news segment on a Minneapolis TV station, wildlife stories accounted for 25 percent of all stories.[62] A study in Britain found that 20 percent of the environmental stories were about wildlife and threats to wildlife habitat.[63]

When do wildlife make the news? Either when someone is making claims about them, or when the boundaries (symbolic or real) between humans and wild animals overlap or blur.

Most of the claims made about wildlife have to do with human developments or conflicts between humans and animals. Many of these situations are the purview of wildlife management, and the animals managed most are game species (legally hunted or fished), or those we consider pests for some reason. In one study of animals in four urban and four rural Midwest newspapers, 81 percent of the news stories were about game animals; only 13 percent were about animals that were threatened or endangered.[64] (Interestingly, these proportions roughly parallel state budget allocations for game and so-called nongame species.) About 59 percent of the news stories were about hunting, fishing, or both, and 46 percent of all wildlife stories appeared on the outdoor recreation page, where such stories are often featured. The most common types of conflict reported were not physical ones between humans and animals, but management conflicts, which were noted in one-third of all stories.

By definition, wildlife is separate and distant from us. So when an animal crosses what we consider the normal human-animal boundary, that's deemed newsworthy. If the duck builds its nest in the wilds, that's not newsworthy; however, if the duck builds its nest next to a downtown building, that's newsworthy. Likewise, when a moose leaves the mountains and wanders through backyards or strip malls, it'll make the evening news. Animals doing what animals normally do (separate from us) isn't newsworthy.

In the world of news, the spokespeople for animals are overwhelmingly government officials. In the same study of Midwest newspapers, 57 percent of all quoted sources in wildlife stories were government officials, particularly state wildlife officials. Conservation or environmental groups spoke for wildlife only 6 percent of the time.

The types of animals most likely to receive news coverage reflect both the dominance of game animals and state wildlife departments and the animals we simply prefer. The animals most frequently featured in news stories bear a striking resemblance to the animals "most liked" by humans. In the study, 36 percent of the news-getters were large mammals, 28 percent birds, 12 percent fish, and 11 percent were small mammals.

If you grew up in a small town, you know that the small weekly or even daily newspaper varies greatly from its urban counterparts. All news media frame issues in terms of the prevailing concerns and values of their immediate social and cultural environment, which differs significantly from large city to small rural town, including the value and concerns placed upon wildlife.

In small towns, not only are residents physically closer to a larger variety of wildlife and presumably have a greater chance for direct contact and interaction, but rural residents also are likely to interpret their wildlife experiences differently from city dwellers. When people are directly dependent on natural resources for a living, animals—both wild and domestic—are highly valued for what they provide. This usefulness may consist merely of enjoyment for their proximity, or the sport of hunting or catching them, or because they provide food for the table. But when animals' presence interferes with the business of making a living—foxes in the chickens or insects in the grain—animals lose their utilitarian value and become "varmints." Thus, a small rural newspaper is likely to reflect the value of wildlife as primarily utilitarian. For example, a common feature of small rural newspapers is the "trophy photo" showing who bagged the big buck or the trophy bass.

For a city dweller, contact with wildlife beyond the backyard squirrel and occasional urban deer is often more deliberate (bird-watching, fishing) or a by-product of other outdoor activities. The day-to-day wildlife experience in the city lacks the utilitarian value and connection to livelihood. Instead, the city is the center of decision-making for wildlife management and the headquarters location for various government agencies. In turn, the urban newspaper is likely to focus more on the stewardship activities of wildlife management.

Regardless of where it's printed, a typical news story about wildlife features a large game animal that is the focus of a management action, and a state wildlife official speaks for the animal. Again, this reflects the powerful role of state wildlife officials in defining wildlife issues, which is evident in the news emphasis on game species and hunting.

### Animals in Advertising

Everything we admire about animals is available for advertisers to exploit and capitalize upon. The grace of a bird, the agility of an otter, the aesthetics of a zebra—all are used to sell you products. You don't need experience with any of these animals to know what a zebra or otter is valued for and what the product, by extension, is supposed to provide.

Animals in particular provide cultural shorthand for advertising. We may not all agree what a forest stands for, but we know what the owl in it is supposed to "mean" and what the deer fawn represents. And when an ad message lasts for only ten or twenty or thirty seconds, "The fastest way to make a point in a TV spot is to use a visual image whose meaning viewers agree upon."[65]

This agreed-upon meaning is more extensive than you might think. "Animals can signify many things: family roles, wildness, unpredictability, power, sexiness. They can signify relationships, attributes, or both."[66] Thus, a black bear licking its cub can be used to depict a parent-child relationship and the jaguar stalking through the grass sends the message that it's wild, unpredictable, and sensual.

Just as people in ads fulfill certain social roles—homemaker, teen, Joe Suburb—animals in ads act as species representatives, not individual animals. Both humans and animals in advertisements are designed to be stereotyped portrayals, and we're not encouraged to think of them as individuals. And in the case of animals—with which we have far less experience than humans—we tend to apply those cultural labels and symbols. Hence, mules are stubborn and foxes are sly.

According to advertising researchers, we like to believe that animals, especially mammals, have families similar to human families. Animals can then "become 'as-if' representations of the viewer's idealized self-image, in terms of both positive attributes and desired relationships."[67] We want to see in animal-families that the parents are good providers but are also capable of tenderness or playfulness.

Part of the self-image portrayed by animals in advertising concerns gender. Studies have found that indeed, women and men respond differently to animal images in ads.[68] A sample of men and women were shown ads where animals were used to help sell cars, beer, and cat and dog food. Women responded most positively to ads where animals represented nurturing relations and identified less when animals were used to express product attributes. On the other hand, to men, animals embodied desirable product attributes, such as power, speed, and strength. When car ads used wild cats, the men responded positively and perceived the product as strong, fast, and controlling the animal's wildness. In these ads, the "wild cats are intercut with sexy, anything-but-domestic women who are iconographic feline representations."[69] Men also rated highly dog food ads where the dogs were used to illustrate qualities such as bravery, spirit, and loyalty. While both men and women thought cats were finicky eaters, women responded most to ads that showed a close, nurturing relationship between the cat and human.

## Zoos

I once was standing in front of the cougar exhibit at the zoo, when a mother and toddler approached. The young girl, pointing at the cougar, said excitedly, "Look Mommy, a big kitty!" Her mother replied, "No honey, that's a bad kitty, that's a big, bad kitty."

Over 100 million Americans make trips to the zoo each year, and most of them recognize the supposed educational mission of zoos. Yet, "the presentation of captive wild animals in the zoo reveals more about the human societies which have constructed them—and whose members roam freely through them—than about the animals which are confined within them."[70] Because a zoo is an artifice, an unnatural created place, what is significant is not the animal itself (which will not behave as if it were in a natural place) but how the animal is thought about and communicated about. Thus the cougar is not a cougar but a "big, bad kitty."

For all their popularity, zoos evoke a range of attitudes and emotions "ranging from a sense of power and domination to negative feelings of guilt and disgust or positive ones like joy and aesthetic appreciation, and finally to beliefs about association with or separation from the animal world."[71] It's inevitable that when we go to the zoo, "we take with us all our worries and our joys, our heroes and our villains, and we dole them out to the various species, casting each one in the role best equipped for it on the basis of accidental human resemblances."[72] For many visitors, the only way to understand or appreciate the animals is to give them human characteristics; in essence, we are observing humans in animal skins.[73]

## The Historical Legs of Zoos

Zoos are not a modern-day or American invention. The practice of viewing captive animals has ancient roots that influence how we approach zoos today. Reportedly, the first zoos were constructed thousands of years ago in ancient Persia, Egypt, and China.[74] As far back as medieval times, carnivals displayed animals as spectacles, and visitors took pleasure in their strangeness, grotesqueness, dangerousness, and otherworldliness. Such displays treated the animals like monsters in a prisonlike setting.

The public menageries of eighteenth and nineteenth century Europe exhibited strange animals as well as *humans*—unusual, deformed, or mentally deranged "madmen." People came to watch both. As one scholar noted, "It is highly significant that what is normal behavior in animals—their unrestrained wildness—is equated with human madness, that is abnormal behavior."[75]

The word "bedlam" denotes a scene of mad confusion, a wild uproar. The word was derived as the nickname of the Bethlem Royal Hospital in London, an asylum for the insane. Historians note that "a Sunday visit to Bedlam was one of London's greatest amusements."[76] Over three hundred visitors a day paid a penny to go in and speak to patients and basically make fun of them. A creature chained in a squalid cell with two elegant visitors staring at him is reminiscent of what?

Another forerunner of the zoo was the private menagerie, a collection of animals owned and displayed by wealthy individuals. By contrast, working-class folk enjoyed gambling on or racing animals, baiting, and cock- and dog-fighting. It wasn't until "nineteenth-century bourgeois reforms"[77] that these pursuits were banned; encouraged in its place was "rational recreation" in the form of parks, playgrounds, and zoos. The Zoological Society of London, which opened in 1827, was modeled after the museum and encouraged education, but in practice provided mere entertainment. At the time, zoos weren't really about animals; "Zoos were about social progress; they were safe diversions, rational recreation, approved leisure."[78] By displaying exotic animals (and non-European humans), zoos were very much a part of colonial condescension and conquest.

By the postwar era and the 1960s, the working class was an increasing proportion of zoo visitors. It was also during this time that "animal rights" first gained notice. So from the 1970s onward, zoos increasingly endeavored to place the interests of animals first and organized their entertainment under very different conditions. The decade also brought two types of innovations: endangered animal zoos and breeding ventures, and simulated ecosystems from which the animals originated. Animals were moved from individual cages to enclosures that were more similar in native climate, vegetation, and terrain, and sometimes included communities of similar species. Some animals were confined by moats and invisible barriers rather than bars. Education messages connected animals and their habitats, encouraged visitor involvement, and presented conservation messages. Recreation not related to the zoo experience was often excluded, though many zoos retained bird shows and marine mammal shows.

*On Display*

Picture for a moment the physical geography of the zoo and what it communicates to you. Animals are grouped either by type (reptiles) or by region of origin (African Savannah). In front of each animal is a sign; at a minimum, each animal is named. Two names are given: the common name (Polar Bear) and the scientific name (Thalarctos maritimus). Just like in a museum, what you are viewing is a specimen of that type, not an individual. It would be like naming you Homo erectus instead of Jacob Jones. By and large, zoos avoid giving personal names to individual animals to avoid anthropomorphizing them. However, pandas are frequently named (Ling Ling and Tian Tian) and the zoo in Salt Lake City has "name the polar bear cubs" contests (before the cubs are removed from their mother and sent to another zoo).

The layout and design of the enclosures also communicates. Rocks and cliffs are likely molded concrete. Trees in the primate enclosure could be plastic. You might even hear mood music, like the calling of jungle birds. Much of what you see is an elaborate and sophisticated attempt to recreate the natural world . . . in a way that fools nobody. One author called these attempts examples of an "architectural guilt"[79] for putting wild animals on permanent display.

There is pressure to give the animals a better stage and more complex scenery to make it appear more satisfactory and morally acceptable.

Zoos are "explicit, even intentional, models of relations between human cultures and the natural world. . . . They are constructed environments that often tell us more about ourselves than they do about what we're ostensibly looking at."[80] Another critic concluded that, "[A]t the most basic level, zoos are institutions of power, in that they reflect the uniquely human ability to hold in captivity and dominate large numbers of diverse wild animals for the purpose of human enjoyment and benefit. The zoo constitutes a gallery of images constructed by man."[81]

What we really learn from a visit to the zoo may be the same thing gained from a visit to a mental institution: how a creature adapts to captivity and institutional routine. Despite the best of intentions, "even the best zoos may be creating animal stereotypes that are not only incorrect but that actually work against the interests of wildlife preservation."[82] Zoos face limited resources and zoo visitors who "do not come predisposed to learn about the animals."[83]

The typical visit to zoo isn't very long—two hours or less. If you observe people moving through the zoo, most just register what they've seen as they move quickly past. They might linger only if the animal is "doing something." Yet when asked in surveys, visitors knew that the purpose of the zoo was primarily educational, but added that the zoo was mainly about entertainment. It seems that the latter model is what guides their behavior when they visit. Studies in the United States found that visitors rarely read the information signs or the exhibit brochures.[84]

We also learn how humans react to the creatures in captivity. Most zoos have signs asking visitors not to tap on the glass or bars to try and get the animal's attention, yet the behavior is common. According to a teacher of abnormal psychology, "One of the most depressing aspects of a visit to the zoo is the amount of petty sadism and exhibitionism displayed by the visitors, adults as well as children. These unfortunate but all too common occurrences make it evident that, by itself, the sight of caged animals does not engender respect for animals."[85]

## Conclusion

When you return from a backpack or visit to a national park, the highlights (beyond the weather and perhaps the scenery) are bound to be what animals you saw. Nothing speaks to us of the natural world as animals do. Animals are powerful place-markers and symbols of what is "natural" and wild, and represent the antithesis of technological culture.

Yet, "when we gaze at animals, we hold up a mirror to ourselves." It is impossible to remove the layers of cultural representations that preceded the encounter. Even when we seek out authentic experience and understanding, we cannot entirely remove the deer from its pop culture communication or the wolf from our historical hatred of it. We use entire species as cultural shorthand for human values and emotions. The communication and the representations of bison or moose occur so often that we think we "know" them.

Yes, we lack knowledge, we stereotype, and we generalize. We have preferences for animals most like us or like children, and for the big and dramatic ones. We may be ignorant of their habitat, their everyday lives, and how our actions affect them. We write about them in our newspapers only when there is conflict over them or when they "trespass" onto land we consider ours.

Yet, we seem to truly need them, to need what is "other" than human, to need them near us and surrounding us—as pets, in zoos, on our clothing and in our movies, and in the wild. Animals—and what they "mean"—mean a great deal to us. We share a common environment and are both subject to the effects of its degradation. The destiny of many animals, therefore, depends not just on our actions, but on the subjective feelings that we communicate about them.

# 8

## News Media

No matter where I go, people like to complain about the media. At social gatherings, meetings on campus, even hiking in the woods, media-bashing is a frequent topic. Some of this is because people know I teach mass media courses and find me a target, in the same way that medical doctors are asked for diagnoses at parties. Conservatives lay the blame on the liberal, biased media. Liberals claim the news media are too conservative, protecting those in power and not questioning their agenda.

What's most striking to me in these conversations is the enormous expectations people have for the media. They believe that because journalists have free speech protection, they should behave more as watchdogs of the public interest. They assume that free speech is inextricably linked to fairness and objectivity—as long as it matches their political leanings. At the same time, most people understand little about the process of news production, and the role of media in society.

Here are just a few of the headlines in my daily newspaper over the course of an average week:

*Lawsuits Shape Bush Forest Policy, Critics Say*
*Moab Celebrates Earth Day by Touting Wind-Power Initiative*
*Cougar Visits Not a Trend*
*Nuclear-Site Alternatives an 'Insult' for Tribe*
*Mosquito-Killing Virus Sought*
*Drought Worries Watered down by Cooler Spring*
*Animal Activists Plan to Disrupt March*

*Conservation Groups Protest Wilderness Deal*
*EPA Honors Mayor with Climate Protection Award*

There were additional stories during this particular week that on the surface may not seem to be environmental stories but still had ramifications for the natural world and our relationship with it, including health risks from bird flu and the rodent-spread hantavirus, lifestyle topics such as vegan diets and planting apple trees, and suburban sprawl. The business section was full of stories with environmental ramifications: oil and natural gas companies, consumer spending, wind power initiatives, mass transit, and even innovative waste-reduction measures by businesses.

The topics ran the gamut of resource issues, but my small sampling of stories emphasized animals, nuclear waste, and water conservation (the fifth year of an ongoing drought). Stories concerned city, county, and national environmental policies, and like news generally, were most often spurred by time-specific events or actions by newsmakers. This level of attention might suggest that the news media (at least this newspaper) consider the environment a highly newsworthy topic and might even be supportive of environmental protection.

But in the grand scheme of daily life, how important is the environment to the mass media? Do journalists report this topic area any differently than other types of news? How and why were these stories chosen and not others? What was it about these topics that made them appear on the media radar screen? And overall, does environmental news affect people and their perceptions or behaviors toward the natural world? In short, what is the role of the media and what should we expect of them? These questions are the focus of this chapter.

## News and Social Reality

By most definitions, news media include newspapers (daily and weekly), magazines, radio, television, and the Internet. News presented by these mediums is generally distinct from entertainment. On TV and radio, news is presented in clear-cut newscasts at set times. In newspapers, news appears on news pages separate from editorial pages and the reporter is clearly identified. Opinion columns are labeled. On the Internet, news can be found on Web sites sponsored by virtually all major newspapers and TV networks, as well as other independent news sites. Obviously, information about the natural world can appear in mass media both as news and as entertainment; however, this chapter considers just media news coverage.

How "real" is this thing we call "news"? Consider this anecdote about the difference between "reality" and "social reality." In his classic book *Public Opinion*, Walter Lippmann told of an island where some French, Germans, and English lived quite peaceably.[1] Then a British mail ship (their only link with the outside world) brought news about six weeks of fighting that had been taking place between their countries at the beginning of World War II. Although the day-to-day "reality" was that island residents were friends, the ship brought news of what Lippmann called "the world outside," or actual events and a mediated (or constructed) knowledge of them. Suddenly, the residents had to contend with a "social reality" that they technically were now enemies, not friends. Were the residents to think and behave on the basis of what their relationships truly were, or on what social reality said they were?

When the news media present this world to us, for the most part we believe what they say. That is, most people consider the mass media to be one of the most credible sources of information, a far more trusted source than advertising, salespersons, and even government. We put stock in the notion that the press is "objective" or at least tries to be. But what many news consumers fail to recognize is that any news report is a constructed version of *social* reality, a report that necessarily includes some facts and ignores others, and presents one version or frame of reality at the expense of another. For example, when the newspaper reports that an air inversion that traps pollutants is "caused" by a stationary high pressure system, we tend to accept this version of reality that air inversions are in a sense natural and beyond our control—ignoring the fact that what makes an inversion a problem is the pollutants that people put into the air during this atmospheric event. When TV news tells us that a cougar was found in a suburban garage, the social reality presented to us is that the animal is trespassing—not the humans. "News" by its very nature is a version of an event or issue constructed by one observer, a version that easily could be recorded differently by another observer. A photographer taking a picture facing north will take a very different picture from the very same location if she turns around and faces south. In a similar way, a journalist presents a snapshot of an event that in essence becomes the social reality of thousands if not millions of people when it is presented as "news."

Over the last eighty years, mass communication scholars have wrestled with the notion of media "power." Research at first concluded that the news media have extremely powerful effects on people and were able to zap propaganda into individuals just like a "magic bullet" or "hypodermic needle." Then, scholars recognized that audiences weren't so passive in receiving media information but were able to evaluate or ignore it. Active audiences sought out media viewpoints that were consistent with their existing beliefs. Current thinking is that news media do indeed have effects on people—influencing their awareness, attitudes, and at times even their behaviors—but the circumstances under which media influence occurs are complex and hard to predict (see Box 8.1).

News media definitely played a role in the development of the environmental social movement and in the fairly high consensus among Americans today about the importance of environmental protection and environmental quality. But does that mean that news media serve as a watchdog for the natural world, sounding the alarm about environmental threats and trumpeting the call for social change? Research suggests not. Do the media rely heavily on environmental activists as news sources and effectively communicate their agendas to the public? Again, no. Although environmental reporting has developed and matured over the decades, such reporting in some measure reflects the same type of role that the news media play regarding social change for other social issues. To understand why this is, we must first look more closely at how news "comes" to journalists, and how they make news decisions and put together news stories.

## How Environmental Stories Reach the Media

Imagine a reporter sitting in the newsroom. How does that reporter figure out what to write? How does a reporter actually find or come across what becomes tomorrow's news? The process is two-fold: first, many news tips come to reporters from outside sources, and second, reporters assigned to a topical "beat" (such as the police beat, education beat, or environment beat) search out news ideas from their known sources or from their knowledge of the topic.

## The Environment Beat

I once made a bet with a fellow reporter that I could rewrite every single story in our local news section as an environmental story; I won the bet. After all, most every news story involves or has implications for air, water, energy, food, paper or wood, minerals or metals, land use, animals, and so on. It's an interesting process for an editor to decide which of those stories should be written by the reporter assigned to the environment beat and which to the business or food editor. (See Box 8.2 for an overview of environmental journalism.)

For many reasons, the environment has never been a comfortable arena of coverage for the media.[2] First of all, "the environment" cuts across all news beats and topics (business, outdoors, legislative, health, science, and so on) and may be in the purview of many different reporters. Also, too often environmental stories are viewed as "a snore," pushed aside in favor of more exciting topics like scandal and celebrities. Because of the complex, scientific nature of many stories, reporters often lack expert training and can be easily influenced by special interests, yet remain suspicious of environmental group spokespersons. In addition, the "the anti-business stance of much of the environmental movement . . . makes reporters and editors leery about whom to use as a source of reliable news."[3]

So structurally, newsrooms may be at a loss as to how to best fit stories about the environment into newsroom organization and routines. As a result, all newspapers and virtually all TV newsrooms may have one (or more) journalist assigned to cover the environment as part of his or her duties. However, on any given day, an environmental story may be assigned to a science specialist, a health care reporter, a general assignment reporter, or even a business reporter. This means that decisions about what environmental stories to cover may be made at numerous levels by editors and individual reporters.

## Box 8.1

### Does Media Coverage Affect Us?

Of great interest to those on both sides of the environmental fence is how media coverage influences us. Overall, studies find fairly weak associations between content and audience "outcomes" like knowledge, attitude, and behavior. One or more stories do not cause an effect perhaps as much as they "prime" an existing attitude or thought.

Why such limited or short-term effects? The effect of messages may be long term and cumulative at the cultural level. Personal factors such as experience, interpersonal communication, selective perception, and message salience also play a role. After all, "social environments are rich places, and it is becoming increasingly clear that the mass media are but a subset of many channels available to individuals."[1]

Our roles as social participants also influence how we interpret media messages. We tend to believe that others are more affected by something than we are (whether pollution or pornography), a so-called optimistic bias or third-person effect. A "spiral of silence" occurs when you perceive that the majority do not hold your belief, so you self-censor and remain quiet. "Bandwagon" effects occur when we perceive that the majority support an issue (or proposal or candidate) and we add our support.

The most widely tested effects theory is "agenda setting,"[2] which holds that the media don't tell us what to think, but are fairly effective in telling us what to think *about*.[3] This is tested by comparing what media report most often with topics that people say are most important. Given the influence of "priming," agenda setting might actually measure coverage *quantity* and media's ability to amplify social concern.[4]

For most people, media are the primary source of information about risks,[5] whether from bird flu, genetically modified foods, or microorganisms in the water. Mass media do a good job of making risk issues salient initially, but interpersonal

### Information Subsidies

On any given day, well over a hundred news releases may arrive in the newsroom of a large daily newspaper. In addition, there may be dozens of meetings scheduled by government agencies, news conferences called by politicians or nonprofit organizations, and phone calls with tips of potential newsworthy happenings. It's a confusing and seemingly unorganized jumble of news for journalists to sort through. But at the same time, such a large, steady supply of news makes the job of a journalist in locating and identifying news much easier.

Although journalists make the ultimate decision of which news tips to act upon and which to ignore, they are nonetheless subject

---

**Box 8.1 con't.**

channels also are used to make judgments about the risk at a later time.[6] Generally, the greater the volume of coverage about a risk, the greater the risk the public believes it to be. However, even when media pay a great deal of attention to a risk, it doesn't guarantee that individuals will know when to be most concerned and change their behavior.[7]

1. Sharon Dunwoody and Hans Peter Peters, "Mass Media Coverage of Technological and Environmental Risks: A Survey of Research in the United State and Germany," *Public Understanding of Science* 1 (1992):199–230, 218.

2. Tony Atwater, Michael B. Salwen, and Ronald B. Anderson, "Media Agenda-Setting with Environmental Issues," *Journalism Quarterly* 62 (1985):393–97.

3. Maxwell E. McCombs and Donald L Shaw, "The Agenda-setting Function of the Mass Media," *Public Opinion Quarterly* 36 (1972):176–187.

4. Allan Mazur, "The Dynamics of Technical Controversy," *Journal of Communication* 31 (2) (1981):106–115.

5. Eleanor Singer and Phyllis M. Endreny, *Reporting on Risk: How the Mass Media Portray Accidents, Diseases, Disasters, and Other Hazards* (New York: Russell Sage Foundation Publications, 1993).

6. Sharon Dunwoody and Kurt Neuwirth, "Coming to Terms with the Impact of Communication on Scientific and Technological Risk Judgments," in *Risky Business: Communicating Issues of Science, Risk, and Public Policy*, eds. L. Wilkins and P. Patterson (Westport, CT: Greenwood Press, 1991), 11–30; T. R. Tyler and F. L. Cook, "The Mass Media and Judgments of Risk: Distinguishing Impact on Personal and Societal Level Judgments," *Journal of Personality and Social Psychology* 47 (4) (1984):693–708.

7. S. Klaidman, *Health in the Headlines: The Stories behind the Stories* (New York: Oxford University Press, 1991).

---

to influence when newsworthy information is presented to them by outside sources, often by public relations officials employed by large organizations. Studies have found that source-instigated news contributes a large portion of the media content. One researcher found that about 60 percent of the news originated from routine channels predominately under source control, such as news conferences, news releases, and official proceedings;[4] it's noteworthy that these channels are primarily controlled by the entity *seeking* news coverage. Another study also found that newspapers depended very heavily on routine channels, which allowed the sources "more control over their news product than when enterprise [reporting] channels are used."[5]

The effectiveness of media relations efforts in obtaining media coverage has been well documented,[6] although the effectiveness of

## Box 8.2
### The Environment as "Beat"

Only after the growth of public awareness and the environmental movement in the 1970s was the environment recognized as an important, ongoing social issue and was granted the status of a reporting "beat" such as the "police beat" or "city hall."

Studies by journalists and academics have noted a series of ups and downs in the amount of environmental news over the past thirty years: "The environmental beat has never really been stable, riding a cycle of ups and downs like an elevator. These cycles, and consequent increases or decreases in numbers of environmental reporters and their space or air time, appear to be driven by public interest and events, as well as economic conditions."[1] In 1989, the year of the *Exxon Valdez* oil spill in Alaska, total news coverage of the environment by the three major TV networks reached an all-time high of 774 combined minutes. By 1998, the TV news minutes fell to 195. In the first quarter of 2001 and George W. Bush's Presidency, TV news minutes climbed to 264. *Columbia Journalism Review* proclaimed in August 2001 that the environment beat had "gotten its groove back."[2] A month later, terrorist attacks diverted media attention from the environment and a host of issues.

Professor Sharon Friedman summarizes: "The 1990s became the decade that environmental journalism . . . grew into its shoes, becoming more sophisticated with the help of the Internet and a professional organization, the Society of Environmental Journalists (SEJ). The field also matured as stories changed from relatively simple event-driven pollution stories to those of far greater scope and complexity . . . Growing into new shoes can be painful if they pinch, however, and environmental coverage, like most other journalism beats during this decade, faced a shrinking news hole brought about by centralization of media ownership, revenue losses and challenges from new media. Environmental journalism's dilemma was dealing with a shrinking news hole while facing a growing need to tell longer, complicated, and more in-depth stories."[3]

SEJ was founded in 1990 to help environmental journalists stay better informed, network, and share information. The group publishes a journal and a Web site (www.sej.org) and hosts an e-mail discussion forum for members. By 2002, SEJ had grown into an active professional group of more than 1,200 members.

1. Sharon Friedman, "And the Beat Goes On: The Third Decade of Environmental Journalism," in *The Environmental Communication Yearbook*, vol. 1, ed. Susan L. Senecah (2004):175–187 at 177.

2. Jane Hall, "How the Environmental Beat Got Its Groove Back," *Columbia Journalism Review* (July–Aug. 2001):10.

3. Friedman, "And the Beat Goes On," 177.

public relations efforts by business and government has been studied more often than efforts by specific social protest groups. (The public relations industry is discussed more in the next chapter.) In a nine-month period, 202 of the 236 news releases issued from a major state agency were placed in some form in daily newspapers.[7] In another study, some state agencies (through their public information officers) were very effective in passing along agency agendas to the public through newspapers. In this study, news releases and tips issued by six state agency public information officers were tracked and tied to news coverage in eight daily newspapers in Louisiana; efforts to get news coverage were successful about half of the time. The study concluded that when agency releases were used, the agencies were generally successful in transmitting both issue salience and raw information.[8]

Many people unfamiliar with news production are amazed that journalists are "handed" so many news ideas rather than pounding the pavement, wearing out shoe leather, and digging out stories themselves. Only fairly recently have researchers begun to look at who significantly influences what the media report.[9] For obvious reasons, it's important to investigate more fully the ways nonmedia actors interact with journalists and influence which items appear on the media agenda.

So why don't journalists reject self-serving publicity materials? Because they save the media time and money. In a sense, a news tip received through a routine channel amounts to an "information subsidy" that reduces the cost and effort of gathering news.[10] At the same time, the more effective an organization is at supplying information subsidies, the greater the potential it has to affect—if not control—the news agenda. The creation of these subsidy items, often by public relations practitioners, has been defined as an attempt to produce influence over reporters' access and use of certain data, facts, or potentially newsworthy events.

But as any public relations practitioner knows, news releases and media contact do not automatically translate into media coverage. Factors such as a reputation for high quality information,[11] prestige of the organization,[12] news judgments by media gatekeepers, and community make-up can all play a role in which information subsidies get selected. In one study, the success of county extension agents in placing news in the media was not related to the amount of personal media contact made by the agents, but it was related to the amount of local employment in agriculture.[13]

When environmental groups approach media with information subsidies, they are already at a disadvantage as a less powerful (and perhaps more threatening) entity in the social system. In a study of media use of news releases for stories concerning the environment in the San Francisco area, business editors depended almost entirely on industry releases although some reporters did use releases from environmental groups.[14] The researcher found that half of environmental news stories written were based on (or relied heavily upon) news releases, most frequently those of government agencies. (We'll revisit this in a moment.)

In addition to a formalized structure, money can help an organization get its information in the hands of reporters, particularly when it comes to producing an information subsidy complete with audio and visual, called a VNR or video news release. Free video (sent on tapes or downloaded by TV stations for free from satellite feeds) greatly decreases the cost of producing TV newscasts. The *Columbia Journalism Review* found that 75 percent of TV news directors used at least one VNR B-roll (video footage and sounds without narration) per week.[15] A station can add its own voice-over narration (often from a script supplied with the VNR) onto the B-roll video, making the story virtually impossible to detect as externally produced. For obvious journalistic reasons, stations continue to resist crediting VNR footage material on-air and do so rarely.[16]

Because the cost of professionally producing a VNR costs tens of thousands of dollars, industry has relied on VNRs most often. (More about VNRs and public relations efforts by business in the next chapter.) That is not to say that environmental groups haven't occasionally produced VNRs; one researcher noted footage supplied by Greenpeace was used in an on-air news segment (without video attribution) about a group protest of whaling.[17]

## How the Media Choose News

If you dial-hop between TV newscasts or compare competing daily newspapers in the same city, it's surprising how similarly the various media outlets define the day's news. You may discover the exact same stories at the top of the newscasts and on the front pages, and perhaps a very similar angle and similar "talking heads." If there are so many more potential news stories than space or time permit, how is it that journalists are choosing virtually the same ones? Assuming that reporters aren't calling each other (and are even hoping to "scoop" the competition), how is it that the news in entirely different mediums looks so much alike?

First, remember that "news is a socially created product, not a reflection of objective reality."[18] News "is produced by people who operate, often unwittingly, within a cultural system, a reservoir of stored cultural meanings. It is organized by conventions of sourcing—who is a legitimate source. . . . It lives by unspoken preconceptions about the audience—less a matter of who the audience actually may be than a projection by journalists of their own social worlds. News, as a form of culture, incorporates assumptions about what matters, what makes sense, what time and place in which we live, and what range of considerations we should take seriously."[19]

Media decisions about what to publish by and large protect dominant cultural values such as existing power and class arrangements. In a study of newspaper content, one researcher concluded that decisions about what *not* to publish protected socio-cultural integration and hid institutional flaws; for example, the newspaper omitted two-thirds of the economic news seen as adverse to the commercial sector.[20] In general, there was a lack of news that might appear offensive to the values of family, religion, community, patriotism, and business.

To help choose the news, journalists rely on things like professional journalistic norms, "news values," and other conventions to help them weed through the reams of potential news and choose what the dominant culture considers the most newsworthy. In this daily (if not hourly) task, the environment is just one of many topics worth covering that must compete with others. As one scholar put it, "What the various news media decide to cover is at one level a daily bargaining game between and among competing interests and topics. That bargaining game is guided partly by tradition, but also by structural patterns within the press that value certain subjects and situations more than others."[21]

Because news is so event-driven, environmental stories some-times don't compete well. Environmental issues are ongoing, om-nipresent, and often too complex to present as two distinct "sides" or as a single, dramatic event. Overall, the news media "still value people and ideas in conflict more than conditions and trends that are omnipresent."[22] Walter Lippmann once described media atten-tion as "a restless spotlight," due to its propensity to focus the glare intensely on a subject, but just as quickly to move on to another topic it finds more "sexy." The media's short attention span con-tributes to its on-again off-again coverage of long-term environmen-tal issues. One study found that news attention to depletion of the ozone layer was strongly tied to specific meetings, reports, and of-ficial announcements, despite the constant nature of the problem.[23] Such media behavior leads environmentalists to see the media as "an occasional ally" but more often "a fickle and unreliable friend."[24]

Environmental issues also are often highly scientific and techni-cal, which makes journalists more susceptible to influence by special interests when they lack the expertise to fully understand concepts, such as global climate change. Some scholars have found media cov-erage of the environment to be a science-oriented discourse, domi-nated by scientific and government officials,[25] although some have found the topic to be far more dominated by government.[26]

The "cultural givens" apparent in environmental coverage of "mastery over nature" and "progress through science" help explain why media discourse on the environment is largely "a science dis-course, drawing on scientists as the primary arbiters of right and wrong, true and false, real and imagined."[27] Some believe that the accumulation of scientific evidence is one factor that can help move the environment to the top of the political agenda. For example, agreement among scientists was considered a prerequisite by many journalists before the media would pay attention to destruction of the ozone layer.[28] More recently, scientific debate about the particu-lars of global warming have led some journalists to question its real-ity as a scientific phenomenon.[29]

### Journalists as "Gatekeepers"

A useful metaphor to describe the entire process of selecting news is "gatekeeping." As a gatekeeper, a journalist controls the gate that lets some potential news items pass through but not others. Ever since the first so-called gatekeeping studies decades ago,[30] researchers have delved into the extent to which individual journalists play a role in what news the public sees, hears, or reads.

As a concept, gatekeeping has been explored from many levels. Some attribute gatekeeping decisions to the economic structure of the news organization or economic influences like advertising. Others point to organizational constraints (such as deadlines) and occupational routines (such as beats) affecting journalists' actions, a sociological perspective that analyzes "news-work" or "making news."[31] Still others emphasize the constraining force of broad cultural symbol systems, power and social control, community norms, and even ideological influences of editors and publishers.

Overall conclusions amassed from gatekeeping studies are that journalists rely on professional values and on cues within the social system regarding the importance of a particular item or event to make their news judgments. Professional values, which involve news values and journalistic norms of objectivity and balance, are discussed in more detail later. Individual attributes or characteristics of journalists have *not* been found to be as important;[32] in other words, we can't say that reporters rely solely on their own personal preferences to sift through and choose news. However, journalists cannot report the news without expressing some values, even if unconsciously, through what some have called "enduring values."[33] These values blind journalists to structural faults in the system and cause them not to question the legitimacy of the existing order, creating news that serves business and political interests.

When people question the influence of owners and/or publishers upon news values, journalists stress how the news operation is separate from the business operation and is free from its bias. However, studies have found that a form of "social control" in the newsroom is structural, subtle, and institutionalized at the organizational level. The most effective form of institutional control is the "conditioned belief"—when a reporter does not realize that he or she is submitting to the organization's norms. In one study about press ideology and organizational control of news, researchers found a high degree of ideological consonance between reporters and the newspaper organization.[34]

What gatekeeping tells us about environmental reporting is that journalists will rely on traditional news values to judge the merits of environmental stories, but they also rely on powerful entities within the social system (whether respected government officials, industry spokespersons, or politicians) for cues as to the importance of environmental news. The ideology of the surrounding community and important economic interests also have an influence on what environmental topics may pass through the news gate.

### Journalistic Norms: Fairness and Objectivity

Within the American system of journalism is a firmly rooted commitment to fairness and objectivity. Great efforts are made to structurally separate "fact" from "opinion." News stories are placed on separate pages from editorials, and columns are labeled and personalized with a small photo. Within a news story, reporters do not insert their own opinions (at least overtly) and must attribute opinions as quotes or paraphrases by chosen sources. (One exception to this strict separation between fact and opinion appears on local TV newscasts where anchors and occasionally reporters engage in editorial "chit-chat" about the stories they air.)[35]

American journalists strive for emotional detachment; an editor of mine was proud of the fact that he didn't vote, which he believed was an important symbol of his fairness and detachment from the political issues he reported. American journalistic tradition differs greatly from the openly partisan press in much of the world's media and the textured interpretive essays found in many European newspapers.

However, objectivity is more an ideological ideal than an operational reality. Naturally, every news selection involves a choice made by an individual, regardless of whether the person relied on professional norms for guidance. As the rest of this chapter demonstrates, a journalist's choice of news sources, a news "frame," and continued attention to an issue all represent subjective choices.

Even if a journalist is careful to avoid injecting overt opinion, the choice and construction of a news story can still introduce bias. One media scholar noted a different kind of bias in news stories, one that's "negative, detached, technical, and official."[36] One way to provide objectivity and balance is the long-standing journalistic tradition of bringing in opposing "sides." A journalist might quote a range of positions (a government official, an industry spokesperson, and an environmental activist) believing that such "balance" provides objectivity. However, such he-said/she-said reporting may give the appearance of all viewpoints having equal merit, or of a de-emphasized viewpoint having less merit. Instead, when "news tends to emphasize conflict, dissension, and battle, out of a journalistic convention that there are two sides to any story, news heightens the appearance of conflict even in instances of relative calm."[37]

According to some, this objectivity-turned-bias is evident in the coverage of global climate change. There is a general worldwide consensus among scientists regarding global warming, including the role of human behavior in the phenomenon; scientific disagreement is centered primarily on the timeframe, location, and particular impacts of the warming. However, media reporting of global climate change has given the issue "an ersatz balance"[38] by giving space to dissenters and suggesting a scientific debate when there is not one. Readers are unable to evaluate where the balance of evidence lies.[39]

## News Values

In addition to journalistic norms of fairness and objectivity, traditional news values play a role in what environmental stories are chosen as news. In beginning news reporting textbooks, there is widespread agreement as to basic news values: proximity, pocketbook, prominent people and places, human interest and drama, unusualness, trends, impact, importance, and currency or "hot topic." Some texts also mention news values of conflict, anniversaries of important events, children, visually compelling things or events, and a local or regional angle to a national or global story.

Identifying the news value(s) of a story allows journalists to select and organize discrete details, choose sources, and emphasize opinions. In the story, the news value is evident in the first paragraph, sometimes in the headline, and throughout much of the story. By hanging the story on a "news peg" a journalist is able to say "this is a story about . . ."

When editors were asked the most important reason why news releases were not used, their number one reason was that the information was "not newsworthy." In order to meet media criteria of newsworthiness, information subsidies must emphasize journalism's accepted news values. For example, if a soil scientist wanted to publicize what she considered exciting new findings about the composition of desert soils, she might have to be creative in packaging her information to better fit traditional news values. She might emphasize what the findings mean in terms of economic impacts for local grazing and ranching. Or, she could enlist a well-known local leader or respected official to stress the ramifications of the findings for recreational use of desert lands.

### Event-driven

News is, to a large degree, event-driven. The public hearing on air quality regulations, the release of a study on recovery efforts of a species, the visit of a top EPA official, the opening day of fishing season—all are time-specific happenings that fit the news criterion of timeliness. The time-bound nature of "hard" news allows the newspaper reporter to define the event as news today, knowing that tomorrow the newspaper will line the bottom of the bird cage.

Events can happen unexpectedly; they also are planned or created.[40] Numerous individuals and organizations have grown savvy at planning and staging events that take advantage of the timeliness criterion. The ribbon cutting and news conference are classic examples of created events, but advocates also may stage the release of a report or study, plan a rally or protest, or adeptly tie a timely national event to a local situation.

A great deal of the daily news diet consists of planned events, including more than half of TV news stories.[41] The attraction of planned events is obvious if you think of newsroom operations: events fit into news routines and take some of the unpredictability out of the news cycle. If an editor knows that her reporters and camera crews are covering a half-dozen events, there is less uncertainty in what the news product will look like and less dependence on the unexpected and unplanned accidental event.

### Economic Constraints and Advertising Influences

As commercial institutions, news media also are constrained by the often-unspoken influence of important advertisers, which makes them less likely to challenge current business operations and conflicts that may arise from them. *Ms.* magazine said that pressure from advertisers upon editorial content was the publication's reason to cancel all advertising and rely solely on subscriber support.[42]

Researchers noted a reluctance by some media to publish news about the health risks of smoking for fear of losing advertising dollars. One research team described the "unhealthy addiction" of media to tobacco advertising dollars and concluded that the media were hampered in conveying smoking risks.[43] A historical study notes the powerful influence of public relations and advertising efforts by tobacco companies to influence coverage of research concerning the health effects of smoking.[44]

Although journalists loudly claim that news production is entirely separate from advertising, the media's dependency on advertising dollars is undeniable. In newspapers, the amount of advertising sold determines the daily "news hole" or allotment of space for news—not the other way around. To anger or alienate a large advertiser could jeopardize the financial health of a news medium.

## How the Media Report Environmental Stories

What we label and discuss as an environmental issue is open to interpretation both in a general sense and in the media. In other words, what we call environmental or environmentalism "is an especially indeterminate, malleable ideological form. In other words, environmentalism is what its current bearers say it is."[45] If that's the case, stories labeled as "environmental" and how they are reported in news media outlets is particularly important.

### Story Construction

Once a journalist decides to report a story, decisions must be made how to construct the story: choosing news sources, selecting facts and quotes, and ordering the pieces into a narrative sequence. The most common organizational structure for a news story is called "inverted pyramid" in which a summary of the most important elements is placed in the first paragraph. Journalists are trained to summarize the "five W's and H" in just the first few sentences: who, what, where, when, why, and how. In subsequent paragraphs, details are added in decreasing order of importance.

This most-important to least-important structure for news stories is said to have developed when news bulletins were delivered via telegraph and operators were never certain whether the entire message would get through. If the connection failed part way through, at least the most important details had arrived. In modern times, the decreasing-importance structure continues to play an important role; very few newspapers readers read each and every story all the way to the end. In the same way, headlines help to attract readers to stories of interest by highlighting a few important words.

Obviously, deciding which facts and viewpoints are the most important (and least important) is a subjective act. If a reporter describes the positions of two opposing sides in an environmental debate in equal amounts, has "balance" been achieved? Not if one side is mentioned in the all-important first paragraph and the other side is mentioned in the last paragraph.

Another disadvantage of this organizational structure is that the concentration on discrete facts such as "where" and "when" often means that important context, historical background, and explanation and interpretation are given short shrift. For example, most stories about social protest focus on who, where, when, and how many, but give little attention to the history of the debate that brought convictions to this level or the ideological message of the protestors. Even initial news of forest fires reports the event in much the same way as an urban fire, focusing on number of personnel, equipment, acres, and threatened structures, neglecting important historical and biological facts.

### News Sources

Perhaps the most crucial decision made in the construction of a news story is who is chosen to speak authoritatively on the subject at hand: the news source. In many ways, news is as much a product of news sources as it is reporters. The interaction between journalists and sources has been described as a dance, and although it takes two to tango, sources more often than not do the leading.[46] Although the journalist-source relationship is a symbiotic one, news-seekers and sources need media more than media need any one news-maker.

To a casual observer, it might seem that there are an infinite number and variety of news sources. But in practice, media content represents a very limited diversity of sources.[47] News media rely most heavily on sources who are powerful "knowns" with economic or political power[48] and return repeatedly to rather small groups of so-called experts.[49] In a two-year study of TV network news, researchers found reliance on a very small, elite, homogeneous group of experts.[50] Elites meet two important criteria for selection as news sources: availability and suitability or legitimacy in the power structure.[51]

Government spokespersons have legitimacy because they are recognizable, credible, and have status. News-workers treat bureaucratic accounts as factual and their sources as "authorized knowers."[52] The tendency to use government releases and quote government sources is what one scholar coined as the "principle of bureaucratic affinity."[53] Other researchers have pointed out that an advantage of a formalized bureaucratic structure is that someone is always around and works regular business hours to maintain contact with the press.[54] In a study of the ability of environmental groups to obtain media coverage in major daily newspapers, groups with a moderate level of bureaucracy fared best; groups with very little formal organization were virtually ignored by the newspapers.[55]

Research has concluded that journalists support and defer to established authority sources and are dependent on those authorities for information. One study found that 60 percent of all news came through routine channels, such as news releases or official proceedings that were under source control.[56] In the same study, government officials accounted for more than three-fourths of all news sources. In a later replication of this study, researchers again found a heavy reliance on official sources: 31 percent of front-page news sources were affiliated with the U.S. government.[57] There also was a strong reliance on men in executive positions and upon veiled sources. In one study, 54 percent of all stories in the *New York Times* and *Washington Post* used one or more unnamed sources, including "officials" and "spokesmen."[58] On Canadian TV news, government and business spokespersons accounted for over half the sources,[59] perhaps because these official sources made it easier for journalists to concentrate on the individuals perceived to be more important.

Newsmakers are predominantly male. According to one research team, "news is made and information controlled almost exclusively by men acting in some official capacity, with official status. . . . Women were infrequently cited as sources, a signal to the reader that they are relatively unimportant in both public and private sector activities and events."[60] In their study, the "maleness frame" that media used not only attached greater importance to male sources but also diminished the importance of women even when they were used as sources. Women journalists were only slightly more sensitive to the "symbolic annihilation of women"[61] in their choices of sources.

If media support government authority, they may ignore conflictive issues[62] and calls for social change. A researcher discovered that seven out of ten sources were administrative officials (usually with government institutions) in stories about marijuana; he concluded that the dominance of social problems depend on the ideological questions determined by the political power structure, which is contrary to the conventional "watchdog" model of the media.[63] One scholar noted that when media concentrate on fleeting, short-term news events, there is a "missing dimension" on deeper, long-term change.[64]

These patterns of news source use also hold true for media coverage of the environment, which is dominated by government sources[65] and often excludes environmental group sources.[66] In a survey called "The Press and the Environment," journalists said they got the majority of their information for environmental stories from government sources. American Opinion Research conducted a survey for the Foundation for American Communication of 512 print and broadcast journalists who reported about the environment.[67] When asked to identify the source they used most often for data and information about the environment, 51 percent of the journalists said government officials or their news releases or reports and 25 percent cited environmental activist groups. The remaining sources used were academics and professional journals (8 percent), consumer groups (4 percent), business executives or publications (4 percent), and other (9 percent). Studies have demonstrated that if government and official experts are considered "knowns" in news coverage, environmental groups often are considered "unknowns," even in news about their specialty areas.

Research on news content supports the dominance of government sources. In a study of newspaper stories about wildlife, government-affiliated sources numbered over 55 percent of news sources, while special interest groups (including wildlife and sportsmen groups) accounted for only 6 percent.[68] In a study of the Canadian press, scientists and government and industry officials greatly outnumbered interest group representatives.[69] A study of Canadian and U.S. newspaper coverage of ozone depletion found a preponderance of government officials as news sources; almost 50 percent were government officials or government scientists.[70]

Similar findings have been discovered in research of TV news sources. In a study of environmental stories on local television news, there were far more stories about (and more sources from) business and government than about environmental group involvement or as news sources.[71] Over 40 percent of all sources in this study of a daily TV segment about the environment were government and 20 percent were business; less than 8 percent were sources from environmental or consumer groups.

The pattern of sources also holds true for TV news in Europe. In a study of TV news in Denmark and Britain, representatives of established environmental groups were among the least prominent sources.[72] The scholar concluded that "While spectacular actions and demonstrations staged by environmental pressure groups may act as catalysts for media coverage . . . the relative absence of spokespersons from [these] groups suggests that the primary articulation and inflection of environmental matters . . . remains firmly anchored within established and 'legitimate' . . . institutions."[73]

As environmental issues grow in complexity, the role of government in those issues is likely to grow. Scholars agree that the regulatory and technical nature of "second-generation" environmental issues such as global warming and ozone depletion will require great involvement and coordination from government at all levels.[74] This may result in even greater reliance on government officials as sources for environmental stories. At the same time, there isn't much to suggest that journalists' reliance on environmentally friendly news sources will greatly increase.

## Community Structure and Self-interest

It's easy to lump all news media together and assume they function in exactly the same way when reporting the news. However, if you've ever read a weekly newspaper from a small town, you know that this type of media outlet views its role in the community much differently than media in a big city. In a small town newspaper, you'll find lots of social news such as who went to Arizona on vacation, who had out-of-town visitors, and who hooked the trophy bass. In a rural community, conflicts are less likely to be treated as news, and decisions are more likely to be made by a handful of powerful town leaders on a consensual basis. This differs greatly from an urban press, which limits or confines the reporting of social events and views conflict as routine and doesn't hesitate airing it.

In different ways, media in each setting are paying attention to community self-interest and helping to guard the social structure. What researchers have found is that the amount and type of control exerted by media varies according to the pluralism of the community.[75] A large urban center is very pluralistic, with a heterogeneous and diverse population and where power is spread among many individuals and institutions. In a pluralistic setting like this, news media serve as conflict managers who help the diverse social system accommodate and respond to conflicts by airing them to the masses. But a small community newspaper functions as an agent of community progress and supports community leaders and values. Because consensus is highly valued in a small, homogeneous community, editors tend to support other community leaders and control conflict information.[76] However, when the conflict involves an external power source (such as a distant seat of government or outside corporation), airing conflict tends to bring more internal cohesion to the community as it battles the outsider.

Numerous studies have investigated what community pluralism has meant for reporting environmental issues. A comparison of rural and urban newspaper coverage of wildlife found that stories about wildlife conflicts were far more common in urban papers. In addition, the theme of wildlife stories in rural newspapers was "utilitarian" (reflecting community self-interest) while the urban paper theme was "stewardship" (also reflecting that community's self-interest as the seat of management decisions).[77]

Another study compared newspaper coverage in the small northern Minnesota town of Ely over the impending designation of the

Boundary Waters Canoe Area Wilderness with coverage in the Minneapolis press two hundred miles to the south.[78] As you might expect, the Ely paper painted a negative picture of the designation because of its potential effect on community self-interest (namely resorts and logging interests) while urban papers, far removed from direct economic impacts, generally supported designation. The Ely newspaper drew a picture of a community united against an outside enemy.

Community structure also played a key part in how three communities reported the environmental risks associated with Superfund sites. In each city, news framing was driven most by community structure and the interpretation championed by the prevailing power structure in town.[79] Yet another study found that newspapers in larger pluralistic communities were more likely to link contamination from local sources to health threats in the community than were papers in smaller, less pluralistic towns.[80]

What if a community is "fragmented," that is, small in size but high in pluralism? In one such fragmented town, newspaper coverage of environmental conflict favored the status quo news sources (government and industry) and cited them far more often than activists and community residents through all stages of the conflict.[81] In the first stage of the conflict, newspaper editorials came out against a proposed hazardous waste plan, but the paper later reversed its position and supported industry. Throughout the conflict, the local press legitimized industry through the positive way it presented the waste plan and provided unbalanced attention to industry concerns. Although the reality of the industry's environmental record was poor and full of citations and violations, the newspaper supported the company, evidence of its support of the power structure.

No matter the size or diversity of the community, there may be times when local environmental issues are simply too sensitive and conflictual to report. If that's the case, media might instead focus on environmental problems "up the road a piece" in an attempt to protect community self-interest.[82] This type of self-protective behavior is also found in public opinion polls when residents report that environmental conditions (air quality, water quality, or toxic waste) are not as bad in their own town or city as in a neighboring area.

## How the Media Frame Environmental Stories

If three journalists attended a protest rally, it's very likely they would report three different versions of the event. Even with "news values" as guidelines, each individual would select and order the information either slightly or much differently. One account might focus on the number of protesters, what they were chanting, and the reaction of police. A second story might tell a personal tale of struggle and conviction waged by the protest leader. A third report might elicit crowd reaction and interpretation as to what the protest was about and whether it was a good idea. None of these stories would be any less "correct" or newsworthy; each journalist merely chose a different piece of the world outside to present as social reality. Each story has a unique "frame" through which to view the same event.

### Subjective Selection of "Objective" Facts

Just as a picture frame or house frame organizes the inner contents and provides an outer boundary, a news frame "is a central organizing idea for news content that supplies a context and suggests what the issue is through the use of selection, emphasis, exclusion, and elaboration."[83] Simply put, framing is the subjective act of selecting and ordering objective facts.

Some sort of ordering and choosing is necessary, of course. Journalists must actively make sense of an immense quantity of information, selecting some points or news sources as critical, while discarding and downplaying others. News frames help "simplify, prioritize, and structure the narrative flow of events"[84] and allow a journalist to say "this is a story about X . . ." Framing is cognitive simplification that makes the world look natural. News frames are almost entirely implicit and taken for granted, not appearing to either journalists or audiences as the social constructions they are, appearing instead as actual attributes of events that reporters are merely reflecting. For example, when we read in the paper that the state wildlife board voted overwhelmingly to extend the spring bear hunt, we assume that the reporter attended the meeting and simply recorded the vote. With this frame, what's been simplified and taken for granted is whether this kind of hunting season is well supported or necessary. Female bears shot in spring may leave behind cubs unable to survive by themselves.

Journalists use frames to organize discourse and bring it into a meaningful structure for quick relay to audiences as news, which is an active process, not a passive one.[85] Frames have the potential to influence audience opinions because a frame stresses specific values and facts, "endowing them with greater apparent relevance to the issue than they might appear to have under an alternative frame."[86] Therefore, it's important to examine the basic conceptual and ideological framework through which a journalist presents an event, as well as how news stories are "given one dominant or primary meaning rather than another."[87] For news consumers, the concern is that frames must tell complex stories with only a narrow range of perspectives and direct people to consider certain things when they think about issues.[88] To a large degree, the frame used to interpret a news event determines what available information is relevant or irrelevant for the consumer.[89]

In a very real sense, frames define the issue, who's responsible, and what the solution is. Let's say a reporter is assigned to write about the latest snow-pack figures in a drought. If she stresses the lingering weather pattern as the problem, the solution that naturally follows is to wait for the pattern to change. If the reporter instead identifies agricultural water use as the problem, that frame obviously suggests an entirely different solution. As one scholar put it:

> Frames define problems (determine what a causal agent is doing with what costs and benefits, usually measured in terms of common cultural values); diagnose causes (identify the forces creating the problem); make moral judgments (evaluate causal agents and their effects); and suggest remedies (offer and justify treatments for the problem and predict their likely effects). . . . To frame is to select some aspects of a perceived reality and make them more salient in a communicating context, in such a way as to promote a particular problem definition, causal interpretation, moral evaluation, and/or treatment recommendation for the item described.[90]

*Internal and External Influences on News Frames*

Obviously, determining what the problem is or even what's important in a news sense is a "negotiated concept."[91] News values and journalistic norms may guide this process, but they don't go far enough in explaining how news frames are both socially constructed and culturally reinforced. One way to think of a news frame is not as the product per se of a journalist and her or his individual values, but as "an invocation of socially created collective universals and traditional understandings."[92] In one sense, news frames and ideologies both rely on an integrated set of frames of reference through which we see and understand the world: "Both frames and ideologies provide the people in a given society with a framework within which to interpret events, define problems, diagnose causes and seek remedies."[93]

Journalists look to the social structure for cues when selecting story frames. If, for example, the state environmental agency, the water district, prominent politicians, and TV meteorologists discuss water availability as a weather-driven phenomenon unrelated to human behavior, the journalist is aware of this collective, constructed understanding of the issue. Since the journalist is dependent upon these institutions and individuals and their "knowing," the journalist is unlikely to advance a story frame that differs drastically from their interpretation of events. In this sense, journalists are fairly conservative or at least cautious in how they view environmental issues. However, if a legitimate challenge or conflict arises regarding culturally accepted views of water use, the journalist may dutifully report the alternative frame (with comment, of course, from its detractors). The point is that the suggestion or "evidence" for news frames originates in the social structure—not solely within the journalist.

Individual journalists construct individual frames, but these frames don't necessarily represent individual characteristics of the journalist. Instead, story frames are reflective of both routine internal forces in news-making[94] as well as external influences, such as cultural values and social power. The result is that journalists tend to construct highly formulated news frames that reconstruct the world in similar ways,[95] a fact that's readily apparent if you watch and compare TV newscasts or daily newspapers. In environmental news, the frames are almost exclusively anthropocentric.

## Types and Characteristics of News Frames

News frames appear not as overt statements but in the "key words, metaphors, concepts, symbols, and visual images" that are emphasized.[96] A reader won't find one sentence that states "the frame is . . . ," but nevertheless will be able to make that conclusion from reading the entire story. Individual story factors that influence frames include syntactic structures (word or phrase patterns), script structures (such as what's highlighted as most newsworthy), thematic structures (that point to a causal theme), and rhetorical devices (stylistic choices).[97] Such factors can be emphasized in quotes chosen, what material is included in the lead or headline, or even the choice of individual words. In the headlines that began this chapter, several provide words that suggest a specific frame, such as "Nuclear-Site Alternatives an 'Insult' to Tribe."

Frames provide other distinctive information in addition to what's the problem, who's responsible, and what's the solution. By story ordering, a frame can judge what's important; placing an environmental group claim in the last paragraph is a judgment that it's less important than other claims. A frame also can identify "victims," whether harmed individuals or an organization harmed by government regulations. Categorizing or labeling incidents or participants either as "concerned citizens" or "deviant lawbreakers" is a powerful framing device. (The last chapter returns to media treatment of social protest and so-called deviant behavior.) By generalizing something as part of a broader context or trend, a frame can link or associate one particular situation to another (even unrelated) phenomenon. For example, calling a requirement to clean up smokestack emissions "an example of an increasingly hostile regulatory environment" is quite a different generalization than calling the requirement "the latest in a series of efforts to protect the health of area residents."

Although researchers have named and labeled a wide variety of news frames, two general categories of frames considered most relevant to environmental issues are status quo frames and challenger frames (see Box 8.3). Obviously, challenger frames[98] support social change regarding current environmental practice and often are advanced by environmental activists, but also occasionally by members of the power structure. Challenger frames can appear in a news story either as one of many viewpoints, or less commonly, as the frame of the entire news story. Status quo frames are most typically utilized by those within the social structure, either in response to a challenger or to evidence that some kind of social change is needed in regards to the environment.

### Frames Influence Audience Perceptions

If journalists actively construct news frames, do audiences actively interpret and process news frames? Numerous researchers have investigated this question with experiments that present participants with different news frames.

---

### Box 8.3
### Common Frames Used by Challengers and the Status Quo

**Challenger Frames**

> Loss   *(rescuers become heroes, "save" creatures or places)*
> Entitlement   *(rights, something needs securing such as access or tradition)*
> Endangerment   *(threats to health or safety of animals, humans, ecosystem, etc.)*
> Unreason   *(being taken advantage of, tricked or fooled, may point out opposition as uninformed or uneducated)*
> Calamity   *(pending doom, utter disaster)*

**Status Quo Frames**

> Responding   *(we're working on it or studying it; often indicates cooptation, not genuine response or change)*
> Powerlessness   *(there's nothing we can do, it's not our jurisdiction, responsibility)*
> Barriers   *(cost, time, expertise)*
> Scientific or technological solutions   *(need more scientific study first; can solve through scientific intelligence, perseverance, ingenuity; can fix or counter environmental damage or mitigate impacts)*
> Avoidance or downplay   *(it's isolated incident and not big problem, don't get hysterical, denial of problem, secrecy over problem, postpone or evade addressing issue)*

One study examined the effect of different frames in TV news coverage of a social protest on audience members who viewed them. In this experiment, participants viewed news stories with frames that gave either a high or low degree of support for the status quo (such as police). The level of status quo support within the news stories did indeed affect the audience's perceptions of the protest, such as whether police should be criticized and whether the audience could identify with the protestors and their demands. Those who viewed the story that had the highest degree of status quo support estimated that public support for the protest was only half as much as the estimate by those who viewed the story with low support for the status quo.[99]

In another experiment, participants were asked to read a newspaper story about an air inversion (which traps pollutants near the ground) with either a status quo frame, a social change frame, or a "balanced" frame. The status quo frame defined the weather as the problem and the solution as waiting for the weather to change. Those who read the story with the social change frame were much more likely to perceive that the air inversion presented a risk to their health.[100]

A large-scale hog farm was the subject of another experiment. Five different news frames presented differing degrees of support for either the farm proponents or farm opponents. Those who read news stories with the frames most favorable to the hog farm were significantly more likely to explain the issue in economic rather than environmental terms. Only those who read the most extreme farm-opponent frame placed an emphasis on an environmental interpretation to the story.[101]

One final experiment concerned news stories about poverty. In stories that personalized poverty (like a human interest frame), viewers assigned responsibility for the circumstances to the individual; in stories that framed poverty as due to economic conditions and social policies, viewers assigned responsibility to society at large.[102]

## "Guard Dog" Media and Social Change

Now that we've discussed how news is discovered, chosen, and reported, let's look at the big picture of the media's role in social change. A good many of us expect media to play the role of "watchdogs" for the environment. The watchdog idea was articulated by Edmund Burke as satire in Great Britain in the 1700s: the press serve as a Fourth Estate to provide checks and balances to the power of the first two estates (church and nobility), and after the French Revolution, to the power of the third estate, the common masses. This views the press as autonomous and independent from government and business, and as a watchdog of the public's interests.

Yet a recent study found that few journalists really believe they fulfill this adversarial watchdog role, and instead see themselves as disseminators and interpreters of news and information.[103] It's also clear from the way that media choose and report news that they are not autonomous and independent. Journalists rely on others to alert them to potential news and provide cues as to its importance. It's more accurate to think of reporters as collection centers for information generated by others.

Therefore, media do not fundamentally challenge the dominant power structure because they are an integrated part of it. Instead, the news media role is primarily one of stability and conflict control. Controlling conflict may seem counterintuitive to the media axiom "if it bleeds, it leads" the newscast or front page. But think of how the media deal with conflict. Let's say a reporter goes to cover a protest about a proposed waste incinerator, a typical high-conflict environmental story. If state officials have granted permits and the sponsoring industry has promised jobs and tax revenues, this support from the power structure is an obvious cue to the reporter, who will likely seek out official comments for the story. At the same time, the reporter recognizes that the protest is newsworthy, though typical reports of protest tend to somewhat marginalize protestors. Although the reporter has given the protesters publicity, airing the conflict helps defuse the threat, diminishes (or ignores) the protesters' viewpoint, and insulates and protects the power structure.

That doesn't mean that "challengers" like environmental activists are always marginalized and the status quo is always supported. At times, news media will criticize groups or individuals in power, especially when there is conflict among these elites. In the previous example, if the state regulatory agency were at odds with the incinerator proponents, media reporting might center around this conflict, airing the disagreement and presenting the opportunity for entities in the social system to respond and negotiate the conflict. If media never responded to or criticized the power structure, they could be considered hegemonic—a situation encountered in countries with state-controlled presses. But even in the United States, if conflict among elites is limited or nonexistent, news media support of the status quo tends to be strong.[104] Depending on where it emanates and how big a threat it poses, social conflict can be "functional" for the social system and help to stabilize and maintain it. The media role in conflict reporting helps ensure that social change occurs in a minimal and orderly way and only with support from the power structure. If media give continued attention to an issue or conflict the system has deemed worthy of change, it increases the likelihood that the larger social system will respond.[105]

The reluctance of news media to support social change describes a "social control" role and says that "the media act generally, but non-purposively, to support the values dominant in a community or nation."[106] In contrast to what many people believe to be a "liberal" news media, mainstream media by and large are conservative institutions, following the lead of prominent social actors and supporting what media perceive to be dominant values and practices. News media support for the status quo is embedded in the processes of news production, so thoroughly embedded that individual journalists may not be consciously aware of them.[107]

Instead of a watchdog, news media can be described more accurately as performing the role of a "guard dog."[108] The job of a guard dog is to protect its owners and their property or person. A guard dog, while friendly to most, may attack someone in a weaker but threatening position. If another master were to claim ownership of the property, the guard dog would switch allegiances. Likewise, news media do not offer equal support to all institutions or authorities. Instead, they protect the established interests and powers as long as the main powers are in agreement. If a challenge appears within the system, most media will attack the most vulnerable individuals, not the entire system.[109]

If you apply that reasoning to the environment, although media may support individual actions to stop pollution or preserve land, they never fundamentally question capitalism and continual growth as the dominant paradigm, nor do they question private property or pollution "rights." Although they may support individual programs like recycling, media would not substantially criticize American consumerism (which is driven by advertising and pays the bills for all mass media). There is quite a bit of evidence that shows that media defer to mainstream values and the status quo rather than an objective airing of conflicts surrounding social problems, including the environment.[110]

If you return to the headlines that opened this chapter, the emphasis on water conservation might sound like a media "watchdog" promoting social change. However, it's important to examine the background of this issue and the media's role in it. As mentioned, these headlines came as Utah was entering the fifth summer of an ongoing drought. In the first several years of the drought, media coverage focused on the drought purely as a weather phenomenon, the solution to which was just to wait it out. By the end of the third year, when a state agency produced a series of public service advertisements featuring the governor and the theme "Slow the Flow, Save $H_2O$," media attention to water conservation immediately increased. At that time, news stories focused almost entirely on the need for individual actions to save water, particularly summertime lawn watering.

As the state approached year five of the drought, numerous political officials and agencies became involved in the issue and media attention remained constant and focused. It wasn't until this point, after sustained timeliness and the involvement of prominent public officials, that the focus of attention changed from voluntary actions by individuals to actions the social structure might take to help the situation—namely, watering restrictions and a change in the water rate structure that encouraged conservation. A state environmental group had been calling for a water rate change for over a decade (but receiving only limited media coverage). This media behavior is one of a guard dog that followed the lead of the power structure, waiting for the cue to climb on the water conservation bandwagon. Even at the critical fifth year, the media did not criticize the basic way in which water was allocated and used. In this case, the role of the media in social change regarding water conservation was one of a follower, not a leader, and involved modest individual behavior—and only later moderate institutional—change.

## Conclusion

How likely is it that in twenty or thirty years we'll see headlines similar to those that opened this chapter? As environmental problems become more severe and important as a social issue, will the media change their role in the reporting of the environment, perhaps to more of a watchdog? Without significant social change in the social structure and the way we value and make decisions about natural resources, it is unlikely.

While some people like to proclaim the news media are liberal and champions of vast social change, the truth is that media are pretty conservative institutions. The media fallback position will guard those in the social system with the most power and legitimacy. If those in power begin to champion and call for significant social change regarding our relationship with the environment, the media will follow—not lead—calls for change. It might be environmental groups who initiate the call to fellow citizens and leaders for change; it might be doctors concerned about health effects of environmental quality; it might be world leaders. But any proponent of social change will have an uphill battle—both with the dominant power structure and with the media—if the desired change differs, even slightly, from the status quo. In that sense, media act as agents of social control. As guard dogs rather than watchdogs, the media dutifully report conflicts so that powers in the social structure may better accommodate them. But airing conflicts and individual transgressions is far different than critiquing wholesale the social system values and institutions on which media are utterly dependent for news.

That is not to belittle the power that news media have to present a constructed social reality of the world beyond, and to influence our perceptions by ignoring some stories and unrelentingly following others. There is quite a body of research that documents that media do indeed have the potential to affect our values, attitudes, and at times, our behaviors. Through media gatekeeping decisions, through individual story framing, and through the use of official and expert news sources, media most definitely create a social reality—not an objective mirror of the world's events. This is not to say that journalists are crusading, opinionated crusaders; they are humans, who necessarily rely on their professional norms and values to do the best job they can. But they are also creatures of a social institution that's a profit-making business that must sell subscriptions and audiences to advertisers. They are employees of a social institution that's very much interdependent on the rest of the social system and the powerful individuals in it to help them create a news product.

# 9

# Battle for Spin: The Public Relations Industry

A woman says to a man at a party, "So you're in public relations. Is that where you get me to like something I wouldn't like at all if you didn't do what you do to make me like it?" This *New Yorker* cartoon that appeared thirty years ago still captures how many people view public relations (PR). To many, PR is that rather mysterious way of getting into our psyches and making us believe or think certain things. When we hear "that was a good PR job" we think of spin, hype, of pulling a fast one. We think something is slimy or manipulative, slick, or good for an organization in a selfish way. When we think of PR practitioners, we think spin doctors and flacks.

Of course that's a gross stereotype and rather unfair. The simplest definition of PR is the formalized communication function in an organization, an organization that might just as easily be an environmental group as a multinational corporation or government agency. The job may or may not be called public relations, but public information, public affairs, or even media relations or community liaison. PR in an organization may be combined with marketing and advertising, or may be largely farmed out to public relations firms or advertising agencies. What distinguishes PR from marketing is that public relations is interested in communicating to noncustomer audiences, whether employees, journalists, government or political officials, or entire communities in which the organization resides.

As benign as this might sound, a PR person is nevertheless an organizational advocate. There is nothing wrong with advocacy per se. But with selling an organization and its aims comes varying degrees of "cheerleading" and the danger of pushing the boundaries of truth and fairness. How far and to whose benefit the push occurs can result in honest communication, manipulation and dishonesty, and everything in-between.

There also is nothing wrong per se with the techniques of PR. Grassroots organizing and the creative utilization of news publicity have been enlisted to support wilderness, expose corporate pollution, and encourage democratic participation. As John Stauber and Sheldon Rampton, two critics of the PR industry, point out, "As individuals, we not only have the right to engage in these activities, we have a responsibility to participate in the decisions that shape our society and our lives." However, because of the very different resources that organizations bring to the table, the same PR tactics are not available to all, in particular the multi-million-dollar PR campaigns undertaken on behalf of large corporations and business associations. It is money that enables some in the PR industry "to mobilize private detectives, attorneys, broadcast faxes, satellite feeds, sophisticated information systems and other expensive, high-tech resources to outmaneuver, overpower and outlast true citizen reformers."[1]

The result of these massive and expensive efforts is that today PR is mediating environmental communication like never before. In particular, corporations are becoming an increasingly active participant in environmental communication.[2] As we've seen in previous chapters, a great deal of PR-instigated communication goes undetected and unscrutinized, making its way into mass media as "news," appearing—unchallenged—as advertisements, or being seamlessly integrated into political and regulatory arenas. And, the PR industry "carefully conceals most of its activities from public view. This invisibility is part of a deliberate strategy for manipulating public opinion and government policy."[3]

This chapter explores the role and function of the PR industry. Most often this industry is working within or on behalf of industry or government, though environmental groups and other nonprofits also practice PR. For the time being, we'll look at how PR is used by government and business and return to environmental groups in the final chapter.

## The PR Goals of Government

"Public relations" work by the federal government is technically pro-hibited. The tacit threshold of government spin from a legal and philosophical standpoint is pure "information"—no lobbying or promotion of an environmental agenda. This is not new. The 1913 Gillett Amendment prohibited the use of federal money for "public-ity or propaganda purposes" not authorized by Congress. (The law also prohibited hiring federal employees with the job title "public relations" for fear the government would be viewed as a propaganda machine.) Though state and local agencies don't face the same re-strictions, they tend to support the philosophy of governments as providing information, not PR or spin. But as we'll see in the next section, government agencies sometimes have creatively maneu-vered their information past these legal and philosophical limita-tions.

As organizational advocates, PR practitioners must represent and communicate the organization's goals, practices, and guiding phi-losophy, including toward the environment. The government rec-ognizes its role in environmental protection and as the most ap-propriate guardian of the public and its resources. Depending on the agency, the environmental philosophy of government has occa-sionally been conservationism or preservationism, but not in a way that threatens other institutions, including business. Government at all levels may recognize its stewardship role, but again not at the expense of its duty to help the commercial sector thrive. Thus, the environmental philosophy of government supports a rather status quo utilitarianism (if not unrestrained instrumentalism) as often as it does conservationism.

The government philosophy of stewardship may even be viewed as the societal response to "market failure,"[4] where the unfettered marketplace leaves the rest of us with environmentally related prob-lems it isn't equipped to solve. The language of such an argument typically says that business activities necessarily impose external costs on society (often because public goods and resources are under-priced), and market mechanisms fail to allocate resources efficiently in such cases. These failures justify government activities to change the behavior of businesses that are pure profit maximizers with the right combination of coercive standards and incentives.[5] After all, the regulatory mindset holds that pollution and a certain number of harms (or deaths) are acceptable costs to pay. (For a discussion of how economic indicators like gross national product [GNP] tally and communicate environmental harms, see Box 9.1.)

In her book *Systems of Survival*, Jane Jacobs says that society has two moral syndromes, the guardian and the commercial.[6] The job of the guardian is to guard boundaries, to be protective of societal possessions (especially those held in common), to value loyalty and tradition, and in general to shun trading and involvement in the commercial. We can see this guardian role in government structure and practice, but also to a large degree in the forms and manner of government communication.

Thus, the PR goals of government are to communicate its guardianship and to involve the citizenry in it. Government agencies solicit comments for "public participation" and write planning documents for public (and business) review. Agencies also produce publications and news releases that communicate programs and goals of its guardian role. But when the public responds and becomes involved in this governance, so do the commercial and political sectors. A common result: the government guardian, attempting to appease more powerful masters, fails to guard the public resources and interest. In the controversy over allowing snowmobiles in Yellowstone National Park, public comment overwhelmingly supported the government's proposed restrictions (as did scientific evidence regarding harm). Yet, political will prevailed, and the guardian backed down and snowmobiles remain.

Just as the guardian has certain roles and duties, Jacobs says that the commercial sector is entirely based on trading and functions best when it is open, innovative, and forward-thinking. Given their important but diametrically opposed purposes, Jacobs says that ideally, society should separate the guardian and the commercial systems as completely as possible.

### The PR Goals of Business

The goals of PR practitioners in the commercial system are to communicate the efficient and industrious way it conducts business. How

## Box 9.1

### Economic Indicators Communicate What?

The news reports that "housing starts" are up, GNP grew, unemployment rate fell, and the rate of inflation was unchanged. But what do these economic indicators communicate about life in our communities? Not as much as one might think. Consider GNP, gross national product, the total value of goods made by U.S. producers (here or overseas). It measures money flow from households to businesses and vice versa and includes money spent on consumer goods, export goods, investment goods, government expenditures, and the money business spends for the costs of production like wages, material costs, and interest on loans. Essentially, GNP is a measure of spending, which is interpreted as "growth" and "progress." The GNP tallies what Americans spend on goods and declares it (literally and rhetorically) to be the total "good."

To the market, spending money on environmental problems is positive and contributes to GNP. Cleaning up toxic waste sites and oil spills "help" the economy. The billions of dollars that Americans spend to cope with environmental and health ills give the market a boost but confuse "progress."

Just before he was assassinated in 1968, Robert Kennedy delivered a speech about GNP: "The gross national product includes air pollution and advertising for cigarettes, and ambulances to clear our highways of carnage. It counts special locks for our doors, and jails for the people who break them. [It] includes the destruction of the redwoods and the death of Lake Superior. It grows with the production of napalm and missiles with nuclear warheads. And if the gross national product includes all this, there is much that it does not comprehend. It does not allow for the health of our families, the quality of our education, or the joy of our play. It is indifferent to the decency of our factories and the safety of streets alike. It does not include the beauty of our poetry or the strength of our marriages, the intelligence of our public debate or the integrity of our public officials. . . . The gross national product measures neither our wit nor our courage, neither our wisdom nor our learning, neither our compassion nor our devotion to country. It measures everything, in short, except that which makes life worthwhile, and it can tell us everything about America—except whether we are proud to be Americans."[1]

To address these shortcomings, alternative indexes like Seattle's "sustainability indicators" assess economic, environmental, and social conditions. In 1995, the Genuine Progress Indicator was introduced, which adds the value of nonpaid work (such as housework, childcare, and volunteering) and subtracts the cost of social ills such as crime, natural resource depletion, and loss of leisure time. Using this calculation, the U.S. economy has declined by 45 percent in the last two decades—in contrast to GDP figures, which showed that the economy more than doubled.[2]

1. Posted on Sustainable Seattle Web site: www.sustainableseattle.org.

2. Linda Baker, "Real Wealth: The Genuine Progress Indicator Could Provide an Environmental Measure of the Planet's Health," *E Magazine* (May–June 1999), 36–41.

this plays out in practice and communication, however, depend on the philosophies and requirements guiding the organization. Large corporations have a legally mandated profit motive that seems forever bound to unrestrained instrumentalism (see Box 9.2). On the opposite end, a handful of businesses see environmental protection and responsibility as their guiding philosophy and have transformed their practices in significant and meaningful ways. Stonyfield Farms, which produces the Number Five brand of yogurt, awards grants to dairy farmers to promote sustainable agriculture and is offsetting two thousand tons of carbon dioxide (100 percent of its emissions) with reforestation projects. Fetzer Vineyards uses only organically grown grapes, aims to completely cut waste from its winemaking process, and was the first wine producer to buy 100 percent renewable energy.[7] CEO Ray Anderson of Interface, the world's largest commercial carpet manufacturer, has totally transformed his business's manufacturing process and is aiming for complete sustainability in its operations.

Obviously, individual businesses interpret "social responsibility" toward the environment very differently. Economist Milton Friedman liked to pronounce that the social responsibility of business began and ended with increasing profits, and businesses should not spend money that didn't contribute to overall profitability. President Dwight Eisenhower once remarked that "What's good for General Motors is good for the USA." Some businesses maintain that social responsibility is an after-profit obligation. Some have gone so far as to argue that social responsibility distorts the market by deflecting business from its primary role of returning profits.

In today's marketplace, if a company undertakes what it believes to be environmentally responsible actions (particularly actions beyond those required by government), it is advantageous to communicate that. The challenge faced by receivers of this kind of communication is knowing when the "talk" indeed matches the "walk." On the Web sites of many major corporations are environmental policy statements. Recent research of these policies found that the "Majority of companies voluntarily publishing a [environmental policy] statement do not commit to most of the specific policies."[8] The authors advised outsiders to "look with a skeptical eye" at any company that commits to a policy without an economic motivation

## Box 9.2
### The Corporate Form: Problems and Solutions

Centuries ago, early business ventures like sailing expeditions faced great risk and the possibility of losing all money invested in them. So, the corporate form—where investors would not be liable for any more than the cost of their investment—was established to encourage risk-taking and speculative investments. Before the sixteenth century, business debts were transgenerational—passed on to the business owners' descendants who were forced to pay or sent to debtors' prisons.

Corporations are thus legally unique: "The charter of limited liability distinguishes a corporation from all other forms of enterprise, because it was (and is) actually a gift of the state—a grant, a covenant, a form of permission that citizens, through their government, delegate to the corporation and its shareholders."[1] Corporate status means that "by nature, by law, and by tradition," corporations have a legal mandate to place shareholders' profit interests above those of the community, the state, and the environment.[2] After the Civil War, courts applied the "due process" clause of the Fourteenth Amendment (protecting the rights of freed slaves) to corporations, granting them the legal status of a natural person. Like a person, a corporation could buy and sell property, borrow money, sue, and be sued—though unlike citizens, corporations could deduct the cost of legal expenses when accused or convicted of crimes. Some argue that the status granted to corporations has turned them into the worst kind of citizen, claiming the rights but not the responsibilities of citizenship.[3]

Since states grant charters, states can revoke them. A group of lawyers asked the state of California to revoke the charter of Unocal for repeated and grievous offenses, which would have dissolved Unocal and sold its assets. Although the California Attorney General refused to revoke the charter, he acknowledged that his office had the power to do so.

Another solution is to amend corporate codes by adding language that requires more than the pursuit of profit. Former corporate attorney Robert Hinkley proposed adding a twenty-eight-word Code for Corporate Citizenship to corporate charters: "The duty of directors henceforth shall be to make money for shareholders, but not at the expense of the environment, human rights, public health and safety, dignity of employees, and the welfare of the communities in which the company operates."[4] Hinkley—and perhaps more Americans like him—believes the public is ready to hold corporations more accountable.

1. Paul Hawken, *The Ecology of Commerce: A Declaration of Sustainability* (New York: HarperCollins, 1993), 106.

2. Ibid., 116.

3. Mark Achbar, Jennifer Abbott, and Joel Bakan, *The Corporation*, (Zeitgeist Films, Canada 2004).

4. Arnie Cooper, "'Twenty-Eight Words that Could Change the World,' an interview with Robert Hinkley," *The Sun* (Sept. 2004).

for implementing it.[9] In a survey of Fortune 500 companies and the relationship between environmental objectives and business strategy, a researcher concluded that despite a small number of "proactive firms," traditional management objectives (such as cost and risk reduction) still dominate. The study also concluded that "coercive government interventions are still the most important policy tools" and drivers of business' environmental decisions.[10]

PR is a major component in the strategic positioning of many businesses in relation to the environment. PR goals include a favorable business climate, which can mean a fairly unfettered ability to seek profit and create positive public sentiment. Although those goals are not mutually exclusive to environmental protection, some companies view them that way. As a result, an increasing focus in some PR departments is "green communication" that seeks to shift the guardian-commercial relationship by arguing for voluntary environmental compliance and oversight, market-driven regulation, and "sustainability." We'll return to this PR strategy later in the chapter.

## Public Relations: Objectives, Strategies, and Tactics

Let's say you come across an ad for the National Wetlands Coalition, whose logo features ducks flying over a marsh. Given the name and visual, a logical conclusion is that this group is trying to protect wetlands and the creatures dependent on them.

How do you know whether this message is authentic? Is it possible to detect what might be called "green spin"? It's not easy and it depends on several things: how public relations functions in the organization, whether the message crosses the line from persuasion to propaganda, and whether the communication stresses merely image or actual performance.

A key distinction is how organizational resources shape what strategies and message channels are used. Even though the tactics of public relations are available to all, the money is not. Financial resources are critical to all kinds of communication, including environmental communication. While some "free" message channels ostensibly are available to all—such as news publicity—expensive channels such as advertising are not. As noted, the government has both legal and financial limits to the type of messages it can transmit and is thus heavily dependent on news media, as are environmental groups. Environmental groups' budgets severely limit their communication choices, and due to their status as challengers may hinder their ability to obtain free news publicity. In contrast, businesses and in particular large corporations have very large PR and advertising budgets. To a certain degree, ample resources can enable an organization's communication efforts to be highly proactive. (For more about the basic terms and elements of PR, see Box 9.3.)

The National Wetlands Coalition, for example, is a front group, crafted to resemble a grassroots conservation organization but in truth is a front for a variety of oil drillers, developers, and natural gas companies who want to weaken wetlands protection. Because the identity, donors, and true purpose are concealed, it's a classic case of propaganda.

## Public Relations within Organizations

One of the first PR men mentioned by virtually every public relations textbook is P. T. Barnum, promoter and circus owner who coined the phrase "there's a sucker born every minute." Barnum began his career in 1863 by buying Joice Heth, an old Negro slave, and putting her on exhibit for the public as the 160-year-old childhood nursemaid to George Washington. Barnum contributed to the hoax by forging letters about the exhibit and sending them to the New York press. When an autopsy upon Heth's death pegged her true age at about eighty, Barnum said he was deeply shocked at the way this woman had deceived him.[11] PR counselors of the time also worked on the image of John D. Rockefeller, Sr., whose family was widely hated for its ruthless, monopolistic business tactics. To soften his image, Rockefeller's PR advisors told him to carry a pocketful of dimes to give away to children whenever he was seen in public.

PR textbooks label such early practices as "press agentry," characterized by manipulation and hype, and which closely resembles propaganda.[12] Today, the PR of Hollywood, sports celebrities, and even some politicians can be characterized as press agentry.

By the early 1900s, some PR practice began to focus on simply putting out factual information, a model labeled "public information" or publicity, which is the model most often practiced by most

**Box 9.3**

PR by the (Text)book

Introductory PR textbooks teach the "four-step process" of PR: research, planning, communication, and evaluation.

In *research*, primary and secondary research collect information on pertinent issues and affected audiences. Conducting systematic, objective research is the foundation for two-way communication.

In the *planning* step, research is utilized to strategize objectives, key messages, and the most appropriate channels to reach target audiences. Another piece of planning is the "situation analysis," or an accounting of the current message and issue environment.

The *communication* stage involves active communication and will vary according to the type of issue. For an emerging issue, communication will focus on raising awareness in a way that allows an organization to help define or frame the new issue. For a long-standing issue of some controversy, the message environment is crowded. Only messages deemed the most credible, newsworthy, shocking, or otherwise unusual will receive much attention. Of course, any message broadcast widely enough and repeated stands a better chance of reaching the most ears and eyeballs.

In the *evaluation* step, the entire process is critiqued for its effectiveness. Depending on the duration of the action or campaign, evaluation may take place throughout and used to make ongoing adjustments in messages, audiences, or channels.

PR textbooks also focus on objectives, strategies, and tactics as the building blocks of communication campaigns. An *objective* is a desired outcome or end result, either in terms of attitude or behavior change or in simple terms of information sent. A well-written objective is measurable, which also is key to effective evaluation.

In its narrowest sense, a *strategy* describes how you will reach an objective conceptually or how the message will be positioned. The advertising campaign by the milk industry positioned milk as healthy for athletic (celebrity) bodies. President Bush's "Healthy Forests Initiative" was a strategy to get the public to support increased logging on federal lands by conveying it as the healthy way to protect forests and prevent massive forest fires.

*Tactics* are the on-the-ground, nuts-and-bolts messages and activities that communicate strategies and help reach objectives. For best effect, tactics involve a mix of channels to reach different audiences but essentially work toward the same end. A campaign to boost recycling might involve tactics such as bill stuffers, community events, news publicity, T-shirts and bumper stickers, billboards, and activities at public schools.

government agencies today. At noted earlier, it is illegal to call government information "public relations," hence the common job titles of public information or public affairs. This model of practice is primarily one-way, meaning information is issued from the organization to the public and interested audiences, but far less information is formally solicited and brought into the organization. A prohibition of spending money on communication research (such as of public attitudes and desires) hinders many government agencies from fully moving beyond the public information model.

From the 1920s onward, a growing body of public opinion and psychology research helped scholars better tap people's opinions and sentiments and shifted the focus of some PR to "scientific persuasion." Although data-gathering made the information exchange between organization and audiences slightly more two-way, the intent remained on persuading individuals to accept organizational practices and products.

Edward Bernays, an early PR practitioner and researcher (and nephew of Sigmund Freud), described this as the "engineering of consent." In his 1928 book *Propaganda*, Bernays argued that such manipulation was simply good science and was needed to overcome societal chaos and conflict:

> The conscious and intelligent manipulation of the organized habits and opinions of the masses is an important element in democratic society. Those who manipulate this unseen mechanism of society constitute an invisible government which is the true ruling power of our country. . . . We are governed, our minds are molded, our tastes formed, our ideas suggested, largely by men we have never heard of. This is a logical result of the way in which our democratic society is organized. . . . In almost every act of our daily lives, whether in the sphere of politics or business, in our social conduct or our ethical thinking, we are dominated by the relatively small number of persons . . . who understand the mental processes and social patterns of the masses. It is they who pull the wires which control the public mind."[13]

Although this form of PR practice emphasizes two-way communication and gathering audience opinions and sentiments, it is considered "asymmetrical" because the burden of change or persuasion rests entirely with individuals outside the organization. In other words, knowledge of opinions or market preferences is used to better "sell" the organization to the audience and persuade changes in audience attitudes or behaviors. Communication is used to align individuals' interests with those of the organization, not the organization's interests with the public's.

Only in the last several decades have PR scholars conceptualized a "two-way symmetric" model of PR practice that truly aligns the organization's and public's interests and expects changes and adjustments in both their behaviors. For example, Interface carpet company—out of concern for the environment and its customers—greatly reduced the amount of raw materials, waste, and toxins in its products. It also redesigned its carpets in a way that allows the replacement of worn areas and not the entire carpet. The goal of two-way symmetric PR is actions that are mutually beneficial to organization and audiences and builds relationships over the long term.

Today, the practice of PR struggles to professionalize itself. Yet, the field has carried forward all of its past practices into the future and all models of PR are present today. And in spite of its push for a more ethical and professional field, when the Public Relations Society of America revised its Code of Ethics in 2000, it placed even less emphasis on enforcement for a code that was nonbinding and lacked teeth to begin with.

### PERSUASION AND PROPAGANDA

The techniques used in environmental communication often go beyond simple "persuasion," which we think of as rather neutral and harmless when compared with "propaganda." As discussed in the advertising chapter, the distinction is far more subtle and concerns the purpose, identity of the sender, and control of information. Persuasion is an interactive attempt to influence by satisfying the needs of both persuader and persuadee. In persuasion, you have access to other information and you know exactly who is trying to persuade you and what his or her purpose is. Propaganda, on the other hand, is communicated with a concealed purpose, concealed identity, and takes place in an environment where the free flow of information is somehow restricted. Unlike persuasion, propaganda seeks to further the goals of the propagandist and is not necessarily in the individual's best interests.

In his classic book *The Prince*, published over four centuries ago, Niccolo Machiavelli recognized that there was power both in using and withholding information. The work of modern-day public relations is quite adept at the control of information for its benefit by:

> Withholding information and releasing it at predetermined times
> Releasing information juxtaposed with other information to influence public perception
> Manufacturing and/or distorting information
> Communicating information only to select audiences
> Controlling the media as a source of information distribution
> Presenting distorted information from what appears to be a credible source

As a key information-generator in this country, government at all levels exercises a great deal of information control. News releases are printed with "release dates." Politicians and agencies alike are known for releasing potentially damaging information late on Friday when news media are disadvantaged in writing comprehensive stories. Yet, given the legitimated authority role of government, its information can be inherently newsworthy. Media may feel controlled and manipulated by such tactics, yet feel compelled not to ignore the information either. The business sector also may engage in these information control practices, but their monetary resources provide them with additional ways to control information.

"Perception management" is an example of the control of information to serve propagandistic ends and frequently includes the deliberate creation of doubt and uncertainty. As described in the critical film *The Corporation*, managing the public perception of a corporation involves making the company appear indispensable, responsible for progress and the good life, and as the most efficient form of business.[14] The film describes the work of the large, international PR firm Burson Marsteller and its efforts to help clients identify resources and barriers and use communication to create public perceptions. The PR firm sees this as helping the corporation "have a voice" and a viewpoint on important issues. In reality, however, managing a perception in this way entails creating or massaging reality. For example, Burson Marsteller created a fake grassroots group called the British Columbia Forest Alliance to combat environmental campaigns critical of Canadian forestry corporations.

### PERCEPTION MANAGEMENT AND SCIENTIFIC UNCERTAINTY

Another method to influence public perception is to question legitimate scientific findings and create uncertainty. This strategy was used extensively by the tobacco industry to question the accumulating scientific evidence regarding the health effects of smoking. A well-known Brown and Williamson tobacco company memo from the late 1960s observed that "Doubt is our product since it is the best means of competing with the 'body of fact' that exists in the mind of the general public. It is also the means of establishing a controversy."[15]

The same tactic was used in the 1970s by DuPont when science revealed the role of CFCs (chlorofluorocarbons) in the destruction of the ozone layer. DuPont, working with the giant PR firm Hill and Knowlton, set up a "quick response" campaign to react to scientific findings and temper critical press accounts. According to one journalist, the campaign successfully "attacked the science behind the ozone depletion fears and delayed government action for two years, enough time for DuPont to bring new, ozone-friendly chemicals to market."[16]

For another issue, DuPont created doubt regarding the spread of a toxic chemical in the environment by editing a state agency's news releases, an example of the propagandistic control of media as an information distributor.[17] In 2002, South Carolina Department of Environmental Protection regulators planned to warn Wood County residents in a news release that the toxic man-made chemical C8 was spreading across the area through air emissions from DuPont's Parkersburg plant. The news release was killed after complaints from a DuPont lawyer. In a sworn statement filed with EPA, an agency spokesperson explained that DuPont regularly reviewed and edited agency news releases concerning C8.

More recently, the manufacture of doubt has been used by the oil and gas industry to forestall action on global climate change. In 2005, the *New York Times* reported that a White House official—a former

American Petroleum Industry lobbyist with no scientific training—had edited government reports on climate change research, inserting numerous expressions of doubt.[18] Shortly after, an article in *Scientific American* by George Washington University epidemiologist David Michaels told how oil and gas industries hired consulting firms to review critical scientific findings about climate change "and pull these studies apart." Michaels said these attacks "outgun" scientists who lack the time and money to defend or replicate their research. He concluded that "The vilification of threatening research as 'junk science' and the corresponding sanctification of industry-commissioned research as 'sound science' has become nothing less than standard operating procedure in some parts of corporate America."[19]

The government (and the political forces that oversee it) also has tried to manage public perception around global climate change. In January 2006, James Hansen, physicist and director of NASA's Goddard Institute for Space Studies, was ordered by his superiors to submit for advance review his scientific papers, speeches, and Web postings. This occurred after Hansen announced two dire findings about climate change. Hansen refused.

The Global Climate Coalition was founded in 1989 by forty-six petroleum and automotive industries and the National Association of Manufacturers to counter the "myth of global warming."[20] The coalition was a client of E. Bruce Harrison's PR firm (who orchestrated the chemical industry attack on Rachel Carson's *Silent Spring*), and fought to weaken the 1992 UN Earth Summit treaty on climate change. The Coalition also opposed Senate ratification of the Kyoto Protocol that would have assigned stringent targets for lowering greenhouse gas emissions. "Drawing upon a cadre of skeptical scientists, during the early and mid-1990s the Global Climate Coalition sought to emphasize the uncertainties of climate science and attack the mathematical models used to project future climate changes. The group and its proxies challenged the need for action on global warming, called the phenomenon natural rather than man-made, and even flatly denied it was happening."[21]

After the Kyoto Protocol emerged in 1997, the Coalition was forced to focus on economic arguments rather than challenge the science. At this point, some corporations that had previously supported "skepticism" were converted. Shell, Texaco, British Petroleum, Ford, General

Motors, and DaimlerChrysler all abandoned the Global Climate Coalition. In 2002, the Coalition was "deactivated," saying on its Web
site that "The industry voice on climate change has served its purpose
by contributing to a new national approach to global warming."[22]

Yet one journalist noted that some "forces of denial"—most notably the American Petroleum Institute (API) and ExxonMobil—remain committed to fighting the idea of climate change and the science supporting it. "In 1998, the *New York Times* exposed an API
memo outlining a strategy to invest millions to 'maximize the impact of scientific views consistent with ours with Congress, the media and other key audiences.' The document stated: 'Victory will be
achieved when . . . recognition of uncertainty becomes part of the
'conventional wisdom.'"[23]

A lengthy investigative article published in *Mother Jones* traced
nearly $9 million of ExxonMobil contributions from 2000 through
2003 to organizations seeking to undermine scientific findings, including "more than 40 think-tanks; media outlets, and consumer, religious, and even civil rights groups that preach skepticism about the
oncoming climate catastrophe."[24] The American Enterprise Institute
(which received $960,000) published an article about global warming
titled "Don't Worry, Be Happy"; the Hoover Foundation (recipient of
$140,000) published one called "Happiness Is a Warm Planet."

The notion that corporations ought to fund think tanks to mold
public perception and support their political agendas (rather than
funding objective research) is a phenomenon of the last few decades.
This allows corporate views to be communicated in arenas less stringent than mass media and public forums, and not subject to scientific controls in peer-reviewed journals. Back in 1977, the influential
neo-conservative Irving Kristol of the American Enterprise Institute
published an essay in the *Wall Street Journal* that advised business to
fund public policy groups that support a laissez-faire, antiregulatory
agenda. He said that "corporate philanthropy should not be, and
cannot be, disinterested," but should serve as a means "to shape or
reshape the climate of public opinion."[25]

### SPIN: IMAGE VERSUS PERFORMANCE

In a Rubes cartoon, two Egyptian-looking men stand in front of what
looks like a completed pyramid. One of them says, "Excellent! Pha-

raoh will be quite pleased to learn that you've completed construction under budget and ahead of schedule." But we can see from behind that the pyramid is actually a cardboard-looking facade that's been propped up. This pyramid is all about image, not performance.

When an organization tries to substitute an environmentally friendly image for a lack of performance, it's called "greenwashing." The *Concise Oxford English Dictionary* defines it as "disinformation disseminated by an organization so as to present an environmentally responsible public image." Typically, messages crafted by public relations are what paint an organization as eco-friendly. But it can take a lot of digging to discern how the publicized tidbit is not representative of overall practice. Royal Caribbean Cruise Lines claimed on its Web site that "nothing gets dumped overboard," but Web site visitors probably wouldn't know that the company pled guilty to twenty-one felony counts for pouring waste oil and hazardous chemicals into U.S. waters, and then falsifying logbooks to cover it up.[26] The Coca Cola Company communicates its sponsorship of America Recycles Day but doesn't tell you that the 20 million plastic bottles Coke sells *every day* are entirely virgin plastic.[27]

The messages most subject to greenwashing are those controlled by the organization, such as Web sites, brochures, and advertisements. Unlike news coverage and other information that receives scrutiny, verification, and comment, these messages are "controlled" because the originator dictates exactly what the message says and where and when it appears. Thus, an ad or a Web site could boast of one small green action, that while true, is a distortion of the organization's environmental record. As discussed in the advertising chapter, image ads focus on the reputation or good deeds of the business and differ from product ads seeking a direct sale. Recent environmental image ads have been bought by a wide range of companies: Phillips Petroleum, GM, Mobil, Weyerhauser, Georgia-Pacific, Chrysler, Mitsubishi, Cattlemen's Association, Dow Chemical, and International Paper.

A leading PR figure in corporate environmental spin is E. Bruce Harrison, who published *Going Green: How to Communicate Your Company's Environmental Commitment* in 1993. According to Harrison, "Good green communication—the open, two-way exchange between parties with interest in a specific environmental matter (the process I call envirocomm)—is a vital part of positive green positioning, or placing the business person and the company squarely on the public-interest green."[28] Yet Harrison counsels readers that becoming green is all about the mental habit of thinking like a good guy and shifting your "green paradigm" for success: "Fortunately, this need not require too much work on your part."[29] Harrison's solution is communication, not action. He also concludes that the environmental movement is dead and that the regulations of the 1970s "have done their job and ought to be let out to pasture—or put out if they won't go peaceably."[30] Instead, "Corporate environmentalism is now more lively than external activist environmentalism . . . and this trend will continue to grow."[31]

Some federal agencies have increasingly turned to PR firms to supplement their internal information efforts and produce controlled messages. By one estimate, in 2004 alone, the federal government spent $88 million on contracts with PR firms.[32] In several instances, these PR contracts were used to sell controversial programs to the public. The Government Accounting Office ruled that publicity produced by a PR firm for the U.S. Forest Service was blatantly one-sided and designed to convince the public that revisions to the Sierra Nevada Forest Plan were necessary and cost-effective for avoiding catastrophic wildfires.

But most of the prominent instances of greenwashing involve advertising and corporations. (For suggestions on how to evaluate image and advocacy ads, see Box 9.4.) A recent ad by Shell in *National Geographic* read, "What do we really need in today's energy-hungry world? More gardeners." The ad copy described Shell's support of the Flower Garden Banks National Marine Sanctuary in the Gulf of Mexico, which sounds very green. The cost of advertising in this magazine runs in the six-figure range; Shell contributed just five thousand dollars a year to the sanctuary. In other words, Shell spent far more touting its contribution than on its performance.

A similar example is Chevron's long-running ad campaign "People Do." One advertisement showed an endangered San Joaquin kit fox escaping a coyote by running into an artificial den of buried pipe, built by Chevron employees "because they care." Yet some biologists say artificial dens don't help foxes much because if chased, a fox is likely to run to the old den location. The cost to Chevron for each ar-

## Box 9.4

### Evaluating Image and Advocacy Advertisements

When you evaluate image and advocacy advertisements, consider three dimensions: portrayal of *adversaries*, type of *appeal*, and the *sponsor's interests*.

Typical *adversaries* are government agencies, special interest groups, competitors, and the general public, which could be portrayed as unnecessarily restricting actions or not acting forcefully, as spreading falsehoods or half truths, or not fully understanding the issue.

*Appeals* come in three types. An *emotional* appeal tries to build readers' sympathies by focusing on general, intangible, or aesthetic concerns: "If we find more ways to turn every day into Earth Day, what a wonderful world it will be" (text from a newspaper ad by Dayton's on Earth Day). An ad using *reasoned persuasion* might present data to rationalize a position and link the advertiser's interests with the reader's: "Kennecott Utah Copper has planted some 30,000 trees and shrubs, and reclaimed more than 9,000 acres of land for wildlife. . . . Kennecott's philosophy is to balance our everyday needs for metals with an environmentally sound approach to mining. Kennecott recognizes that being a good steward of the land . . . is essential to our business success" (in a print ad by Kennecott). In an *informational* appeal, the reader might be urged to decide for herself: "People start pollution. People can stop it" (slogan of the Keep America Beautiful campaign).

There are a number of ways that the *sponsor's* interest in the issue can be identified. A *disinterested* or *benevolent* sponsor is identified, but connected only generally to an issue presented as a broad public concern, such as litter in the Keep America Beautiful ad. Benefits to the sponsor are either indirect or not mentioned. The Dayton's Earth Day ad is an example of a benevolent sponsor. A *self-righteous* sponsor will openly associate its self-interest with the issue and may openly defend that self-interest by criticizing opponents' arguments; Kennecott is a self-righteous sponsor. Although the identity of a *participative sponsor* may be clear, the sponsor's self-interest is carefully disguised and the issue is presented as a problem common to industry and in the public interest. Many of the ads in Mobil's long-standing advocacy advertising campaign present Mobil as a participative sponsor, arguing a stance on national energy policy yet not mentioning what the position means for Mobil specifically. Finally, the self-interests (and sometimes identity) of an *elusive* sponsor may be carefully disguised, focusing instead on general social concern and public benefit. Lobbying groups or industry front groups are frequently elusive sponsors. For example, the average person would not know that the U.S. Council for Energy Awareness is an industry lobbying group.

Source: Adapted from S. P. Sethi, *Advocacy Advertising and Large Corporations: Social Conflict, Big Business Image, the News Media, and Public Policy* (Lexington, MA: Lexington Books, 1977).

tificial den was less than three thousand dollars, while the estimated cost of the People Do campaign during the year this ad was run $5 to $6 million.[33] In addition, artificial den construction is a standard mitigation procedure for oil companies operating where kit foxes live. The American Petroleum Institute (of which Chevron is member) supports lobbying to gut some of the laws that require projects like kit fox den construction. According to one critic, Chevron wants to hide its forty-nine Superfund sites and the millions of dollars paid for environmental infractions behind its People Do ads.[34]

Naturally, any organization will accentuate and communicate the positive over the negative. But over time and with repeated exposure, the public may be persuaded that a company is a responsible environmental steward when it is not. In a poll of Californians after Chevron's People Do campaign had been running for about five years, Chevron was named as the oil company consumers trust most to protect the environment. The trend toward communicating a green image is red hot. Today all large and many smaller PR firms have environmental divisions for their corporate clients, divisions which in the 1990s generated more than $86 million in fees.[35]

Green image ads also create the illusion that corporations take pro-environmental actions voluntarily, which "serves to defeat or marginalize environmental activism"[36] and makes corporations appear responsible and taking care of things independent of regulation by the guardian. Thus greenwashing can have a pointed political agenda: "to persuade the public that strict environmental laws are no longer needed, because America's environmental problems have been solved and the only thing left to fear is regulation itself."[37]

In 2003, a confidential memo from Republican consultant Frank Luntz to party leaders was leaked to the press. The memo detailed the party's greenwash strategy and warned Republicans that they had "lost the communication battle" over the environment. It encouraged them to gain control by seizing the "window of opportunity to challenge the science" on global warming. Luntz recommended safe yet evocative buzz words (like safer, cleaner, healthier) and a focus on the "fair balance between the environment and economy." Luntz concluded that "A compelling strategy, even if factually inaccurate, can be more emotionally compelling than a dry recitation of the truth."

Another PR strategy that can result in spin is to shift blame from an organization to individuals. In the 1970s, a popular ad by Keep America Beautiful and the Ad Council featured Native American actor Iron Eyes Cody with a tear running down his cheek at the sight of litter along roadways and streams. This campaign sent the message that *individuals* were the ones most responsible for pollution. This fit with the self-interest of Keep America Beautiful, which has lobbied against mandatory recycling and bottle deposit laws that would make businesses more responsible for the final disposal of their products.[38] The Keep America Beautiful campaign (funded by Coke, McDonalds, Scott Paper, and landfill and incinerator companies) frames litter clean-up as a superficial solution that's preferable to substantive action.

Greenwashing in ads has become so popular that nonprofit organizations buy counter-ads and give greenwash "awards" to expose the large gaps between environmental image and performance. The July 2005 "Greenwasher of the Month," named by the nonprofit watchdog group The Green Life, was ExxonMobil, the world's largest publicly traded oil company, whose net earnings are $25.3 billion and whose products and operations give rise to about 5 percent of the global human-made $CO_2$ emissions.[39]

One Exxon ad features a tea kettle whose steam swirls in a circle back to the kettle under the headline "We're all for reducing emissions." The ad says that Exxon uses cogeneration to harness steam from power plants to use in its refining process. What's left unsaid, however, is that other oil companies spend far more on renewable and alternative energy. When ExxonMobil announced a stunning $10 billion in profit for the third quarter of 2005, it said it had no plans to invest any of those earnings in developing alternative or renewable energy.[40] To counter its greenwashing, "Exxpose Exxon" is a grassroots campaign calling for Exxon to stop lobbying to open the Arctic National Wildlife Refuge, to pay outstanding damages from the 1989 *Exxon Valdez* spill, to increase investment in renewables, and to withdraw funding from groups arguing against the existence of global warming.

Two automakers are examples of greenwash advertising, according to the California-based nonprofit Bluewater Network. Bluewater's 2005 ad campaign asked, "Is Toyota a wolf in sheep's clothing?"

Bluewater questions why the automaker is fighting tougher standards on fuel economy and emissions. While Toyota's overall fuel economy is the best in the industry (27.5 mpg), it is worse than it was twenty years ago (30 mpg).[41]

In 2004, Bluewater launched its "Jumpstart Ford" campaign for Ford's last-place ranking in fuel economy standards.[42] Some Ford image ads tout the "living" roof of its Dearborn, Michigan, truck plant, which manufactures Ford F-150s, which get the *lowest* fuel economy in its class (11.9 city and 15.2 highway mpg). The Green Life gave its greenwash award in May 2004 for Ford's "The Greening of the Blue Oval" campaign, saying that the ten acres of plants grown on the Dearborn plant roof are "not nearly large enough to absorb the carbon dioxide emissions created by the gas-guzzling F-150s that roll off the assembly line below." Green Life said that "Based on Ford's ranking at the bottom of the fuel economy rankings, the absurdity of building worst-in-class pickups within a supposedly sustainable manufacturing facility, and its preference for voluntary targets over concrete benchmarks for long-term emissions reductions, it appears that the blue oval has not yet been greened, just greenwashed."[43] Although Ford now sells a hybrid SUV, the company's environmental performance is far from "green" (see Figure 9.1).

In 2000, British Petroleum began a $200 million "rebranding" campaign, replacing its traditional shield logo with a green and yellow sunburst and shortening its name to BP. The campaign positioned BP at the vanguard of environmental reform in the energy industry—"Beyond Petroleum." Part of the campaign was "Plug in the Sun" and featured the installation of solar panels in two hundred gas stations around the world. The ad campaign said "we can fill you up by sunshine" and put "some sun in your life."

Unlike many oil and gas companies, BP has recognized climate change and tried to get mileage with environmentally savvy customers. A recent BP ad in national U.S. magazines proclaimed, "Reducing our footprint: here's where we stand." The copy talks of deep water drilling technology, pipeline construction that "helps preserve wetlands," and cogeneration at "one of our largest facilities." Nevertheless for every sixteen dollars BP spends on solar energy, it spends ten thousand more on oil exploration and development.[44] According to the nonprofit CorpWatch, "Below the surface of their public rela-

**Figure 9.1**

tions efforts, however, BP continues to steamroll ahead with gas and oil production, prompting questions about just how serious they are about climate change."[45] BP also is the lead shareholder in the Baku-Ceyhan oil pipeline, which runs 1,100 miles from Azerbaijan through Georgia to a Turkish seaport. Nongovernmental organizations monitoring this project found 173 violations of World Bank environmental and social standards in the Turkish section alone during the design stage.

Chevron continues to be extremely active on the greenwashing front in ads, its Web site, and as a supplier of "supplemental educational materials" provided free of charge to classrooms. A leaked memo said the purpose of these materials was "informing teachers/ students about uncertainties in climate science." The American Petroleum Institute (of which Chevron is a member) supplies a K-8 module called "Energy and Society" which includes a CD called "Energy and Me." The CD integrates music and dance with energy education and teaches that global warming is still scientifically controversial.

### Strategies and Tactics: Getting the Green Word Out

A skillful PR practitioner in government or business has a lot of tactical options for communicating the strategies of his or her organization. In addition to Web sites, ads, and news releases, there is e-mail and snail mail, newsletters, pamphlets and brochures, film and photo, interpersonal communication to one or many, special events, demos, and field trips, to name a few. Here we'll discuss three of note to government and business that have potential to greenwash and cross the persuasion-propaganda line: video news releases (VNRs), trade association campaigns, and front groups and fake grassroots organizations.

#### VIDEO NEWS RELEASES

Most of us watching the evening news would not recognize a VNR when we saw it. VNRs (discussed briefly in the news media chapter) are designed to be seamless, either as fully produced audio-video packages or just videos with scripts. Today, VNRs are distributed via satellite to almost all of the approximately 750 television newsrooms in the nation. Because a professionally produced VNR can cost fifteen to twenty-five thousand dollars to produce and another ten to fifteen thousand dollars to distribute and get on the air, corporations were once the primary producers. However, a great deal of the scrutiny in the last couple of years has concerned VNR production by the federal government.

What makes VNRs controversial is that they almost always are aired without attribution or source identification. Editors don't want to label the source because it is at odds with journalism's mission to verify independently the claims of its news sources. VNRs became prevalent at a time when more and more television stations were cutting news budgets and were glad to have packaged news to call their own, even if prepared by organizations seeking to sell products or programs. VNR sponsors and producers are reluctant to label their videos or on-camera spokespeople because they want the media's stamp of legitimacy. Richard Edelman, CEO of Edelman Public Relations, said he prefers the easy "compromise" of requiring on-screen disclosure for government-produced VNRs but no such requirement for the larger and more lucrative corporate VNR market.

Neither cost nor legal restrictions has prevented the federal government from playing the VNR game. As mentioned, the Gillett Amendment prohibited the use of federal money for "publicity or propaganda purposes" not authorized by Congress. In past cases, federal agencies violated this restriction if they failed to identify clearly the source of editorials and newspaper articles disseminated to the media. The departments of Interior and Agriculture have been some of the biggest producers of VNRs. According to the independent watchdog group Center for Media and Democracy, USDA's Broadcast Media and Technology Center has a $2.8 million annual budget that it has used to produce over ninety VNRs and two thousand ANRs (audio news releases for radio).

*USA Today* reported that in the past decade, the Department of Interior had distributed nearly three hours worth of VNRs to news stations. Two videos concerned U.S. Geological Survey research into West Nile virus. In one VNR produced in September 2003, the narrator signed off "Porter Versfelt reporting," sounding like a bona fide journalist.[46]

The U.S. Forest Service hired the PR firm One-World Communication to produce VNRs and printed materials for "Forests with a

Future" concerning the Sierra Nevada Forest Plan. Not mentioned in the publicity materials was that the new plan replaced a Clinton-era plan that represented ten years of scientific study and public input. Timber removal would increase from 111 million board feet in the old plan to 330 million board feet in the new one.

The Government Accountability Office (GAO), an investigative arm of Congress, ruled that some government VNRs in 2004 violated federal laws prohibiting "covert propaganda" by the government. The GAO said that the VNRs themselves did not state the agencies that produced them—although the TV stations that aired them certainly did know who was responsible.[47] Regarding the Sierra Nevada VNR, the GAO ruled that it wasn't illegal; even though it was one-sided, the Forest Service wasn't obligated to offer opposing opinions (as would a news medium). The report also noted that promotion of agency policy was allowable, but that promotion of the agency or officials in it was not.[48]

All this recent print media attention to government-produced VNRs diverts attention from the far more numerous corporate VNRs that also lack scrutiny and identification.

Apparently there is a new trend in the broadcasting industry to air VNRs for a fee, blurring the line even further between news and paid advertising. An article in *Broadcasting & Cable* described "secured placement," which allows a VNR producer to pay a TV station to run the VNR "news." The author said, "secured VNR buys are much more cost-effective than conventional ad buys," because the average cost of a secured VNR was fifteen to twenty-five thousand dollars to produce and ten to fifty thousand dollars for airtime. In comparison, the cost of an average thirty-second TV commercial in 2003 of was $372,000 to produce and $5 to $20 million for airtime.[49]

### TRADE ASSOCIATION CAMPAIGNS

Trade associations have long provided PR services to their members in the form of industry advertising, marketing, and lobbying. Increasingly, these associations are promoting and publicizing the voluntary steps taken by industry in the name of the environment. However, some association campaigns qualify as greenwashing designed to relieve industry of regulatory requirements.

One early example was the "Responsible Care" campaign of the Chemical Manufacturers Association. The campaign pushed the industry's voluntary standards program and was touted for its commitment to sustainable development. But the campaign also sought to throw out the Community-Right-to-Know Act (providing citizens information about the processes and pollutants produced at a plant in their community) and to reduce or eliminate the Toxic Release Inventory that manufacturers were required to submit.[50] The campaign called for a rewrite of the Clean Water Act and the Superfund Reform bill (which would exempt companies from retroactive liability for toxic sites). At the same time that Responsible Care was trying to rollback environmental protections, they were running green image ads: "As an animated dove flies from factory smokestack to factory smokestack, each stack emits a puffy white cloud into a sky of robin's-egg blue. 'When one chemical company starts cleaning up its act, that's good. When two chemical companies do it, that's better,' says the narrator, over the sound of chirping birds and a jazz combo. 'And when 200 companies get together, they can make a real difference.'"[51]

Business Roundtable, an association of almost two hundred corporate CEOs, formed "Climate Resolve" in response to President George W. Bush's challenge to the private sector to help reduce global greenhouse gases. However, Climate Resolve supports a reduction in *emissions intensity* of 18 percent by 2012—a ratio of emissions to gross domestic product (GDP), which allows emissions to continue to increase, as long as corporate revenues keep growing. This reduction is fairly easy; industry emissions dropped 21 percent in 1980s before the campaign had even begun. If a member of Climate Resolve can't meet the 18 percent, there are no consequences because participation is voluntary. In stark contrast, the Kyoto Protocol mandates *absolute reductions* below 1990 levels. In an ad for Climate Resolve, it asked, "Why are we volunteering to do this? Because what's good for the environment is good for business." The Green Life named Business Roundtable Greenwasher of the Month in September 2004 for lobbying against the Kyoto Protocol and openly questioning the validity of climate change science for nearly ten years.[52]

In Climate Resolve's first report, General Motors was noted under "Exemplary Company Actions" for removing the bulbs illuminating front panels on over one hundred vending machines. Meanwhile, GM's fleetwide fuel economy remained the same as ten years ago. GM's Web site says, "GM is dedicated to protecting human health, natural resources, and the global environment. . . . That is why we are constantly improving the performance of today's vehicles, as well as the processes used to manufacture them."[53]

A pesticide industry lobbying association called CropLife America has argued that the Environmental Protection Agency (EPA) should be free of scientific input from both the U.S. Fish and Wildlife Service and National Marine Fisheries Service. CropLife America maintains that the EPA should get to decide without consultation when pesticides might harm species protected by the Endangered Species Act. EPA already has the discretion to override pesticide restrictions in the Northwest by announcing emergency declarations of pest outbreaks. EPA also made a deal with the manufacturer of altrazine requiring them to monitor only 40 of 1,172 watersheds "at risk" for contamination. (Altrazine is an endocrine disruptor and has been banned in the European Union because of its harmful effects.) The advice that EPA might get from the federal Insecticide, Fungicide, and Rodenticide Act Task Force also is not free from bias. The task force has no members of the public, but its membership does overlap with CropLife America, with members representing BASF, Bayer CropScience, Dow AgroSciences, DuPont Ag Products, Monsanto, and Syngenta. This gives the pesticide industry influence over government decisions affecting endangered species.

In 2000, the National Ski Areas Association launched a voluntary "beyond compliance" program called Sustainable Slopes. After receiving "broad input" from ski companies, government agencies, environmental nonprofits, and others, the association identified principles in twenty-one areas of environmental management such as water resources and energy conservation. Sustainable Slopes now has 175 participants. On its Web site, an Environmental Vision Statement says the goal of the program is "To be leaders among outdoor recreation providers through managing our businesses in a way that demonstrates our commitment to environmental protection and stewardship while meeting expectations of the public." Its mission states, "We are committed to improving environmental performance in all aspects of our operations and managing our areas to allow for their continued enjoyment by future generations."

But like other voluntary compliance programs, this one lacks "specific performance-based standards, third-party oversight, and penalties for failed compliance. In other words, it allows ski areas to unsparingly sanction their own sustainability."[54] In a separate and independent study published in the *Policy Studies Journal* titled "Is Greener Whiter? Voluntary Environmental Performance of Western Ski Areas," two researchers found that ski areas participating in Sustainable Slopes actually performed worse environmentally than nonparticipating ski areas.[55]

## FRONT GROUPS AND FAKE GRASSROOTS

A key element in our democratic system of governance is that people can organize, speak up, and seek a redress of grievances from their government. In order for the government to maintain power, we expect officials to listen and respond to the wishes of the governed. This trust is violated when organizations with considerable resources corrupt the citizen-centered democratic process with front groups.

A front group, explained briefly already, is a fake grassroots group. It was not founded by a group of citizens rising from the grassroots and organizing to raise awareness and seek change. Rather it was crafted by a profit-making enterprise to look citizen-driven. The two forms are as different as Kentucky bluegrass and astroturf. The names and identities given to these groups, however, sound like the real pro-environmental thing. The Alliance for Environment and Resources supports clear-cutting in national forests. The goal of Citizens for the Environment is to eliminate federal environmental laws. The Abundant Wildlife Society lobbies for continued trapping and shooting of coyotes, mountain lions, and other predators.

Typical message strategies for front groups include casting doubt on the severity of social or environmental problems, creating doubt by magnifying uncertainty, and promoting superficial solutions that preempt changes necessary to adequately solve problems. Front groups, through name or message, portray themselves as reasonable, middle ground, and moderate. Doubt (or at least confusion) is a major strategy of the American Council on Science and Health. The Council poses its industry-funded "experts" as independent scientists. One Council health expert claimed that the Whopper wasn't unhealthy; Burger King is a donor to the Council.

Citizens for Sensible Energy Choices never had any bona fide citizens in it. Instead, the biggest donor to the group—which amassed about $1 million for polling, consulting, and TV and radio ads—was Xcel Energy. Ostensibly, the group was opposed to renewable energy mandates in Colorado, and said that sound renewable policy could be based on voluntary initiatives and not the enforceable targets proposed in a state ballot initiative. Despite the group's publicity, Coloradans passed Amendment 37, which forced large Colorado utilities (including Xcel) to produce 3 percent of their electricity from renewable sources by 2007, 6 percent by 2011, and 10 percent by 2015. Citizens for Sensible Energy Choices was named Greenwasher of the Month by The Green Life in October 2004 for getting "the world's governments to allow corporations to police themselves through voluntary codes of conduct, win-win partnerships and best practices learning models, rather than binding legislation and regulation."

Front groups have existed for decades. A 1994 article titled "Public Interest Pretenders" in *Consumer Reports* magazine said, "Today, inventing phony 'citizens' groups is an industry in its own right. . . . Public relations specialists have discovered countless ways to create at least the illusion of citizen involvement."[56] One PR firm that specializes in manufacturing grassroots-looking support is Bonner & Associates, profiled in William Greider's *Who Will Tell the People* (1992) and Stauber and Rampton's *Toxic Sludge* (1995). Jack Bonner's PR operation has three hundred phone lines, a sophisticated computer system, and employees who dial around the country looking for "white hat" citizens. Without knowing exactly who is paying for this operation, citizens are persuaded to endorse the political objectives of corporations like Dow Chemical and the Chemical Manufacturers Association.

Manufactured citizen support also has been used to combat bona fide citizen groups, particularly NIMBY (Not in My Back Yard) groups fighting the siting of a particular polluting or undesirable business. Davies Communication specializes in this area. According to critics, "John Davies helps neutralize these groups on behalf of corporate clients."[57] An ad by Davies Communication showed a photo of a white-haired lady holding a sign that said, "Not in My Backyard!" Copy accompanying the photo said: "Don't leave your future in her hands. Traditional lobbying is no longer enough. . . . To outnumber your opponents, call Davies Communications."[58] In other promotional material, Davies claims "he can make a strategically planned program look like a spontaneous explosion of community support."[59] Once a citizen is on the phone, the employee says that writers are standing by to help write a letter, or offers to patch the citizen through (for free) to the appropriate politician or official. Paid letter writers use a variety of "kitty cat" stationery, stamps, and envelopes in order to better match the caller and look like an individual response. Through the use of mass-orchestrated, manufactured support, businesses buy the appearance of widespread support and citizen advocacy.

## Conclusion

When you go to a job interview or on a first date, you are an advocate. When you turn your "best side" to the camera and accentuate the positive, you are attempting to portray yourself in the most favorable light. And why not? We are all advocates for something, someone, some belief.

PR is an advocacy profession that uses communication as its primary tool. There is nothing implicitly wrong with PR or its strategies and tactics, which are available to all. But throughout the past century, there has been a lot of dirt on the face of this profession. Saying "that was a good PR move" smacks of deceit or a smooth sleight of hand. Examples of unethical practices abound in all sectors—government and commercial, but also nonprofit.

Advocates—including those doing PR for organizations—seek companions and converts. A public information officer in the state wildlife agency and a PR director in a timber company both believe in their organizations and the roles they play, and this is apparent in all their communication. The PR practitioner probably doesn't think every time he or she sits at the keyboard, "I represent the guardian" or "I need to stress the role of the commercial sector," but the influence of organization-based advocacy is undeniable. Naturally, PR in government and business will see environmental issues according to their self-interests, and their messages and positioning will define what the problem is, who's responsible, and what's the solution.

What is problematic about the PR profession is that when seeking to gain companions and converts, the persuasion frequently gets heavy-handed and prompts observers to shout "spin!" A VNR gets distributed without an identifying tagline, which therefore conceals the messenger's identity and qualifies as a piece of propaganda. Or, a million-dollar ad campaign stresses a lovely green image that isn't representative of performance, but by virtue of repetition (and lacking refutation) the message becomes accepted reality. Both manipulate our perception, including of the natural world.

Since its founding, our country has believed itself well equipped to deal with spin. We set up a government of both representative and direct democracy, of checks and balances, of power divided between federal and state governments, and with a Bill of Rights that protects free speech and a free press. We trust that all these things will dampen divisive conflict but also will allow citizens to speak up, organize, and seek social change. James Madison's hope was that the balances would help to control "mischievous factions." Thomas Jefferson thought that as the country grew and changed, it was likely we would add articles to the Bill of Rights and perhaps write an entirely new Constitution. But no matter where our founders placed their faith, there was a strong belief that with free speech and press, in the marketplace of ideas, truth would prevail and the nation's interests would be protected. With a fair and engaged discussion of all the viewpoints, we would logically and eventually arrive at good solutions.

In practice, this has never worked perfectly. But today, our vaunted "marketplace of ideas" faces threats, including from the practice of PR. As practiced by some, advocacy communication blurs the boundaries of the guardian and corrupts the democratic process. According to one critic, greenwashing disseminates public apathy and undermines an informed citizenry. Even when tactics like front groups are exposed, they are still detrimental to the public debate and "engender profound public cynicism about the political process."[60] And, speech is not free; it's expensive. In sheer dollars—for advertising, PR firms, VNRs, and front groups—for-profit businesses are winning the PR spin battle about the environment. Buttressed by a supportive political environment, many corporations and associations tell us that they should be allowed to regulate themselves, instead of the guardian.

Government agencies are at a disadvantage in countering this. They lack large PR budgets and have legal restrictions on their publicity and information gathering, which destines them to a one-way "public information" model of PR. When truly acting as guardians of public interest and resources, they practice two-way symmetric PR, fully researching and aligning the public's interests with their own. Commercial sector PR practice, on the other hand, often follows the two-way asymmetrical model, intent on persuading the public that its actions are green, but with little intention of making substantive internal, organizational change in its environmental practice. And many companies are putting millions into green spin ads and actions instead of pro-environmental actions. Environmental groups also can play the PR game, but they are hampered by a lack of resources and other constraints, as discussed in the next chapter.

# 10

## Communication and Social Change

Think of something you once tried to change. Even if the change just involved yourself—exercising more, volunteering, watching less TV—you still faced obstacles, fought tradition and habit, and perhaps needed new skills or attitudes. If you attempted to change something beyond yourself—your brother's opinion, a city regulation, a corporate practice—what did you face? All of the above, plus resistance or outright opposition.

When someone seeks change, it signals a dissatisfaction with the way things are now—with the status quo, if you will. The person seeking change perceives a gap between the existing state of affairs and something more desirable. And there's a reason for the familiar ring of what we call the "status quo"—what exists now is comfortable and known, and to some degree it "works" and makes sense. At some point, the attitude, the policy, or the practice made sense to adopt (at least for some person or institution), so changing it to something new and unknown will require a considerable shift.

When you try and change an opinion or policy, what do you utilize? Communication. Though some may view change as a political or social process, the primary tool is nevertheless communication. On the surface, efforts to effect environmental change may seem like battles over physical things like wilderness or air or fish. But in a larger sense, the communicative battle is over the meaning and value attached those physical things, which affects their destiny. In essence, it's a struggle of rhetoric and persuasive argument and the ability to have your values and problem definition prevail and become the accepted cultural viewpoint, the new status quo.

But it's not just a matter of individual messages aimed at individual people. As noted in similar ways in previous chapters, messages compete in a cultural arena that's designed to favor some messages over others, making it very much a struggle at the level of social institutions and culture. And, what makes a message persuasive is a combination of factors: what the person was thinking about when she read the message, and whether those thoughts were reinforced by economics, the physical environment, friends and family, the entire social context.

When it comes to environmental change, the environmental social movement is the largest, most organized force for change. For over a century, movement activists have sought change of the status quo to varying degrees and have encountered varying degrees of social control, cooptation, and even outright suppression. (See Box 10.1 to learn about the countering "wise use" movement.) The environmental movement has achieved some grand successes yet failed to reach more comprehensive goals. Social movement scholars recognize that drastic social change of any kind is exceedingly rare, and even moderate social change is very difficult to achieve.

This chapter examines the entire landscape of communication and social change, bringing together lessons from the previous chapters with lessons of social movement theory to help understand what environmental activists face today. First, what could be called the "dominant social paradigm" is contrasted with an "environmental paradigm" as a marker of the type of changes being sought. Next, we put the lessons from previous chapters in the context of what they tell the environmental movement about successful communication. This leads of to a taxonomy of environmental groups; like any organization, a group's structure, history, and goals affect the kind of communication in which it engages. In turn, groups make tactical choices for their communication, relying on a variety of channels, actions, and positioning to get their messages across; here we examine member communication and news media. Finally, we consider a new vision for the communication of environmental change.

## Box 10.1

The Counter Movement: "Wise Use"

When the environmental movement achieved success, it encountered opposition from well-organized and often well-funded groups rallied around the
banners of "wise use" and "property rights." Wise use adherents claim that
environmentalists and environmental regulations destroy free enterprise, private property rights, jobs, and force industries out of business. A classic symbol was the endangered spotted owl, blamed for problems encountered by
the timber industry. Such concerns are felt most intensely in the West by re-
source-extractive industries[1] but wise use philosophy gets support throughout the country from those who feel impacted by environmental reforms or
perceived attempts by outsiders to change traditional rural ways of life.[2]

Some wise users consider themselves the true conservationists who hunt
and fish and oppose "locking up" public lands. However, most wise use
groups also want relaxed environmental protections. Wise use groups run
the gamut of anti-environmental perspectives. The most zealous wise use
activists see environmental laws as a conspiracy to allow the United Nations
to take over, the position of the Utah-based National Federal Lands Conference, which supports antifederal "militias."[3]

The wise use movement had its roots in the 1980s Sagebrush Rebellion, a backlash against environmentalism and land management policies by
conservative and largely Western landowners. In response, the BLM began
a push to privatize some public lands and halted a proposal to raise grazing
fees. Although privatization was never fully implemented, it shifted relationships between land managers, residents, and environmentalists. In the mid-
1990s, the Republicans' Contract with America provided another boost to
wise use groups.

Wise use groups use the same tactics as the environmental movement:
letter-writing, phone campaigns, media stunts, and political involvement.
But wise use sympathizers also have reportedly intimidated and assaulted environmental activists.[4] A favored legal tactic was SLAPPs, "strategic lawsuits
against public participation." Hundreds were filed by developers, polluters,
wise use groups, and sympathetic law firms to impede the work of environmentalists or slow law enforcement.

## Changing the Dominant Social Paradigm to an Environmental One

Table 10.1 contrasts the Dominant Social Paradigm with the Environmental Paradigm. Environmental scholars created this dualism
to help articulate between environmental worldviews.[1] The domi-

**Box 10.1 continued**

Wise use groups have received support from far-right media personalities (like Rush Limbaugh), and are funded by industry groups,[5] conservative think tanks (such as Heritage Foundation and Cato Institute), law firms (like the Mountain States Legal Foundation), and PR firms. Some wise use groups are outright front groups for industry; the Chicago-based Environmental Conservation Organization is a front for real estate and development interests.[6] Others, like the Maryland-based Fairness to Land Owners Coalition, are simply small property owners concerned over government restrictions.

The wise use movement has about 1,500 member organizations with considerably fewer than a hundred thousand members.[7] But since the 1980s, their priorities dovetailed with Republican efforts to deregulate and defund environmental policy, which means they carry clout. According to one critic, wise use groups have "the power to impede and occasionally sidetrack attempts at environmental protection."[8] Even if the movement gains no additional size, it has weakened, if not coopted, some problem definitions that once belonged to the environmental movement.

1. David Helvarg, "Grassroots for Sale: The Inside Scoop on (Un)wise Use," *Amicus Journal* 16 (1994).

2. Christopher J. Bosso, "Seizing Back the Day: The Challenge to Environmental Activism in the 1990s," in *Environmental Policy in the 1990s*, 3rd ed., eds. Norman Vig and Michael Kraft (Washington, D.C.: CQ Press, 1997), 53–74.

3. Bosso, "Seizing Back the Day," 60.

4. Mark Dowie, *Losing Ground: American Environmentalism at the Close of the Twentieth Century* (Cambridge, MA: MIT Press, 1995).

5. Phil Brick, "Determined Opposition: The Wise Use Movement Challenges Environmentalism," *Environment* 37 (8) (1995):17–20, 36–42.

6. Bosso, "Seizing Back the Day," 59.

7. Phil Brick, "Determined Opposition."

8. Helvarg, "Grassroots For Sale," 25.

---

nant paradigm supports the most anthropocentric ideology of unrestrained instrumentalism: hierarchical relationships and human dominion over nature, growth equated with progress, and resources having only instrumental value for humans. In contrast, the environmental paradigm supports interdependence and nonhierarchical relationships and values the natural world in all its diversity and complexity.

Think of how the dominant paradigm is firmly ingrained in our

**Table 10.1**

**The Dominant Social Paradigm versus the Environmental Paradigm**

| Dominant social paradigm | Environmental paradigm |
|---|---|
| Emphasizes human dominion over nature (Judeo-Christian tradition, roots) | Emphasizes humans as interdependent part of nature |
| Growth represents progress; environment is a resource that funds this progress | Growth is not itself valuable—sustainability and conservation preferred |
| Humans are the dominant species with access and rights to "resources" | Humans are merely one species among many, not the highest order |
| Only humans have rights | All entities that act purposively have rights |
| Things have value according to standards set by humans | Things valued: diversity, complexity, integrity, harmony, stability |
| Individuals act in their own best interest | Individual behavior contributes to collective, community good |
| More conservative politically | More liberal politically |

psyches, embedded in our institutions, and present in the ways we use, value, and manage natural resources. We use the gross national product (GNP) and other economic indicators based on growth as a yardstick for how the country is doing. We "manage" animals based on those we like, those that threaten or bother us, and those we hunt and fish. Where humans want to live and play and work are the primary considerations in how land and resources are used. With this cultural reinforcement, it's hard to imagine what an environmental paradigm might even look like and the kinds of change needed to reach it.

If you grew up in a democratically governed society, you perhaps take the notion of "social change" for granted. You can vote for your preferred candidate and ballot initiative. You can write letters, voice your opinion, or sign a petition if you believe some injustice should be righted. You can give money to groups working for change and you can show up at a public hearing, rally, or march. And if the social system is working, it will at least pay attention.

Since the earliest days of our country, our founders were concerned with crafting a system of governance that had both stability but also adaptability. A democratic system (through representative and direct democracy) must be able to handle two problems at the same time: it must avoid tyranny or domination by a minority, and it also must be responsive to the unmet or changing needs of its citizens. If a democracy is successful in handling these two problems, it will bring about regular, orderly change with the consent of the governed. If a group rises up to challenge the status quo and if other individuals or institutions judge the group's challenge as legitimate, the system must respond in some way. Does this mean that any challenge or protest brings significant social change? No. One of the primary flaws in the "pluralist heaven" of our democracy is that the heavenly chorus sings with a strong upper-class accent. That is, the dominant social structure is more responsive to powerful upper-class interests and less likely to heed the call for change when it comes from outside its own class.

Thus, challengers have always faced an uphill battle. In the 1500s, Machiavelli wrote of the arduous task of the social reformer: "There is nothing more difficult to carry out, nor more doubtful of success, nor more dangerous to handle, than to initiate a new order of things. For the reformer has enemies in all those who profit by the old order, and only lukewarm defenders in all those who would profit by the new order. This lukewarmness [arises] partly from . . . the incredulity of mankind, who do not truly believe in anything new until they have had actual experience of it."[2]

Social change inevitably benefits some and disadvantages others — and those disadvantaged will attempt to thwart change and foil any challenge that threatens its advantages or existing power relationships. The response of those in power to a proposed social change may be to exert some form of "social control," such as ignoring or marginalizing the challengers, or appeasing or accommodating them symbolically but not substantively. Social institutions continually walk this tightrope: recognizing the need for change and simultaneously controlling the way it is aired and occurs. As discussed in the news chapter, the media exert tremendous social control pressure.

## A Taxonomy of Environmental Groups

What defines a social movement is that it is a collection of individual movement groups that collectively provide a more-or-less persistent and organized effort to bring about—or resist—social change. To differing degrees, social movements represent change from the bottom up, meaning that movements grow from the grassroots and operate outside the power structure. In addition, movements begin with relatively little social power or recognition and seek both legitimation and change from existing social institutions, like government, politics, the legal system, education, and business. What distinguishes a "social movement" from a one-time response (like a concert to benefit victims of a hurricane or a loose collection of citizens calling for a change) is organization and ongoing operation.

Thus, what most distinguishes a movement group is *how formally organized* it is, which affects how it operates and communicates. This is turn affects a host of other factors, such as the role of leaders and members, group communication with members and the larger public, and the tactics utilized. Here, we examine organization in two simple camps—informal or "grassroots" groups, and formal or "institutional" groups.

### Informal or Grassroots Groups

Almost all environmental groups began as informally organized grassroots groups. Oftentimes, a group emerges to oppose a local environmental hazard or plan (such as a proposed incinerator or dam), or to change a broader-based problem or threat (such as insecticide spraying or whaling practices). One component in the emergence of a grassroots group is the involvement of one or more charismatic leaders. These leaders can be ordinary citizens, but research has also shown a high number of so-called intellectual or social elites.

Structurally, a grassroots group's greatest "resource" may be its passion and determination. An informal group lacks money, which will mean few (if any) paid staff, few (if any) dues-paying members, and no office space. Obviously, a new grassroots group will lack training and expertise—both in how to mobilize and run a movement group, and how to engage in specialized skills such as filing a lawsuit, collecting scientific data, and writing a news release.

There is a tendency for larger, established environmental groups to look down on unskilled grassroots groups as narrow and even selfish in focus.[3] But, the focus by some grassroots groups on so-called LULUs (locally unwanted land uses) and NIMBY (not in my back yard) efforts has broadened environmentalism to concern for the environment as a lived-in place. In that sense, grassroots groups really symbolize a fight of NIABY (not in anybody's back yard) because they recognize the need for economic, social, and regulatory reform and the reduction of hazards.

Grassroots environmental activism often is not as constrained in its tactics as the big "nationals," which permits communication strategies that are less compromising. Local activists do not have to worry about offending large, diverse constituencies and must "literally, live with the decisions made."[4] Grassroots activists working on issues of "environmental justice" have several distinguishing characteristics: a personal stake in the outcome, backgrounds that may be working class and/or people of color, and the ability to see environmental degradation as just one way their communities are under attack.[5]

### Formal or Institutional Groups

The factor most tied to the formalization of a social movement group is time. Social movement researchers have found that the longer a group exists, the greater the chance it will formalize its structure and operation. If a group achieves a certain amount of success over time—evidenced by legitimation, money, members, or media attention—the likely result is a change in the group and its structure. Success may feed a rather circular upward spiral: a small group of activists successfully blocks the spraying of pesticides in a court appeal, which garners significant media attention, which attracts more members, which brings in more money, which enables more appeals and protests, which attracts yet more media coverage, more members, more money . . . Eventually, the group will need additional staff to keep track of the money, communication, expanded issue agenda, and members. The charismatic initial leader may be replaced with a professional manager, who may bring in additional grants to hire specialists such as a staff attorney or media relations experts.

Every now and then, a group initially emerges as a formalized group, perhaps with a significant source of money and trained leaders and little connection to the grassroots level. (This roughly describes the founding of the Environmental Defense Fund and the Natural Resources Defense Council; each was assisted by a Ford Foundation grant and their first leaders were attorneys.[6] These groups were scientifically and legally based and more dependent on attracting grant money than grassroots members.)

But generally, the process of formalization occurs rather naturally over time. Social movement scholars note that the typical lifecycle of a successful movement moves from emergence and initial mobilization to significant growth and thus group "maintenance." The grand successes of environmental groups in the 1960s and early '70s spurred a move to maintenance for many established groups that suddenly had many new members to communicate with and keep happy; membership increased sevenfold from 123,000 in 1960 to 819,000 by 1969.[7]

The mainstream environmental movement in this country fits the profile of a movement that has become formal and highly institutionalized over time. The Audubon Society and Sierra Club are over a century old and other large groups have survived for a half-century. Early amateurism gradually evolved into more professionally run groups. Initial charismatic leaders (such as the Sierra Club's David Brower) were replaced by professional organizers. Older, formalized groups typically rely less on grassroots action by their members and more on paid staffs of lobbyists, attorneys, and full-time scientists.[8] Large numbers of distant members need regular communication and must be persuaded to continue to support the organization. Communication also is devoted to direct mail appeals and other efforts to raise money. Pressures for environmental groups to professionalize have come from several directions: the amount and complexity of environmental legislation and issues, rapidly expanding membership, and monetary resources that required complex financial management.[9]

Social movement scholars have found that the older and more formalized the group, the more wary it is not to alienate existing bases of support—whether members, funders, or even its target institutions. This may prompt a shift to "tamer" action[10] that resembles the operation of the surrounding social institutions: bureaucratic, legalistic, and scientific. This shift also may produce radical splinter groups.[11] Thus "success" is a double-edged sword both to social change and the groups that seek it, for success can initiate a maturation that makes the group appear less firmly *outside* the social institutions from which it seeks change.

## Lessons for Movement Communication

Before we focus on the specific tactical communication choices of informal and formal environmental groups, let's review some of the lessons that research has provided us for communication in general. First, communication depends on a message being successfully sent and received in a very competitive message environment; "receiving," however, is not the same as understanding and accepting. Consider three broad but crucial factors that affect how any one message is interpreted: the belief systems and the personal contexts within the individual sender and receiver, the message and how it is crafted and sent, and the message environment in which an individual message is sent and received.

### Within the Individual

A Los Angeles business executive, a cattle rancher in Texas, a teacher in rural Kentucky, a Native American tribal leader in northern Wisconsin, a realtor in Florida, and an environmental activist in Nevada. What does each individual bring to the table? A unique set of childhood experiences with nature, geographically relevant attachments, ideologies both environmental and political, and historical and cultural contexts. It is impossible to divorce these contexts from the way that these individuals send and receive messages about the environment.

Also consider the social role and position of each individual. The realtor, rancher, and activist will view and value a wooded piece of land differently. Some of these individuals are firmly inside status quo institutions, while others are outside. The teacher and the sheriff live in rural communities where communication and conflict about environmental issues play out very differently than they do in Los Angeles. And of course, each individual uniquely perceives his or her self-interest, with some believing that "the environment" has very little to do with everyday life and its concerns.

### Within the Message

Each of these geographic areas no doubt has a wildlife issue, so imagine the form a wildlife message might take. Who is likely to instigate the message, and what channel might deliver it, affect the message's reception. A news story prompted by an activist and an advertisement purchased by a realtor vary in their authority and perceived bias. Yet neither message might have the persuasive power of interpersonal communication from a tribal leader or teacher.

Through its story frame, each message will define the problem, who's responsible, and the solution differently. The frame might tap underlying cultural values, might employ animals as symbols of human characteristics, or might be dissonant with the existing beliefs of the recipient. According to theories of message reception, what's going on *inside* the head of the recipient might be far more important than the message itself.

### Within the Message Environment

The present landscape for environmental communication includes extremely widespread support for environmental protection and quality, and even a willingness to pay more for that protection. Yet scholars have found that environmental concern tends to be mile wide but inch deep—meaning that either favorable opinions do not match behaviors, or that opinions are not connected to on-the-ground conditions and choices of the individual, government, business, and so on. At the same time, more and more people—including environmental professionals—have tried to distance themselves from "e" words like environmentalist and environmentalism.

Some of the disconnects we create may be due to the lack of knowledge of the environment and what supports or harms it. Most Americans live in cities and may not have the same level of direct environmental experience that engenders understanding and support. American lifestyles are marked by consumerism and "living large" with housing, energy use, and so on. The marketplace and pop culture encourage us to relate to the natural world as a commodity for entertainment, something to hold at a distance and idealize and that is only tangentially related to everyday life. The message environment also contains very real physical and social constraints, such as auto dependency over mass transit, undervalued natural resources, environmental racism from unequal externalized costs, and so on.

The message environment of the status quo tends to lull us into thinking that change is not really necessary. TV ads and programming, the operation of business and government, and what we see in our neighborhoods and in our stores tell us that status quo behavior toward the environment is okay. Our belief systems historically have supported human hierarchy and domination of the natural world as the appropriate relationship. Thus, the social structure is more accepting of messages that support the status quo than messages that advocate social change. Part of this is human nature, but part is due to who benefits most from existing conditions and power relationships. Social change messages must constantly fight marginalization.

## Tactical Communication Choices

The array of communication tactics available to environmental groups are the same as those available to other organizations such as business and government. But when the communication comes from challengers seeking social change, how and when the tactics are used differs.

Environmental group communication targets multiple audiences: members and potential members, "the general public," and of course individuals and institutions in the social structure in which change is sought. The stage of the issue or problem affects the message; emerging issues require awareness and education, while ongoing problems might need constant action-oriented communication. The stage of the environmental group itself also affects communication. In the earliest stages of formation, a group may even avoid public communication, whereas a well-established group might prefer behind-the-scenes lobbying to mass media messages.

Finally, the internal structure of environmental groups—formal or informal—greatly affects communication choices. Formalized and relatively resource-rich groups with specialized divisions of labor have a much larger array of communication tactics available to them: conducting scientific research (and publicizing results in reports), large-scale merchandizing, advertising campaigns, extensive lobbying of political and regulatory arenas, filing (and publicizing) lawsuits and briefs, publishing, and of course hiring staffs of communication and marketing specialists. Sierra Club publishes an extensive book list. Both the Sierra Club and Audubon Society publish well-known magazines that are available in bookstores, not just to members.

In a study of public relations (PR) and media staffs in sixteen national environmental groups (a mix of informal and formal), all groups had issued a news release in the last month and all but one had held a news conference.[12] Nine of the sixteen groups said they initiated contact with the media daily, and twelve said that the media contacted them daily for information or a response. Three of the groups did not have any paid staff devoted to PR, while three of the groups had over twenty paid PR staff members. In half the groups, more than 50 percent of the PR staffers had more than ten years of communication experience. About half of the groups said they had a communication plan and half had issued a video news release. The groups also showed a high degree of sophistication in skill level and techniques in their communication; groups as varied as Earth First! and the World Wildlife Fund said they produced video news releases.[13]

As an example of the creativity employed to gain publicity through non-news channels, video messages attached to rented movies are a recent fundraising and publicity tactic of some environmental groups. *Environment Writer* reported that the movie *A Few Good Men* is preceded by a six-minute message about the work of the Natural Resources Defense Council and is delivered by Tom Cruise, Whoopi Goldberg, Warren Beatty, Billy Crystal, and Demi Moore. *A River Runs Through It* has a plug for The Wilderness Society. And Earth Island Institute managed to get an 800-number plugged into the movie version of *Free Willy*.[14]

We'll take a much closer look at communication with news media, but first, how and why environmental groups communicate with their members.

## Member Communication

The very definition of a social movement group implies that it gets its power and voice from its grassroots—its members. It is a group's ability to mobilize a response from many "ordinary" individuals—rather than appearing as a singular group and solitary voice—that can be an effective call for social change. Movement groups are member organizations first and foremost, and virtually all communication must be crafted with members in mind. It is communication that sparks people to join environmental groups, and communication that urges them to take action, give money, and renew membership. Even the mention of a group in the news media is important communication for its members, telling them that their dollars are providing an important voice. Perhaps the most traditional channels of member communication include newsletters and magazines, direct mail, and nowadays, e-mail and Web sites.

People join an environmental group for many different reasons, such as a love of outdoor places and activities, a desire for social connection with like-minded people, strong values (environmental or political), guilt, social status, self-esteem from "making a difference," and a sense of belonging. Communication is needed to reinforce a sense of group solidarity and the importance of each individual to the collective goal. But "belonging" looks very different in a small local group with no office and a barebones budget than in a national environmental group with a half-million members and a budget of $40 million.

It's safe to say that the smaller the group, the greater the dependence on interpersonal communication among members and the more active the participation. In an informal group, the greatest resource is usually "people power" in the form of personal contributions of time, muscle, and money. When I was active in the Idaho Conservation League in the 1980s, our chapter held spaghetti dinner fundraisers, mobilized members through a phone-tree, leafleted, and drove across the state to the capitol to lobby. We bought group T-shirts, sold note cards, stuffed envelopes, wrote letters to editors and agencies, and testified at hearings. Today, the Wyoming Outdoor Council organizes outdoor activities and social gatherings for its members as a way to promote group solidarity. (Incidentally, the

Sierra Club was originally a hiking club when it formed in the late 1800s.)

Large national environmental groups with a strong chapter structure (such as National Audubon Society, Sierra Club, and sportsmen's groups like Izaak Walton League and Trout Unlimited) are able to capitalize on such active participation and personal communication tactics. But large, formal groups without chapters often must contend with a large "paper membership" of far-flung members who need other forms of communication or feedback to feel connected and valuable.

A large paper membership is often recruited via a direct-mail campaign and then encouraged to contribute additional funding. Aided by the purchase of targeted mailing lists, environmental groups have discovered that direct mail for mass mobilization is well suited to recruiting supporters. Some organizations, like Audubon, support chapters and also use direct mail successfully (and have since the early 1970s) to attract members and dollars, while others such as the Izaak Walton League stick to a chapter structure and don't use direct mail to seek a mass membership. A membership recruited by mass mail, however, is not necessarily a highly committed one, and often exerts little influence on decision-making within the organization.[15]

Many national groups use their Web sites to speak to members and encourage their action through phone calls, letters, and increasingly, e-mail. Greenpeace's Web site allows members (and nonmembers) to click on the words "act now" and then choose from several issues. The links lead you to a letter that's already written that you are free to edit and then send. The Audubon Web site has action alerts and printable petitions. The Web site of the Southern Utah Wilderness Alliance lets you click on "write a letter to the editor."

Some politicians and agencies dismiss the receipt of standardized mass appeals from environmental group members as ineffective. As noted in the last chapter, Bonner and Associates uses different stationery and language specifically to avoid the appearance of an interest group-prompted mass response, believing that individual-looking responses carry far more weight. Nevertheless, formal environmental groups know they can't abandon the "participation orientation" provided by their members to focus solely on their "power orientation." The latter focuses communication and energy more directly at the targets of social change, whether Congress or the Environmental Protection Agency (EPA).

## APPEALS TO ACTIVISTS

The particular type of appeals made to members deserves some discussion. We've all seen the slogans: "Save the _____" and "Stop the _____." They might appeal to our guilt, fear, moral outrage, urgency, or personal concern. As we saw in chapter 3, a mix of factors can be effective in bringing about behavior, including social and moral norms, altruistic and ecocentric beliefs, knowledge, self-efficacy, personal experience, and perceived control.

A few additional pieces of research contribute to this picture. In one experiment, a variety of appeals for environmentally responsible behavior were tested.[16] The appeals varied in how they defined the problem (framed either as in danger of losing something or as gaining something), whether it appealed to concern for current or future generation, and whether the recommended actions involved "taking less" (i.e., restraining one's use) or "doing more" (i.e., active contribution). The researcher discovered that the communication with the most positive responses discussed losses to the current generation; it didn't matter whether the action concerned "taking" or "giving." Other researchers have concluded that a message about the current generation might appeal more to self-interest and is therefore more relevant to the individual.[17]

If messages emphasizing loss are more persuasive, does that mean that "guilt works"? In other words, if an environmental group appeals to you to act now to prevent more loss, won't you feel guilty if you choose inaction? And are repeated "guilt trips" productive—especially in motivating paper members from a distance?

In an analysis of activist-oriented publications of Environmental Defense Fund (EDF) and Audubon Society, one researcher asked, "might the larger community be worn out and down by the rhetorical strategy of guilt" and moved instead into numbness, "inertia and apathy"?[18] The scholar began by citing an appeal in an EDF message: "YES, I want to help save the seals, sea birds and rare sea turtles from death-dealing plastics at sea."

It's true that shame and guilt are social emotions that serve important functions. Guilt can indeed motivate reparative action as long as following "successful" guilt "is an action which can mediate the guilty feelings . . . [for] guilt demands an outlet."[19]

But she wondered whether guilt appeals might be productive in the short term but not necessarily in the long run: "Does the long-term effect of the discourse of guilt tend to work against maintaining those publications' goals—a growing group of active people committed to the cause?"[20] After all, "if consensus-building is a long-term goal, if dialogue between differing parties is desired as a rhetorical strategy, guilt can have an enormous cost."[21]

This analysis noted that one of the first widespread appeals of "doom" was that of Rachel Carson's apocalypse in *Silent Spring*, which she effectively communicated to a lay public. Though some environmental groups resist a "rhetoric of gloom," many are "looking instead to the motivational force of guilt." We've all seen photos of injured animals, damaged lands, and polluted sites in various environmental publications and have all read "overused phrases"[22] such as "You can make a difference" and "We can make a difference." When you combine the two, guilt will derive from inaction and the blame is placed on the inactive reader.

It's a difficult conundrum. An organization appeals to the implied shared attitudes of its members, believes it knows its members, and continuously refers to its community of concerned people. Yet the author noted that the studied publications had a "storehouse of unquestioned cultural givens, a sense of shared values and history, even a belief in the rightness of the community's perception that can be seen by the predominance of direct calls to action, coupled with a lack of detailed explanation why."[23]

According to other scholars, "such rhetoric . . . fails to meet the continuing need for dialogue, deliberation, and consensus-building."[24] They conclude that much environmental group communication has "polarized language reflecting entrenched positions," which is how much of the public views the environmental movement.[25]

Thus, member communication for environmental groups is extremely important in attracting and retaining members, yet calls for action to avoid guilt have the potential to turn off members (and others). A key element of interpersonal communication is constant feedback and adjustment, which of course is difficult with a large and distant membership. At the very least, environmental groups could heed the first step of the four-step process of public relations, which is research. Precisely identifying member attitudes and values, and the action appeals that are productive and not, could help environmental groups better communicate with the grassroots from which their power emanates.

## Communication with News Media

It's apparent from environmental group Web sites—national, state, local, and international—that though they have many avenues for communication, one of the most important is the news media. Even on Web sites you'll find banks of news releases, video news releases, reprinted stories, and position papers. The Southern Utah Wilderness Association Web site even provides news tips for reporters and offers them B-roll video and photos.

News coverage is vital to the mobilization of new members and overall public opinion. In many cases, "the public's perception of a movement's intensity of action may reflect media coverage rather than the actual membership strength or the scope and intensity of grievances."[26] Television coverage in particular has the power to influence support or opposition to social movements, but TV also is more dependent upon image and impression, which can hinder a movement group's ability to convey issue substance and context. When a group receives news coverage, it has gained access to a mass audience for "free," it has gotten the media's stamp of third-party legitimacy, and the media pass along the group's viewpoints or actions to policy makers and targets of their social change efforts.

News coverage of an environmental group may be absent (or marginalized) until a group has received minimal legitimization in the system. Initial legitimization can come through attention in specialized media,[27] from public concern, from governmental agencies and procedures,[28] or from organized size and strength.

Mass media publicity is perhaps more important for nonmembers than environmental group members. One study found that those most concerned and knowledgeable about the environment (including those most active) tended to use specialized media (such as particular magazines and Web sites) rather than mass media for environmental information.[29] Nevertheless, news media in large

**Figure 10.1**

measure mediate between large environmental groups and their isolated and far-flung members.[30] Even if a large group uses a great deal
of direct mail and other communication channels, it still relies on
news media to communicate with members.[31]

Environmental group actions present two things to the news
media. First, the very nature of protest and environmental conflict
makes it fit the textbook definition of news: it's dramatic, emotional,
or unusual; is timely; concerns current events, trends, or changes;
concerns politics or pocketbook issues; and contains either local
interest or widespread, universal interest.[32] Second, environmental
conflict presents some degree of "threat" to the status quo; protest
goals usually seek to rearrange in some way the existing power relationships, distribution of resources, bases of authority, or other components of the social structure. That's why media find it hard to
ignore something like protesters chaining themselves to equipment
and also report the filing of a lawsuit.

News coverage is important at all stages of a movement and is
important (though for different reasons) to both informal and formal groups. "In today's society, it is extremely difficult for a widespread social movement to emerge without gaining access to the mass
media."[33] In early stages, when the cause is new to the media, groups

(whether resource-rich or resource-poor) can stage dramatic events or align themselves with newsworthy people or institutions. News coverage during the early stages of movement groups can even substitute for resources, organizational structure, or grassroots organizing.[34]

For an established (and likely formal) group, the interactive nature of media coverage both sustains groups and changes their internal dynamics.[35] In essence "the medium becomes the movement" because media coverage pursued by a group shapes its leadership, its goals, and ultimately its success.[36] Some argue that the media's process of gathering news has a moderating and conservatizing influence on social movement groups because "newsmaking puts a premium on organizational characteristics, typically found in the relatively conservative groups of a movement," forcing movement groups to "redefine their issues to make them more palatable to a larger public."[37] As noted earlier, environmental groups reported that journalists contact them daily, often to be "responders" to official information.[38] Official responses and institutional protest tactics are easily accommodated in a formal structure and less likely to offend a large, diverse membership. Media staff also can help capitalize on events (both planned and unforeseen), which make up a large portion of media news.

Part of the process of group formalization may be due to their need for sustained media attention, attention that can greatly contribute to the group's success in expanding its concerns to the general public and onto the policy-makers' agenda. A public relations apparatus "can make news on demand without resorting to the extreme tactics that might prove counterproductive."[39] But at the same time, there is also a danger that media may not view highly formalized groups as representative of the environmental movement and able to speak for it. In one study, environmental groups with a medium level of formalized organization were significantly better than highly formalized and informal groups in obtaining news coverage.[40]

### AVENUES FOR NEWS

There essentially are two ways to get news: create news, or piggyback onto someone else's news. One advantage of playing piggyback is that the news media (or some news-maker) has already defined and legitimated something as newsworthy. At times, a protracted dispute remains newsworthy for its entire life, though new developments must provide the spark for coverage to return. Once an emerging issue has received initial coverage, the media's restless spotlight is likely to direct its beam elsewhere on seemingly new material. To maintain the restless (but purposeful) spotlight, an environmental group can escalate its rhetoric and protest strategies, or try and strengthen its position as an established, legitimate news source.

In a study about protests surrounding a proposal to build a high voltage power line across rural Minnesota, three phases of news media involvement were documented.[41] In the early stages, protesters received coverage primarily in rural newspapers in the geographically affected area. When the issue reached court action, the more distant metro newspapers began extensive coverage. Media coverage during this phase was centered on the legal procedures and adversarial relations between the protesters and the utility. During the final phase, when the courts had decided the power line could be built, media editorials supported the decision and declared that the protesters had had their day in court. Ensuing violent protests were portrayed as illegitimate acts of vandalism in newspapers, and at this stage, in television news. Information flow through the media depended on the stage of the controversy and was highest during times of intense conflict.

Advantages of creating news can be creativity, timing, and perhaps a stronger hand in framing it. News creation for environmental groups includes two kinds of tactics: taking direct action and institutional action. Direct actions include boycotts, marches, protests, sit-ins, strikes, and nonviolent and nondestructive things like treesitting, blocking roads, and chaining oneself to fences or equipment. (Violent or destructive actions have been used by a couple of radical animal rights groups but rarely by typical environmental groups.) Institutional actions are directed at institutions: filing lawsuits, testifying at hearings, writing letters or petitions, educating, releasing studies, and so on. Both types of actions have advantages and disadvantages, and in the case of the power line protesters mentioned above, direct action and institutional action may happen simultaneously.

The relatively tame institutional actions are the vast majority undertaken by environmental groups and have been since the movement's founding. Here's one example of institutional action used to get news coverage by a media-savvy environmental group. The Natural Resources Defense Council (NRDC), a national group devoted to legal action and scientific research of environmental issues, was frustrated by what it saw as the EPA's foot dragging in banning the use of Alar (a plant growth regulator) on fruits, primarily apples. Although the EPA acknowledged Alar's potential cancer risk as early as 1973, in 1989 the NRDC decided to wait no longer for action.[42] They hired an outside communication firm to conduct a "well-planned and effective public relations campaign"[43] centered around the NRDC report, "Intolerable Risk: Pesticides in Our Children's Food." One of NRDC's key points was that federal pesticide limits were established on the basis of adult metabolism and consumption, while children ingest far greater amounts of fruits such as apples.

The communication firm hired by NRDC succeeded in getting CBS's *60 Minutes* to break the story, which led to an immediate and widespread reaction by the public. There was heavy media coverage both locally and nationally, including cover stories in *Time* and *Newsweek* and stories on network TV newscasts. Although the campaign had many critics—from Congressmen to the apple industry—it illustrated an effective, planned media campaign by an environmental movement group. NRDC received media coverage again when the National Academy of Sciences published its long-awaited report, *Pesticides in the Diets of Infants and Children* in 1993. Interestingly, Congress had requested the study in 1988, a year before NRDC's media campaign. The report recommended regulatory changes so that exposure to pesticide residues reflected the quantitative and qualitative differences in toxicity between children and adults.

That doesn't mean that institutional actions are always gobbled up by news media or other social institutions. Because all environmental group actions challenge the status quo, they can be ignored, marginalized, or subverted. In 1996, senior scientist Theodora Colborn of the World Wildlife Fund published *Our Stolen Future*, a book about an array of endocrine-disrupting chemicals. The Ph.D. zoologist was called by some "the Rachel Carson of the '90s" for her book discussed scientific findings for many of the same chemicals. The political PR firm Fenton Communication was hired to publicize the book. In a study of magazine coverage of the book, critics attacked Colborn's scientific credentials, called her work not objective, and dismissed her as an environmentalist.[44] Similar to the reaction to Carson's work, the chemical industry mounted a news media counter-campaign to Colborn's book with "third party experts" and front groups.[45] In part due to industry actions, the book never received a great deal of attention by news media or the public.

But it's direct action that's most likely to be the target of "social control" by news media. The environmental groups most likely to engage in direct action tactics are small, informal grassroots groups that have few resources, lack legitimacy, and find it hard to gain the attention of journalists. There is often little to lose with an attention-getting protest but a lot to gain in terms of new members, money, and results. These groups (such as the power line protestors above) don't have to worry about offending donors or alienating a power structure that has not yet recognized them. A march, boycott, or rally may successfully gain media and public attention, though they also carry risks of marginalization.

One exception to only grassroots groups undertaking direct action is Greenpeace, a large, formalized, international group that has always relied on dramatic protests and has been fairly successful in obtaining news coverage of them. Greenpeace distributes photos and videos to publicize their direct action tactics—chasing whaling ships, plugging effluent pipes, scaling smokestacks—when journalists are not present to see them.[46] Greenpeace relies on the Quaker principle of "bearing witness" in its confrontational, nonviolent resistance (a protest strategy borrowed from the civil rights movement) by putting their bodies on the line to stop nuclear testing or prevent ocean dumping.

A group that has faded from view but helped popularize direct action was Earth First! Protests by Earth First! are often meant to be shocking and absurd—and to garner media attention. One of its first media "stunts" (which received widespread coverage) was in April of 1980 and featured Earth First-ers unfurling a three-hundred-foot-long plastic "crack" down the face of Arizona's Glen Canyon Dam, a dam that represented a compromise between the Sierra Club and the Bureau of Reclamation. During a protest of U.S. Forest Service policy in Montana, Earth First-ers smeared themselves and the Forest Service building with feces.

But like other groups that engage in dramatic protests, Earth First! has often been ignored by the media. As discussed in the news media chapter, reporting of social protest is part of the process of social control and conflict management.[47] When the media ignore or marginalize protest they exercise social control, and are most likely to do so in the name of growth and/or profit, which is also the basis of the media's existence.[48] The very open-ended quality of news gives media discretion in defining and framing news events as they see fit.[49] Depending on the frame, journalists may treat activists as threatening the social fabric, or as legitimate, concerned citizens alerting the public to a serious problem deserving of attention. Regardless, protest news meets the media's goals of being interesting to their audiences and helping to produce timely news products.

Several researchers have studied the news portrayal of so-called deviant behavior and have discovered that the media tend to exaggerate the activities of deviants and overstate the danger they pose, thus promoting a conservative ideology and generating support for law and order.[50] Such coverage provides society with objects of moral indignation and scapegoats, diverting attention from the underlying institutional causes of the problem. In one study, the more that journalists thought certain protest groups were deviant, the less favorably the media reported their actions, although the deviant behavior sometimes still received prominent coverage.[51] Overall, the study found a significant relationship between a group's deviance and its media treatment as a legitimate political contender. In other words, the more deviant the group was perceived to be by editors, the less favorable the stories and the less legal and viable the group was portrayed to be.

Thus a protest group and the media can form a symbiotic and interactive relationship. The protest group strives to present challenger tactics that are interesting, likely to be portrayed as legitimate, and meet the news needs of media; news coverage also serves to recruit members and advance the group's goals. In turn, the media receive an information subsidy from the group that reduces the cost and uncertainty of news-work, alerts audiences to a social issue, and serves as a method of social control. Environmental groups can meet news needs and fit news routines when they plan scheduled, predictable events, produce dramatic visuals, strive for geographic balance, and do so within reporter deadlines.

An important point needs to be emphasized: the news media do not create social movements (nor the groups in them). Mass media coverage of social protest can either accelerate or decelerate social movements, but the media do not initiate movements.[52] Conversely, the media are more likely to control or suppress news of social protest until the conflict has been legitimized in some way. Media may accelerate social protest by placing items on the social agenda and giving them priority and repeated attention. But media reporting also may be part of a process of deceleration of movement activity if it denies attention to social protest. Media reporting may perform "damage control" and "cool out" protests perceived as threatening to the established order. While the media do tend to reinforce established authority, media information can be expected to increase during intense conflicts.[53]

## Partial Success for the Environmental Movement

As a social movement, the environmental movement today little resembles the one that began over a hundred years ago. Some environmental groups are as large as small corporations, preferring as tactics "paper protests" and behind-the-scenes negotiation. The biggest groups sponsor their own credit cards and product lines and have large, specialized staffs of scientists, attorneys, and PR directors. This differs markedly from the modest storefront nature of early groups, who accomplished their goals with few volunteers and few resources. The movement now is best known for its large national groups, although today there also are thousands of grassroots groups run entirely by passionate volunteers with nonprofessional leaders and shoestring budgets.

In social movement parlance, there are three possible outcomes for a movement and the groups within it: total failure (achieving no social change), total success (successfully enacting a new ideology and practice), or partial success. Most would agree that the environmental movement in this country has achieved partial success.

What limits success stems in large part from how the social structure reacts to movement goals. One partial successful outcome is a *becalmed* social movement, or one that survives over a period of time but fails to achieve major success or failure. A second outcome is a movement that is *accommodated* and/or *coopted*. If a social movement changes its own structure and ideology to be more congruent with the surrounding social system, it has succumbed to accommodation. If authorities attempt to bring movement groups over to their side, convincing group leaders that their demands are being met yet without providing significant sought-after social change, the movement has been coopted. Authorities may try and convince movement groups that they are listening and are on the same side, yet not concede to the challengers' demands. Scholars say that both partial-success outcomes diffuse protest and control the degree to which social change occurs.[54]

One can see these partial-success outcomes in communication from the current environmental movement. As the mainstream movement aged, it increasingly resembled the government bureaucracy: professional, legal, and seeking only modest change. Favored legal strategies have not secured the desired environmental protection. J. William Futrell of the Environmental Law Institute said that environmental laws "have made only spotty changes in the social and economic values that lead to pollution, and the results they have produced in restoring the environment fall far short of the expectations . . ."[55] Author and critic Mark Dowie charged that movement leaders continued to put too much faith in the federal and state government to protect the environment, yet had built up a sizeable force of registered lobbyists who were still trying to convince legislators and the government to enforce its own environmental laws.[56] Research also has documented the tendency of groups to professionalize and conservatize over time, which has certainly happened in the environmental movement.

But according to resource mobilization theory, regardless of what happens within the movement, conditions in the social structure also have to be optimal for a movement to be successful. Clearly, environmental groups have faced since 1980 a political climate that has been either mildly supportive or moderately hostile to environmental change. And for the past five years, the country has been distracted by wars and related issues.

One of the more ironic things about the process of social change is that the more successful the movement, the more likely that movement ideals and language will be coopted. This is apparent in the "green communication" of the corporate world and the often superficial support of political leaders. From the 1970s onward, while the American public accepted the most basic premise of environmental protection, the very meaning of environmentalism and environmentalists was being diluted and appropriated. The percentage of citizens expressing support for the environment (which does not equate with support of the movement, however) is phenomenally high. This is due to the environmental movement's success—not its failure—in permeating its message into the public psyche.

Yet now, there are numerous institutions and individuals who realize that the environment is a bandwagon not just to climb on, but to try to drive. After all, there is money to be made in associating one's organization or products with a green image, and there is the status quo to maintain (and thus environmental change to be subverted). Some charge that the movement has lost control of crucial problem definition to corporate and even popular sentiment; just look at what the "dirty words" "environmentalist"and "environmentalism" have come to mean in the public's mind.

## A New Vision for the Communication of Environmental Change

In his popular book *Don't Think of an Elephant!*, George Lakoff calls the process of attaching meaning and values to our communication "framing,"[57] a concept that was discussed in the news chapter in relation to how journalists construct their storylines. Those who study social movements call this process "problem definition." Either way, our words about the natural world both interpret and define it and give it meaning at numerous levels. The struggle is not just how we use and treat things like trees and tree frogs but over the meaning attached to physical things. In essence, it's a clamor to have your values and problem definition prevail.

We see meanings of nature and environment constructed in all messages. Advertising messages frame the environment as an idealized commodity. A political speech might position the environment as something that costs humans money. Tourism brochures define nature as that outdoor place you escape to play. Environmentalists might label the environment as pristine nature in the Arctic or wilderness areas. Why these frames or labels matter to environmental communication is because, first of all, they appear natural and are therefore taken for granted. And second, they have the ability to powerfully communicate "this is the problem, this is who's responsible, and this is the solution."

But from a communication standpoint, successful environmental communication is not just about shifting a frame of reference and "talking" about the natural world in a different way. There is no magic bullet message or strategy that will transform the environmental movement and "save" the natural world. Given the public's reaction to "environmentalists," the hostile political environment, and the becalmed and coopted nature of some movement groups, what's needed is an entirely new modality for how we think, speak, and act toward the natural world. What's needed is a new vision.

In the fall of 2004, an essay called "The Death of Environmentalism" questioned the effectiveness of the current environmental movement and its ability to bring about social change.[58] Although it's beyond the scope of this book to address all the policy implications, it is clear that for whatever reason, the current mainstream movement has defined and communicated the environment and environmental issues in a somewhat restricted fashion. Throughout its history, the movement has concentrated on preservation and pollution, and historically it has used institutional tactics. Since its beginnings, the movement has formed partnerships with government and business as often as it has fought them. Choosing certain issues and battles over others is naturally a matter of practicality. And, environmental activists bear a tremendous burden as the primary and most visible challengers and advocates for social change regarding the environment. It's also true that from its inception, the environmental movement (like other movements) has attracted leaders and members who are white, middle or upper class, and well-educated social and intellectual elites. Appealing to a broader base has fallen to the relatively resource-poor, informal grassroots groups, such as those working for environmental justice.

In part due to the success of the issue agenda of the environmental movement, our culture has accepted very limited definitions: wilderness is an environmental issue, but consumerism is not.

Nature worthy of protection is the pristine places where people are not. Distant nature is more valued than everyday nature. The most appropriate spheres for protecting nature are the political, legal, and governmental bureaucracies.

These definitions or frames of what environment is and is not have served a role. Frames facilitate communication because they carry a great deal of symbolic meaning and help organize and structure our social world. To be useful, they must remain somewhat stable and not change overnight, a stability to which our social institutions contribute. The stability of the definition of "environment" has given it its widespread recognition in the general public: "All communication is dependent upon shared meaning among communicators. . . . The greater the difference in their individual understanding of symbols, the less able they are to communicate. Frames, as part of the deep structure of a culture, provide a significant portion of the shared meaning among society's members. Frames provide the unexpressed but shared knowledge of communicators that allows each to engage in discussions that presumes a set of shared assumptions."[59]

It's important to think of frames not just as cognitive phenomena that give us rules for thinking about and processing information. Successful frames are more aptly cultural phenomena that penetrate virtually all institutions and individuals and influence relevant communication and practices. As positive and inclusive as this sounds, frames are ultimately very limiting. Just as a picture frame includes some scene, it excludes even more. Framing environmental issues as matters of preservation or pollution defines those concerns as relevant to the discussion, but a whole host of other concerns as less so. When a frame groups an array of phenomena as either "economics" or "environment," it's partially arbitrary and ultimately helps to define the roles of social actors as relevant or peripheral or marginalized. "Choosing what frame problematic social phenomena are to be placed in may do more to determine their meaning than lengthy discussions of the facts of or arguments toward them."[60]

Frames further structure our understanding by outlining the ways that various beliefs, values, and actions are related: "Certain kinds of relationships are privileged by the frame—presenting them as likely and appropriate, whereas others are portrayed as inappropriate, illegitimate, or impossible. That is, even among those concepts that are deemed relevant to a topic, certain kinds of relationships are more or less likely, more or less appropriate, more or less valued."[61] In this light, it's easy to see why we so often disconnect our sentiments for the natural world from our actions, not understanding that lawn care and food choices have significant connections to a healthy environment.

Once firmly established, a frame may likewise inhibit the process of social change and serve the status quo. "Social activist groups faced with a commonly held frame that impairs their ability to communicate their case may find it difficult to successfully advance their cause. Like a team playing on a steep slope, regardless of their effort or their abilities, the outcome is preordained, the odds too long, the competition weighted too heavily against them. When the applied frame is too detrimental to the group's efforts, it may be wiser to attempt to reframe the debate so that the odds are more in its favor. This is a difficult task and usually unsuccessful, but it represents a major improvement in the group's chances for ultimate success if it can be accomplished."[62]

Thus, environmental issues today reside in the existing definitions of what environment means and therefore encounter trouble being communicated in any other terms. What may prove more successful than putting energy into shifting and redefining the current frame of environment is instead conceptualizing a compelling, positive vision that reconnects us and brings environment home. An encompassing vision for environmental relationships would not just be a frame with new language, but a comprehensive cultural framework for how we see our daily lives on the earth.

Albert Einstein once said, "We cannot solve our problems with the same thinking we used when we created them." Likewise, we need new ways of doing, seeing, and communicating about human relationships and responsibilities toward natural world. We need new ways of talking, of being with all that is "other," a humbler and more reciprocal recognition of our interdependency and connectedness. For all that it has accomplished, environmentalism today has not altered or shifted our basic relationships and ideologies. Ideologies that move beyond anthropocentrism and truly alter human hierarchy and dominance and that stand for intrinsic value in significant ways are part of a new environmental vision. As one scholar put it, in current-day environmental thinking, "No recognition is given to ecological sensibilities, the necessity of providing an ecocentric critique of industrial society, or of exploring the 'wild self' and transforming society."[63]

In terms of environmental messages and how to communicate them, it would be wise to look well beyond the current movement. We need a new set of "articulators" to communicate a fresh, broad view of human relationships and actions toward the natural world. We need charismatic visionaries to spark new social change groups, even a new movement. The struggle over what environment means, the values it holds for all of us, and how we speak and act toward it, is being lost. As Lakoff wisely argues, it's not effective to employ others' greenwashed words or argue against other's values. A common perception of environmentalists is that they stand against things far more than they stand for things. Simply reframing environmentalism is insufficient; we need a compelling re-vision of environment.

We need to bring the environment home. The environment needs to be reconnected to our everyday lives, in work and leisure, in words and actions. The average person has been schooled to think of "the environment" as something out there, distant, of little consequence for health and happiness, and that environmentalists and politicians haggle over. The average individual is not aware of her integral participation in and communication about the natural world in her home, her neighborhood, her city. She doesn't realize that City Creek Park communicates as much as *Sierra* magazine or a Senate hearing. An advertisement for a car communicates, as does the purchase of it, as does the fact that radio stations relay commuter traffic information, as does the news story about the price of oil half a world away. In this message environment, one message from an environmental group about an air pollution lawsuit is just that: one message.

Whether through an environmental movement or not, we need to create a "participation orientation" regarding humans and the natural world. We need to communicate the role that individuals play through their voluntary actions and choices, and their responsibilities and rights as citizens to have and make choices. Relying solely on a strong "power orientation" that wields political power and influence to generate pro-environmental laws and regulations leaves its beneficiaries behind: the people affected.[64] And as the last several decades have demonstrated, a power orientation is especially vulnerable to political change.

One of the key components of behavior change (and communication itself) is an appeal to self-interest: How am I affected and what's in it for me? Environmentalism of any stripe should communicate to me not how I must suffer and sacrifice, but how I will benefit. While I might care about something far away, I'll care more about something right here. I need to hear messages of personal relevance and self-efficacy, that indeed environmental issues affect me and there are choices I can make, big and small, and choices I can seek in my leaders and institutions. The traditional guilt appeals and gloom and doom feel inevitable, and I have engaged in some of them myself. But in today's world, those burdens are too heavy to carry far or for very long. Communicate a positive vision, give me a direction, and enable direct experience with the natural world throughout my life. Experience can be a far better teacher than any amount of talking.

Some people have suggested that words like "environmentalism" be abandoned and replaced because they have been coopted and denigrated. What I suggest instead is that both the word and practice truly be brought home. If anything, the conversation needs to be broaden and expanded, not shut down or avoided. Part of the solution to the environmental changes we must make is a bigger and broader understanding of how we "talk" to each other—in word, thought, and practice—about natural resources and our relationship with them. We must enlarge the definition of environmental messages and where we find them, and to be encouraged to go beyond their face value.

# Endnotes

## Introduction

1. William Cronon, "The Trouble with Wilderness; or, Getting Back to the Wrong Nature," in *Uncommon Ground: Rethinking the Human Place in Nature*, ed. William Cronon (New York: W.W. Norton, 1996), 69–90, 88.

2. Cronon, "The Trouble with Wilderness," 81.

3. Kevin M. DeLuca and Anne Demo, "Imaging Nature: Watkins, Yosemite, and the Birth of Environmentalism," *Critical Studies in Media Communication* 17 (2000):241–60

4. William Cronon, "Introduction: In Search of Nature," in *Uncommon Ground: Rethinking the Human Place in Nature*, ed. William Cronon (New York: W.W. Norton, 1996), 23–56, 25.

## Chapter 1: The Formation of Environmental Beliefs

1. Wallace Stegner, "It All Began with Conservation," *Marking the Sparrow's Fall: Wallace Stegner's American West*, ed. Page Stegner (New York: Henry Holt, 1998), 121.

2. Gary Snyder, *The Practice of the Wild* (New York: North Point Press, 1990), 26.

3. Peter H. Kahn, Jr. and Stephen R. Kellert, eds., *Children and Nature: Psychological, Sociocultural, and Evolutionary Investigations* (Cambridge, MA: MIT Press, 2002), viii.

4. Harold F. Searles, *The Nonhuman Environment* (New York: International Universities Press, 1959), 27.

5. Peter H. Kahn, Jr., "Children's Affiliations with Nature: Structure, Development, and the Problem of Environmental Generational Amnesia," in *Children and Nature: Psychological, Sociocultural, and Evolutionary Investigations*, eds. P. H. Kahn, Jr. and S. R. Kellert (Cambridge, MA: MIT Press, 2002) 93–116.

6. Louise Chawla, "Childhood Place Attachments," in *Human Behavior and Environments: Advances in Theory and Research. Vol. 12: Place Attachments*, eds. I. Altman and S. Low (New York: Plenum Press, 1992), 63–84.

7. R. Sebba, "The Landscapes of Childhood: The Reflections of Childhood's Environment in Adult Memories and in Children's Attitudes," *Environment and Behavior* 23 (1991):395–422, 400.

8. Definitions derived from Stephen R. Kellert, "Experiencing Nature: Affective, Cognitive, and Evaluative Development in Children," in *Children*

*and Nature: Psychological, Sociocultural, and Evolutionary Investigations*, eds. P. H. Kahn, Jr. and S. R. Kellert (Cambridge, MA: MIT Press, 2002), 117–51.

9. Will Nixon, "How Nature Shapes Childhood: Personality, Play, and a Sense of Place," *Amicus Journal* (Summer 1997):31–35.

10. C. Fishman, "The Smorgasbord Generation," *American Demographics* (1999):54–60.

11. David W. Orr, "Political Economy and the Ecology of Childhood," in *Children and Nature: Psychological, Sociocultural, and Evolutionary Investigations*, eds. P. H. Kahn, Jr. and S. R. Kellert (Cambridge, MA: MIT Press, 2002), 279–303.

12. Robert M. Pyle, *The Thunder Tree: Lessons from an Urban Wildland* (Boston: Houghton Mifflin, 1993), 145–47.

13. Kellert, "Experiencing Nature," 139.

14. Antony S. Cheng, Linda E. Kruger, and Steven E. Daniels, "'Place' as an Integrating Concept in Natural Resource Politics: Propositions for a Social Science Research Agenda," *Society and Natural Resources* 16 (2003):87–104, 87–88.

15. D. Kemmis, *Community and the Politics of Place* (Norman: University of Oklahoma Press, 1990), 119.

16. Lynne C. Manzo, "Beyond House and Haven: Toward a Revisioning of Emotional Relationships with Places," *Journal of Environmental Psychology* 23 (2003): 47–61.

17. R. Hester, "Sacred Structures and Everyday Life: A Return to Manteo, North Carolina," in *Dwelling, Seeing and Designing: Toward a Phenomenological Ecology*, ed. D. Seamon (New York: State University of New York Press, 1993), 271–98.

18. T. Hartig, M. Mang, and G. Evans, "Restorative Effects of Natural Environmental Experiences," *Environment and Behavior* 23 (1991):3–26; Rachel Kaplan and Stephen Kaplan, *The Experience of Nature: A Psychological Perspective.* (Cambridge: Cambridge University Press, 1989).

19. R. D. Sack, *Place, Modernity, and the Consumer's World: A Relational Framework for Geographical Analysis* (Baltimore, MD: Johns Hopkins University Press, 1992), 1.

20. Cheng, Kruger, and Daniels, "'Place' as an Integrating Concept," 90.

21. Ibid., 92.

22. Example from Ibid.

23. Ibid., 93.

24. Ibid.

25. Ibid., 98.

26. J. Dixon and K. Durrheim, "Displacing Place Identity: A Discursive Approach to Locating Self and Other," *British Journal of Social Psychology* 39 (2000):27–44.

27. W. M. Denevan, "The Pristine Myth: The Landscape of the Americas in 1492," *Annals of the Association of American Geographers* 82 (1992):362–85.

28. Annie L. Booth and Harvey M. Jacobs, "Ties That Bind: Native American Beliefs as a Foundation for Environmental Consciousness," *Environmental Ethics* 12 (Spring 1990):27–43.

29. Kirkpatrick Sale, *The Conquest of Paradise: Christopher Columbus and the Columbian Legacy* (New York: Penguin, 1990), 301.

30. Jerry Mander, *In the Absence of the Sacred: The Future of Technology and the Survival of the Indian Nations* (San Francisco: Sierra Club Books, 1991).

31. William Cronon and Richard White, "Indians in the Land," *American Heritage* 37 (5) (1986):18–25.

32. Cronon and White, "Indians in the Land," 22.

33. Freda Rajotte, *First Nations Faith and Ecology* (London: Cassell, 1998), 45.

34. Ronald Wright, *Stolen Continents: The New World through Indian Eyes* (London: Penguin Books, 1993), 14.

35. Mander, *In the Absence of the Sacred.*

36. Sale, *The Conquest of Paradise*, 75 (italics in original).

37. Ibid., 86.

38. Ibid., 88.

39. John Rodman, "Four Forms of Ecological Consciousness Reconsidered," in *Ethics and the Environment*, eds. D. Scherer and T. Attig (Englewood Cliffs, NJ: Prentice-Hall, 1983), 82–92.

40. Sale, *The Conquest of Paradise*, 79.

41. Ibid., 286.

42. John Young, *Sustaining the Earth: The Past, Present and Future of the Green Revolution* (Kensington: New South Wales University Press, 1991), 56.

43. Peter Hay, *Main Currents in Environmental Thought* (Bloomington: Indiana University Press, 2002), 104.

44. R. Attfield, *The Ethics of Environmental Concern* (Athens: University of Georgia Press, 1991), 25.

45. J. Baird Callicott and Roger T. Ames, "Introduction: The Asian Tradition as a Conceptual Resource for Environmental Philosophy," in *Nature in Asian Traditions of Thought: Essays in Environmental Philosophy*, eds. J. B. Callicott and R. T. Ames (Albany: State University of New York Press, 1989), 3–4.

46. Lynn White Jr., "The Historical Roots of Our Ecologic Crisis," *Science* 155 (1967):1203–1207, 1205.

47. Ibid., 1206.

## Chapter 2: A Spectrum of Environmental Ideologies

1. George Sessions, "Ecocentrism and the Anthropocentric Detour," *ReVISION* 13 (3) 1991:109–15.

2. Paul Shephard, *The Tender Carnivore and the Sacred Game* (New York: Scribner's, 1973).

3. James Shanahan and Katherine McComas, *Nature Stories: Depictions of the Environment and Their Effects* (Cresskill, NJ: Hampton Press,1999).

4. Elizabeth M. Harlow, "The Human Face of Nature: Environmental Values and the Limits of Non-anthropocentrism," *Environmental Ethics* 14 (1992):27–42.

5. K. Vishwanath and David Demers, *Mass Media, Social Control, and Social Change: A Macrosocial Perspective* (Ames: Iowa State University Press, 1999), 9.

6. R. V. Young, Jr. in the *National Review* (cited in S. Fox, *John Muir and His Legacy* (Boston: Little, Brown and Co., 1981), 373.

7. Peter Hay, *Main Currents in Environmental Thought* (Bloomington: Indiana University Press, 2002), 112–13.

8. Former Secretary of Interior James Watt, *The Washington Post*, May 24, 1981.

9. Bureau of Land Management Director Pat Shea, quoted in the *Salt Lake Tribune*, April 18, 1998, A1.

10. John Rodman, "Four Forms of Ecological Consciousness Reconsidered," in *Ethics and the Environment*, eds. D. Scherer and T. Attig (Englewood Cliffs, NJ: Prentice-Hall, 1983), 82–92.

11. Grandberg-Michaelson, *Redeeming the Creation: The Rio Earth Summit:*

*Challenges for the Churches* (Geneva, Switzerland: World Council of Churches Publication, 1992), 78–79.

12. "Degrading the Environment is a Sin, Orthodox Christian Leader Declares," *Los Angeles Times* (printed in *Salt Lake Tribune*), Nov. 12, 1997.

13. Terry Tempest Williams "Statement before the Senate Subcommittee on Forest and Public Lands Management Regarding the Utah Public Lands Management Act of 1995," in *American Nature Writing 1997* (San Francisco: Sierra Club Book, 1997), 170.

14. Rodman, "Four Forms of Ecological Consciousness Reconsidered," 247.

15. Ibid., 247.

16. Ibid., 245.

17. Ibid., 246.

18. Aldo Leopold, *A Sand County Almanac* (New York: Oxford University Press, 1949).

19. J. P. Sterba, "From Biocentric Individualism to Biocentric Pluralism," *Environmental Ethics* 17 (1995):191–207; Peter Singer, "Animal Liberation," *Island* 54 (1993):62–66.

20. Rodman, "Four Forms of Ecological Consciousness Reconsidered."

21. Hay, *Main Currents in Environmental Thought*.

22. Rodman, "Four Forms of Ecological Consciousness Reconsidered," 249.

23. Peter Marshall, *Nature's Web: An Exploration of Ecological Thinking* (London: Simon & Schuster, 1992), 434.

24. J. Baird Callicott, "Elements of an Environmental Ethic: Moral Considerability and the Biotic Community," *Environmental Ethics* 1 (1979):71–81; J. Baird Callicott, "The Conceptual Foundations of the Land Ethic," in *Companion to a Sand County Almanac: Interpretive and Critical Essays*, ed. J. B. Callicott (Madison: University of Wisconsin Press, 1987),186–217.

25. Rodman, "Four Forms of Ecological Consciousness Reconsidered," 251.

26. Annie L. Booth and Harvey M. Jacobs, "Ties That Bind: Native American Beliefs as a Foundation for Environmental Consciousness," *Environmental Ethics* 12 (Spring 1990):27–43, 29.

27. Rodman, "Four Forms of Ecological Consciousness Reconsidered," 250.

28. Ibid.

29. Ibid., 253.

30. Ibid., 250.

31. Booth and Jacobs, "Ties That Bind."

32. Hay, *Main Currents in Environmental Thought*.

33. Sessions, "Ecocentrism and the Anthropocentric Detour," 70.

34. Marshall, *Nature's Web*, 437.

35. Mary Mellor, *Feminism and Ecology* (New York: New York University Press, 1997), 150.

36. Ibid., 151.

37. James O'Connor, "Socialism and Ecology," *Capitalism, Nature Socialism* 2 (3) (1991):1–12.

38. Mellor, *Feminism and Ecology*, 154.

39. Val Plumwood, "The Ecopolitics Debate and the Politics of Nature," in *Ecological Feminism*, ed. Karen Warren (London: Routledge, 1994), 69.

40. Hay, *Main Currents in Environmental Thought*, 82.

41. Mellor, *Feminism and Ecology*.

42. Karen J. Warren, "The Power and the Promise of Ecological Feminism," *Environmental Ethics* 12 (1990):125–46, 137.

43. Robin Eckersley, *Environmentalism and Political Theory: Toward an Ecocentric Approach* (Albany: State University of New York Press, 1992), 68.

44. Such as Starhawk, La Chapelle, and Spretnak. See Peter Hay, *Main Currents in Environmental Thought*.

45. Ibid., 79.

46. Karen J. Warren, "A Feminist Philosophical Perspective on Ecofeminist Spiritualities," in *Ecofeminism and the Sacred*, ed. C. J. Adams (New York: Continuum, 1993), 119–32, 124.

47. Quoted in Joni Seager, *Earth Follies: Feminism, Politics and the Environment* (London: Earthscan, 1993), 219.

48. Connie Bullis, "Retalking Environmental Discourses from a Feminist Perspective: The Radical Potential of Ecofeminism," in *The Symbolic Earth: Discourse and Our Creation of the Environment*, ed. James Cantrill and Christine Oravec (Lexington: University of Kentucky Press, 1996), 123–148, 132.

49. Luther Standing Bear, *Land of the Spotted Eagle* (Lincoln: University of Nebraska Press, 1993), 45.

50. Eugene C. Hargrove, "Introduction," in *Nature in Asian Traditions of Thought: Essays in Environmental Philosophy*, eds. J. B. Callicott and R. T. Ames (Albany: State University of New York Press, 1989), xiii–xxi.

51. Mander, *In the Absence of the Sacred*.

52. Freda Rajotte, *First Nations Faith and Ecology* (London: Cassell, 1998), 35.

53. Booth and Jacobs, "Ties That Bind."

54. Vine Deloria, Jr. *God Is Red* (New York: Grosset & Dunlap, 1973), 39.

55. Rajotte, *First Nations Faith and Ecology*, 23.

56. Ibid., 25.

57. Hay, *Main Currents in Environmental Thought*.

58. Booth and Jacobs, "Ties That Bind," 31.

59. J. D. Hughs, *American Indian Ecology* (El Paso: Texas Western Press,1983).

60. Mander, *In the Absence of the Sacred*.

61. Booth and Jacobs, "Ties That Bind," 33.

62. Deloria, *God Is Red*.

63. Paula Gunn Allen, "Iyani: It Goes This Way," in *The Remembered Earth*, ed. Geary Hobson (Albuquerque, NM: Red Earth Press, 1979), 191.

64. Paula Gunn Allen, "The Sacred Hoop: A Contemporary Indian Perspective on American Literature," in *The Remembered Earth*, ed. Geary Hobson (Albuquerque NM: Red Earth Press, 1979), 225.

65. Hargrove, "Introduction."

66. Hay, *Main Currents in Environmental Thought*, 116.

67. Ibid.

68. David Edward Shaner, "The Japanese Experience of Nature," in *Nature in Asian Traditions of Thought: Essays in Environmental Philosophy*, eds. J. B. Callicott and R. T. Ames (Albany: State University of New York Press, 1989), 163–81.

69. Joanna Macy, *World as Lover, World as Self* (London: Random House, 1993), 53.

70. Martine Batchelor and Kerry Brown, eds. *Buddhism and Ecology* (New York: Cassell, 1992), ix.

71. Gary Synder, "Buddhism and the Possibilities of a Planetary Culture," in *Deep Ecology: Living as if Nature Mattered*, eds. Bill Devall and George Sessions (Salt Lake City, UT: Gibbs Smith, 1985), 251.

72. Sale, *The Conquest of Paradise*, 88–89.

73. Bill Devall and George Sessions, eds. *Deep Ecology: Living as if Nature Mattered*. (Salt Lake City, UT: Gibbs Smith, 1985), 11.

74. Marshall, *Nature's Web*, 19.

75. Shaner, "The Japanese Experience of Nature."

76. Sale, *The Conquest of Paradise*, 88–89.

77. Tu Wei-ming, "The Continuity of Being: Chinese Visions of Nature," in *Nature in Asian Traditions of Thought: Essays in Environmental Philosophy*, eds. J. B. Callicott and R. T. Ames (Albany: State University of New York Press, 1989), 67–78.

78. Wei-ming, "The Continuity of Being," 70.

79. Ibid., 71.

80. Ibid.

81. Shaner, "The Japanese Experience of Nature," 175.

82. Francis H. Cook, "The Jewel Net of Indra," in *Nature in Asian Traditions of Thought: Essays in Environmental Philosophy*, eds. J. B. Callicott and R. T. Ames (Albany: State University of New York Press, 1989), 213–29, 215.

83. Example from Cook, "The Jewel Net of Indra," 225.

## Chapter 3: The Links between Environmental Attitudes and Behaviors

1. Paul C. Stern, "Toward a Coherent Theory of Environmentally Significant Behavior," *Journal of Social Issues* 56 (3) (2000):407–24.

2. Denton E. Morrison and Riley E. Dunlap, "Environmentalism and Elitism: A Conceptual and Empirical Analysis," *Environmental Management* 10 (5) (1986):581–89.

3. Linda Kalof, Thomas Dietz, and Gregory Guagnano, "Race, Gender, and Environmentalism: The Atypical Values and Beliefs of White Men," *Race, Gender & Class* 9 (2) (2002):112.

4. Riley E. Dunlap and Robert E. Jones, "Environmental Concern: Conceptual and Measurement Issues," in *Handbook of Environmental Sociology*, eds. Riley E. Dunlap and William Michelson (Westport, CT: Greenwood, 2002), 485.

5. Dunlap and Jones, "Environmental Concern," 485.

6. Riley E. Dunlap and Rik Scarce, "The Polls—Poll Trends: Environmental Problems and Protection," *Public Opinion Quarterly* 55 (1991):713–34.

7. Riley E. Dunlap and Kent D. Van Liere, "The 'New Environmental Paradigm': A Proposed Measuring Instrument and Preliminary Results," *Journal of Environmental Education* 9 (1978):10–19; Riley E. Dunlap, Kent D. Van Liere, Angela G. Mertig, and Robert Emmet Jones, "Measuring Endorsement of the New Ecological Paradigm: A Revised NEP Scale," *Journal of Social Issues* 56 (3) (2000):425–42.

8. Riley E. Dunlap, "Trends in Public Opinion toward Environmental Issues: 1965–1990," in *American Environmentalism: The U.S. Environmental Movement, 1970–1990*, eds. Riley E. Dunlap and Angela G. Mertig (Philadelphia: Taylor and Francis, 1992).

9. Dunlap, "Trends in Public Opinion," 89.

10. Willett Kempton, James S. Boster, and Jennifer A. Hartley, *Environmental Values in American Culture* (Cambridge, MA: MIT Press, 1999), 4.

11. Kempton, Boster, and Hartley, *Environmental Values in American Culture*, 4.

12. Dunlap and Scarce, "The Polls—Poll Trends."

13. Lydia Saad, "Environmental Concern Down This Earth Day," The Gallup Organization, April 13, 2003. At www.gallup.com/poll/releases.

14. Kevin Coyle, *Environmental Literacy in America* (Washington, D.C.: National Environmental Education & Training Foundation, 2005).

15. Coyle, *Environmental Literacy in America*, 16.

16. T. Marcinkowski, *Using a Logic Model to Review and Analyze an Environmental Education Program* (Washington, D.C.: North American Association for Environmental Education, 2004).

17. Maria Lane, "Environmentally Responsible Behavior: Does it Really Matter What We Believe?" *Planning Forum* 6 (1) (1996):33–39.

18. Coyle, *Environmental Literacy in America*, 42.

19. Ibid., 35.

20. A. Eagly and S. Chaiken, *The Psychology of Attitudes* (Fort Worth, TX: Harcourt Brace, 1993); D. Scott and F. K. Willits, "Environmental Attitudes and Behaviors: A Pennsylvania Survey," *Environment and Behavior* 26: 239–60.

21. Paul Stern and Thomas Dietz, "The Value Basis of Environmental Concern," *Journal of Social Issues* 50 (1994):65–84.

22. Stern, "Toward a Coherent Theory," 410.

23. Paul C. Stern, "Psychology, Sustainability, and the Science of Human-environment Interactions," *American Psychologist* 55 (2000):523–30; Paul C. Stern and G. T. Gardner, "Psychological Research and Energy Policy," *American Psychologist* 36 (1991):329–42.

24. Stern, "Toward a Coherent Theory," 410.

25. Carroll J. Glynn, Susan Herbst, Garrett J. O'Keefe, and Robert Y. Shapiro, *Public Opinion* (Boulder, CO: Westview Press, 1999), 107.

26. M. Rokeach, *The Nature of Human Values* (New York: Free Press, 1973).

27. Paul Stern, Thomas Dietz, Linda Kalof and Gregory Guagnano, "Values, Beliefs, and Proenvironmental Action: Attitude Formation toward Emergent Attitude Objects," *Journal of Applied Social Psychology* 25:1611–1636.

28. Stern, "Toward a Coherent Theory."

29. Julia B. Corbett, "Motivations to Participate in Riparian Improvement Programs: Applying the Theory of Planned Behavior," *Science Communication* 23 (3) (2002):243–63.

30. Richard M. Perloff, *The Dynamics of Persuasion* (Hillsdale, NJ: Lawrence Erlbaum, 1993), 85.

31. Ibid., 86.

32. M. Fishbein and I. Ajzen, *Belief, Attitude, Intention and Behavior: An Introduction to Theory and Research* (Reading, MA: Addison-Wesley, 1975).

33. Craig Trumbo and Garrett O'Keefe, "Understanding Environmentalism and Information Effects in Water Conservation Behavior: A Comparison of Three Communities Sharing a Watershed" (Paper presented to the Association for Education in Journalism and Mass Communication, August, Phoenix, AZ, 2000); Corbett, "Motivations to Participate in Riparian Improvement Programs."

34. Garrett Hardin, "The Tragedy of the Commons," *Science* 162 (1968):1243–1248.

35. Raymond S. Nickerson, *Psychology and Environmental Change* (Mahwah, NJ: Lawrence Erlbaum, 2003), 90.

36. Robert J. Griffin, Sharon Dunwoody, and Kurt Neuwirth, "Proposed Model of the Relationship of Risk, Information Seeking and Processing to the Development of Preventive Behaviors," *Environmental Research* 80 (1999):230–45.

37. Trumbo and O'Keefe, "Understanding Environmentalism and Information Effects."

38. M. Fishbein, "Introduction," in *The Theory of Reasoned Action: Its Application to AIDS-Preventive Behaviour*, eds. D. J. Terry, C. Gallois, and M. McCamish (Oxford, UK: Pergamon, 1993), xv–xxv.

39. Gregory A. Guagnano, Paul C. Stern, and Thomas Dietz, "Influences on Attitude-Behavior Relationships: A Natural Experiment with Curbside Recycling," *Environment and Behavior* 27 (1995):699–718.

40. Stern, "Toward A Coherent Theory," 415.

41. J. Boldero, "The Prediction of Household Recycling of Newspapers: The Role of Attitudes, Intentions, and Situational Factors," *Journal of Applied Social Psychology* 25 (5) (1995):440–62; K. Chan, "Mass Communication and Pro-environmental Behavior: Waste Recycling in Hong Kong," *Journal of Environmental Management* 52 (1998):317–25; S. F. Cheung, D. K.-S. Chan, and Z. S.-Y. Wong, "Reexamining the Theory of Planned Behavior in Understanding Wastepaper Recycling," *Environment and Behavior* 31 (5) (1999):587–612.

42. B. Verplanken, H. Aarts, and A. van Knippenberg, "Habit, Information Acquisition, and the Process of Making Travel Mode Choices," *European Journal of Social Psychology* 27 (1997):539–60.

43. J. A. Bargh, "Auto-motives: Preconscious Determinants of Thought and Behavior," in *Handbook of Motivation and Cognition: Foundation of Social Behavior*, vol. 2, eds. E. T. Higgins and R. M. Sorrentino (New York: Guilford, 1990), 93–130.

44. Stern, "Toward a Coherent Theory."

45. *Green Gauge 2001: Americans Focus on the Environment* (New York: Roper, 2001).

46. P. Wesley Schultz, "Knowledge, Information, and Household Recycling: Examining the Knowledge-Deficit Model of Behavior Change," in *New Tools for Environmental Protection*, National Research Council (Washington, D.C.: National Academy Press, 2002).

47. Stephen Kaplan, "Human Nature and Environmentally Responsible Behavior," *Journal of Social Issues* 56 (3) (2000):491–508.

48. Kaplan, "Human Nature," 496.

49. J. J. Mansbridge, "On the Relation of Altruism and Self-interest," in *Beyond Self-interest*, ed. J. J. Mansbridge. (Chicago: University of Chicago Press, 1990), 133–43.

50. B. S. Low and J. T. Heinen, "Population, Resources and Environment: Implications of Human Behavioral Ecology for Conservation," *Population and Environment* 15 (1993):7–41.

51. Kaplan, "Human Nature."

52. The Reasonable Person Model was put forth in Kaplan, "Human Nature."

53. Examples from Julia B. Corbett, "Altruism, Self-interest, and the Reasonable Person Model of Environmentally Responsible Behavior," *Science Communication* 26 (4) (2005):368–89.

54. Kaplan, "Human Nature," 502.

55. P. C. Stern, E. Aronson, J. M. Darley, D. H. Hill, E. Hirst, W. Kempton, and T. J. Wilbanks, "The Effectiveness of Incentives for Residential Energy Conservation," *Evaluation Review* 10 (2) (1986):147–76.

## Chapter 4: Work and Consumer Culture

1. Ed Andrew, *Closing the Iron Cage: The Scientific Management of Work and Leisure* (Montreal: Black Rose Books, 1981), 19.

2. Geoffrey Godbey, *Leisure in Your Life*, 5th ed. (State College, PA: Venture Publishing, 1999).

3. Andrew, *Closing the Iron Cage*, 19–20.

4. Richard K. Brown, ed., *The Changing Shape of Work* (New York: St. Martin's Press, 1997).

5. Brown, *The Changing Shape of Work*, 64.

6. Godbey, *Leisure in Your Life*.

7. Donald G. Reid, *Work and Leisure in the 21st Century: From Production to Citizenship* (Toronto: Wall & Emerson, 1995), 11.

8. Robert E. Land, *The Loss of Happiness in Market Democracies* (New Haven: Yale University Press, 2000), 71.

9. Ibid., 16.

10. Godbey, *Leisure in Your Life*.

11. Reid, *Work and Leisure*, 21.

12. Juliet B. Schor, *The Overworked American: The Unexpected Decline of Leisure* (New York: BasicBooks/Harper Collins, 1991), 2.

13. Schor, *The Overworked American*, 2.

14. Ibid., 110.

15. Ibid.

16. Ibid.

17. Ibid., 114.

18. Ibid.

19. Reid, *Work and Leisure*, 11–12.

20. Schor, *The Overworked American*, 7.

21. Godbey, *Leisure in Your Life*.

22. Stephen M. Fjellman, *Vinyl Leaves: Walt Disney World and America* (Boulder, CO: Westview Press, 1992), 7.

23. Mike Featherstone, *Consumer Culture and Postmodernism* (Newbury Park, CA: Sage, 1991), 83.

24. Thomas Hine, *I Want That! How We All Became Shoppers* (New York: HarperCollins, 2002), xiv–xv.

25. Steven Miles, *Consumerism as a Way of Life* (London: Sage, 2004), 1.

26. Z. Bauman, *Legislators and Interpreters* (Cambridge: Polity Press, 1987), 166.

27. Arthur Asa Berger, *Shop 'Til You Drop: Consumer Behavior and Consumer Culture* (Lanham, MD: Rowman & Littlefield, 2005), 1.

28. Miles, *Consumerism as a Way of Life*, 148.

29. The derogatory term "banana republic" was coined to describe a small tropical (and usually Central or South American) country that was economically dependent on fruit-exporting or similar small-scale trade, yet the same inequity of wealth and power of these countries could easily be "exported" as a model.

30. Berger, *Shop 'Til You Drop*.

31. Ibid., 6.

32. Simon Patten, *The Consumption of Wealth* (New York, 1892), 34.

33. Stuart Ewen, *Captains of Consciousness* (New York: McGraw-Hill, 1976).

34. Stuart Ewen, *All Consuming Images: The Politics of Style in Contemporary Culture* (New York: Basic Books, 1988), 243, emphasis added.

35. J. Gordon Lippincott, *Designs for Business* (Chicago, 1947), 14–15.

36. Ewen, *All Consuming Images*.

37. Ibid., 248.

38. Ibid.

39. Ibid., 251.

40. Berger, *Shop 'Til You Drop*.

41. Ibid.

42. Concepts from Ibid., 75.

43. Ibid., 15.

44. Jean Baudrillard, *Selected Writings*, ed. M. Poster (Cambridge, UK: Polity Press, 1988).

45. Paul du Gay, *Consumption and Identity at Work* (London: Sage, 1996), 80.

46. Baudrillard, *Selected Writings*.

47. Thorstein Veblen, *The Theory of the Leisure Class* (London: George Allen and Unwin, 1957).

48. Ibid., 85.

49. Pierre Bourdieu, *Distinction*, trans. R. Nice (London: Routledge, 1984), 30.

50. Ewen, *All Consuming Images*.

51. Ibid., 234.

52. Ibid., 242–43.

53. Miles, *Consumerism as a Way of Life*, 150.

54. Richard White, "'Are You an Environmentalist or Do You Work for a Living?': Work and Nature," in *Uncommon Ground: Rethinking the Human Place in Nature*, ed. William Cronon (New York: W.W. Norton, 1996), 171–185.

55. White, "Are You an Environmentalist," 184.

56. Figures found at www.svtc.org/hightech_prod/desktop.htm, which cited source of table as "Electronics Industry Environmental Roadmap," (Austin, TX: Microelectronics and Computer Technology Corporation, 1996).

57. White, "Are You an Environmentalist," 181.

58. Ibid., 174.

59. Ibid., 173.

60. Ibid., 179.

61. Ibid., 177.

62. Ibid., 174.

## Chapter 5: Leisure in Nature as Commodity and Entertainment

1. Geoffrey Godbey, *Leisure in Your Life*, 5th ed. (State College, PA: Venture Publishing, 1999).

2. Ed Andrew, *Closing the Iron Cage: The Scientific Management of Work and Leisure* (Montreal: Black Rose Books, 1981), 22.

3. Ibid., 23.

4. Ibid., 33.

5. Paul Shepard, *Where We Belong: Beyond Abstraction in Perceiving Nature* (Athens: University of Georgia Press, 2003), 159.

6. Michelle Scollo Sawyer, "Nonverbal Ways of Communicating with Nature: A Cross-Case Study," in *The Environmental Communication Yearbook*, vol. 1, ed. Susan L. Senecah (Mahwah, NJ: Lawrence Erlbaum, 2004), 227–249, 235.

7. Henry David Thoreau, *Walden and Other Writings* (New York: The Modern Library, 1937), 597.

8. Sawyer, "Nonverbal Ways of Communicating with Nature," 236.

9. Michael Lundblad, "Patagonia, Gary Snyder, and the 'Magic' of Wilderness," in *Imagining the Big Open: Nature, Identity, and Play in the New West*, eds. Liza Nicholas, Elaine M. Bapis, and Thomas J. Harvey (Salt Lake City: University of Utah Press, 2003), 73–91.

10. Ibid.

11. Ibid., 82.

12. Ken Owens, "Fishing the Hatch," in *Imagining the Big Open: Nature, Identity, and Play in the New West*, eds. Liza Nicholas, Elaine M. Bapis, and Thomas J. Harvey (Salt Lake City: University of Utah Press, 2003), 111–121).

13. Ibid.

14. Liza Nicholas, "1-800-Sundance," in *Imagining the Big Open: Nature, Identity, and Play in the New West*, eds. Liza Nicholas, Elaine M. Bapis, and Thomas J. Harvey (Salt Lake City: University of Utah Press, 2003), 259–271, 259.

15. Ibid.

16. Ibid., 265.

17. Ibid.

18. Jennifer Price, "Looking for Nature at the Mall: A Field Guide to the Na-

ture Company," in *Uncommon Ground: Rethinking the Human Place in Nature*, ed. William Cronon (New York: W.W. Norton, 1996), 186–203, 198.

19. Ibid., 201.

20. Shepard, *Where We Belong*, 34.

21. Ibid., 32.

22. Ibid., 52.

23. Thomas Greider and Lorraine Garkovich, "Landscapes: The Social Construction of Nature and the Environment," *Rural Sociology* 59 (1) (1994):1–24, 1.

24. Galen Cranz, "Changing Role of Urban Parks: From Pleasure Garden to Open Space," *Landscape* 22 (3) (1978):9–18, 9.

25. Ibid., 11.

26. Ibid., 12.

27. Ibid., 15.

28. Stephen M. Fjellman, *Vinyl Leaves: Walt Disney World and America* (Boulder, CO: Westview Press, 1992), 2.

29. Ibid., 6.

30. Ibid., 13.

31. Ibid., 329.

32. Steve Birnbaum, *Steve Birnbaum Brings You the Best of Walt Disney World* (New York: Houghton-Mifflin, 1989), 124.

33. Fjellman, *Vinyl Leaves*, 6.

34. Alan Bryman, *The Disneyization of Society* (London: Sage, 2004).

35. Ibid.

36. Ibid.

37. Ibid., 38.

38. Arthur Asa Berger, *Shop 'Til You Drop: Consumer Behavior and Consumer Culture* (Lanham, MD: Rowman & Littlefield, 2005).

39. Bryman, *The Disneyization of Society*, 41.

40. Jim Krane (Associated Press), "Building Islands from Scratch Rough on Sea Life, Divers," *Salt Lake Tribune*, Feb. 27, 2005, A21.

41. Andrew, *Closing the Iron Cage*.

42. Katherine A. McComas, James Shanahan, and Jessica S. Butler, "Environmental Content in Prime-Time Network TV's Non-News Entertainment and Fictional Programs," *Society and Natural Resources* 14 (2001):533–542.

43. A Gallup poll found that respondents who most favored environmental protection over economic growth were nonwhite females, ages 18–29, and who earned $20–29,000 a year. From D. W. Moore, "Public Sense of Urgency about Environment Wanes," *Gallup Poll Monthly* 355 (1995):17–20.

44. McComas et al., "Environmental Content in Prime-Time," 533.

45. James Shanahan, Michael Morgan, and Mads Stenbjerre, "Green or Brown? Television and the Cultivation of Environmental Concern," *Journal of Broadcasting and Electronic Media* 41 (1997):305–323.

46. R. Lance Holbert, Nojin Kwak, and Dhavan V. Shah, "Environmental Concern, Patterns of Television Vision, and Pro-Environmental Behaviors: Integrating Models of Media Consumption and Effects," *Journal of Broadcasting and Electronic Media* 47 (2):177–196 (2003).

47. Alexander Wilson, *The Culture of Nature* (Cambridge, MA: Blackwell, 1992), 129.

48. Ibid., 122.

49. Ibid.

50. Colin Turnbull, "East African Safari," *Natural History* 5 (1981):26, 29–34.

51. Jim Motavalli, "Taking the Natural Path," *E: The Environmental Magazine*, 13 (4), July/Aug. 2002, 26–26.

52. Martha Honey, "Protecting Eden: Setting Green Standards for the Tourism Industry," *Environment* 45 (6) (July-Aug. 2003):9–21, 10.

53. Tom Selwyn, ed., *The Tourist Image: Myths and Myth Making in Tourism* (Chichester, UK: John Wiley, 1996), 9–10.

54. Ibid., 9.

55. Wilson, *The Culture of Nature*, 22.

56. Selwyn, *The Tourist Image*, 7.

57. Ibid., 21.

58. Graham Dann, "The People of Tourist Brochures," in *The Tourist Image: Myths and Myth Making in Tourism* ed., Tom Selwyn (Chichester, UK: John Wiley, 1996), 61–82.

59. Ibid., 63.

60. Elizabeth Edwards, "Postcards: Greetings from Another World," in *The Tourist Image: Myths and Myth Making in Tourism*, ed. Tom Selwyn (Chichester, UK: John Wiley, 1996), 197–222.

61. Christine Macy and Sarah Bonnemaison, *Architecture and Nature: Creating the American Landscape* (New York: Routledge, 2003), 107.

62. Wilson, *The Culture of Nature*, 22.

63. Ibid., 25.

64. Macy and Bonnemaison, *Architecture and Nature*.

65. Ibid., 71.

66. Ibid., 79.

67. Ibid., 84–85.

68. Ibid., 111.

69. Ibid., 123.

70. Wilson, *The Culture of Nature*.

71. Shepard, *Where We Belong*, 158.

72. "A Moment of Truth for User Fees," *High Country News* 36 (1) (Jan. 19, 2004):4.

73. E. Boo, *Ecotourism: The Potentials and Pitfalls* (Washington, D.C.: World Wildlife Fund, 1990), 3.

74. Honey, "Protecting Eden," 13–14.

75. E. Jane Luzar and Assane Diagne, "Profiling the Nature-Based Tourist: A Multinomial Logit Approach," *Journal of Travel Research* 37 (1) (1998):48–55.

76. Honey, "Protecting Eden," 14.

77. Jill M. Belsky, "Misrepresenting Communities: The Politics of Community-based Rural Ecotourism in Gales Point Manatee, Belize," *Rural Sociology* 64 (4) (1999):641–666.

78. Belsky, "Misrepresenting Communities," 641.

## Chapter 6: Faint-Green: Advertising and the Natural World

1. J. B. Twitchell, *Adcult USA: The Triumph of Advertising in American Culture* (New York: Columbia University Press, 1996).

2. E. Iyer, B. Banerjee, and C. Gulas, "An Expose on Green Television Ads," *Advances in Consumer Research* 21 (1994):292–98; L. J. Shrum, J. A. McCarty, and T. M. Lowrey, "Buyer Characteristics of the Green Consumer and Their Implications for Advertising Strategy," *Journal of Advertising* 24 (2) (1995):71–82.

3. S. Banerjee, C. S. Gulas, and E. Iyer, "Shades of Green: A Multidimensional Analysis of Environmental Advertising," *Journal of Advertising* 24 (2) (1995):21–32.

4. L. M. Benton, "Selling the Natural or Selling Out? Exploring Environmental Merchandizing," *Environmental Ethics* 17 (1) (1995):3–22.

5. Michael Schudson, "Advertising as Capitalist Realism," in *Advertising in Society*, eds. R. Hovland and G. B. Wilcox (Lincolnwood, IL: NTC Business Books, 1989), 73–98.

6. B. J. Phillips, "Advertising and the Cultural Meaning of Animals," *Advances in Consumer Research* 23 (1996):354–60.

7. D. L. Dadd and A. Carouthers, "A Bill of Goods? Green Consuming in Perspective," in *Green Business: Hope or Hoax?*, eds. C. Plant and J. Plant (Philadelphia: New Society Publishers, 1991).

8. Will Nixon, "The Color of Money: Cashing in on Green Business," *Amicus Journal* 20 (2) (1998):16–18.

9. J. Greer and K. Bruno, *Greenwash: The Reality behind Corporate Environmentalism* (New York: Apex Press, 1996).

10. S. P. Sethi, *Advocacy Advertising and Large Corporations: Social Conflict, Big Business Image, the News Media, and Public Policy* (Lexington, MA: Lexington Books, 1977).

11. J. A. Ottman, *Green Marketing: Challenges and Opportunities for the New Marketing Age* (Lincolnwood, IL: NTC Business Books, 1993).

12. T. W. Luke, "Green Consumerism: Ecology and the Ruse of Recycling,"in *In the Nature of Things: Languages, Politics and the Environment*, eds. J. Bennett and W. Chaloupka (Minneapolis: University of Minnesota Press, 1993), 154–72, 166.

13. E. Iyer and B. Banerjee, "Anatomy of Green Advertising," *Advances in Consumer Research* 20 (1993):484–501.

14. Banerjee, Gulas, and Iyer, "Shades of Green."

15. Iyer and Banerjee, "Anatomy of Green Advertising."

16. Banerjee, Gulas, and Iyer, "Shades of Green."

17. Arne Naess, "The Shallow and the Deep, Long-range Ecology Movement: A Summary," *Inquiry* 16 (1973):95–100.

18. Banerjee, Gulas, and Iyer, "Shades of Green."

19. C. Obermiller, "The Baby Is Sick/the Baby Is Well: A Test of Environmental Communication Appeals," *Journal of Advertising* 24 (2) (1995):55–70.

20. M. E. Schuhwerk and R. Lefkoff-Hagius, "Green or Non-green? Does Type of Appeal Matter When Advertising a Green Product?" *Journal of Advertising* 24 (2) (1995):45–54.

21. E. Fink, "Biodegradable Diapers Are Not Enough in Days like These: A Critique of Commodity Environmentalism," *EcoSocialist Review* 4 (2) (1990), 212.

22. James Shanahan and Katherine McComas, *Nature Stories: Depictions of the Environment and Their Effects* (Cresskill, NJ: Hampton Press, Inc.,1999).

23. Ibid., 108.

24. W. E. Kilbourne, "Green Advertising: Salvation or Oxymoron?" *Journal of Advertising* 24 (2) (1995):7–20, 15.

25. Ibid.

26. Dadd and Carouthers, "A Bill of Goods?"

27. L. Carlson, S. J. Grove, and N. Kangun, "A Content Analysis of Environmental Advertising Claims: A Matrix Method Approach," *Journal of Advertising* 22 (3) (1993):28–39.

28. Ibid.

29. D. L. Scammon and R. N. Mayer, "Agency Review of Environmental Marketing Claims: Case-by-Case Decomposition of the Issues," *Journal of Advertising* 24 (2) (1995):33–44.

30. Dadd and Carouthers, "A Bill of Goods?"

31. Luke, "Green Consumerism."

32. Twitchell, *Adcult USA*.

33. Schudson, "Advertising as Capitalist Realism."

34. Twitchell, *Adcult USA*, 11.

35. J. Turow, *Breaking up America: Advertisers and the New Media World* (Chicago: University of Chicago Press, 1999), 194.

36. Ibid., 16.

37. Ibid., 13.

38. J. U. McNeal, "Billions at Stake in Growing Kids Market," *Discount Store News* 41 (Feb. 7, 1994).

39. "Zillions: For Kids from Consumer Reports," in *Captive Kids: Commercial Pressures on Kids at School* (New York: Consumers Union Education Services, 1995).

40. A. Molnar, "Schooled for Profit," *Educational Leadership* 53 (1) (1995):70.

41. "Zillions: For Kids from Consumer Reports," 13.

42. Ibid., 13.

43. L. M. Benton, "Selling the Natural or Selling Out? Exploring Environmental Merchandising," *Environmental Ethics* 17 (1) (1995):3–22.

44. A. Braithwaite, "Situations and Social Action: Applications for Marketing of Recent Theories in Social Psychology," *Journal of the Market Research Society* 25 (1983):19–38, 33.

45. Schudson, "Advertising as Capitalist Realism."

46. Twitchell, *Adcult USA*, 13.

47. Phillips, "Advertising and the Cultural Meaning of Animals."

48. Twitchell, *Adcult USA*.

49. C. Lasch, *The Culture of Narcissism* (New York: W. W. Norton, 1978).

50. R. W. Pollay, "The Distorted Mirror: Reflections on the Unintended Consequences of Advertising," in *Advertising in Society*, eds. R. Hovland and G. B. Wilcox (Lincolnwood, IL: NTC Business Books, 1989), 437–476.

51. J. Price, "Looking for Nature at the Mall: A Field Guide to the Nature Company," in *Uncommon Ground: Rethinking the Human Place in Nature*, ed. W. Cronon (New York: W.W. Norton, 1996), 186–203, 189.

52. C. Lasch, *The Culture of Narcissism*.

53. Pollay, "The Distorted Mirror."

54. Lasch, *The Culture of Narcissism*.

55. Schudson, "Advertising as Capitalist Realism," 79.

56. Christine L. Oravec, "To Stand outside Oneself: The Sublime in the Discourse of Natural Scenery," in *The Symbolic Earth: Discourse and Our Creation of the Environment*, eds. J. G. Cantrill and C. L. Oravec (Lexington: University Press of Kentucky, 1996), 58–75.

57. Ibid., 68.

58. Ibid., 69.

59. Schudson, "Advertising as Capitalist Realism," 77.

60. Ibid., 87.

61. Pollay, "The Distorted Mirror."

62. Ibid.

63. Price, "Looking for Nature at the Mall," 189.

64. Schudson, "Advertising as Capitalist Realism," 83.

65. Price, "Looking for Nature at the Mall."

66. Ibid., 197.

## Chapter 7: Communicating the Meaning of Animals

1. Adrian Franklin, *Animals and Modern Cultures: A Sociology of Human-Animal Relations in Modernity* (London: Sage Publications, 1999), 62.

2. Alexander Wilson, *The Culture of Nature* (Cambridge, MA: Blackwell, 1992).

3. Bob Mullan and Garry Marvin, *Zoo Culture* (London: Weidenfeld & Nicolson, 1987).

4. Ibid.

5. Paul Shepard, *Thinking Animals* (New York: Viking Press, 1978).

6. Barry Lopez, *Of Wolves and Men* (New York: Charles Scribner's Sons, 1978).

7. J. E. S. Sokolow, *The Role of Animals in Children's Literature*, unpublished manuscript, School of Forestry and Environmental Studies, Yale University, 1980.

8. Stephen R. Kellert, "Affective, Cognitive, and Evaluative Perceptions of Animals," in *Behavior and the Natural Environment*, eds. Irwin Altman and Joachim Wohlwill (New York: Plenum Press, 1983), 243.

9. David E. Cooper, "Human Sentiment and the Future of Wildlife," in *Attitudes to Animals: Views in Animal Welfare*, ed. Francine L. Dolins (Cambridge, UK: Cambridge University Press, 1999), 231–43.

10. Ibid.

11. Ibid., 239.

12. Ibid., 240.

13. Lisa Mighetto, *Wild Animals and American Environmental Ethics* (Tucson: University of Arizona Press, 1991).

14. Erich Klinghammer, "The Wolf: Fact and Fiction," in *Perceptions of Animals in American Culture*, ed. R. J. Hoage (Washington, D.C.: Smithsonian Institution Press, 1989), 77–91, 82.

15. Mighetto, *Wild Animals and American Environmental Ethics*, 78–79.

16. Ibid., 79.

17. Klinghammer, "The Wolf: Fact and Fiction."

18. Mighetto, *Wild Animals and American Environmental Ethics*.

19. Ibid., 82.

20. Ibid., 83–84.

21. Mark N. Trahant, "The Wolf as Story, Both Old and New," *Salt Lake Tribune*, Jan. 1, 2003, A-1, A-10.

22. Tore Bkerke and Bjorn P. Kaltenborn, "The Relationship of Ecocentric and Anthropocentric Motives to Attitudes toward Large Carnivores," *Journal of Environmental Psychology* 19 (1999):415–421.

23. Klinghammer, "The Wolf: Fact and Fiction," 81.

24. Trahant, "The Wolf as Story," A10.

25. L. David Mech, *The Wolf* (Garden City, NJ: Natural History Press, 1970).

26. Farley Mowatt, *Never Cry Wolf* (New York: Dell Publishing, 1963).

27. Mighetto, *Wild Animals and American Environmental Ethics*, 90.

28. Trahant, "The Wolf as Story," A10.

29. Ibid.

30. Klinghammer, "The Wolf: Fact and Fiction."

31. Kellert, "Affective, Cognitive, and Evaluative Perceptions of Animals," 260.

32. Stephen R. Kellert, "Perceptions of Animals in America," in *Perceptions of Animals in American Culture*, ed. R. J. Hoage (Washington, D.C.: Smithsonian Institution Press, 1989), 5–24.

33. Stephen R. Kellert, "Attitudes toward Animals: Age-Related Development among Children," *Journal of Environmental Education* 16 (3) (1995):29–39.

34. Ibid., 33.

35. Kellert, "Perceptions of Animals in America."

36. Ibid., 19–20.

37. Ibid.

38. Kellert, "Attitudes toward Animals."

39. Elizabeth A. Lawrence, "Neoteny in American Perceptions of Animals," in *Perceptions of Animals in American Culture*, ed. R. J. Hoage (Washington, D.C.: Smithsonian Institution Press, 1989), 57–75.

40. Kellert, "Perceptions of Animals in America."

41. Helga Olkowski and William Olkowski, "Entomophobia in the Urban Ecosystem, Some Observations and Suggestions," *Bulletin of the Entomological Society of America* 22 (3) (1976):313–317.

42. Lawrence, "Neoteny in American Perceptions of Animals."

43. Mullan and Marvin, *Zoo Culture*.

44. Stephen J. Gould, *The Panda's Thumb* (New York: W.W. Norton, 1980).

45. R. Morris and D. Morris, *The Giant Panda* (London: MacMillan, 1981), 26.

46. Lawrence, "Neoteny in American Perceptions."

47. Ibid., 71.

48. Randall Lockwood, "Anthropomorphism Is Not a Four-letter Word," in *Perceptions of Animals in American Culture*, ed. R. J. Hoage (Washington, D.C.: Smithsonian Institution Press, 1989), 41–55.

49. Ibid., 43.

50. Ibid., 49.

51. Ibid.

52. Tom Regan, "Ethical Perspectives on the Treatment and Status of Animals," in *Encyclopedia of Bioethics*, vol, 1, ed. Warren Thomas Reich (New York: Simon & Schuster: MacMillan, 1978), 159–71.

53. Lilly-Marlene Russow, "Changing Perceptions of Animals: A Philosophical View," in *Perceptions of Animals in American Culture*, ed. R. J. Hoage (Washington, D.C.: Smithsonian Institution Press, 1989), 25–39, 35–36.

54. Gordon M. Burghardt and Harold A. Herzog, "Animals, Evolution, and Ethics," in *Perceptions of Animals in American Culture*, ed. R. J. Hoage (Washington, D.C.: Smithsonian Institution Press, 1989), 129–51.

55. R. Morris and D. Morris, *Men and Snakes* (New York: McGraw-Hill, 1965).

56. Burghardt and Herzog, "Animals, Evolution, and Ethics," 148.

57. Regan, "Ethical Perspectives."

58. Burghardt and Herzog, "Animals, Evolution, and Ethics," 148.

59. Julia B. Corbett, "When Wildlife Make the News: An Analysis of Rural and Urban North-Central U.S. Newspapers," *Public Understanding of Science* 4 (1995):397–410; T. Rose, *Freeing the Whales: How the Media Created the World's Greatest Non-Event* (New York: Birch Lane Press, 1989), preface.

60. Cooper, "Human Sentiment and the Future of Wildlife."

61. Portions of this discussion first appeared in Corbett, "When Wildlife Make the News"; and Julia B. Corbett, "Rural and Urban Newspaper Coverage of Wildlife: Conflict, Community, and Bureaucracy," *Journalism Quarterly* 69 (4) (1992):929–37.

62. Julia B. Corbett, "The Environment as Theme and Package on a Local Television Newscast," *Science Communication* 19 (3) (1998):222–37.

63. S. Cottle, "Mediating the Environment: Modalities of TV News," in *The Mass Media and Environmental Issues*, ed. Anders Hansen, (Leicester: Leicester University Press, 1993), 107–33.

64. Corbett, "When Wildlife Make the News."

65. JoAnn Magdoff and Steve Barnett, "Self-imaging and Animals in TV Ads," in *Perceptions of Animals in American Culture*, ed. R. J. Hoage (Washington, D.C.: Smithsonian Institution Press, 1989), 93–100.

66. Magdoff and Barnett, "Self-imaging and Animals in TV Ads," 100.

67. Ibid., 94.

68. Ibid.

69. Ibid., 97.

70. Mullan and Marvin, *Zoo Culture*, xiv.

71. Ibid., xv–xvi.

72. Morris and Morris, *The Giant Panda*, 172.

73. Mullan and Marvin, *Zoo Culture*.

74. Wilson, *The Culture of Nature*.

75. Mullan and Marvin, *Zoo Culture*, 33.

76. Henri F. Ellenberger, "The Mental Hospital and the Zoological Garden," in *Animals and Man in Historical Perspective*, eds. J. Klaits and B. Klaits (New York: Harper & Row, 1974), 59–93, 69–70.

77. Franklin, *Animals and Modern Cultures*, 67.

78. Ibid., 68.

79. Mullan and Marvin, *Zoo Culture*, 159.

80. Wilson, *The Culture of Nature*, 246.

81. Mullan and Marvin, *Zoo Culture*, 160.

82. Robert Sommer, "What Do We Learn at the Zoo?" *Natural History* (1972):26–29, 84–85, 26.

83. Mullan and Marvin, *Zoo Culture*, 127.

84. Ibid.

85. Sommer, "What Do We Learn at the Zoo?" 26.

## Chapter 8: News Media

1. Walter Lippmann, *Public Opinion*, (New Brunswick, NJ: Transaction Publishers, [1922] 1991).

2. Everett E. Dennis, "In Context: Environmentalism in the System of News," in *Media and the Environment*, eds. C. L. LaMay and E. Dennis (Washington, D.C.: Island Press)(1991), 55–64, 59.

3. Everett E. Dennis, "In Context," 62.

4. Leon V. Sigal, *Reporters and Officials: The Organization and Politics of Newsmaking* (Lexington, MA: D.C. Heath, 1973).

5. Jane Delano Brown, Carl R. Bybee, Stanley T. Wearden, and Dulcie Murdock Straughan, "Invisible Power: Newspaper News Sources and the Limits of Diversity," *Journalism Quarterly* 64 (1) (1987):45–54, 51.

6. W. P. Martin and M. Singletary, "Newspaper Treatment of State Government Releases," *Journalism Quarterly* 58 (1981):93–96; Judy Van Slyke Turk, "Information Subsidies and Media Content: A Study of Public Relations Influence on the News," *Journalism Monograph* No. 100 (1986).

7. Lynne Masel Walters and Timothy N. Walters, "Environment of Confidence: Daily Newspaper Use of Press Releases," *Public Relations Review* 18 (1) (1992):31–46.

8. Turk, "Information Subsidies and Media Content," 24.

9. Judy Van Slyke Turk and Bob Franklin, "Information Subsides: Agenda-setting Traditions," *Public Relations Review* (Winter 1987):29–41.

10. O. H. Gandy, Jr., *Beyond Agenda Setting: Information Subsidies and Public Policy* (Norwood, N.J.: Ablex, 1982).

11. S. Dunwoody and M. Ryan, "Public Information Persons as Mediators between Scientists and Journalists," *Journalism Quarterly* 60 (4) (1983):647–48.

12. S. Holly Stocking, "Effect of Public Relations Efforts on Media Visibility of Organizations," *Journalism Quarterly* 62 (2) (1985):358–66, 450.

13. Philip J. Tichenor, Clarice N. Olien, and George A. Donohue, "Predicting a Source's Success in Placing News in the Media," *Journalism Quarterly* 44 (1) (1967):32–42.

14. David B. Sachsman, "Public Relations Influence on Coverage of Environment in San Francisco," *Journalism Quarterly* 53 (1) (1976):54–60.

15. B. Sonenclar, "The VNR Top Ten," *Columbia Journalism Review* March–April 14:(2001).

16. E. E. Chang, "The Video News Release: Public Relations and the Television News Business," (Paper presented to the annual conference of the Association for Education in Journalism and Mass Communication, Aug. 1995, Washington, D.C.); A. Hunt, "Is It Really News? An Analysis of Video News Releases," (Paper presented at annual conference of the Association for Education in Journalism and Mass Communication, Aug. 1997, Chicago.)

17. Julia B. Corbett, "The Environment as Theme and Package on a Local Television Newscast," *Science Communication* 19 (3) (1998):222–237.

18. Pamela J. Shoemaker and Stephen D. Reese, *Mediating the Message: Theories of Influence on Mass Media Content*, (New York: Longman, 1991), 21.

19. Michael S. Schudson, "The 1996 New News Bias," *Public Relations Strategist* 1 (4) (1995):37–41, 40.

20. Warren Breed, "Mass Communication and Socio-Cultural Integration," *Social Forces* 37 (1958):109–16.

21. Dennis, "In Context," 55.

22. Ibid., 60.

23. Julia B. Corbett, "Atmospheric Ozone: Global or Local Issue? Coverage in Canadian and U.S. Newspapers," *Canadian Journal of Communication* 18 (1993):81–87.

24. Dennis, "In Context," 61.

25. Sharon M. Friedman, Sharon Dunwoody, and Carol L. Rogers, *Scientists and Journalists: Reporting Science as News* (New York: Free Press,1986); Dorothy Nelkin, *Selling Science: How the Press Covers Science and Technology* (New York: W.H. Freeman, 1987); Lee Wilkins and Philip Patterson, *Risky Business: Communication Issues of Science, Risk and Public Policy* (New York: Greenwood Press, 1991).

26. Julia B. Corbett, "Rural and Urban Newspaper Coverage of Wildlife: Conflict, Community and Bureaucracy." *Journalism Quarterly* 69 (4) (1992):929–937; Corbett, "The Environment as Theme and Package."

27. Anders Hansen, "The Media and the Social Construction of the Environment," *Media, Culture and Society* 13 (4) (1991):443–458, 452.

28. Alison Anderson, "Source Strategies and the Communication of Environmental Affairs," *Media, Culture and Society* 13(4) (1991): 459–476.

29. Julia B. Corbett and Jessica L. Durfee, "Testing Public (Un)certainty of Science: Media Representations of Global Warming," *Science Communication* 26 (2) (2004):129–151; Kris Wilson, "Drought, Debate, and Uncertainty: Measuring Reporters' Knowledge and Ignorance about Climate Change," *Public Understanding of Science* 9 (2000):1–13.

30. W. Gieber, "News Is What Newspapermen Make It," in *People, Society and Mass Communications*, eds. A. Dexter and D. M. White (New York: The Free Press, 1964); D. M. White, "The Gatekeeper: A Case Study in the Selection of News," *Journalism Quarterly* 27 (1950):383–90.

31. Mark Fishman, *Manufacturing the News* (Austin: University of Texas Press, 1980); Gaye Tuchman, *Making News: A Study in the Construction of Reality* (New York: The Free Press, 1978).

32. Pamela J. Shoemaker, Martin Eichholz, Eunyi Kim, and Brenda Wrigley, "Individual and Routine Forces in Gatekeeping," *Journalism & Mass Communication Quarterly* 78 (2) (2001):233–246.

33. Herbert L. Gans, *Deciding What's News: A Study of CBS Evening News, NBC Nightly News, Newsweek and Time* (New York: Pantheon, 1979).

34. Joseph Man Chan and Chin-Chuan Lee, "Press Ideology and Organizational Control in Hong Kong," *Communication Research* 15 (2) (April 1988):185–97.

35. Corbett, "The Environment as Theme and Package."

36. Schudson, "The 1996 New News Bias," 37.

37. Ibid., 38.

38. Wilson, "Drought, Debate, and Uncertainty."

39. Corbett and Durfee, "Testing Public (Un)certainty of Science."

40. Molotch and Lester, "Accidental News."

41. D. Berkowitz, "TV News Sources and News Channels: A Study in Agenda-Building," *Journalism Quarterly* 3 (1987):507–513; R. L. Carroll, "Content Values in TV News Programs in Small and Large Markets," *Journalism Quarterly* 62 (1985):877–882.

42. Gloria Steinem, "Sex, Lies and Advertising," *Ms.* (1990 July/August):18–28.

43. W. L. Weis and C. Burke, "Media Content and Tobacco Advertising: An Unhealthy Addiction," *Journal of Communication* 36 (4) (1986):59–69.

44. Karen Miller, "Smoking up a Storm: Public Relations and Advertising in the Construction of the Cigarette Problem, 1953–1954," *Journalism Monograph* 136 (Dec. 1992).

45. Frederick H. Buttel, "Environmentalization: Origins, Processes, and Implications for Rural Social Change," *Rural Sociology* 57 (1) (1992):1–27, 15.

46. Gans, *Deciding What's News.*

47. Leon V. Sigal, *Reporters and Officials: The Organization and Politics of Newsmaking* (Lexington, MA: D.C. Heath, 1973).

48. Gans, *Deciding What's News.*

49. J. E. Steele, "Experts and the Operational Bias of Television News: The Case of the Persian Gulf War," *Journalism and Mass Communication Quarterly* 72 (4) (1995):700–811.

50. Marc Cooper and Lawrence C. Soley, "All the Right Sources," *Mother Jones* (Feb./Mar. 1990):20–27, 45–48.

51. Gans, *Deciding What's News.*

52. Fishman, *Manufacturing the News.*

53. Ibid., 143.

54. Suzanne Staggenborg, "The Consequences of Professionalization and Formalization in the Pro-Choice Movement," *American Sociological Review* 53 (1988):585–606.

55. Julia B. Corbett, "Media, Bureaucracy, and the Success of Social Protest: Newspaper Coverage of Environmental Movement Groups." *Mass Communication & Society* 1 (1–2) (1998):41–61.

56. Sigal, *Reporters and Officials.*

57. Jane Delano Brown, Carl R. Bybee, Stanley T. Wearden, and Dulcie Murdock Straughan, "Invisible Power: Newspaper News Sources and the Limits of Diversity," *Journalism Quarterly* 64 (1) (1987):45–54.

58. Hugh M. Culbertson, "Veiled News Sources—Who and What Are They?" *News Research Bulletin*, American Newspaper Publishers Association (May 1975):2–23.

59. Robert A. Hackett, "A Hierarchy of Access: Aspects of Source Bias in Canadian TV News," *Journalism Quarterly* 62 (1985):256–265, 277.

60. Lynn M. Zoch and Judy VanSlyke Turk, "Women Making News: Gender as a Variable in Source Selection and Use," *Journalism & Mass Communication Quarterly* 75 (4) (1998):762–775, 771.

61. Zoch and Turk, "Women Making News," 772.

62. David L. Paletz, Peggy Reichert, and Barbara McIntyre, "How the Media Support Local Government Authority," *Public Opinion Quarterly* 35 (1971):80–92.

63. R. Gordon Shepherd, "Selectivity of Sources: Reporting the Marijuana Controversy," *Journal of Communication* 31 (2) (1981):129–37.

64. P. Golding, "The Missing Dimension: News Media and the Management of Social Change," in *Mass Media and Social Change*, eds. E. Katz and T. Szescko (Beverly Hills, CA: Sage Publications, 1981).

65. Corbett, "Rural and Urban Newspaper Coverage"; Michael R. Greenberg, David B. Sachsman, Peter M. Sandman, and Kandice L. Salomone, "Network Evening News Coverage of Environmental Risk," *Risk Analysis* 9(1) (1989):119–126; C. M. Liebler and J. Bendix. "Old-Growth Forests on Network News: News Sources and the Framing of Environmental Controversy," *Journalism and Mass Communication Quarterly* 73 (1):53–65; Conrad Smith, "News Sources and Power Elites in News Coverage of the *Exxon Valdez* Oil Spill," *Journalism Quarterly* 70(1993):750–52.

66. Corbett, "The Environment as Theme and Package"; Edna Einsiedel, "The Canadian Press and the Environment," Paper presented at International Association for Mass Communication Research, Barcelona, Spain 1988.

67. Survey results reported in *Environment Writer*, May/June 1993, a newsletter published by the Environmental Health Center, a division of the National Safety Council.

68. Corbett, "Rural and Urban Newspaper Coverage of Wildlife."

69. Edna Einsiedel and Eileen Coughlan, "The Canadian Press and the Environment," in *The Mass Media and Environmental Issues*, ed. A. Hansen (Leicester: Leicester University Press, 1993).

70. Corbett, "Atmospheric Ozone."

71. Corbett, "The Environment as Theme and Package."

72. Anders Hansen, "Socio-political Values Underlying Media Coverage of the Environment," *Media Development* 37 (2) (1990):3–6.

73. Hansen, "Socio-political Values," 4–5.

74. Robert Cameron Mitchell, Angela G. Mertig, and Riley E. Dunlap, "Twenty Years of Environmental Mobilization: Trends among National Environmental Organizations," in *American Environmentalism: The U.S. Environmental Movement, 1970–1990*, eds. Dunlap and Mertig (Philadelphia: Taylor & Francis, 1992).

75. M. Janowitz, *The Community Press in an Urban Setting* (New York: Macmillan, 1952); Alex Edelstein and B. Schulz, "The Weekly Newspaper's Leadership Role as Seen by Community Leaders," *Journalism Quarterly* 40 (1963):565–74.

76. Philip J. Tichenor, George A. Donohue, and Clarice N. Olien, *Community Conflict and the Press* (Beverly Hills, CA: Sage Publications, 1980).

77. Corbett, "Rural and Urban Newspaper Coverage of Wildlife."

78. Julia B. Corbett, "Whooping It up over Wilderness: Media Coverage of the Boundary Waters Wilderness Act, *Minneapolis Tribune* and *Ely Echo*" (1987), unpublished research.

79. Sharon Dunwoody and Robert Griffin, "Journalistic Strategies for Reporting Long-Term Environmental Issues: A Case Study of Three Superfund Sites," in *The Mass Media and Environmental Issues*, ed. A. Hansen (Leicester, UK: University of Leicester Press, 1993).

80. Robert J. Griffin, Sharon Dunwoody, and Christine Gehrmann, "The Effects of Community Pluralism on Press Coverage of Health Risks from Local Environmental Contamination," (Paper presented to the annual conference of the Association for Education of Journalism and Mass Communication, Montreal, 1992.)

81. Claire E. Taylor, Jung-Sook Lee, and William R. Davie, "Local Press Coverage of Environmental Conflict," *Journalism & Mass Communication Quarterly* 77 (1) (2000):175–192.

82. S. E. Hungerford and J. B. Lemert, "Covering the Environment: A New 'Afghanistanism,'" *Journalism Quarterly* 50 (1973):457–481,508.

83. J. Tankard, L. Henrickson, J. Silberman, K. Bliss, and S. Ghanem, "Media Frames: Approaches to Conceptualization and Measurement," (Paper presented to the Association for Education in Journalism and Mass Communication, 1991), 1.

84. P. Norris, "The Restless Search: Network News Framing of the Post-Cold-War World," *Political Communication* 12 (1995): 357–370, 357.

85. Todd Gitlin, *The Whole World Is Watching,* (Berkeley: University of California Press, 1980).

86. Thomas E. Nelson, Rosalee A. Clawson, and Zoe M. Oxley, "Media Framing of a Civil Liberties Conflict and Its Effect on Tolerance," *American Political Science Review* 91(Sept. 1997):567–583, 569.

87. D. Morley, "Industrial Conflict and the Mass Media," *Sociological Review* 24 (1976):245–268, 246.

88. David Tewskbury, Jennifer Jones, Matthew W. Peske, Ashlea Raymond, and William Vig, "The Interaction of News and Advocate Frames: Manipulating Audience Perceptions of a Local Public Policy Issue," *Journalism & Mass Communication Quarterly* 77 (4) (2000):804–829.

89. James K. Hertog and Douglas M. McLeod, "Anarchists Wreak Havoc in Downtown Minneapolis: A Multi-level Study of Media Coverage of Radical Protest," *Journalism and Mass Communication Monographs* 151 (June 1995):4.

90. Robert M. Entman, "Framing: Toward Clarification of a Fractured Paradigm." *Journal of Communication* 43 (4) (1993):51–58, 52 (dashes in original changed to parentheses).

91. Tewskbury, Jones, Peske, Raymond, and Vig, "The Interaction of News," 806.

92. Roya Akhavan-Majid and Jyotika Ramaprasad "Framing and Ideology: A Comparative Analysis of U.S. and Chinese Newspaper Coverage of the Fourth United Nations Conference on Women and the NGO Forum," *Mass Communication & Society* 1 (3–4) (1998):131–152, 133.

93. Ibid., 133–34.

94. Shoemaker, Eichholz, Kim, and Wrigley, "Individual and Routine Forces in Gatekeeping."

95. Tewskbury, Jones, Peske, Raymond, and Vig, "The Interaction of News," 806.

96. Robert M. Entman, "Framing U.S. Coverage of International News: Contrasts in the Narratives of the KAL and Iran Air Incidents." *Journal of Communication* 41 (4) (1991):6–27, 7.

97. Zhongdang Pan and Gerald M. Kosicki, "Framing Analysis: An Approach to News Discourse," *Political Communication* 10 (1993):55–75.

98. Charlotte Ryan, *Prime Time Activism: Media Strategies for Grassroots Organizing* (Boston: South End Press, 1991).

99. McLeod and Detenber, "Framing Effects of Television News."

100. Jessica L. Durfee, *Framing Effects on Public Perceptions of Environmental Health Risks: Air Quality in Salt Lake City*, Master's Thesis, University of Utah Department of Communication, 2003.

101. Tewskbury, Jones, Peske, Raymond, and Vig, "The Interaction of News."

102. Shanto Iyengar, *Is Anyone Responsible? How Television Frames Political Issues* (Chicago: University of Chicago Press, 1991).

103. D. H. Weaver and G. C. Wilhoit, *The American Journalist* (Bloomington: Indiana University Press, 1986).

104. McLeod and Detenber, "Framing Effects of Television News."

105. George A. Donohue, Philip J. Tichenor, and Clarice N. Olien, "Gatekeeping: Mass Media Systems and Information Control," in *Current Perspectives in Mass Communication Research*, eds. F. G. Kline and P. J. Tichenor (Beverly Hills, CA: Sage, 1972); George A. Donohue, Philip J. Tichenor, and Clarice N. Olien, "Mass Media Functions, Knowledge and Social Control," *Journalism Quarterly* 50 (1973):652–659; Hebert Spencer, *The Principles of Sociology*, vol. 1 (New York: D. Appleton and Co., 1898).

106. Denis McQuail, *Mass Communication Theory* (London: Sage Publications Inc., 1987), 285.

107. Shoemaker and Reese, *Mediating the Message.*

108. George A. Donohue, Philip J. Tichenor, and Clarice N. Olien, "A Guard Dog Perspective on the Role of Media," *Journal of Communication* 45 (1995):115–32.

109. Ibid.

110. Julie J. Andsager and Leiott Smiley, "Evaluating the Public Information: Shaping News Coverage of the Silicone Implant Controversy," *Public Relations Review* 24 (1998):183–201; Edward S. Herman and Noam Chomsky, *Manufacturing Consent* (New York: Pantheon, 1988); Harvey Molotch and Marilyn Lester, "Accidental News: The Great Oil Spill as Local Occurrence and National Event," *American Journal of Sociology* 81 (2) (1975):235–260; David Paletz and Robert Entman, *Media Power Politics* (New York: Free Press, 1981).

## Chapter 9: Battle for Spin

1. John Stauber and Sheldon Rampton, *Toxic Sludge Is Good for You! Lies, Damn Lies, and the Public Relations Industry* (Monroe, ME: Common Courage Press, 1995), 14.

2. Alison Anderson, "Source Strategies and the Communication of Environmental Affairs," *Media, Culture and Society* 13 (4) (1991):459–476; Alison Anderson, "Source-Media Relations: The Production of the Environmental Agenda," in *The Mass Media and Environmental Issues*, ed. A. Hansen (Leicester, England: Leicester University Press, 1993), 51–68; J. A. Ottman, *Green Marketing: Challenges and Opportunities for the New Marketing Age* (Chicago, IL: NTC Publishing, 1995); E. Bruce Harrison, *Going Green: How to Communicate Your Company's Environmental Commitment* (Burr Ridge, IL: Irwin Professional Publishing, 1993).

3. Stauber and Rampton, *Toxic Sludge*, 14.

4. M. E. Kraft and N. J. Vig, *Environmental Policy in the 1990s*, 2nd ed., (Washington, D.C.: CQ Press, 1994).

5. Clinton J. Andrews, "Environmental Business Strategy: Corporate Leaders' Perceptions," *Society & Natural Resources* 11 (1998):531–540.

6. Jane Jacobs, *Systems of Survival* (New York: Random House, 1993).

7. Jennifer Bogo, "Business Savvy: Making Room on the Shelves for a New Generation of Greener Goods," *E Magazine* (July/August 2000):26–33, 29.

8. Catherine A. Ramus and Ivan Montiel, "When are Corporate Environmental Policies a Form of Greenwashing?" *Business & Society* 44 (4) (2005):377–414, 400.

9. Ibid., 408.

10. Andrews, "Environmental Business Strategy," 539.

11. Stauber and Rampton, *Toxic Sludge*.

12. For a full discussion of the four models of PR practice, see for example: Dan Lattimore, Otis Baskin, Suzette T. Heiman, Elizabeth L. Toth, and James K. Van Leuven, *Public Relations: The Profession and the Practice* (Boston: Mc-Graw Hill, 2004); Dennis L. Wilcox and Glen T. Cameron, *Public Relations: Strategies and Tactics*, 8th ed. (Boston: Allyn & Bacon, 2006); Doug Newsom, Judy VanSlyke Turk, and Dean Kruckeberg, *This Is PR: The Realities of Public Relations*, 8th ed. (Belmont, CA: Wadsworth/Thompson Learning, 2004).

13. Edward L. Bernays, *Propaganda* (New York: 1928), 9.

14. Mark Achbar, Jennifer Abbott, and Joel Bakan, *The Corporation* (Zeitgeist Films, Canada, 2004).

15. Chris Mooney, "Some Like It Hot," *Mother Jones* (May/June 2005).

16. Jeff Nesmith, "New Product for U.S. Industry: 'Manufactured Doubt': Industries Growing Adept at Manipulating Science to Suit Their Needs," *Austin American-Statesman* (June 26, 2005).

17. Ken Ward Jr., "Dupont Lawyer Edited DEQ's C8 Media Releases," *Charleston Gazette* (July 03, 2005).

18. Reported in Nesmith, "New Product for U.S. Industry."

19. Reported in Ibid.

20. David Helvarg, "The Big Green Spin Machine: Corporations and Environmental PR," *Amicus Journal* (Summer 1996):13–21, at 21.

21. Mooney, "Some Like It Hot."

22. See www.globalclimate.org.

23. Mooney, "Some Like It Hot."

24. Ibid.

25. Reported in Ibid.

26. Bogo, "Business Savvy."

27. Ibid.

28. Harrison, *Going Green*, 16.

29. Ibid., 18.

30. Ibid., 301.

31. Ibid., 14.

32. See www.thegreenlife.org.

33. Helvarg, "The Big Green Spin Machine."

34. Bogo, "Business Savvy."

35. Helvarg, "The Big Green Spin Machine."

36. Ibid., 15.

37. Ibid., 14.

38. Ibid.

39. See www.thegreenlife.org.

40. James R. Healey, "Alternate Energy Not in the Cards at ExxonMobil," *USA Today* (Oct. 28, 2005).

41. Sarah A. Webster, "Ad Attacks Toyota's Record: Environmental Group Questions Efficiency," *Detroit Free Press* (October 24, 2005).

42. Joan Lowry, "Environmentalists Bypass Washington to Pressure Corporations," *Scripps Howard News Service* (May 25, 2005).

43. See www.thegreenlife.org.

44. Bogo, "Business Savvy."

45. See CorpWatch Web site: www.corpwatch.org.

46. Mark Memmott, "'Reports': Not Necessarily the News," *USA Today* www.usatoday.com/news/washington/2005-03-20-vnr-notnews_x.htm.

47. Ibid.

48. Mark Blaine, "This Message Brought to You By . . . , " *Forest Magazine* 7 (3) (Summer 2005):32–37.

49. Joe Mandese, "The Art of Manufactured News," *Broadcasting & Cable* (March 28, 2005), see www.broadcastingcable.com/article/CA513090.html.

50. Helvarg, "The Big Green Spin Machine."

51. Ibid., 20.

52. See www.thegreenlife.org.

53. See GM Web site www.gm.com (June 2005).

54. The Green Life, Aug. 2004 Greenwasher of Month, see www.thegreenlife.org.

55. Jorge Rivera and Peter de Leon, "Is Greener Whiter? Voluntary Environmental Performance of Western Ski Areas," *Policy Studies Journal* 32 (3): 417–37

56. "Public Interest Pretenders," *Consumer Reports* (May 1994).

57. Stauber and Rampton, *Toxic Sludge*, 89.

58. Ibid.

59. Ibid.

60. Helvarg, "The Big Green Spin Machine," 21.

## Chapter 10: Communication and Social Change

1. Riley E. Dunlap and Kent D. Van Liere, "The 'New Environmental Paradigm,'" *Journal of Environmental Education* 9 (4) (1978):10–19; Riley E. Dunlap, Kent D. Van Liere, Angela G. Mertig, and Robert Emmet Jones, "Measuring Endorsement of the New Ecological Paradigm: A Revised NEP Scale," *Journal of Social Issues* 56 (3) (2000):425–42; James Shanahan and Katherine McComas, *Nature Stories: Depictions of the Environment and Their Effects* (Cresskill, NJ: Hampton Press,1999).

2. Niccolo Machiavelli, *The Prince* (New York: Oxford University Press, 1532 [1952]), 55.

3. Angela G. Mertig, Riley E. Dunlap, and Denton E. Morrison, "The Environmental Movement in the United States," In *Handbook of Environmental Sociology* (2002):448–481.

4. Kirkpatrick Sale, *The Green Revolution: The American Environmental Movement, 1962–1992* (New York: Hill & Wang, 1993), 58.

5. Luke W. Cole and Sheila R. Foster, *From the Ground Up: Environmental Racism and the Rise of the Environmental Justice Movement* (New York: New York University Press, 2001), 33.

6. Robert Mitchell, "Since *Silent Spring*: The Institutionalization of Counter-Expertise by the United States Environmental Law Groups," (Washington, D.C.: Resources for the Future, Inc., Discussion Paper D-56, 1979).

7. Robert Cameron Mitchell, Angela G. Mertig, and Riley E. Dunlap, "Twenty Years of Environmental Mobilization: Trends among National Environmental Organizations," in *American Environmentalism: The U.S. Environmental Movement, 1970–1990*, eds. Dunlap and Mertig (Philadelphia: Taylor & Francis, 1992), 15.

8. Ibid., 21.

9. Ibid., 22.

10. Suzanne Staggenborg, "The Consequences of Professionalization and Formalization in the Pro-Choice Movement," *American Sociological Review* 53 (1988):585–606; Julia B. Corbett, "Media, Bureaucracy, and the Success of Social Protest: Newspaper Coverage of Environmental Movement Groups," *Mass Communication & Society* 1 (1–2) (1998):41–61.

11. Mayer N. Zald and Roberta Ash, "Social Movement Organizations: Growth, Decay and Change," *Social Forces* 44 (1966):327–41.

12. Julia B. Corbett, *Media, Bureaucracy, and the Success of Social Protest: Media Coverage of Environmental Movement Groups*, Ph.D. dissertation, University of Minnesota, School of Journalism and Mass Communication, 1994.

13. Julia B. Corbett, "Media Relations and Media Success of Environmental Movement Groups," (Paper presented at the annual conference of the International Communication Association, Chicago, IL, May 1996).

14. Julia B. Corbett, *Media, Bureaucracy and the Success of Social Protest.*

15. R. K. Godwin and R. C. Mitchell, "The Impact of Direct Mail on Political Organizations," *Social Science Quarterly* 65 (1984):829–39.

16. Joel J. Davis, "The Effects of Message Framing on Response to Environmental Communication," *Journalism & Mass Communication Quarterly* 77 (2) (1995):285–299.

17. James Cantrill, "Communication and Our Environment: Categorizing Research in Environmental Advocacy," *Journal of Applied Communication Research* 21(1993):66–95.

18. Arlene Plevin, "Green Guilt: An Effective Rhetoric or Rhetoric in Transition?" *Technical Communication Quarterly* 6 (2) (1997):125–139.

19. Ibid., 127.

20. Ibid., 136.

21. Ibid., 137.

22. Ibid., 134.

23. Ibid., 133.

24. M. Jimmie Killingsworth and Jacqueline S. Palmer, "The Discourse of Environmentalist Hysteria," *Quarterly Journal of Speech* 81 (1995):1–19, 15.

25. Ibid.

26. Mayer N. Zald and John D. McCarthy, eds., *Social Movements in an Organizational Society* (New Brunswick, NJ: Transaction Publishers, 1987), 372.

27. Glenn G. Strodthoff, Robert P. Hawkins, and A. Clay Schoenfeld, "Media Roles in a Social Movement: A Model of Ideology Diffusion," *Journal of Communication* 35 (2) ( 1985):134–153.

28. Clarice N. Olien, Philip J. Tichenor, and George A. Donohue, "Media Coverage and Social Movements," in *Information Campaigns: Balancing Social Values and Social Change*, ed. C. T. Salmon (Newbury Park, CA: Sage, 1989), 139–163, 149.

29. Mark A. Larson, "Communication Behavior by Environmental Activists Compared to Non-Active Persons," *Journal of Environmental Education* 14 (1) (1992):11–20.

30. Zald and McCarthy, *Social Movements*, 375.

31. Will C. Van den Hoonaard, "Numbers and 'Social Forms': The Contributions of Simmel to Social Movement Theory," in *Research in Social Movements, Conflicts and Change*, vol. 13, eds. Louis Kriesberg and Metta Spencer (Greenwich, CT: JAI Press, 1991), 31–43.

32. Melvin Mencher, *Basic News Writing* (Dubuque, Iowa: William C. Brown Publishers, 1986); M. L. Stein, *Getting and Writing the News* (New York: Longman, 1985).

33. Richard B. Kielbowicz and Clifford Scherer, "The Role of the Press in the Dynamics of Social Movements," in *Research in Social Movements, Conflicts and Change*, vol. 9, ed. Louis Kriesberg (Greenwich, CT: JAI Press, 1986), 71–96; 90–91, 84.

34. Anthony Oberschall, *Social Movements: Ideologies, Interests and Identities* (New Brunswick, NJ: Transaction Publishers, 1993), 281.

35. Todd Gitlin, *The Whole World Is Watching*, (Berkeley: University of California Press, 1980).

36. Harvey Molotch, "Media and Movements," in *The Dynamics of Social Movements: Resource Mobilization, Social Control and Tactics*, eds. Mayer N. Zald and John D. McCarthy (Cambridge, MA: Winthrop Publishers, Inc., 1979), 71–93, 81.

37. Kielbowicz and Scherer, "The Role of the Press in the Dynamics of Social Movements."

38. Anderson, "Source-Media Relations," 65.

39. Kielbowicz and Scherer, "The Role of the Press in the Dynamics of Social Movements," 86.

40. Corbett, "Media, Bureaucracy, and the Success of Social Protest."

41. Clarice N. Olien, Philip J. Tichenor and George A. Donohue, "Media and Stages of Social Conflict," *Journalism Monograph* 90 (1984).

42. Julia B. Corbett, "Apples, Alar, PR and the Media: Accelerating a Public Policy Issue," unpublished research, 1991.

43. Sharon M. Friedman, Kara Villamil, Robyn Suriano, and Brenda Egolf, "Alar and Apples: Newspaper Coverage of a Major Risk Issue." *Public Understanding of Science* 5 (1996):1–20.

44. Julia B. Corbett, "Women, Scientists, Agitators: Magazine Portrayal of Rachel Carson and Theo Colborn," *Journal of Communication* 51 (4) (2001):720–749.

45. David Helvarg, "Poison Pens," *Sierra* 82 (Jan. 1997):31–35.

46. Fred Pearce, *Green Warriors: The People and the Politics behind the Environmental Revolution* (London: The Bodley Head, 1991), 19.

47. Olien, Tichenor, and Donohue, "Media Coverage and Social Movements."

48. Harvey Molotch, "The City as a Growth Machine: Toward a Political Economy of Place," *American Journal of Sociology* 82 (2) (1976):309–332.

49. Molotch, "Media and Movements," 91.

50. S. Cohen, *Folk Devils and Moral Panics* (London: McGibbon and Kee, 1972); S. Cohen and J. Young, eds., *The Manufacture of News* (London: Constable, 1973).

51. Pamela J. Shoemaker, "Media Treatment of Deviant Political Groups," *Journalism Quarterly* 60 (1984b):66–75, 82.

52. Olien, Tichenor, and Donohue, "Media Coverage and Social Movements."

53. Ibid., 160.

54. Ibid., 149.

55. Quoted in Philip Shabecoff, *A Fierce Green: The American Environmental Movement* (New York: Hill and Wang, 1993), 134.

56. Jim Motavalli, "Flying High, Swooping Low: Assessing the Environmental Movement at the Close of the 'E Decade,'" *E Magazine* (Jan/Feb. 2000), 24–30, 26.

57. George Lakoff, *Don't Think of an Elephant! Know Your Values and Frame the Debate* (White River Junction, VT: Chelsea Green, 2004).

58. The authors of the essay, Michael Shellenberger and Ted Nordhaus, originally presented the paper at a conference. The essay has since become widely available on various Web sites, such as www.thebreakthrough.org.

59. James K. Hertog and Douglas M. McLeod, "A Multi-perspectival Approach to Framing Analysis: A Field Guide," in *Framing Public Life: Perspectives on Media and Our Understanding of the Social World*, eds. Stephen D. Reese, Oscar H. Gandy, Jr., and August E. Grant (Mahwah, NJ: Lawrence Erlbaum, 2001), 139–161, 141.

60. Ibid., 147.

61. Ibid., 143.

62. Ibid., 147.

63. Bill Devall, "Deep Ecology and Radical Environmentalism," in *American Environmentalism: The U.S. Environmental Movement, 1970–1990*, eds. Riley E. Dunlap and Angela G. Mertig (Philadelphia: Taylor & Francis, 1992), 55–56.

64. Mertig, Dunlap, and Morrison, "The Environmental Movement," 455.

# Index